Imagination
and Intellect

Imagination
and Intellect

READINGS FOR COMPOSITION

Edward G. McGehee
Edgar L. McCormick
Kent State University

PRENTICE-HALL, INC., *Englewood Cliffs, N.J.*
1962

© 1962
PRENTICE-HALL, INC.
Englewood Cliffs, N.J.

Library of Congress Catalog Card No. 62-9292

PRINTED IN THE UNITED STATES OF AMERICA

45119-C

Preface

This anthology, intended to stimulate the imagination and challenge the intellect of its readers, begins with selections expressing the individual's awareness of himself and his reactions to the realities he encounters in his immediate environment. It advances from such personal perceptions to more abstract considerations of education, science, art, and moral values. Such progression from knowledge of the self to more universal wisdom presents a natural order for the developing thinker and writer to follow.

We have chosen selections that will stimulate a student's reading, thinking, and writing. Most of the fifty-eight essays and narratives have been published within recent years; some, however, are writings which are older, yet contemporary in their approach. Form and content, far more than an author's reputation, governed our choice. We asked that a writer be mature and responsible, that he reveal individuality, and that he organize his thoughts in an appropriate, impressive totality. Avoiding ephemeral and hackneyed material, we selected prose that reveals an author's imagination, intellect, and his ability to write. Having used these selections, we know that they offer a wide variety of writing assignments, serve as models for the successful organization of papers, and by presenting the student with new concepts and unexpected points of view, they stimulate thought and discussion both in and out of the classroom.

Imagination and Intellect will help develop the student's ability to read analytically and critically, and to communicate information, ideas, and attitudes in clear, effective prose. In addition to the readings themselves, the book contains questions and suggestions that will benefit the student in his study of a writer's meaning, organization, and expression. Numerous ideas for writing, varying in difficulty, accompany each selection. These aids are included primarily for the benefit of the student; they are not intended to be a substitute for a rhetoric or general handbook. In addition to biographical material, we have provided suggestions for additional reading that will either continue an author's idea, offer a contradictory view, or clarify the statements he has made. We expect this anthology to provide the student with added incentive to avail himself of the materials offered by his library.

Our aim has been to produce a superior anthology. Our success in achieving this goal is due largely to what we have learned from our own teachers and students. Although we cannot name all those to whom we are indebted, we acknowledge, especially, the help we have received from Esther Bone, Dean Keller, Ralph Tutt, Margaret Stopher, John Keating, Chester Satterfield, Julia Neal, Harry Wheeler, James Poe, and Diana Powers and other members of the editorial staff of Prentice-Hall.

E.G.M.

E.L.M.

The Discerning Eye

SOME INTRODUCTORY REMARKS ABOUT WRITING

Thoughtful observers of parents and children, of teachers and pupils, of nature and man's creations speak to you in the first four sections of this book. As you read these essays and stories, you will see that vivid and significant topics for writing exist all about you. Familiar subjects and personal experiences furnish the best subject matter for all who wish to improve their writing. As an initial step in improving your skill, emulate these authors and try recording your experiences as a member of a family, as a student, and as an individual in the midst of society. You will soon discover that you have a great amount of knowledge to draw upon—much more than you at first realize. It is natural to want to tell others of your observations and insights, just as it is normal to want to hear what others have felt and learned. Each of us has his own perspective, and the exchange of our views reveals the diversity and immensity of the human experience.

To have many initial subjects for papers, you need to pay attention only to who you are, where you live, and whom you meet. The suggestions for writing given at the end of each essay are, as you will soon discover, just a few of the many possibilities. If you keep alive but a fraction of that sense of wonder that prompted you to ask many questions when you were a child, you will never say, as students sometimes do, "I've nothing to write about." It is extremely important for you to be a perceptive observer; an absorbing interest in your immediate world will enable you to portray your surroundings graphically and will also lead you to speculate about the meaning inherent in even the most ordinary events and situations. As a vivid writer you will note color and movement, feel warmth and joy, sense satisfaction and disappointment; and catching these impressions firmly in your imagination, you will translate them into words.

Early in this freshman course your most effective writing, rather than merely reporting or describing, will often reveal your attitude toward significant experiences. For example, Jesse Stuart, the first author in this anthology, who has an eye for accurate portrayal, sees more than a mountain farmer in his father. Stuart creates a portrait of a Kentucky hillman who is endowed with poetic wisdom. You need not be a Jesse Stuart to have this awareness of human qualities, but you may need practice in capturing them in words and recording them on paper. A freshman, interested in majoring in mathematics, wrote the following appreciation of his grandfather. This student based his essay upon what he himself had observed and upon what his curiosity had prompted him to learn from his parents:

"SKINNER" JOHN

All the neighbors had high respect for old Skinner McFall. Although he was a "square shooter," his round, hard, skinny head always "figgered" out how to make one dollar bring in another. His name didn't indicate that he made his dollars through sharp practices but rather that as a lad he made money by novel methods. In his youth he had been teased and cajoled in the village blacksmith shop when he boasted of the polecats he had trapped and skinned. He had stated simply and concisely, "I skun 'em." The burly, good-natured smith always greeted him, "Well, here comes Skinner John who skun a skunk." To his embarrassment, the name stuck.

At the age of seventy, when other men were nodding on the porches and complaining of "rheumatiz," old Skinner hung up a square, black-and-gold sign in the front window of the parlor. The passers-by saw it across the green lawn, glittering between the white, ruffled curtains and were amused. It read:

JOHN C. McFALL

REALTOR

Old John had left his farm and had come to live in town. No one saw any reason why he should continue to work. For fifty years he had been a thrifty farmer. His pastures had fed flocks of sheep and herds of cattle. Acres were brown-furrowed in March and golden-stubbled in August. His barns were full of hay to the cupolas and the granaries were overflowing with wheat and corn. To the neighbors his uncanny ability to sow wheat when the price of corn hit bottom and to buy ewes when the pasture was lush suggested Moses in the land of Egypt. "Skinner John," one of them would say, "seems to 'figger' out what the Almighty's going to do about the weather. Even if snow'd come in May, I'll bet John would get advance notice and have the young lambs in the pasture lot by the barn."

Now, the lock box in the First National Bank was full of government bonds and this tall, white house, trimmed in green with honeysuckle-covered porches, was to be his haven until. . . . But John never said much about that. He could see from his bedroom window the cemetery stretching over the smooth, green hills. His wife had always tended to the religious duties for the family. She asked the blessing at the table and led the family in worship. On a hot, sultry morning old John would say, "Now, don't choose the longest chapter in the Bible. Make it short. It's going to rain and we've got to get that hay before it spoils." But Skinner wrote a check in three figures to cancel the debt on the church. He gave because he wanted to be respected, not because he feared God or loved the hypocritical men who said long prayers but didn't pay their part towards the upkeep of the building.

Old John expressed his contempt for such men by the way he spat his tobacco juice. In fact, his years of experience enabled him to spit expressively; a long, rangy arc denoted reflection on a cash offer; a short, explosive shot indicated quick acceptance; and when the deal just didn't go through, the dark juice dribbled and he wiped it away with the back of his hand.

Not knowing Skinner John, the other real estate dealers in the town laughed up their sleeves when they saw the sign in the parlor window. Before three months, they were eating their chagrin. The old man had sold the gasoline station on the corner of East Main and Liberty, the Smith house, and half a dozen empties the agents had been listing for years. They rode around in speedy cars and used high pressure salesmanship. Old John walked, one trouser leg swishing against the other. He also spent a lot of time with his village cronies in front of the Ace Barber Shop or the town hall. He listened and learned. "The heirs are going to sell the Feed Store." "The Widow Grimes is going to sell the old home place and go to live with her son out in Montana," or, "I hear the new manager of the co-op is coming the first of the month."

He particularly liked the widows. He would mow the lawn for one; take sweet corn to another; and tease the one whose period of mourning had long since passed, telling her about the "good looking man I was a-talking to the other day who was a-looking for a good cook."

The real estate men smiled contemptuously when they saw the skinny little man painting a house. They smiled crookedly "on the other sides of their faces" when, almost before the owner knew it, John was showing the house to somebody who was *thinking* of buying a house and was *looking*. Soon John was spitting a long parabola of rich, dark tobacco juice.

The years having made him a little more skinny and his blue eyes a trifle more faded, he was eighty-two when I went along with him to the cemetery to look over "some lots Jim Nelson is a-thinking of buying for the Ingersolls." Standing on the wind-swept hill, the old veteran pointed out to Jim the advantages and disadvantages of man's whole estate.

"There're a few good lots right on this knoll and the drainage is good. And I reckon you'll hear Gabriel blow his trumpet that much sooner." Old John chuckled. "You won't have to buy such big monuments either, for on the hill this-a-way a small one'll stand up above the taller ones lower down. Now, me, I've got a lot over here. I had one over in that corner by the gate where I could see the folks a-coming and a-going." He twinkled pleasantly. "But somebody got buried in it a-fore I knew it. Of course, it was a mistake but

I couldn't ask them to dig him up. That's why I got this one over here right by Dr. Mann, the old president of the college, thinking I might mix with the educated folks. And do you know, derned if a man I was a-suing for a commission didn't up and die and there he is on the other side of me. I reckon he's going to feel cheap when he sees me rising up beside him on resurrection day. He'll wish then he'd paid me my money. Maybe he'll fork it over before Saint Peter sees him. You see, it's a heap more important to choose your neighbors in a cemetery than on a village street. Now, Jim, I'll tell you another thing. Look," and he pointed at his lot. "I got my tombstone up. Right nice pink marble, isn't it? I saved nearly the price of the lot by buying the stone myself. The children can't drive a bargain like I can. I told old man Wenslow, 'Now, look-a-here, I may not die a-tall and you'll never make the sale, but for cash right now you can sell me right now. Take it or leave it.' He wanted to split the difference, but I said, 'You throw off one half and I'll throw off the other.' Nice carving thrown in too. 'In my Father's house are many mansions.' " The blue-veined hand wiped the dust from the smooth, glowing marble.

There flashed before my mind that other inscription in the parlor window and I knew it wouldn't be long before old Skinner would be telling the world-weary pilgrims: "There's some right good mansions up here on a golden street. No upkeep required. No taxes. I tell you, you get good neighbors and a harp thrown in with every mansion."

Such writing is true to life, but not in the usual sense of being like a photograph or an accurate drawing. It captures the old man's speech, appearance, movement, and personality; and, because it is not a one-dimensional portrait, it also penetrates into such qualities of human behavior as perseverance, humor, and thrift.

Value your own experiences and use them as a basis for your writing. If you choose subject matter with which you are well acquainted, you will be prompted to vigorous and graphic expression. Since you cannot possibly know from first-hand experience all that is likely to attract your interest, you must rely, at times, upon the observations of others. Already you have learned much through discussions with your contemporaries; now you must learn to rely even more than you have in the past upon the knowledge that you can derive from books. As Emerson says, books become the great repositories of wisdom. From them we learn vicariously.

When you turn to books for information and enlightenment, it is important to remember that the mark of your intellectual growth and your achievement as a writer will become evident as you go beyond the facts and make your own evaluations. In your readings you will notice that others do not always agree with you; however, you should be sure to understand their perspectives before you decide that you have nothing to learn from them. Different points of view will sometimes challenge your earlier concepts, revealing new ways of looking at older ideas.

The essays and narratives in the last three sections of this an-thology are devoted particularly to the intangible values that are associated with science, art, and self-realization. Your reading, your discussion, and your writing will turn increasingly towards thought and analysis. You will see the need of being receptive to new ideas, of qualifying and modifying old beliefs or hastily acquired new ones, and of becoming more subjective in your writing. For example, Albert Gardner, the student who wrote the following theme, based his paper upon his own experience, but he went a step further than the student who described his grandfather. Gardner's paper reveals his interest in the complexities of life:

THE CARILLON AND THE TURKEY

There is a tall bell tower on the campus here, and everyday it rings out the hours, half-hours, and quarter-hours. Each noon and evening a carillonneur plays a short piece on its bells, and it is pleas-ing to hear its music chiming faintly in the distance. It is a kind of prologue that sets the stage and mood for dinner.

Today, November 23, the carillonneur has played short pieces off and on throughout the day. He has just finished "A Hymn of Thanks-giving." Some of the boys in the Williamson Library are thumbing magazines, some are writing letters home, and some are just relaxing comfortably. When the bell tower strikes one, they will all walk leisurely to dinner. That dinner will be their whole day, even though it may not last over an hour. There will be turkey and cranberry sauce and good fellowship. After the coffee and pump-kin pie, they may thumb through some more magazines, write some more letters, or go to the lounge and watch a television show. After that they will joke about the turkey or about how full they are. Later, they will say good-night. Just before they go to sleep, they will make an unconscious mental readjustment, readying themselves for history lectures and French classes in the morning. Thanksgiving Day is one of the best holidays of the year.

On this day the turkey has received the spice of holiday spirit, garnished with a full day's devotions. Though it can appear and disappear within an hour, we fondly remember and anticipate it, year after year. I cannot help being aware today of this atmosphere which surrounds the simple act of eating a turkey dinner.

Just now I also remember the times when I had dinner under different conditions.

I once worked sixty hours a week at a menial job and received trivial wages. However, I had half an hour free for lunch. Then I would sit on a shipping crate in the jumbled stock room, take out of a paper bag some dried-out sandwiches which my mother had made and wrapped in paper napkins, open a bottle of pop, and dine. For half an hour the hubbub of those working beyond the door of that stock room would find no ears. Mr. Gardner was not to be disturbed. He was dining. Where? At a delightful spot. A portable radio diffused soft music, and there, over a book, vigorous conversation took place between Mr. Gardner and Tolstoi. What did Mr. Gardner eat? He never looked at menus. How long did Mr. Gardner take to dine? Half an hour, but after those thirty minutes Mr. Gardner became just "Al" again.

I always rather enjoyed dining. I could use the top of another shipping crate for my table, or I could eat a filet mignon at a damask covered table, glowing in candle light, a whole series of proper knives and forks being displayed beside my plate. Mealtimes are a state of mind.

I recall the ritual on the continent—coffee at eleven. In England —tea at four. It wasn't the coffee or the tea that mattered; eleven and four o'clock meant relaxation. In the Yankee stadium at the seventh inning the people just get up and stretch. This may appear strange, necessary, or warmly human. We may sense the atmosphere so that it clothes the bare act with significance, or we may not sense the atmosphere at all and leave the act merely to carry out its function.

It was always rather distasteful to eat in New York at those slot-machine cafeterias where one puts two or three dimes into a slot and pulls out a sandwich. They served good food, but the places always made me think of human filling stations or food dispensaries, cold, without atmosphere or character. Sometimes, however, an Italian family would come in, and the children would noisily and excitedly see slabs of pie they wanted. Their mother would have to hush them. Then the father would say. "Luigi, wanta a salami sandwich? Mama, you gotta some dimes?"

Mama would open her bag and from an inner purse take out some coins and give them to Papa who would put them into the proper slot. Luigi got to take his own sandwich out of the compartment. Then, what would Angela want? Sometimes a feast but not necessarily for the belly.

We could easily reduce our lives, I feel, to a series of almost "negative" actions. We eat so that we shall *not* be hungry. We drink so that we shall *not* be thirsty. We sleep so that we shall *not* be tired. We could easily say that we eat so that we can work, so that we can eat, and so on in a meaningless circle. We could easily reduce our daily lives to that series of negative actions which only erase the deficiencies.

But mealtimes are a state of mind. I like to look over the rim of the glass of milk I've raised to my lips and see Mama take the dimes out of her inner purse and give them to Papa. I don't eat to live. I can hate the food but love the dinner.

This is the sentiment of aesthetics. It is the appreciative recognition of the atmosphere around us. Its importance lies not in any practical action nor in any monetary value, but, instead, in the state of mind which "marks the quick from the dead." Life breathes more fully with it. I sometimes feel this way while riding on a train or waiting outside an office. The train not only carries me somewhere, but I am already somewhere on the train itself. Waiting outside an office is the pure action. There are, if you will pardon the poor metaphor, harmonics in that pure action which give it tone and color and vibrancy. What kind of place is this office? Who else is waiting? What kind of people do they appear to be? That journey on the train and that waiting outside the office I might elaborate as symbols for our constant journey through the days and our waiting for events to come.

Thanksgiving Day may call to mind only the picture of a turkey on a table, but it is really a whole day. I can't recognize the piece that the carillonneur is now playing, but soon the clock will strike one. I shall walk leisurely to dinner, go to the movies afterwards, joke about the turkey, and finally go to bed. Perhaps the bell tower will then be chiming out eleven o'clock.

This student's essay moves beyond what might have been merely a lifelike account of dining, towards a revelation of an attitude, an expression of what mealtimes mean when viewed aesthetically. As you develop your skills you too will become more concerned with such ideas or abstractions. You will learn to present them in the context of the specific situations that embody them.

Whether you are expressing an experience chiefly as the senses know it, or as the mind confronts it, you must always find the best possible form for conveying your view of the experience to interested and intelligent readers. As you write and observe the work of other writers, you will learn to select a topic of the right size or magnitude—one neither too inconsequential nor too ponderous—for proper development in a relatively short essay. Usually you will devote the paper to a specific situation, a particular person, or a single idea or emotion. Choosing a subject of proper size enables you to expand it fully, to include all explanations, illustrations, and details which your readers, who have not shared in your experience, will find essential if they are to recreate it for themselves, with your help.

The forms of discourse will not be a major factor in your choice of the proper means of expression. Normally you will not have to decide whether you will use description, narration, or argumentation. Most of your writing will be expository, for its purpose will be to explain, inform, and clarify. Writers use exposition to record events, analyze ideas, define difficult terms, and to give directions. They may incorporate descriptive elements as they focus on particular scenes, people, or events. They may also include narration, the form common to biography and to history, when they recall a sequence of events. Dialogue can often be a part of such accounts when the writer needs to emphasize the dramatic moments and the people who are involved in the action. In some of your papers later in the course you may present one side of an argument as you come upon an idea which you would like to defend or to persuade others to accept. But in all of your papers you will be chiefly concerned with using exposition. Through it you will learn to be systematic, clear, and vivid. When you need to be particularly specific about people and places you will find yourself incorporating narration and description into your expository prose.

Once you have a subject clearly in mind (you may have to state it in a simple sentence to be sure that you have set its proper bounds), you must consider what plan or pattern of organization will be most natural for its development. If you are elaborating upon a thesis, pay particular attention to logic and coherence. After defining your subject, discuss its divisions and subdivisions thoroughly, giving each the emphasis it merits. You will need to use adequate illustrations and examples to bring your points close to your reader's own experience or to give him the definite evidence he will need if he is to grasp your argument. Sometimes you may find that contrasting different ideas or drawing analogies will serve as effective means of clarifying your subject. Outlines, particularly those using sentences for the major and minor points, will also help you to determine the most logical and effective arrangement of your ideas.

Less complex papers, those which are chiefly concerned with what we discover through the senses, will be easier for you to plan. Chronological and spatial orders are natural to them; thus, you can use a time sequence to explain a process and a spatial order to describe your surroundings. Another device you can use within these patterns allows you to move from the specific to the general, or vice versa. You should consult your rhetoric for additional advice about organizing your essays most effectively, always remembering that each subject will call for its own method and that no rules will ever fully suffice as your guide.

After clearly determining your purpose and plan, you must turn to a consideration of the techniques of writing. Paragraphs will represent the units of your thought; there must be smooth continuity between them as well as between the sentences they contain. It is of the utmost importance that you achieve clarity and concreteness. To do this you must add those pertinent details which will develop the portrait, scene, or belief to provide the exact information the reader will need. You must recapture what you saw, felt, heard, tasted, and smelled. Remember how "Skinner" McFall spat and how his trouser legs swished against each other? You must achieve something of the same effect if you expect others to visualize what you are describing.

You can often convey less tangible experiences by comparing them with experiences that you are sure your readers will know. Such parallels will reveal the nature of the particular situations that you want your readers to understand. Allied to this use of comparison are the metaphor and the simile. When you try these means of being definite, be sure to avoid those well-worn, conventional comparisons (*e. g.,* "like a million dollars," or "like a duck out of water"). Also, before you become overbold in your use of metaphors, be sure to acquaint yourself with the danger of mixing them (*e.g.,* "The ship of state waded like a duck in low gear as it sashayed through the troubled waters," or, "The anthill of bickering sprouted into a mountain of hate and chased, like cats after a ball of twine, all love out of the Smiths' house").

Writing is a difficult art for anyone to master. In addition to choosing a subject wisely, organizing it effectively, and developing it fully, you must also consider various other fundamentals. You should make use of fresh and vivid diction, not necessarily multisyllabic. You should consider the rhythm and variety of your sentences, avoiding an overuse of the passive voice. Only by paying accurate attention to the mechanics (spelling, grammar, punctuation) and by thoroughly revising the essay several hours after you have written the first draft can you polish your act of creation.

Having studied these matters long before you came to college, you can now easily consult a handbook or rhetoric to refresh your mind if this knowledge has lain fallow too long. The most important thing for you to do at present is to write and to profit from the suggestions for revision that your instructor may offer.

Contents

Part Two   *Seeing Ourselves and Others*

Part Three   *The Realms of Place*

part one ✂ *Views of family life*

EARTH POET

JESSE STUART

Jesse Stuart (1907–), who was born in W-Hollow, near Riverton, Kentucky, always wanted to be a writer. A graduate of Vanderbilt, he gave up a teaching career to return to farming, at first writing poems only for his own pleasure. However, with the publication of *Man With a Bull-Tongue Plow* he became well-known as a poet. Since then he has written numerous prize stories, popular novels, several autobiographical volumes, and many poems.

Many people thought my father was just a one-horse farmer who had never got much out of life. They saw him, a little man, dressed in clean, patched overalls, with calloused and briar-scratched hands. They often saw the beard long on his face. And they saw him go away and just stand and look at something. They thought he was

From *Esquire,* January 1960. Copyright © 1959 by Esquire, Inc. Reprinted by permission of Esquire, Inc.

moody. Well, he was that all right, but when he was standing there and someone thought he was looking into space, he was looking at a flower, plant, mushroom, or a new bug he'd discovered for the first time. And every time he looked up into a tree, he wasn't searching for hornets' or birds' nests. And he wasn't trying to find a bee tree. He was just looking at the beauty in one of a million trees. Among the millions of trees, he always found one different enough to excite him.

My father was an earth poet who loved the land and everything on it. He liked to watch things grow. From the time I was big enough for him to lead me by the hand, I went with him over the farm. If I couldn't walk all the way in those early days, he'd carry me on his back. I learned to like many of the things he loved.

I went with him to so many fields over the years and listened to him talk about the beauty and growth of plants, I know now that my father had some wonderful thoughts which should have been written down. And thoughts came to him faster than hummingbirds go from one flower to another.

Somewhere in the dim past, among the unforgotten years of childhood, I remember my father's unloading me from his back under some white oak trees that were just beginning to leaf.

"Look at this hill, son," he said, gesturing broadly with a sweep of his hand. "Look up that steep hill toward that sky. See how pretty that new ground corn is."

This was the first field I can ever remember my father's taking me to see. The rows of corn were like dark green rainbows around a high slope with a valley and its little tributaries down through the center. The ground was clean of woods, and the young corn was dark, stalwart, and beautiful. The corn blades rustled in the wind, and the reason I remember this is that my father said he could understand what the corn blades were saying. He told me they whispered to each other, and this was hard for me to believe. Although I was a child, I thought before anything could speak or make a sound, like a cow, horse or chicken, it had to have a mouth. When my father said the corn could talk, I got down on my knees and looked a stalk over.

"This corn's not got a mouth," I told him. "How can anything talk when it doesn't have a mouth?"

And he laughed like the wind in the corn.

Then, on a Sunday, when my mother and sisters were at a country church, he took me by the hand and led me across two valleys and the ridge between them to a cove where giant beech timber once had stood.

He was always restless on Sundays, eager to get back to the fields in which he worked all week. He had cleared a piece of this land to raise white corn which he planned to have ground for meal to make our bread. He thought this cove was suited to white corn, which he called Johnson County corn. Someone had brought the seed from the Big Sandy River, in the country where my father was born and lived until he was sixteen. And when he had cleared this cove, set fire to the giant beech tops and left ash over the new ground, he thought this earth would produce wonderful cornfield beans too. In every other hill of corn he had planted beans. Now these beans ran up the cornstalks and weighted them with hanging pods of young tender beans. Pictures I saw later in life of Jack and the Beanstalk always reminded me of this tall corn with bean vines winding around the stalks up to the tassels.

But what my father had brought me to see that delighted him most were the pumpkins. I'd never seen so many pumpkins with long necks and small bodies. Pumpkins as big around as the bottom of a flour barrel were sitting beneath the tall corn, immovable as rocks in the furrows. There were pumpkins, and more pumpkins, of all colors—yellow, green and white and green and brown.

"Look at this, won't you?" my father said. "Look what corn, beans, and pumpkins! Corn ears so big they lean the cornstalks. Beans as thick as honey locust beans on the honey locust tree. And pumpkins thicker than the stumps of this new ground. I could walk all over that field stepping on pumpkins. I could go all the way over it and never step on the ground. It's something to see, don't you think? Did you ever see anything as pretty?"

He looked upon the beauty of this cove he had cleared and his three crops growing there before he figured how many bushels of corn and beans and how many pumpkins he would have. He never figured a field in dollars and cents, although he was close and frugal with money. He never wasted a dollar. But dollars didn't mean everything to him. He liked to see pictures of growing things on the land. He carried these pictures in his mind. He never forgot one that interested him.

Once, on a rainy Sunday afternoon when we were walking between cornfields, he motioned for me to step up beside him and look. He pointed to a redbird on its nest in a locust tree. Here sat a redbird with shiny red feathers upon the dark background of a nest. It was just another bird's nest to me until he whispered, "Ever see anything as pretty as that redbird's sitting on that dark nest in the white drops of rain?" From this time on, I have liked to see birds, especially redbirds, sitting on their nests in the rain. My father was the first one ever to make me see the beauty in these little things about me.

He used to talk about the beauty of a rooster redbird, pheasant, chicken hawk, hoot owl, and turkey gobbler. He pointed out the color of the neck, tail, and wing feathers. Then he taught me how to tell a stud terrapin from a female, a male turtle from the female, a bull black snake from a female. My father knew all of these things. He learned them in his own way. He observed so closely that he could tell the male from the female in any species, even the grey lizard, which was most difficult.

"A black snake is a pretty thing," he once said to me. "He is so shiny and black in the spring sun after he sheds his winter skin."

He was the first man I ever heard say a snake was pretty. I never forgot his saying this, and the sumac thicket where we saw the black snake.

He saw more beauty in trees than any man I have ever known. He would walk through a strange forest laying his hand upon the trees, saying this oak and that pine, beech or poplar were beautiful trees. Then he would single out trees and say they should be cut. He would always give his reasons for cutting a tree: too many trees on a root stool; too thick; one damaged by fire at the butt; one leaning against another tree; too many on the ground; or the soil not deep enough above a ledge of rocks to support them.

Then there were the hundreds of times my father took me, when I was a growing boy, to the hills just to see wild flowers. I thought it was silly at first, but as I continued to go with him, I learned more about wild flowers, and appreciated their beauty.

He could sit on a dead log somewhere under the tall beech trees, listen to the wind in the canopy of beech leaves above, look at a clump of violets or at percoon growing beside a rotted log and enjoy himself indefinitely. He didn't want to get up and move. He wanted to sit there and look and love the color in the wild flower's blossom and the noises the wind made rustling the green beech leaves.

So many times when I went with him, we sat on a log, maybe one covered with wild moss, looked at a wild flower for hours, listened to the wind in the leaves, and then got up from the log when the sun went down and started for home.

He always had a lot of feeding to do—livestock, mules, horses, hogs, chickens, and dogs. These animals looked forward to seeing him at feeding time. And he was always there to feed them.

My father wouldn't break the Sabbath by working unless it was an emergency, something he had to do. Often he followed a cow that was overdue to calve. And he watched over ewes in the same manner. He followed them to the high cliffs and often helped them deliver their lambs to save their lives. He did these things and fought forest fires on Sunday. But he always said he could make a living working six days in the week. However, he was restless on Sundays. He just had to walk around and look over his fields and enjoy them.

I've been with him many a time going to the field when we'd cross a stream. He'd stop the horse, sit down on the bank in the shade and watch the flow of water. He'd watch minnows in a deep hole. He wouldn't say a word and I wouldn't either. I'd look all around, for I'd wonder what he'd seen to make him stop. But I never would ask him. When he got through looking, sometimes he'd tell me why he'd stopped. Sometimes he wouldn't. Then we'd go on to the field together, and he'd work furiously to make up for the time he had lost while we sat beside the stream and watched the cool, clean water flowing over the sand and gravel to some far-off destiny beyond his little hill world.

My father didn't have to travel over the country like other people searching for something beautiful to see. Not until very late in his life was he ever over a hundred miles from home. My father didn't have to go away to find beauty, for he found it everywhere around him. He had eyes to find it. He had a mind to know it. He had a heart to appreciate it. He was an uneducated poet of this earth. He didn't know that he was a poet either. If anybody had told him in so many words that he was, he wouldn't have understood. He would have turned and walked away without saying anything.

In the winter, when snow was over the ground and the stars glistened, he'd go to the barn to feed the livestock at four in the morning. I've gone with him to help. I have seen him put corn in the feed-boxes for the horses and mules, and then go out and stand and look at the morning moon. He once told me he always kept a horse with a flaxen mane and tail because he liked to see one run in the moonlight with his mane arched high and his tail floating on the wind. He said he always liked to ride a horse with a flaxen mane and tail.

Then I've gone out early in the morning with him, and he's shown me Jack Frost's nice architecture, which lasted only until the sun came up. This used to be one of the games my father played with me on a cold, frosty morning. He showed me all of these designs that I would never have found without him. Today, I cannot look at white fields of frost on early autumn and winter mornings and not think about him.

When spring returned, he was always taking me someplace to show me a new tree, or a very pretty red mushroom growing somewhere on a rotting stump in some deep hollow. And all summer long he took me so many places, all within a few minutes' walking distance of our home, to show me flowers, plants, trees, things that crawled, walked, rode through the air on wings and swam in the creeks and rivers. He was always finding these strange and beautiful things until I tried to rival him by making discoveries too. I looked over the little and unexpected places to find the beautiful and the unusual.

Once, in autumn, we went to the pasture field to hunt pawpaws.

"Look at the golden meat in one and the big brown seeds like the seeds of a melon or a pumpkin," he said. "Did you ever taste a banana in your life that was as good as a pawpaw? Did you ever see anything prettier than the clean, sweet, golden fruit of a pawpaw?"

I never forgot how he described a pawpaw, and this has made me like pawpaws the rest of my life.

He took me to the first persimmon grove I ever saw. This was after frost, and the persimmons had ripened and had fallen from the trees. "They're wonderful," he said. "The persimmon is a candy tree. It really should have been called the gumdrop tree." His saying this to me, a small boy then, has made me see ripe persimmons after frost always as brown gumdrops. I have always thought of the persimmon as the gumdrop tree.

I didn't get my first thought of dead leaves as being golden ships on the sea from a storybook. And neither did my father, for he had never read a book in his life—he couldn't read. He'd never had a book read to him either. I'd not been in a schoolhouse then, and I couldn't read either. It was in October, and we were sitting on the bank of W-Branch. We were watching the blue, autumn water slide swiftly over the slate rocks. My father picked up leaves that were shaped like little ships and dropped them into the water, and we both watched their graceful movement.

"These are ships on swift water," he told me. "These are going to far-off lands and strange places where strangers will see them."

I never forgot this. I never forgot his love of autumn leaves and the many species he'd pick up when we were out walking and ask me to identify. He'd talk about how pretty each leaf was and that a leaf was prettier after it was dead than it was when it was alive and green and growing.

And no one would have ever felt sorry for my father in his small world—if he had known him. The feeling of sorrow would have turned to envy. For my father had a world of his own. This world went beyond the vast earth that world travelers know. He found more beauty in his acres and square miles than poets who have written a half-dozen books. Only my father couldn't write down the words to express his thoughts. He had no known symbols with which to declare his thoughts. If he had had I don't know what he would have done. But I do know that he would have done something.

If he was not a poet, who lived his life upon this earth and never left a line of poetry, there never was one.

Questions and Suggestions:

1. How do the father's specific comments about the natural world reveal him as being a close observer of nature?
2. What evidence do you find that Stuart himself has learned to be acutely aware of his surroundings?
3. Choose a passage that presents an especially vivid picture. Study it for detail and diction.
4. Examine carefully the construction of the sentences in the first paragraph. What examples do you find of colloquial patterns of speech?
5. Explain how the use of dialogue helps develop the portrait of the father. Does he differ from the other people mentioned in the essay?
6. Compare Stuart's father as an observer of nature with John Burroughs, Loren Eiseley, Richard Jefferies, Sigurd Olson, or Ernest Thompson Seton.

Ideas for Writing:

1. Write a character sketch of your father or mother, focusing upon several incidents that reveal a significant trait.
2. Relate how one of your parents made you aware of something beautiful or unusual, or how you realized that something which you once considered insignficant or ugly was in reality significant or attractive.
3. Contrast a person who is interested in his work with one who is not; be sure to use individuals whom you know and not creations of your imagination.
4. On the basis of this account, how would you define a poet, an educated man, a good farmer, or a wise father?
5. Recreate the comic effects of a telephone conversation you

have overheard, the way in which one of your parents drives,
or the preparations a younger brother made for his first date.

6. If you think that you will have difficulty in finding topics for
    papers, then consider the following example of a student's
    theme that Prof. Tyler liked:

Tyler lighted his pipe and picked up one of the freshman themes.
They had been reading La Fontaine's Fables this week and the assignment had been to write four hundred words on the master's model,
using a beast to point a moral or sharpen an irony. The title of this
one, neatly printed with a stub pen, was *Antaeus in Parvo.* Tyler remembered the boy's face, long as an El Greco, brown eyes, glasses, thin
light hair: Jimmy Lawlor, a true introvert. "I shall not follow," Jimmy
had written, "the model of La Fontaine. Instead I will tell a true
anecdote about an ant I saw last summer. He was so strong for his size
that he reminded me of the giant Antaeus in classical mythology. But
he was just an ordinary black ant, neither very large nor very small.

"When I first saw him I was sitting on the lowest of a flight of nine
stone steps in a neighbor's garden. Over the top of the book I was reading I saw the movement of something white. It was an ugly, ghostly
thing; it seemed to be the front part of a bleeched-out grasshopper's
body. The feelers were missing and both the eye-sockets were empty.
Of course the only reason it was moving at all was that my friend the
ant, who was about one eighth its size, had clamped his jaws firmly
on one of those pale legs and was dragging his prize back home, walking backwards all the way. While I watched, he backed his way up
the first riser. The grasshopper-body must have been much heavier on
the vertical than it had been on the horizontal because now the whole
dead weight hung free from the ant's jaws. But the ant backed right up
the riser of the second step as if nothing could ever stop him.

"The ant had real trouble getting the body over the square edge of
the second step. He had to yank and yank, then move sidewise, retreat
a half-inch down the vertical plane to get another start, and then yank
some more before he found a place where he could get real traction.
He must have worked for three or four minutes right on that edge alone.
At last he heaved the body onto the horizontal plane of the second step,
and you expected him to stop, get out his handkerchief, mop his brow,
maybe look back over the great distance he had covered. But he didn't.

From Carlos Baker, *A Friend in Power,* pp. 45-57. Copyright © 1958
by Carlos H. Baker. Reprinted by permission of Charles Scribner's Sons.

He never even stopped. He never relaxed his hold and he just kept on pulling.

"I must have watched him work for five minutes. Then I forgot about him and read my book for ten minutes. At first, when I looked again, I couldn't see the ant at all. Then halfway up the sixth stone riser I saw the moving fleck of white, and I knew the ant was still pulling away, heading up the nine steps. Each of them was as big for him as a mountain would be to a cliffdweller lugging home the front half of a cow. I saw him once more just starting up the seventh riser, then I didn't see him any more. But I have not forgotten him.

"He did not speak, like the animals of La Fontaine. His mouth was too full of grasshopper-leg, and if ants breathe he must have been puffing hard. But he is an insect who could represent something to mankind. Go to Antaeus, thou sluggard. He is a fable in himself." The theme was signed neatly at the bottom: *James Whitcomb Lawlor.*

Tyler corrected the spelling of "bleached" with a red pencil. "A," he wrote at the top. "This rates a top grade because you have both observed and written a genuine fable on the theme of indefatigability. It could apply very well to a variety of situations."

FATHER AND I

PÄR LAGERKVIST

Shunning publicity, Pär Fabian Lagerkvist (1891–), who was born in southern Sweden, now lives on an island near Stockholm. Long before others were aware of the increasing dangers of totalitarianism, Lagerkvist had become an outspoken critic of dictatorships. Poet, playwright, essayist, and novelist, Lagerkvist, who won the Nobel Prize for Literature in 1951, has over thirty-five books to his credit, only some of which have been translated into English.

When I was getting on toward ten, I remember, Father took me by the hand one Sunday afternoon, as we were to go out into the woods and listen to the birds singing. Waving good-by to Mother, who

From *The Atlantic Monthly,* September 1952. Alan Blair, tr. Copyright 1952 by Pär Lagerkvist. Reprinted by permission of *The Atlantic Monthly.*

had to stay at home and get the evening meal, we set off briskly in the warm sunshine. We didn't make any great to-do about this going to listen to the birds, as though it were something extra special or wonderful; we were sound, sensible people, Father and I, brought up with nature and used to it. There was nothing to make a fuss about. It was just that it was Sunday afternoon and Father was free. We walked along the railway line, where people were not allowed to go as a rule, but Father worked on the railway and he had a right to. By doing this we could get straight into the woods, too, without going a round-about way.

Soon the bird song began and all the rest. There was a twittering of finches and willow warblers, thrushes and sparrows in the bushes, the hum that goes on all round you as soon as you enter a wood. The ground was white with wood anemones, the birches had just come out into leaf, and the spruces had fresh shoots; there were smells on all sides, and under foot the mossy earth lay steaming in the sun. There were noise and movement everywhere; bumblebees came out of their holes, midges swarmed wherever it was marshy, and birds darted out of the bushes to catch them and back again just as quickly.

All at once a train came rushing along and we had to go down onto the embankment. Father hailed the engine driver with two fingers to his Sunday hat and the driver saluted and extended his hand. It all happened quickly; then on we went, taking big strides so as to tread on the sleepers and not in the gravel, which was heavy going and rough on the shoes. The sleepers sweated tar in the heat, everything smelled, grease and meadowsweet, tar and heather by turns. The rails glinted in the sun. On either side of the line were telegraph poles, which sang as you passed them. Yes, it was a lovely day. The sky was quite clear, not a cloud to be seen, and there couldn't be any, either, on a day like this, from what Father said.

After a while we came to a field of oats to the right of the line, where a crofter we knew had a clearing. The oats had come up close and even. Father scanned them with an expert eye and I could see he was satisfied. I knew very little about such things, having been born in a town. Then we came to the bridge over a stream which most of the time had no water to speak of but which now was in full spate. We held hands so as not to fall down between the sleepers. After that it was not long before we came to the platelayer's cottage lying embedded in greenery, apple trees, and gooseberry bushes. We called in to see them and were offered milk and saw their pig and hens and fruit trees

in blossom; then we went on. We wanted to get to the river, for it was
more beautiful there than anywhere else; there was something special
about it, as further upstream it flowed past where Father had lived as
a child. We usually liked to come as far as this before we turned back,
and today, too, we got there after a good walk. It was near the next
station, but we didn't go so far. Father just looked to see that the
semaphore was right—he thought of everything.

We stopped by the river, which murmured in the hot sun, broad
and friendly. The shady trees hung along the banks and were reflected
in the backwater. It was all fresh and light here; a soft breeze was
blowing off the small lakes higher up. We climbed down the slope and
walked a little way along the bank, Father pointing out the spots for
fishing. He had sat here on the stones as a boy, waiting for perch all
day long; often there wasn't even a bite, but it was a blissful life. Now
he didn't have time. We hung about on the bank for a good while,
making a noise, pushing out bits of bark for the current to take, throwing pebbles out into the water to see who could throw farthest; we were
both gay and cheerful by nature, Father and I. At last we felt tired;
we had had enough, and we set off for home.

It was beginning to get dark. The woods were changed—it wasn't
dark there yet, but almost. We quickened our steps. Mother would be
getting anxious and waiting with supper. She was always afraid something was going to happen. But it hadn't; it had been a lovely day,
nothing had happened that shouldn't. We were content with everything.

The twilight deepened. The trees were so funny. They stood listening
to every step we took, as if they didn't know who we were. Under one
of them was a glowworm. It lay down there in the dark staring at us.
I squeezed Father's hand, but he didn't see the strange glow, just walked
on. Now it was quite dark. We came to the bridge over the stream. It
roared down there in the depths, horribly, as though it wanted to
swallow us up; the abyss yawned below us. We trod carefully on the
sleepers, holding each other tightly by the hand so as not to fall in. I
thought Father would carry me across, but he didn't say anything; he
probably wanted me to be like him and think nothing of it.

We went on. Father was so calm as he walked there in the darkness,
with even strides, not speaking, thinking to himself. I couldn't understand how he could be so calm when it was so murky. I looked all
round me in fear. Nothing but darkness everywhere. I hardly dared
take a deep breath, for then you got so much darkness inside you, and
that was dangerous. I thought it meant you would soon die. I remember

quite well that's what I thought then. The embankment sloped steeply down, as though into chasms black as night. The telegraph poles rose, ghostly, to the sky. Inside them was a hollow rumble, as though someone were talking deep down in the earth, and the white porcelain caps sat huddled fearfully together listening to it. It was all horrible. Nothing was right, nothing real; it was all so weird.

Hugging close to Father I whispered: "Father, why is it so horrible when it's dark?"

"No, my boy, it's not horrible," he said, taking me by the hand.

"Yes, Father, it is."

"No, my child, you mustn't think that. Not when we know there is a God."

I felt so lonely, forsaken. It was so strange that only I was afraid, not Father, that we didn't think the same. And strange that what he said didn't help me and stop me from being afraid. Not even what he said about God helped me. I thought He too was horrible. It was horrible that He was everywhere, in the darkness, under the trees, in the telegraph poles which rumbled—that must be He—everywhere. And yet you could never see Him.

We walked in silence, each with his own thoughts. My heart contracted, as though the darkness had got in and was beginning to squeeze it.

Then, as we were rounding a bend, we suddenly heard a mighty roar behind us! We were wakened out of our thoughts in alarm. Father pulled me down onto the embankment, down into the abyss, held me there. Then the train tore past, a black train. All the lights in the carriages were out, and it was going at frantic speed. What sort of train was it? There wasn't one due now! We gazed at it in terror. The fire blazed in the huge engine as they shoveled in coal; sparks whirled out into the night. It was terrible. The driver stood there in the light of the fire, pale, motionless, his features as though turned to stone. Father didn't recognize him, didn't know who he was. The man just stared straight ahead, intent on rushing into the darkness, far into the darkness that had no end.

Beside myself with dread, I stood there panting, gazing after the furious vision. It was swallowed up by the night. Father took me up onto the line; we hurried home. He said: "Strange, what train was that? And I didn't recognize the driver." Then he walked on in silence.

But my whole body was shaking. It was for me, for my sake. I sensed what it meant: it was the anguish that was to come, the unknown, all that Father knew nothing about, that he wouldn't be able to protect me against. That was how this world, this life, would be for me; not like Father's, where everything was secure and certain. It wasn't a real world, a real life. It just hurtled, blazing, into the darkness that had no end.

Questions and Suggestions

1. What is the theme of the story?
2. If the narrator reveals his youthful view of his father when he says that "he thought of everything," what is his mature view? Explain.
3. When do you recognize that the train is both actual and symbolic? Explain why the final paragraph is necessary.
4. Why does Lagerkvist repeat the word *horrible?*
5. What is the topic sentence of the second paragraph? Is it stated or implied?
6. In the third paragraph does the sudden switch to *you*, the indefinite second person, weaken the impact of the specific point of view?

Ideas for Writing

1. This short story offers several clear contrasts: the rural man, the city-child; the peaceful afternoon, the horrible night; the safe past, the uncertain future. Attempt similar contrasts in an autobiographical sketch.
2. Construct a paper around what a city-child knows that a rural-youth does not, or the opposite. Or contrast your father's world with your own.
3. How did the date you had last Friday night differ from a previous one?
4. What effect did school consolidation have upon your high school group of friends?
5. Reveal a friend through the device of a single walk or talk, or develop one episode in such a way that your paper reveals how your companion was more knowing than yourself.
6. Were you ever afraid of the unknown?

THE KITCHEN

LAURIE LEE

In 1944, Laurie Lee (1914–) published his first volume of poetry, *The Sun My Monument*. He received his education at the Slad Village School and at Stroud Central School, both of which are located in Gloucestershire towns. From 1935 to 1939, he traveled around the Mediterranean; during World War II he served in the Crown Film Unit and with the British Ministry of Information. Concerning *Rose for Winter: Travels in Andalusia*, one English reviewer stated, "One believes Mr. Lee. The quality of his writing compels it."

Our house, and our life in it, is something of which I still constantly dream, helplessly bidden, night after night, to return to its tranquillity and nightmares: to the heavy shadows of its stone-walled rooms creviced between bank and yew trees, to its boarded ceilings and gaping mattresses, its bloodshot geranium windows, its smells of damp pepper and mushroom growths, its chaos, and rule of women.

We boys never knew any male authority. My father left us when I was three, and apart from some rare and fugitive visits he did not live with us again. He was a knowing, brisk, evasive man, the son and the grandson of sailors; but having himself no stomach for the sea, he had determined to make good on land. In his miniature way he succeeded in this. He became, while still in his middle teens, a grocer's assistant, a local church organist, an expert photographer, and a dandy. Certain portraits he took of himself at that time show a handsome though threadbare lad, tall and slender, and much addicted to gloves, high collars, and courtly poses. He was clearly a cut above the average, in charm as well as ambition. By the age of twenty he had married the beautiful daughter of a local merchant, and she bore him eight children —of whom five survived—before dying herself, still young. Then he married his housekeeper who bore him four more, three surviving, of which I was one. At the time of this second marriage he was still a

grocer's assistant, and earning nineteen shillings a week. But his dearest
wish was to become a civil servant and he studied each night to this
end. The First World War gave him the chance he wanted, and though
properly distrustful of arms and battle he instantly sacrificed both himself and his family, applied for a post in the Army Pay Corps, went off
to Greenwich in a bullet-proof vest, and never permanently lived with
us again.

He was a natural fixer, my father was, and things worked out pretty
smoothly. He survived his clerk-stool war with a War Office pension
(for nervous rash, I believe), then entered the civil service, as he had
planned to do, and settled in London for good. Thus enabling my
Mother to raise both his families, which she did out of love and pity,
out of unreasoning loyalty and a fixed belief that he would one day
return to her. . . .

Meanwhile, we lived where he had left us, a relic of his provincial
youth; a sprawling, cumbersome, countrified brood too incongruous to
carry with him. He sent us money, and we grew up without him; and
I, for one, scarcely missed him. I was perfectly content in this world
of women, muddle-headed though it might be, to be bullied and tumbled
through the hand-to-mouth days, patched or dressed-up, scolded, admired, swept off my feet in sudden passions of kisses, or dumped forgotten among the unwashed pots.

My three half-sisters shared much of Mother's burden, and were
the good fortune of our lives. Generous, indulgent, warm-blooded and
dotty, these girls were not hard to admire. They seemed wrapped, as
it were, in a perpetual bloom, the glamour of their grown-up teens,
and expressed for us boys all that women should be in beauty, style
and artifice.

For there was no doubt at all about their beauty, or the naturalness
with which they wore it. Marjorie, the eldest, a blond Aphrodite, appeared quite unconscious of the rarity of herself, moving always to
measures of oblivious grace and wearing her beauty like a kind of sleep.
She was tall, long-haired and dreamily gentle, and her voice was low
and slow. I never knew her to lose her temper, or to claim any personal
justice. But I knew her to weep, usually for others, quietly, with large
blue tears. She was a natural mother, and skilled with her needle,
making clothes for us all when needed. With her constant beauty and
balanced nature she was the tranquil night-light of our fears, a steady
flame reassuring always, whose very shadows seemed thrown for our
comfort.

Dorothy, the next one, was a wispy imp, pretty and perilous as a firework. Compounded equally of curiosity and cheek, a spark and tinder for boys, her quick dark body seemed writ with warnings that her admirers did well to observe. "Not to be held in the hand," it said. "Light the touch paper, but retire immediately." She was an active forager who lived on thrills, provoked adventure and brought home gossip. Marjorie's were the ears to which most of it came, making her pause in her sewing, open wide her eyes and shake her head at each new revelation. "You don't mean it, Doth! He *never!* NO! . . ." was all I seemed ever to hear.

Dorothy was as agile as a jungle cat, quick-limbed, entrancing, noisy. And she protected us boys with fire and spirit, and brought us treasures from the outside world. When I think of her now she is a coil of smoke, a giggling splutter, a reek of cordite. In repose she was also something else: a fairy-tale girl, blue as a plum, tender and sentimental.

The youngest of the three was cool, quiet Phyllis, a tobacco-haired, fragile girl, who carried her good looks with an air of apology, being the junior and somewhat shadowed. Marjorie and Dorothy shared a natural intimacy, being closer together in age, so Phyllis was the odd one, an unclassified solitary, compelled to her own devices. This she endured with a modest simplicity, quick to admire and slow to complain. Her favourite chore was putting us boys to bed, when she emerged in a strange light of her own, revealing a devout, almost old-fashioned watchfulness, and gravely singing us to sleep with hymns.

Sad Phyllis, lit by a summer night, her tangled hair aglow, quietly sitting beside our beds, hands folded, eyes far away, singing and singing of "Happy Eden," alone with her care over us—how often to this did I drop into sleep, feel the warmth of its tide engulf me, steered by her young hoarse hymning voice and tuneless reveries? . . .

These half-sisters I cherished; and apart from them I had two half-brothers also. Reggie, the first-born, lived apart with his grandmother; but young Harold, he lived with us. Harold was handsome, bony and secretive, and he loved our absent father. He stood somewhat apart, laughed down his nose, and was unhappy more often than not. Though younger than the girls, he seemed a generation older, was clever with his hands, but lost.

My own true brothers were Jack and Tony, and we three came at the end of the line. We were of Dad's second marriage, before he flew, and were born within the space of four years. Jack was the eldest, Tony the youngest, and myself the protected centre. Jack was the sharp one, bright as a knife, and was also my close companion. We played together, fought and ratted, built a private structure around us, shared the same bed till I finally left home, and lived off each other's brains. Tony, the baby—strange and beautiful waif—was a brooding, imaginative solitary. Like Phyllis, he suffered from being the odd one of three; worse still, he was the odd one of seven. He was always either running to keep up with the rest of us or sitting alone in the mud. His curious, crooked, suffering face had at times the radiance of a saint, at others the blank watchfulness of an insect. He could walk by himself or keep very still, get lost or appear at wrong moments. He drew like an artist, wouldn't read or write, swallowed beads by the boxful, sang and danced, was quite without fear, had secret friends, and was prey to terrible night-mares. Tony was the one true visionary amongst us, the tiny hermit no one quite understood. . . .

With our Mother, then, we made eight in that cottage and disposed of its three large floors. There was the huge white attic which ran the length of the house, where the girls slept on fat striped mattresses; an ancient, plaster-crumbling room whose sloping ceilings bulged like tent-cloths. The roof was so thin that rain and bats filtered through, and you could hear a bird land on the tiles. Mother and Tony shared a bedroom below; Jack, Harold and I the other. But the house had been so patched and parcelled, that it was now almost impossible to get to one's room without first passing through someone else's. So each night saw a procession of pallid ghosts, sleepily seeking their beds, till the candle-snuffed darkness laid us out in rows, filed away in our allotted sheets, while snores and whistles shook the old house like a roundabout getting up steam.

But our waking life, and our growing years, were for the most part spent in the kitchen; and until we married, or ran away, it was the common room we shared. Here we lived and fed in a family fug, not minding the little space, trod on each other like birds in a hole, elbowed our ways without spite, all talking at once or all silent at once, or cry-ing against each other, but never, I think, feeling overcrowded, being as separate as notes in a scale.

That kitchen, worn by our boots and lives, was scruffy, warm and low, whose fuss of furniture seemed never the same but was shuffled around each day. A black grate crackled with coal and beech twigs, towels toasted on the guard; the mantel was littered with fine old china, horse brasses and freak potatoes. On the floor were strips of muddy matting, the windows were choked with plants, the walls supported stopped clocks and calendars, and smoky fungus ran over the ceilings. There were also six tables of different sizes, some armchairs gapingly stuffed, boxes, stools and unravelling baskets, books and papers on every chair, a sofa for cats, a harmonium for coats, and a piano for dust and photographs. These were the shapes of our kitchen landscape, the rocks of our submarine life, each object worn smooth by our constant nuzzling, or encrusted by lively barnacles, relics of birthdays and dead relations, wrecks of furniture long since foundered, all silted deep by Mother's newspapers which the years piled round on the floor.

Waking up in the morning I saw squirrels in the yew trees nibbling at the moist red berries. Between the trees and the window hung a cloud of gold air composed of floating seeds and spiders. Farmers called to their cows on the other side of the valley and moorhens piped from the ponds. Brother Jack, as always, was the first to move, while I pulled on my boots in bed. We both stood at last on the bare wood floor, scratching and saying our prayers. Too stiff and manly to say them out loud we stood back to back and muttered them, and if an audible plea should slip out by chance one just burst into song to cover it.

Singing and whistling were useful face-savers, especially when confounded by argument. We used the trick readily, one might say monotonously, and this morning it was Jack who began it.

"What's the name of the King, then?" he said, groping for his trousers.

"Albert."

"No, it's not. It's George."

"That's what I said you, didn't I? George."

"No, you never. You don't know. You're feeble."

"Not so feeble as you be, any road."

"You're balmy. You got brains of a bedbug."

"Da-da-di-da-da."

"I said you're brainless. You can't even count."

"Turrelee-turrelee . . . Didn't hear you."

"Yes, you did then, blockhead. Fat and lazy. Big faa—"

"Dum-di-dah! . . . Can't hear. . . . Hey nonnie! . . ."

Well, that was all right; honours even, as usual. We broke the sleep from our eyes and dressed quickly.

Walking downstairs there was a smell of floorboards, of rags, sour lemons, old spices. The smoky kitchen was in its morning muddle, from which breakfast would presently emerge. Mother stirred the porridge in a soot-black pot, Tony was carving bread with a ruler, the girls in their mackintoshes were laying the table, and the cats were eating the butter. I cleaned some boots and pumped up some fresh water; Jack went for a jug of skimmed milk.

"I'm all behind," Mother said to the fire. "This wretched coal's all slack."

She snatched up an oilcan and threw it all on the fire. A belch of flame roared up the chimney. Mother gave a loud scream, as she always did, and went on stirring the porridge.

"If I had a proper stove," she said. "It's a trial getting you off each day."

I sprinkled some sugar on a slice of bread and bolted it down while I could. How different again looked the kitchen this morning, swirling with smoke and sunlight. Some cut-glass vases threw jagged rainbows across the piano's field of dust, while Father in his pince-nez up on the wall looked down like a scandalized god.

At last the porridge was dabbed on our plates from a thick and steaming spoon. I covered the smoky lumps with treacle and began to eat from the sides to the middle. The girls round the table chewed moonishly, wrapped in their morning stupor. Still sick with sleep, their mouths moved slow, hung slack while their spoons came up; then they paused for a moment, spoon to lip, collected their wits, and ate. Their vacant eyes stared straight before them, glazed at the sight of the day. Pink and glowing from their dreamy beds, from who knows what arms of heroes, they seemed like mute spirits hauled back to the earth after paradise feasts of love.

"Golly!" cried Doth. "Have you seen the time?"

They began to jump to their feet.

"Goodness, it's late."

"I got to be off."

"Me too."

"Lord, where's my things?"

"Well, ta-ta, Ma; ta boys—be good."

"Anything you want up from the Stores? . . ."

They hitched up their stockings, patted their hats, and went running up the bank. This was the hour when walkers and bicyclists flowed down the long hills to Stroud, when the hooters called through the morning dews and factories puffed out their plumes. From each crooked corner of Stroud's five valleys girls were running to shops and looms, with sleep in their eyes, and eggy cheeks, and in their ears night voices fading. Marjorie was off to her Milliner's Store, Phyllis to her Boots-

and-Shoes, Dorothy to her job as junior clerk in a decayed cloth mill by a stream. As for Harold, he'd started work already; his day began at six, when he'd leave the house with an angry shout for the lathe work he really loved.

But what should we boys do, now they had all gone? If it was school-time, we pushed off next. If not, we dodged up the bank to play, ran snail races along the walls, or dug in the garden and found potatoes and cooked them in tins on the rubbish heap. We were always hungry, always calling for food, always seeking it in cupboards and hedges. But holiday mornings were a time of risk, there might be housework or errands to do. Mother would be ironing, or tidying-up, or reading books on the floor. So if we hung round the yard we kept our ears cocked; if she caught us, the game was up.

"Ah, there you are, son. I'm needing some salt. Pop to Vick's for a lump, there's a dear."

Or: "See if Granny Trill's got a screw of tea—only ask her nicely, mind."

Or: "Run up to Miss Turk and try and borrow half-crown; I didn't know I'd got so low."

"Ask our Jack, our Mother! I borrowed the bacon. It's blummin'-well his turn now."

But Jack had slid off like an eel through the grass, making his sly getaway as usual. He was jumpy, shifty, and quick-off-the-mark, an electric flex of nerves, skinny compared with the rest of us, or what farmers might call a "poor doer." If they had, in fact, they would have been quite wrong, for Jack did himself very well. He had developed a mealtime strategy which ensured that he ate for two. Speed and guile were the keys to his success, and we hungry ones called him the Slider.

Jack ate against time; that was really his secret; and in our house you had to do it. Imagine us all sitting down to dinner; eight round a pot of stew. It was lentil stew usually, a heavy brown mash made apparently of plastic studs. Though it smelt of hot stables, we were used to it, and it was filling enough—could you get it. But the size of our family outstripped the size of the pot, so there was never quite enough to go round.

When it came to serving, Mother had no method, not even the law of chance—a dab on each plate in any old order and then every man for himself. No grace, no warning, no starting-gun; but the first to finish what he'd had on his plate could claim what was left in the pot. Mother's swooping spoon was breathlessly watched—let the lentils fall where they may. But starveling Jack had worked it all out; he followed the spoon with his plate. Absentmindedly Mother would give him first dollop, and very often a second, and as soon as he got it he swallowed it whole, not using his teeth at all. "More please, I've finished"—the bare plate proved it, so he got the pot scrapings too. Many's the race I've lost to him thus, being just that second slower. But it left me marked with an ugly scar, a twisted, food-crazed nature, so that still I am calling for whole rice puddings and big pots of stew in the night.

The day was over and we had used it, running errands or prowling the fields. When evening came we returned to the kitchen, back to its smoky comfort, in from the rapidly cooling air to its wrappings of warmth and cooking. We boys came first, scuffling down the bank, singly, like homing crows. Long tongues of shadows licked the curves of the fields and the trees turned plump and still. I had been off to Painswick to pay the rates, running fast through the long wet grass, and now I was back, panting hard, the job finished, with hayseeds stuck to my legs. A plate of blue smoke hung above our chimney, flat in the motionless air, and every stone in the path as I ran down home shook my bones with arriving joy.

We chopped wood for the night and carried it in, dry beech sticks as brittle as candy. The baker came down with a basket of bread slung carelessly over his shoulder. Eight quartern loaves, cottage-size, black-crusted, were handed in at the door. A few crisp flakes of pungent crust still clung to his empty basket, so we scooped them up on our spit-wet fingers and laid them upon our tongues. The twilight gathered, the baker shouted good night, and whistled his way up the bank. Up in the road his black horse waited, the cart lamps smoking red.

Indoors, our Mother was cooking pancakes, her face aglow from the fire. There was a smell of sharp lemon and salty batter, and a burning hiss of oil. The kitchen was dark and convulsive with shadows, no lights had yet been lit. Flames leapt, subsided, corners woke and died, fires burned in a thousand brasses.

"Poke round for the matches, dear boy," said Mother. "Damn me if I know where they got to."

We lit the candles and set them about, each in its proper order: two on the mantelpiece, one on the piano, and one on a plate in the window. Each candle suspended a ball of light, a luminous fragile glow, which swelled and contracted to the spluttering wick or leaned to the moving air. Their flames pushed weakly against the red of the fire, too tenuous to make much headway, revealing our faces more by casts of darkness than by any clear light they threw.

Next we filled and lit the tall iron lamp and placed it on the table. When the wick had warmed and was drawing properly we turned it up full strength. The flame in the funnel then sprang alive and rose like a pointed flower, began to sing and shudder and grow more radiant, throwing pools of light on the ceiling. Even so the kitchen remained mostly in shadow, its walls a voluptuous gloom.

The time had come for my violin practice. I began twanging the strings with relish. Mother was still frying and rolling up pancakes; my brothers lowered their heads and sighed. I propped my music on the back of a chair and sliced through a Russian Dance while sweet smells of resin mixed with lemon and fat as the dust flew in clouds from my bow. Now and then I got a note just right, and then Mother would throw me a glance. A glance of piercing, anxious encouragement as she side-stepped my swinging arm. Plump in her slippers, one hand to her cheek, her pan beating time in the other, her hair falling down about her ears, mouth working to help out the tune—old and tired though she was, her eyes were a girl's, and it was for looks such as these that I played.

"Splendid!" she cried. "Top hole! Clap-clap! Now give us another, me lad."

So I slashed away at "William Tell" and when I did that, plates jumped; and Mother skipped gaily around the hearth-rug, and even Tony rocked a bit in his chair.

Meanwhile Jack had cleared some boots from the table and started his inscrutable homework. Tony, in his corner, began to talk to the cat and play with some fragments of cloth. So with the curtains drawn close and the pancakes coming, we settled down to the evening. When the kettle boiled and the toast was made, we gathered and had our tea. We grabbed and dodged and passed and snatched, and packed our mouths like pelicans.

Mother ate always standing up, tearing crusts off the loaf with her fingers, a hand-to-mouth feeding that expressed her vigilance, like that of a wireless operator at sea. For most of Mother's attention was fixed on the grate, whose fire must never go out. When it threatened to do so she became seized with hysteria, wailing and wringing her hands, pouring on oil and chopping up chairs in a frenzy to keep it alive. In fact it seldom went out completely, though it was very often ill. But Mother nursed it with skill, banking it up every night and blowing hard on the bars every morning. The state of our fire became as important to us as it must have been to a primitive tribe. When it sulked and sank we were filled with dismay; when it blazed all was well with the world; but if—God save us—it went out altogether, then we were clutched by primeval chills. Then it seemed that the very sun had died, that winter had come for ever, that the wolves of the wilderness were gathering near, and that there was no more hope to look for. . . .

But tonight the firelight snapped and crackled, and Mother was in full control. She ruled the range and all its equipment with a tireless, nervous touch. Eating with one hand, she threw on wood with the other, raked the ashes and heated the oven, put on a kettle, stirred the pot, and spread out some more shirts on the guard. As soon as we boys had finished our tea we pushed all the crockery aside, piled it up roughly at the far end of the table and settled down under the lamp. Its light was warm and live around us, a kind of puddle of fire of its own. I set up my book and began to draw. Jack worked at his notes and figures. Tony was playing with some cotton reels, pushing them slowly round the table.

All was silent except for Tony's voice, softly muttering his cotton-real story.

". . . So they come out of this big hole see, and the big chap said fie he said we'll kill 'em see, and the pirates was waiting up 'ere, and they had this gurt cannon and they went bang fire and the big chap fell down wheeee! and rolled back in the 'ole and I said we got 'em and I run up the 'ill and this boat see was comin' and I jumped on board whooosh cruump and I said now I'm captain see and they said fie and I took me 'atchet 'ack 'ack and they all fell plop in the sea wallop and I sailed the boat round 'ere and round 'ere and up 'ere and round 'ere and down 'ere and up 'ere and round 'ere and down 'ere . . ."

Now the girls arrived home in their belted mackintoshes, flushed from their walk through the dark, and we looked up from our games and said: "Got anything for us?" and Dorothy gave us some liquorice. Then they all had their supper at one end of the table while we boys carried on at the other. When supper was over and cleared away, the kitchen fitted us all. We drew together round the evening lamp, the vast and easy time. . . . Marjorie began to trim a new hat, Dorothy to write a love letter, Phyllis sat down with some forks and spoons, blew ah! and sleepily rubbed them. Harold, home late, cleaned his bike in a corner. Mother was cutting up newspapers.

We talked in spurts, in lowered voices, scarcely noticing if anyone answered.

"I turned a shaft to a thou' today," said Harold.

"A what?"

"He said a 'thou'.' "

Chairs creaked awhile as we thought about it. . . .

"Charlie Revell's got a brand-new suit. He had it made to fit. . . ."

"He half fancies himself."

"Charlie Revell! . . ."

Pause.

"Look, Doth, I got these bits for sixpence. I'm going to stitch 'em all round the top here."

"Mmmmm. Well. Tccch-tcch. S'alright . . ."

"Dr. Green came up to the shop this morning. Wearing corduroy bloomers. Laugh! . . ."

"Look, Ma, look! I've drawn a church on fire. Look, Marge, Doth! Hey, look! . . ."

"If x equals x, then y equals z—shut up!—if x is y . . ."

"O Madeline, if you'll be mine, I'll take you o'er the sea, di-dah . . ."

"Look what I've cut for my scrapbook, girls—a Beefeater—isn't he killing?"

"Charlie Revell cheeked his dad today. He called him a dafty. He . . ."

". . . You know that boy from the Dairy, Marge—the one they call Barnacle Boots? Well, he asked me to go to Spot's with him. I told him to run off home."

"No! You never!"

"I certainly did. I said I don't go to no pictures with butter-wallopers. You should have seen his face . . ."

"Harry Lazbury smells of chicken-gah. I had to move me desk."

"Just hark who's talking. Dainty Dick."

"I'll never be ready by Sunday . . ."

"I've found a lovely snip for my animal page—an old seal—look girls, the expression! . . ."

"So I went round 'ere, and down round 'ere, and he said fie so I went 'ack 'ack . . ."

"What couldn't I do to a nice cream slice . . ."

"Charlie Revell's had 'is ears syringed . . ."

"D'you remember, Doth, when we went to Spot's, and they said, 'Children in Arms Not Allowed,' and we walked little Tone right up the steps and he wasn't even two? . . ."

Marge gave her silky, remembering laugh and looked fondly across at Tony. The fire burned clear with a bottle-green light. Their voices grew low and furry. A farm dog barked far across the valley, fixing the time and distance exactly. Warned by the dog and some hooting owls, I could sense the night valley emptying, stretching in mists of stars and water, growing slowly more secret and late.

The kitchen, warm and murmuring now, vibrated with rosy darkness. My pencil began to wander on the page, my eyes to cloud and clear. I thought I'd stretch myself out on the sofa—for a while, for a short while only. The girls' muted chatter went on and on; I struggled to catch the drift. "Sh! . . . Not now . . . When the boys are in bed . . . You'll die when you hear . . . Not now . . ."

The boards on the ceiling were melting like water. Words broke and went floating away. Chords of smooth music surged up in my head, thick tides of warmth overwhelmed me, I was drowning in languors of feathered seas, spiralling cozily down. . . .

Once in a while I was gently roused to a sound amplified by sleep: to the fall of a coal, the sneeze of the cat, or a muted exclamation. "She couldn't have done such a thing. . . . She did. . . . Done what? . . . What thing? . . . Tell, tell me. . . ." But helpless I glided back to sleep, deep in the creviced seas, the blind waters stilled me, weighed me down, the girls' words floated on top. I lay longer now, and deeper far; heavier weeds were falling on me. . . .

"Come on, Loll. Time to go to bed. The boys went up long ago." The whispering girls bent over me; the kitchen returned upside down. "Wake up, lamb. . . . He's wacked to the wide. Let's try and carry him up."

Half-waking, half-carried, they got me upstairs. I felt drunk and tattered with dreams. They dragged me stumbling round the bend in the landing, and then I smelt the sweet blankets of bed.

It was cold in the bedroom; there were no fires here. Jack lay open-mouthed, asleep. Shivering, I swayed while the girls undressed me, giggling around my buttons. They left me my shirt and my woollen socks, then stuffed me between the sheets.

Away went the candle down the stairs, boards creaked and the kitchen door shut. Darkness. Shapes returning slow. The window a square of silver. My bed-half was cold—Jack hot as a bird. For a while I lay doubled, teeth chattering, blowing, warming against him slowly.

"Keep yer knees to yerself," said Jack, turning over. He woke. "Say, think of a number!"

" 'Leven-hundred and two," I groaned, in a trance.

"Double it," he hissed in my ear.

Double it . . . twenty-four hundred and what? Can't do it. Something or other . . . A dog barked again and swallowed a goose. The kitchen still murmured downstairs. Jack quickly submerged, having fired off his guns, and began snorkling away at my side. Gradually I straightened my rigid limbs and hooked all my fingers together. I felt wide awake now. I thought I'd count to a million. "One, two . . ." I said; that's all.

Questions and Suggestions

1. Should the early passages describing the family include a portrait of the mother? Do you get to know her anyway? If so, how?

2. Is the title appropriate?

3. How does Lee use time as a means of organizing the essay? Is it the main device for achieving unity?

4. After studying the organization of this selection, make a topic outline that indicates the main divisions and subdivisions.

5. Is there evidence in the choice of subjects and the use of language that Lee and Stuart regard life in much the same manner?

6. Cite examples of Lee's use of sounds, smells, and sights that evoke the past.

7. Study his use of verbs and see what they contribute to the total effect.

8. Does Lee overdo his use of remembered dialogue? Does it have a quality of being accurately recalled?

9. Are you ever reminded of a play as you read this essay? If so, why?

10. Consult the *New English Dictionary (NED)* for the definitions of such words as *dotty, cordite, fug, scruffy, horse brass, treacle,* and *quartern.*

Ideas for Writing

1. Describe a room in your home in such a way that your paper

reveals the personality of the member of your family most closely associated with it.

2. Using events that occurred in a brief sequence of time, show one of your parents at work or leisure. Choose action that is significant and revealing.

3. How does one of your parents exhibit tact or patience?

4. Write a descriptive paragraph that evokes the appearance, sounds, and odors of a kitchen, workshop, garage, or laundry.

5. Contrast the "voices" in the Lee household with those heard in the modern home depicted in D. H. Lawrence's "The Rocking-Horse Winner."

GUEST TOWELS

EVAN S. CONNELL, JR.

After two years at Dartmouth, Evan S. Connell, Jr. (1924–), a native of Kansas City, joined the Air Force. Upon his discharge, he resumed his studies, graduating from the University of Kansas. He has also studied at Columbia, Stanford, and San Francisco State College. Some of the short stories that he included in *The Anatomy Lesson* had won prizes and had been included in *The Best American Short Stories,* edited by Martha Foley, and the O. Henry *Prize Stories of 1949* and *1951.*

Boys, as everyone knew, were more trouble than girls, but to Mrs. Bridge it began to seem that Douglas was more trouble than both the girls together. Ruth, silent Ruth, was no trouble at all; Mrs. Bridge sometimes grew uneasy over this very fact, because it was slightly unnatural. Carolyn made up for Ruth, what with temper tantrums and fits of selfishness, but she was nothing compared to Douglas, who, strangely enough, never actually appeared to be attempting to make trouble; it was just that somehow he *was* trouble. Invariably there was something about him that needed to be corrected or attended to, though he himself was totally oblivious to this fact, or, if he was aware of it, was unconcerned. Whenever she encountered him he was either hungry, or dirty, or late, or needed a haircut, or had outgrown something, or had a nosebleed, or had just cut himself, or had lost something, or was just generally ragged and grimy looking. Mrs. Bridge could not understand it. She could take him down to the Plaza for a new pair of corduroy knickers and a week later he had worn a hole through the knee. He was invariably surprised and a little pained by her dismay; he felt fine—what else mattered?

He was hostile to guest towels. She knew this, but, because guest towels were no concern of his, there had never been any direct conflict over them. She had a supply of Margab, which were the best, at least in the opinion of everyone she knew, and whenever guests were coming to the house she would put the ordinary towels in the laundry and place several of these little pastel towels in each of the bathrooms. They were quite small, not much larger than a handkerchief, and no one ever touched them. After the visitors had gone home she would carefully lift them from the rack and replace them in the box till next time. Nobody touched them because they looked too nice; guests always did as she herself did in their homes—she would dry her hands on a piece of Kleenex.

One afternoon after a luncheon she went around the house collecting the guest towels as usual, and was very much surprised to find that one of the towels in Douglas's bathroom had been used. It was, in fact, filthy. There was no question about who had used this towel. She found Douglas sitting in a tree in the vacant lot. He was not doing anything as far as she could tell; he was just up in the tree. Mrs. Bridge approached the tree and asked him about the towel. She held it up. He gazed down at it with a thoughtful expression. Yes, he had dried his hands on it.

"These towels are for guests," said Mrs. Bridge, and felt herself unaccountably on the verge of tears.

"Well, why don't they use them then?" asked Douglas. He began to gaze over the rooftops.

"Come down here where I can talk to you. I don't like shouting at the top of my lungs."

"I can hear you okay," said Douglas, climbing a little higher.

Mrs. Bridge found herself getting furious with him, and was annoyed with herself because it was all really so trivial. Besides, she had begun to feel rather foolish standing under a tree waving a towel and addressing someone who was probably invisible to any of the neighbors who might be watching. All she could see of him were his tennis shoes and one leg. Then, too, she knew he was right, partly right in any event; even so, when you had guests you put guest towels in the bathroom. That was what everyone did, it was what she did, and it was most definitely what she intended to continue doing.

"They always just use their handkerchief or something," said Douglas moodily from high above.

"Never mind," said Mrs. Bridge. "From now on you leave those towels alone."

There was no answer from the tree.

"Do you hear me?"

"I hear you," said Douglas.

Questions and Suggestions

1. From whose point of view is this anecdote told? Why is it humorous? Do Mrs. Bridge and Douglas remind you of any persons whom you know?
2. Which of Mrs. Bridge's attributes and thoughts show that she goes along with the crowd?
3. What kind of mother do you assume her to be?
4. How successful do you find the inclusion of the scene at the tree, the use of dialogue, and the selection of specific details?
5. Contrast Mrs. Bridge with Mrs. Lee. Why do you prefer one mother more than the other?
6. See what H. L. Mencken says in *The American Language: Supplement One* about the popularity of such a coined trade name as *Kleenex,* which appeared in the 1920's.

Ideas for Writing

1. Contrast Connell's presentation of his material with a similarly short episode that appears in the first chapter of Sinclair Lewis's *Babbitt,* when George F. Babbitt also decides to use a guest towel. Do the purposes and methods of the authors vary? In what respect do they agree?
2. Recall an episode from your childhood when you went against the accepted customs of your family or social group, especially if you thought the convention was a foolish one.
3. Recall the difficulty and the resulting family scenes when

you failed to keep your clothes in good condition, neglected to clean your room, or left the bathroom in a mess.

4. Describe the difficulties you have even now in getting ready for your first class.

5. Show how your mother resembles Mrs. Bridge, or how she is quite the opposite.

6. Do you believe that parents love their children equally? If not, why do your parents show some preference?

THE KAGGS FAMILY

ANDREW HALLIDAY

Essayist and dramatist, Andrew Halliday (1830–1877) dropped his surname, Duff, when he moved to London. A Scot by birth and the son of a preacher, Halliday received his education at the University of Aberdeen. Shortly after he arrived in London, in 1849, he began writing for a number of periodicals. Later he was to write numerous travesties, farces, burlesques, domestic dramas, and adaptations of novels. Dickens himself praised Halliday's version of *Little Em'ly*. Although a recent edition of Henry Mayhew's *London's Underworld* makes no mention of the fact, Halliday contributed to the fourth volume of *London Labour and the London Poor* the section that deals with "Beggars and Cheats."

In a paved court, dignified with the name of a market, leading into one of the principal thoroughfares of London, dwelt a family whom, from fear of an action for libel which, should they ever read these lines, they would assuredly bring, I will call Kaggs. Mr. Kaggs, the head of the family, had commenced life in the service of a nobleman. He was a tall, portly man, with a short nose, broad truculent mouth, and a light, moist eye. His personal advantages and general conduct obtained him promotion, and raised him from the servants' hall to the pantry. When he was thirty years of age, he was butler in the family of a country gentleman, whose youngest daughter fell in

From *London Labour and the London Poor,* 1862.

love, ran away with, and—married him. The angry father closed his doors against them, and steeled his heart to the pathetic appeals addressed to him by every post. Mr. Kaggs, unable to obtain a character from his last place, found himself shut out from his former occupation. His wife gave promise of making an increase to the numbers of the family, and to use Mr. Kaggs's own pantry vernacular, "he was flyblown and frost-bitten every joint of him."

It was then that he first conceived the idea of making his wife's birth and parentage a source of present income and provision for old age. She was an excellent penwoman, and for some months had had great practice in the composition of begging letters to her father. Mr. Kaggs's appearance being martial and imposing, he collected what information he could find upon the subject, and passed himself off for a young Englishman of good family, who had been an officer in the Spanish army, and served "under Evans!" Mrs. Kaggs's knowledge of the county families stood them in good stead, and they begged themselves through England, Scotland, and Wales, and lived in a sort of vulgar luxury, at no cost but invention, falsehood, and a ream or so of paper.

It was some few years ago that I first made their acquaintance. Mrs. Kaggs had bloomed into a fine elderly woman, and Mr. Kaggs's nose and stomach had widened to that appearance of fatherly responsibility and parochial importance that was most to be desired. The wife had sunk to the husband's level, and had brought up her children to tread in the same path. Their family, though not numerous, was a blessing to them, for each child, some way or other, contrived to bring in money. It was their parents' pride that they had given their offspring a liberal education. As soon as they were of an age capable of receiving instruction, they were placed at a respectable boarding-school, and, although they only stayed in it one half-year, they went to another establishment for the next half-year, and so managed to pick up a good miscellaneous education, and at the same time save their parents the cost of board and lodging.

James Julian Kaggs, the eldest and only son, was in Australia, "doing well," as his mamma would often say—though in what particular business or profession was a subject on which she preserved a discreet silence. As I never saw the young man in question, I am unable to furnish any information respecting him.

Catherine Kaggs, the eldest daughter, was an ugly and vulgar girl, on whom a genteel education and her mother's example of elegance and refinement had been thrown away. Kitty was a sort of Cinderella in the family, and being possessed of neither tact nor manner to levy contributions on the charitable, was sentenced to an out-door employment, for which she was well fitted. She sold flowers in the thoroughfare, near the market.

The second daughter, Betsey, was the pride of her father and mother, and the mainstay of the family. Tall, thin, and elegant, interesting rather than pretty, her pale face and subdued manners, her long eyelashes, soft voice, and fine hands, were the very requisites for the personation of beggared gentility and dilapidated aristocracy. Mrs. Kaggs often said, "That poor Kitty was her father's girl, a Kaggs all over—but that Bessie was a Thorncliffe (her own maiden name) and a lady every inch!"

The other children were a boy and girl of five and three years old, who called Mrs. Kaggs "Mamma," but who appeared much too young to belong to that lady in any relation but that of grandchildren. Kitty, the flower girl, was passionately fond of them, and "Bessie" patronised them in her meek, maidenly way, and called them her dear brother and sister.

In the height of the season Miss Bessie Kaggs, attired in shabby black silk, dark shawl, and plain bonnet, would sally forth to the most aristocratic and fashionable squares, attended by her father in a white neck-cloth, carrying in one hand a small and fragile basket, and in the other a heavy and respectable umbrella. Arrived at the mansion of the intended victim, Miss Bessie would give a pretentious knock, and relieve her father of the burthen of the fragile basket. As the door opened, she would desire her parent, who was supposed to be a faithful retainer, to wait, and Mr. Kaggs would touch his hat respectfully and retire to the corner of the square, and watch the placards in the public-house in the next street.

"Is Lady —— within?" Miss Betsey would inquire of the servant.

If the porter replied that his lady was out, or that she could not receive visitors, except by appointment, Miss Betsey would boldly demand pen, ink, and paper, and sit down and write, in a delicate, lady's hand, to the following effect: —

"Miss Thirlbrook presents her compliments to the Countess of ——, and most respectfully requests the honour of enrolling the Countess's name among the list of ladies who are kindly aiding her in disposing of a few necessaries for the toilette.

"Miss Thirlbrook is reduced to this extreme measure from the sad

requirements of her infirm father, formerly an officer in his Majesty's
—d Regiment, who, from a position of comfort and affluence, is now
compelled to seek aid from the charitable, and to rely on the feeble
exertions of his daughter: a confirmed cripple and valetudinarian, he
has no other resources.

"The well-known charity of the Countess of —— has induced Miss
Thirlbrook to make this intrusion on her time. Miss T. will do herself
the honour of waiting upon her ladyship on Thursday, when she
earnestly entreats the favour of an interview, or an inspection of the
few articles she has to dispose of."

Monday.

This carefully concocted letter—so different from the usual appeals
—containing no references to other persons as to character or ante-
cedents, generally had its effect, and in a few days, Miss Betsey would
find herself tête-à-tête with the Countess ——.

On entering the room she would make a profound curtsey, and,
after thanking her ladyship for the honour, would open the fragile
basket, which contained a few bottles of scent, some fancy soaps,
ornamental envelopes, and perforated notepapers.

"Sit down, Miss Thirlbrook," the Countess would open the conversation. "I see the articles. Your note, I think, mentioned something
of your being in less fortunate——"

Miss Betsey would lower her eyelashes and bend her head—not
too deferentially, but as if bowing to circumstances for her father—
her dear father's sake—for this was implied by her admirably concealed histrionic capability.

The lady would then suggest that she had a great many claims
upon her consideration, and would delicately inquire into the pedigree
and circumstances of Lieutenant Thirlbrook, formerly of his Majesty's —d Regiment.

Miss Betsey's replies were neither too ready nor too glib. She suffered herself to be drawn out, but did not advance a statement, and
so established in her patroness's mind the idea that she had to deal
with a very superior person. The sum of the story of this interesting
scion of a fallen house was, that her father was an old Peninsular
officer—as would be seen by a reference to the Army List (Miss Betsey had found the name in an old list); that he had left the service
during the peace in 1814; that a ruinous lawsuit, arising from railway speculations, and an absconding agent, had reduced them to—to—
to their present position—and that six years ago, an old wound—

received at Barossa—had broken out, and laid her father helpless on a sick bed. "I know that these articles," Betsey would conclude, pointing to the fancy soaps and stationery, "are not such perhaps as your ladyship is accustomed to; but if you would kindly aid me by purchasing some of them—if ever so few—you would materially assist us; and I hope that—that we should not prove—either undeserving or ungrateful."

When, as sometimes happened, ladies paid a visit to Lieut. Thirlbrook, everything was prepared for their reception with a dramatic regard for propriety. The garret was made as clean and as uncomfortable as possible. Mr. Kaggs was put to bed, and the purpled pinkness of his complexion toned down with violet powder and cosmetics. A white handkerchief, with the Thirlbrook crest in a corner, was carelessly dropped upon the coverlid. A few physic bottles, an old United Service paper, and a ponderous Bible lay upon a ricketty round table beside him. Mrs. Kaggs was propped up with pillows in an arm-chair near the fireplace and desired to look rheumatic and resigned. Kitty was sent out of the way; and the two children were dressed up in shabby black, and promised plums if they would keep quiet. Miss Betsey herself, in grey stuff and an apron, meek, mild and matronly beyond her years, glided about softly, like a Sister of Mercy connected with the family.

My readers must understand that Mr. Kaggs was the sole tenant of the house he lived in, though he pretended that he only occupied the garrets as a lodger.

During the stay of the fashionable Samaritans, Lieut. Thirlbrook —who had received a wound in his leg at Barossa, under the Duke— would say but little, but now and then his mouth would twitch as with suppressed pain. The visitors were generally much moved at the distressing scene. The gallant veteran—the helpless old lady—the sad and silent children—and the ministering angel of a daughter, were an impressive spectacle. The ladies would promise to exert themselves among their friends, and do all in their power to relieve them.

"Miss Thirlbrook," they would ask, as Miss Betsey attended them to the street-door, "those dear children are not your brother and sister, are they?"

Betsey would suppress a sigh, and say, "They are the son and daughter of my poor brother, who was a surgeon in the Navy—they are orphans. My brother died on the Gold Coast, and his poor wife soon followed him. She was delicate, and could not bear up against the shock. The poor things have only us to look to, and we do for them what lies in our power."

This last stroke was a climax. "She never mentioned them before!" thought the ladies. "What delicacy! What high feeling! These are not common beggars, who make an exaggerated statement of their griefs."

"Miss Thirlbrook, I am sure you will pardon me for making the offer; but those dear children upstairs do not look strong. I hope you will not be offended by my offering to send them a luncheon now and then—a few delicacies—nourishing things—to do them good."

Miss Betsey would curtsey, lower her eyelids, and say, softly, "They *are not* strong."

"I'll send my servant as soon as I get home. Pray use this trifle for the present," (the lady would take out her purse,) "and good morning, Miss Thirlbrook. I must shake hands with you. I consider myself fortunate in having made your acquaintance."

Betsey's eyes would fill with tears, and as she held the door open, the expression of her face would plainly say: "Not only for myself, oh dear and charitable ladies, but for my father—my poor father—who was wounded, at Barossa, in the leg—do I thank you from the depths of a profoundly grateful heart."

When the basket arrived, Miss Betsey would sit down with her worthy parents and enjoy whatever poultry or meat had not been touched; but anything that had been cut, anything "second-hand," that dainty and haughty young lady would instruct her sister Kitty to give to the poor beggars.

This system of swindling could not, of course, last many years, and when the west end of London became too hot to hold them, the indefatigable Kaggses put an advertisement into the *Times* and *Morning Post,* addressed to the charitable and humane, saying that "a poor, but respectable family, required a small sum to enable them to make up the amount of their passage to Australia, and that they could give the highest references as to character."

The old certificates were hawked about, and for more than two years they drove a roaring trade in money, outfits, and necessaries for a voyage. Mr. Kaggs, too, made a fortunate hit. He purchased an old piano, and raffled it at five shillings a head. Each of his own family took a chance. At the first raffle Miss Betsey won it, at the second, Miss Kitty, on the third, Mr. Kaggs, on the fourth, his faithful partner, and on the fifth and last time, a particular friend of Miss Kitty's, a young lady in the green-grocery line. This invaluable piece of furniture was eventually disposed of by private contract to a dealer in Barret's Court, Oxford Street, and, a few days later, the Kaggs family really sailed for Melbourne, and I have never since heard of them.

Questions and Suggestions

1. A writer uses irony when he says one thing but means the opposite. When Mrs. Kaggs claims that her son is successful, what does the author want you to understand about the young man? Explain those examples of irony that you locate in the opening paragraphs.

2. Is Halliday sympathetic toward the family? Does he preach or moralize? Does he advocate strict adherence to the Commandment "Honor thy Father and thy Mother"?

3. Specific scenes follow the introductory summary details. How many specific scenes do you find?

4. If the details of the garret help you to visualize the room and its occupants, do these same descriptive elements also offer any explanation for the topic sentence of the paragraph and the idea of "dramatic regard for propriety"?

5. Some people maintain that by using the same ingenuity that he does in cheating, a successful swindler could turn his energy to some account and become a worthy member of society. Do you find any evidence in this sketch that would warrant such a claim?

6. Consult your dictionary for the meaning of *character, truculent, vernacular, valetudinarian, tête-à-tête,* and *scion.* To what does the term *Peninsular* refer? Who was the *Duke* under whom Mr. Kaggs was supposed to have served?

Ideas for Writing

1. Define one: son, daughter, mother, father, brother, sister, guardian, or grandparent. In addition to pointing out the significant quality of character, consider also the individual's relationship to the rest of the family.

2. Contrast the home life of the Kaggses with that of the Lees.

3. Some writers claim it is easier to write about "bad" people than about "good" people. Contrast a useful citizen whom you know with an irresponsible one, remembering to do justice to the former individual.

4. Contrast the Kaggs family with the Micawber family in *David Copperfield.* See especially chapters XI-XII.

5. Do you have a friend who, when quite young, was forced to help support his family? What effect did the work have upon him?

NOTES OF A NATIVE SON

JAMES BALDWIN

Since the publication in 1953 of his first novel, Go Tell It on the Mountain, which is, in part, based on his personal experiences of growing up in Harlem, James Baldwin (1924–) has continued to receive critical acclaim. Winner of a Guggenheim Fellowship, he has also published a novel about Americans in Paris. He is a frequent contributor to some of the better magazines.

On the twenty-ninth of July, in 1943, my father died. On the same day, a few hours later, his last child was born. Over a month before this, there had been, in Detroit, one of the bloodiest race riots of the century. A few hours after my father's funeral, a race riot broke out in Harlem. On the morning of August third we drove him to the graveyard through a wilderness of smashed plate glass.

The day of my father's funeral had also been my nineteenth birthday. It seemed to me that God Himself had devised, to mark my father's end, the most sustained and brutally dissonant of codas. And it seemed to me, too, that the violence which rose all about us as my father left the world had been devised as a corrective for the pride of his eldest son. I had inclined to be contemptuous of my father for the conditions of his life, for the conditions of our lives. When his life had ended I began to wonder about that life and also, in a new way, to be apprehensive about my own.

I had not known my father very well. We had got on badly, partly because we shared, in our different fashions, the vice of stubborn pride. When he was dead I realized that I had hardly ever spoken to him. It seems to be typical of life in America, where nothing, as yet, is stratified, and where opportunities, real and fancied, are thicker than anywhere else on the globe, that the second generation has no time to talk to the first. No one, including my father, seems to have known exactly how old he was, but his mother had been born during slavery. He was of the first generation of free men. He, along with thousands of other Negroes, came North after 1919 and I was part of that generation which had never seen the landscape of what Negroes sometimes call the Old Country.

He had been born in New Orleans and had been a young man there during the time that Louis Armstrong, a boy, was running errands for the dives and honky-tonks of what was always presented to me as one of the most wicked of cities. He was, I think, very handsome. Handsome, proud, and ingrown, "like a toenail," somebody said. But he looked to me, as I grew older, like pictures I had seen of African tribal chieftains: he really should have been naked, with warpaint on and barbaric mementos, standing among spears. He could be chilling in the pulpit and indescribably cruel in his personal life and he was certainly the most bitter man I have ever met; yet it must be said that there was something else buried in him, which lent him his tremendous power and, even, a rather crushing charm. It had something to do with his blackness, I think—he was very black— and his beauty, and the fact that he knew that he was black but did not know he was beautiful.

He claimed to be proud of his blackness but it had also been the cause of much humiliation. He was not a young man when we were growing up and he had already suffered many kinds of ruin; in his outrageously demanding and protective way he loved his children, who were black like him and menaced like him; and all these things sometimes showed in his face when he tried, never to my knowledge with any success, to establish contact with any of us.

When he took one of his children on his knee to play with them, they always became fretful and began to cry; when he tried to help one of us with our homework, the absolutely unabating tension which emanated from him caused our minds and our tongues to become paralyzed, so that he, scarcely knowing why, flew into a rage and the child, not knowing why, was punished. If it ever entered his head to bring a surprise home for his children, it was, almost unfailingly, the wrong surprise, and even the big watermelons he often brought home on his back in the summer led to the most appalling scenes.

I do not remember, in all those years, that a single one of his children was ever glad to see him come home. From what I was able to gather of his early life, it seemed that this inability to establish contact with other people had always marked him. There was something in him, therefore, groping and tentative, which was never expressed. One saw it most clearly when he was facing new people and hoping to impress them. But he never did, not for long. We went from church to smaller and more improbable church, he found himself in less and less demand as a minister, and by the time he died none of his friends had come to see him for a long time. He had lived and died in an intolerable bitterness of spirit and it frightened me, as we drove him to the graveyard through those unquiet, ruined streets, to see how powerful and overflowing this bitterness could be and to realize that it now was mine.

When he died I had been away from home for a little over a year. In that year I had had time to become aware of the meaning of all my father's warnings, had discovered the secret of his proudly pursed lips and rigid carriage: I had discovered the weight of white people in the world.

He had been ill a long time—in the mind, as we now realized, reliving instances of his fantastic intransigence in the new light of his affliction and endeavoring to feel a sorrow for him which never, quite, came true. We had not known that he was being eaten up by paranoia, and the discovery that his cruelty, to our bodies and our minds, had been one of the symptoms of his illness was not, then, enough to enable us to forgive him. The younger children felt, quite simply, relief that he would not be coming home any more. My mother's observation that it was he, after all, who had kept them alive all these years meant nothing because the problems of keeping children alive are not real for children. The older children felt, with my father gone, that they could invite their friends to the house without fear of insult.

His illness was beyond all hope of healing before anyone realized that he was ill. He had always been so strange and had lived, like a prophet, in such unimaginably close communion with the Lord that his long silences, punctuated by moans and hallelujahs and snatches of old songs while he sat at the living-room window, never seemed odd to us. It was not until he refused to eat because, he said, his family was trying to poison him that my mother was forced to accept as a fact what had, until then, been only an unwilling suspicion. When he was committed, it was discovered that he had tuberculosis, and the disease of his mind allowed the disease of his body to destroy him. For the doctors could not force him to eat, either, and, though he was fed intravenously, it was clear from the beginning that there was no hope for him.

In my mind's eye I could see him sitting at the window, locked up in his terrors; hating and fearing every living soul, including his children who had betrayed him too, by reaching toward the world which had despised him. There were nine of us. I began to wonder what it could have felt like for such a man to have had nine children whom he could barely feed. He spent great energy keeping us away from the people who surrounded us, people who had all-night rent parties to which we listened when we should have been sleeping, people who cursed and drank and flashed razor blades on Lenox Avenue. He could not understand why, if they had so much energy to spare, they could not use it to make their lives better. He treated almost everybody on our block with a most uncharitable asperity and neither they, nor, of course, their children were slow to reciprocate.

The only white people who came to our house were welfare workers and bill collectors. It was clear that my father felt their very presence in his home to be a violation: this was conveyed by his carriage, almost ludicrously stiff, and by his voice, harsh and vindictively polite. When I was around nine or ten I wrote a play which was directed by a young, white schoolteacher named Orilla Miller, who then took an interest in me, gave me books to read, and decided to take me to see what she somewhat tactlessly referred to as "real" plays. Theater-going was forbidden in our house, but, with the really cruel intuitiveness of a child, I suspected that the color of this woman's skin would carry the day for me. When, at school, she suggested taking me out, I agreed that she should pick me up at my house one evening. I then, very cleverly, left all the rest to my mother, who suggested to my father, as I knew she would, that it would not be very nice to let such a kind woman make the trip for nothing. Also, since it was a schoolteacher, I imagine that my mother countered the idea of sin with the idea of "education," which word, even with my father, carried a kind of bitter weight.

Before the teacher came, my father took me aside to ask *why* she was coming, what *interest* she could possibly have in a boy like me. And I understood that my father was waiting for me to say something —I didn't quite know what; perhaps that I wanted his protection against this teacher and her "education."

I said none of these things and the teacher came and we went out. It was clear, during the brief interview in our living-room, that my father would have refused permission if he had dared. The fact that he did not dare caused me to despise him; I had no way of knowing that he was facing in that living-room a wholly unprecedented and frightening situation.

Later, when my father had been laid off from his job, this woman went to a great deal of trouble to be of help to us. My mother called her by the highest name she knew: she said she was a "Christian." My father could scarcely disagree but during the four or five years of our relatively close association he never trusted her. In later years, particularly when it began to be clear that this "education" of mine was going to lead me to perdition, he became more explicit and warned me that my white friends in high school were not really my friends and that I would see, when I was older, how white people would do anything to keep a Negro down. Some of them could be nice, he admitted, but none of them were to be trusted. I did not feel this way and I was certain, in my innocence, that I never would.

But the year which preceded my father's death had made a great change in my life. I had been living in New Jersey, working in defense plants, working and living among Southerners, white and black. I knew about the South, of course, and how Southerners treated Negroes and expected them to behave; but it had never entered my mind that anyone would look at me and expect *me* to behave that way. I learned in New Jersey that to be a Negro meant, precisely, that one was never looked at but was simply at the mercy of the reflexes the color of one's skin caused in other people. I acted in New Jersey as I had always acted, that is as though I thought a great deal of myself—I had to *act* that way—with results that were, simply, unbelievable. I had scarcely arrived before I had earned the enmity of all my superiors and nearly all my co-workers. In the beginning, to make matters worse, I simply did not know what was happening, I did not know what I had done, and I shortly began to wonder what *anyone* could possibly do, to bring about such unanimous, active, and unbearably vocal hostility.

I knew about Jim Crow but I had never experienced it. I went to the same self-service restaurant three times and stood with all the Princeton boys before the counter; it was always an extraordinarily long time before anything was set before me; but it was not until the fourth visit that I learned that, in fact, nothing had ever been set before me: I had simply picked something up. Negroes were not served there, I was told, and they had been waiting for me to realize that I was always the only Negro present.

It was the same story all over New Jersey, in bars, bowling alleys, diners, places to live. I very shortly became notorious and children giggled behind me when I passed and their elders whispered or shouted —they really believed that I was mad. And it did begin to work on my mind, of course; I began to be afraid to go anywhere and to compensate for this I went places to which I really should not have gone and where, God knows, I had no desire to be.

My reputation in town naturally enhanced my reputation at work, and my working day became one long series of acrobatics designed to keep me out of trouble. I was fired once and contrived, with the aid of a friend from New York, to get back on the payroll; was fired again, and bounced back again. It took a while to fire me for the third time, but the third time took.

That year in New Jersey lives in my mind as though it were the year during which my veins were, daily, pumped full of poison. Or as though it were the year in which, having an unsuspected predilection for it, I first contracted some dread, chronic disease, the unfailing symptoms of which are a kind of blind fever, a pounding in the skull, and fire in the bowels. Once this disease is contracted, it can, without an instant's warning, recur at any moment. There is not a Negro alive who does not have this rage in his blood—one has the choice, merely, of living with it consciously or surrendering to it. As for me, this fever has recurred in me, and does, and will until the day I die.

My last night in New Jersey, a white friend took me to the nearest big town, Trenton. Almost every detail of that night stands out very clearly in my memory. I even remember the name of the movie we saw because its title impressed me as being so aptly ironical. It was about the German occupation of France, and it was called "This Land Is Mine." I remember the name of the diner we walked into when the movie ended: the *American Diner*. The counterman asked what we wanted and I remember answering with the casual sharpness which had become my habit: "We want a hamburger and a cup of coffee, what do you think we want?"

I do not know why, after a year of such rebuffs, I completely failed to anticipate his answer, which was, of course, "We don't serve Negroes here." I made some sardonic comment about the name of his diner, and we walked out into the streets.

This was the time of the "brown-out," when the lights in all American cities were very dim. When we re-entered the streets something happened to me which had the force of an optical illusion, or a nightmare. People were moving in every direction but it seemed to me, in that instant, that all of the people I could see, and many more, were moving toward me, against me, and that everyone was white. I remember how their faces gleamed. And I felt, like a physical sensation, a *click* at the nape of my neck as though some interior string connecting my head to my body had been cut. I began to walk. I heard my friend call after me, but I ignored him. Heaven only knows what was going on in his mind, but he had the good sense not to touch me—I don't know what would have happened if he had—and to keep me in sight.

I don't know what was going on in my mind, either—I certainly had no conscious plan. I wanted to do something to crush these white faces, which were crushing me. I walked until I came to an enormous, glittering restaurant in which I knew not even the intercession of the Virgin would cause me to be served. I pushed through the doors and took the first vacant seat I saw, at a table for two, and waited.

I rather wonder what I could possibly have looked like. Whatever I looked like, I frightened the waitress who shortly appeared, and the moment she appeared all of my fury flowed toward her. I felt that if she found a black man so frightening I would make her fright worthwhile.

She did not ask me what I wanted, but repeated, as though she had learned it somewhere, "We don't serve Negroes here." She did not say it with the blunt, derisive hostility to which I had grown so accustomed, but rather with a note of apology in her voice and fear. This made me colder and more murderous than ever. I felt I had to do something with my hands. I wanted her to come close enough for me to get her neck between my hands.

So I pretended not to have understood her, hoping to draw her closer. And she did step a very short step closer, with her pencil poised incongruously over her pad, and repeated the formula: ". . . don't serve Negroes here."

Somehow, with the repetition of that phrase, I realized that she would never come any closer. There was nothing on the table but an ordinary mug, half full of water, and I picked this up and hurled it at her. She ducked and it shattered against the mirror behind the bar. With that sound, my frozen blood abruptly thawed, I returned from wherever I had been, I *saw*, for the first time, the restaurant, the people, with their mouths open, already, as it seemed to me, rising as one man, and I realized what I had done, and I was frightened. I rose and began running for the door. A round, potbellied man grabbed me by the nape of the neck and began to beat me about the face. I kicked him and got loose and ran into the streets. My friend whispered *"Run!"* and I ran.

My friend stayed outside the restaurant long enough to misdirect my pursuers. I do not know what I said to him when he came to my room that night. I felt, in the oddest, most awful way, that I had somehow betrayed him. I lived it over and over and over again. I could not get over two facts, both equally difficult for the imagination to grasp, and one was that I could have been murdered. But the other was that I had been ready to commit murder. My life, my real life, was in danger, and not from anything other people might do but from the hatred I carried in my own heart.

I returned home around the second week in June—in great haste because it seemed that my father's death and my mother's confinement were both but a matter of hours. In the case of my mother, it soon became clear that she had simply made a miscalculation. I don't believe that a single one of us arrived in the world, or has since arrived anywhere else, on time. But none of us dawdled so intolerably about the business of being born as did my baby sister. We sometimes amused ourselves, during those endless stifling weeks, by picturing the baby sitting in the safe, warm dark, bitterly regretting the necessity of becoming a part of our chaos and stubbornly putting it off as long as possible.

Death, however, sat as purposefully at my father's bedside as life stirred within my mother's womb, and it was harder to understand why he so lingered in that long shadow. It seemed that he had bent, and for a long time, too, all of his energies toward dying. Now death was ready for him but my father held back.

All of Harlem, indeed, seemed to be infected by waiting. I had never before known it to be so violently still. Racial tensions throughout this country were exacerbated during the early years of the war, partly because the labor market brought together hundreds of thousands of ill-prepared people and partly because Negro soldiers, regardless of where they were born, received their military training in the South. What happened in defense plants and Army camps had repercussions, naturally, in every Negro ghetto. The Harlem police force had been augmented in March, and the unrest grew. Perhaps the most revealing news item, out of the steady parade of reports of muggings, stabbings, shootings, assaults, gang wars, and accusations of police brutality, was the item about six Negro girls who set upon a white girl in the subway because, as they all too accurately put it, she was stepping on their toes. Indeed she was, all over the nation.

I had never before been so aware of policemen, on foot, on horseback, on corners, everywhere, always two by two. Nor had I ever been so aware of small knots of people. Never, when I passed these groups, did the usual sound of a curse or a laugh ring out. Neither did there seem to be any hum of gossip. There was certainly, on the other hand, occurring between them communication extraordinarily intense.

Another thing that was striking was the unexpected diversity of the people who made up these groups. Usually one would see a group of sharpies standing on the street corner, or a group of older men, usually, for some reason, in the vicinity of a barber shop, discussing baseball scores, or the numbers, or the women they had known. Women, in a general way, tended to be seen less often together—unless they were church women, or very young girls, or prostitutes. But that summer I saw the strangest combinations: large, respectable, churchly matrons standing on the stoops or the corners with their hair tied up, together with a girl in sleazy satin whose face bore the marks of gin and the razor, or heavy-set, abrupt, no-nonsense older men in company with the most disreputable and fanatical "race" men, or these same "race" men with the sharpies, or these sharpies with the churchly women. And on each face there seemed to be the same strange, bitter shadow.

The churchly women and the matter-of-fact no-nonsense men had children in the Army. The sleazy girls they talked to had lovers there; the sharpies and the "race" men had friends and brothers there. It would have demanded an unquestioning patriotism, happily as uncommon in this country as it is undesirable, for these people not to have been disturbed by the letters they received, by the newspaper stories they read. It was only the "race" men, to be sure, who spoke ceaselessly of being revenged—how this vengeance was to be exacted was not clear—for the indignities and dangers suffered by Negro boys in uniform; but everybody felt a directionless, hopeless bitterness, as well as that panic which can scarcely be suppressed when one knows that a human being one loves is beyond one's reach, and in danger. Perhaps the best way to sum all this up is to say that the people I knew felt, mainly, a peculiar kind of relief when they knew that their boys were being shipped out of the South, to do battle overseas. Now, even if death should come, it would come with honor and without the complicity of their countrymen. Such a death would be, in short, a fact with which one could hope to live.

It was on the twenty-eighth of July that I visited my father for the first time during his illness and for the last time in his life. The moment I saw him I knew why I had put off this visit so long. I had told my mother that I did not want to see him because I hated him. But this was not true. It was only that I *had* hated him and I wanted to hold on to this hatred. I did not want to look on him as a ruin; it was not a ruin I had hated. I imagine that one of the reasons people cling to their hates so stubbornly is that they sense, once hate is gone, that they will be forced to deal with pain.

We traveled out to him, his older sister and myself, to what seemed to be the very end of Long Island. It was hot and dusty and we wrangled all the way out over the fact that I had recently begun to smoke and, as my aunt said, to give myself airs. But I knew that she wrangled with me because she could not bear to face the fact of her brother's dying. Neither could I endure the reality of her despair, her unstated bafflement as to what had happened to her brother's life, and her own. From time to time she fell into a heavy reverie. Covertly, I watched her face, which was the face of an old woman; soon she would be dying, too.

In my childhood—it had not been so long ago—I had thought her beautiful. At one time one of my brothers and myself had thought of running away to live with her. Now she made me feel pity and revulsion and fear; it was awful to realize that she no longer caused me to feel affection.

She began to cry the moment we entered the hospital room and she saw him lying there, all shriveled and still, like a little black monkey. The great, gleaming apparatus which fed him and would have compelled him to be still even if he had been able to move brought to mind, not beneficence, but torture; the tubes entering his arm made me think of colored pictures I had seen when a child of Gulliver tied down by the pygmies. My aunt wept and wept, there was a whistling sound in my father's throat; nothing was said; he could not speak.

I wanted to take his hand, to say something. But I do not know what I could have said, even if he could have heard me. He was not really in that room with us, he had at last really embarked on his journey; and though my aunt told me that he said he was going to meet Jesus, I did not hear anything except that whistling in his throat.

In the morning came the telegram saying that he was dead. Then the house became absolutely hideous with relatives, friends, hysteria, and confusion, and I left my mother and the children to the care of those impressive women who, in Negro communities at least, automatically appear at times of bereavement armed with lotions, proverbs, and patience, and an ability to cook. I went downtown. By the time I returned, later the same day, my mother had been carried to the hospital and the baby had been born.

For my father's funeral I had nothing black to wear and this posed a nagging problem all day long. It was one of those problems to which the mind insanely clings in order to avoid the mind's real trouble. I spent most of that day at the downtown apartment of a girl I knew, celebrating my birthday with whisky and wondering what to wear that night. This girl had anticipated taking me out for a big dinner and a night club afterward. Sometime during the course of that long day we decided that we would go out anyway, when my father's funeral service was over. I imagine *I* decided it, since, as the funeral hour approached, it became clearer and clearer to me that I would not know what to do with myself when it was over. The girl found a black shirt for me somewhere and ironed it, and, dressed in the darkest pants and jacket I owned, and slightly drunk, I got to my father's funeral.

The chapel was full, but not packed, and very quiet. There were, mainly, my father's relatives, and his children, and here and there I saw faces I had not seen since childhood, the faces of my father's friends. Chief among the mourners was my aunt, who had quarreled with my father all his life. I suppose that she was one of the few people in the world who had loved him, and their incessant quarreling proved, precisely, the strength of the tie that bound them. The only other person in the world, as far as I knew, whose relationship to my father rivaled my aunt's in depth was my mother, who was not there.

It seemed to me that it was a very long funeral. But it was, if anything, a rather shorter funeral than most, nor, since there were no overwhelming, uncontrollable expressions of grief, could it be called— if I dare use the word—successful. The minister who preached my father's funeral sermon was one of the few my father had still been seeing as he neared his end. He presented to us in his sermon a man whom none of us had ever seen—a man thoughtful, patient, and forbearing, a Christian inspiration to all who knew him, and a model for his children. And no doubt the children, in their disturbed and guilty state, were almost ready to believe this; he had been remote enough to be anything.

His sister moaned and this was taken as corroboration. The other faces held a dark, non-committal thoughtfulness. This was not the man they had known, but they had scarcely expected to be confronted with *him;* this was, in a sense deeper than questions of fact, the man they had not known, and the man they had not known may have been the real one. The real man, whoever he had been, had suffered and now he was dead: this was all that was sure and all that mattered now.

While the preacher talked and I watched the children—years of changing their diapers, scrubbing them, slapping them, taking them to school, and scolding them had had the perhaps inevitable result of making me love them, though I am not sure I knew this then—my mind was busily breaking out with a rash of disconnected impressions. Snatches of popular songs, indecent jokes, bits of books I had read, movie sequences, faces, voices, political issues—I thought I was going mad; all these impressions suspended, as it were, in the solution of the faint nausea produced in me by the heat and liquor. For a moment I had the impression that my alcoholic breath, inefficiently disguised with chewing gum, filled the entire chapel. Then someone began singing one of my father's favorite songs and, abruptly, I was with him, sitting on his knee, in the hot, enormous, crowded church which was the first church we attended. It was the Abyssinia Baptist Church on 138th Street. We had not gone there long.

With this image, a host of others came. I had forgotten, in the rage of my growing up, how proud my father had been of me when I was little. Apparently, I had a voice and my father had liked to show me off before the members of the church. I had forgotten what he had looked like when he was pleased but now I remembered that he had always been grinning with pleasure when my solos ended. I even remembered certain expressions on his face when he teased my mother— had he loved her? I would never know. And when had it all begun to change? For now it seemed that he had not always been cruel. I remembered being taken for a haircut and scraping my knee on the foot-rest of the barber's chair and I remembered my father's face as he soothed my crying and applied the stinging iodine. Then I remembered our fights, fights which had been of the worst possible kind because my own technique had been silence.

I remembered the one time in all our life together when we had ever really spoken to each other.

It was on a Sunday and it must have been shortly before I left home. We were walking, just the two of us, in our usual silence, to or from church. I was in high school and had been doing a lot of writing. But I had also been a Young Minister and had been preaching from the pulpit. Lately, I had been taking fewer engagements and preached as rarely as possible.

My father asked me abruptly, "You'd rather write than preach, wouldn't you?"

I was astonished at his question—because it was a real question. I answered, "Yes."

That was all we said. It was awful to remember that that was all we had *ever* said.

The casket now was opened and the mourners were being led up the aisle to look for the last time on the deceased. The assumption was that the family was too overcome with grief to make this journey alone. I disapproved of forcing the children to look on their dead father, considering that the shock of his death, or, more truthfully, the shock of death as a reality, was already a little more than a child could bear, but my judgment in this matter had been overruled and there they were, bewildered and frightened and very small, being led, one by one, to the casket. But there is also something very gallant about children at such moments. It has something to do with their silence and gravity and with the fact that one cannot help them. Their legs, somehow, seem *exposed,* so that it is at once incredible and terribly clear that their legs are all they have to hold them up.

I had not wanted to go to the casket myself and I certainly had not wished to be led there, but there was no way of avoiding either of these forms. One of the deacons led me up and I looked on my father's face. I cannot say that it looked like him at all. His blackness had been equivocated by powder and there was no suggestion in that casket of what his power had, or could have been. He was simply a corpse, and it was hard to believe that he had ever given anyone either joy or pain. Yet his life filled that room. Further up the avenue his wife was holding his new-born child. Life and death so close together, and love and hatred, and right and wrong, said something to me which I did not want to hear concerning man, concerning the life of man.

After the funeral, while I was downtown, desperately celebrating my birthday, a Negro soldier in the lobby of the Hotel Braddock got into a fight with a white policeman over a Negro girl. This was certainly not the first time such an incident had occurred. It was destined, however, to receive an unprecedented publicity, for it ended with the shooting of the soldier. Rumor, flowing immediately to the streets outside, stated that the soldier had been shot in the back, and that he had died protecting a Negro woman. The facts were somewhat different

—the soldier had not been shot in the back, and was not dead—but no
one was interested in the facts. They preferred the invention because
it expressed and corroborated their hates and fears so perfectly. It is
just as well to remember that people are always doing this. Perhaps
many of those legends, including Christianity, to which the world
clings, began their conquest of the world with just some such concerted
surrender to distortion. The effect, in Harlem, of this particular legend
was like the effect of a lit match in a tin of gasoline. The mob gathered
before the doors of the Hotel Braddock simply began to swell and to
spread in every direction, and Harlem exploded.

The mob did not cross the ghetto lines. It seems to have been mainly
interested in something more potent and real than the white face, that
is, in white power, and the principal damage was to white business
establishments in Harlem. It might have been a far bloodier story, of
course, if, at the hour the riot began, these establishments had still
been open. Bars, stores, pawnshops, restaurants, even little luncheon-
ettes were smashed open and looted—looted, it might be added, with
more haste than efficiency. Cans of beans and soup and dog food, along
with toilet paper, corn flakes, sardines, and milk, tumbled every which
way, and abandoned cash registers and cases of beer leaned crazily out
of the splintered windows and were strewn along the avenues. Sheets,
blankets, and clothing of every description formed a kind of path, as
though people had dropped them while running. I truly had not
realized that Harlem *had* so many stores until I saw them all smashed
open; the first time the word *wealth* ever entered my mind in relation
to Harlem was when I saw it scattered in the streets. But one's first,
incongruous impression of plenty was countered immediately by an impression of waste. It would have been better to have left the plate glass
as it had been and the goods lying in the stores.

It would have been better, but it would also have been intolerable,
for Harlem had needed something to smash. To smash something is
the ghetto's chronic need—most of the time it is the members of the
ghetto who smash each other, and themselves. But as long as the ghetto
walls are standing there will always come a moment when these outlets do not work. If ever, indeed, the violence which fills Harlem's
churches, pool-halls, and bars erupts outward in a more direct fashion,
Harlem and its citizens are likely to vanish in an apocalyptic flood.

That this is not likely to happen is due to a great many reasons, most
hidden and powerful among them the Negro's real relation to the white
American. This relation prohibits, simply, anything as uncomplicated

and satisfactory as pure hatred. In order really to hate white people, one has to blot so much out of the mind—and the heart—that this hatred itself becomes an exhausting and self-destructive pose. But this does not mean that love comes easily: the white world is too powerful, too complacent, too ready with gratuitous humiliation, and, above all, too ignorant and too innocent for that. One is absolutely forced to make perpetual qualifications and one's own reactions are always canceling each other out. It is this, really, which has driven so many people mad, both white and black. One is always in the position of having to decide between amputation and gangrene. Amputation is swift but time may prove that the amputation was not necessary—or one may delay the amputation too long. Gangrene is slow, but it is impossible to be sure that one is reading one's symptoms right. The idea of going through life as a cripple is more than one can bear, and equally unbearable is the risk of swelling up slowly, in agony, with poison. And the trouble, finally, is that the risks are real even if the choices do not exist.

But "As for me and my house," my father had said, "we will serve the Lord." I wondered, as we drove him to his resting place, what this line had meant for him. I had heard him preach it many times. I had preached it once myself, proudly giving it an interpretation different from my father's. Now the whole thing came back to me, as though my father and I were on our way to Sunday school and I were memorizing the golden text:

> And if it seem evil unto you to serve the Lord, choose you this day whom you will serve: whether the gods which your fathers served that were on the other side of the flood, or the gods of the Amorites, in whose land ye dwell: but as for me and my house, we will serve the Lord.

I suspected in these familiar lines a meaning which had never been there for me before. All of his texts and songs, which I had decided were meaningless, were arranged before me at his death like empty bottles, waiting to hold the meaning which life would give them for me. This was his legacy: nothing is ever escaped. That bleakly memorable morning I hated the unbelievable streets and the Negroes and whites who had, equally, made them that way. But I knew that it was folly, as my father would have said, this bitterness was folly. It was necessary to hold on to the things that mattered. The dead man mattered, the new life mattered; blackness and whiteness did not matter; to believe that they did was to acquiesce in one's own destruction.

It began to seem that one would have to hold in the mind forever two ideas which seemed to be in opposition. The first idea was acceptance, the acceptance of life as it is, and men as they are: in the light of this idea, it goes without saying that injustice is a commonplace. But this did not mean that one could be complacent, for the second idea was of equal power: that one must never, in one's own life, accept these injustices as commonplace but must fight them with all one's strength. This fight begins, however, in the heart, and it now had been laid to my charge to keep my own heart free of hatred and despair. This intimation made my heart heavy and, now that he was irrecoverable, I wished that my father had been beside me so that I could have searched his face for the answers which only the future would give me now.

Questions and Suggestions

1. Trace the changes in Baldwin's attitudes toward his father? Does he present them in a logical sequence?

2. Why is it necessary for the reader to understand the social conditions, including the violence in Harlem, if he is to interpret the effect of the father's death and if he is to comprehend some of the son's problems?

3. In what ways does the author arouse your sympathy for the father, mother, aunt, and children, as well as for himself?

4. Do you appreciate the author's forthrightness?

5. Do the father and son hold similar feelings for whites?

6. Baldwin suggests that man likes to cling to his hates. Why do you agree or disagree?

7. What is the purpose of the paragraphs that cover the year Baldwin worked in New Jersey?

8. Study the use of such key words as *bitterness, betrayal,* and *cruelty; life* and *death; innocence* and *poison; conversation* and *silences; natives* and *immigrants; disease, love,* and *hate.*

9. Learn the meanings and pronunciations of *intransigence, paranoia, intravenously, asperity, exacerbated, ghetto, reverie, covertly, apocalyptic,* and *gratuitous.*

Ideas for Writing

1. Imagine yourself as an individual who has lived all of his life as a member of a minority group. (The works of Saul Bellow, Ralph Ellison, Lorraine Hansberry, Langston Hughes, Philip Roth, Lillian Smith, and Richard Wright will help you understand what such a life is like.) Present your reaction to a

chance remark, a thoughtless statement, or an intentionally
derogatory criticism.

2. Organize a paper around the contrast inherent in one of the
   following: (a) Baldwin's and Stuart's fathers; (b) Baldwin's
   father and the father in C. P. Snow's "The Stars": (c) and
   home life in Harlem and that in Lee's Cotswold village.

3. Discuss a conflict you have had with a narrow-minded person,
   whether parent, teacher, or friend.

4. How does one learn to tolerate the intolerant individual?
   Should one?

5. Baldwin, who attended a high school in Harlem, learned to
   write through trial and error, not through college training.
   What do you expect your classes in composition to teach you?

FATHERS OF GREAT MEN

GILBERT HIGHET

A native of Glasgow, Gilbert Highet (1906–) graduated from the
University of Glasgow. Later he studied at Oxford, eventually becoming Fellow and Lecturer in Classics at St. John's College. In
1937 he received an invitation to teach at Columbia, but from
1941 to 1946 he was involved with war-time duties. Four years
later, however, he was appointed Anthon Professor of Latin. A
well-known critic, essayist, translator, and broadcaster, Professor
Highet is married to Helen MacInnes, the novelist.

The last group of teachers to discuss is one of the most important and effective. However, it is not really a group, but a collection
of individuals, hardly any of whom knows or cares anything about the
others. It exists now. It is self-perpetuating. It is given far less credit
than it earns. Usually it is forgotten altogether by the public and sometimes by its pupils. But its work has been invaluable, and ranks as
teaching of the very finest type.

These teachers are the fathers of great men, who taught them much
of what they needed to become great. The idea that a "genius" is a

human being of a superior species who creates himself like a ghost materializing is a poor oversimplification. So is the opposite mistake that every eminent man is nothing but the product of his social environment, as brass is the product of zinc and copper, or diabetes the result of a pancreas deficiency. Individuals differ far more widely than their environments. All great men do a good deal of work on themselves. By their long exertion of will, their disregard of others, and their development of slowly maturing plans, certain existentialists would say that they really create themselves. And obviously their social life affects them very deeply. But the first influences upon them, which often create the most lasting impressions, are received from their own families. When the parents deliberately set out to teach them, these impressions are deeper and certainly more systematic. Many distinguished men were produced not only physically but also spiritually by their fathers.

For a woman the physical act of producing a child is a long, tremendous enterprise, which fills her (whether she likes it or not) with purpose and responsibility and vitality. For a man it is brief and, in feeling, almost purposeless. The rest of his share in the child's life before birth is auxiliary at best. But after it is born he can begin to share equally with the mother in helping it to live and learn. As it grows able to think and talk, he will share that job more and more, whether he knows it or not, whether he wants to or not. Large numbers of fathers do not know this, do not care, and hope it is not true. They try to live as though the child had never been born. They leave it to its mother, or to the schools, or to the other children. Sometimes they try completely ignoring it. Nearly always they refuse to adapt themselves to it when it brings in new ideas and lets loose new forces in their home. Yet by doing all that they are teaching the child just as carefully and emphatically as though they were concentrating on it several hours a day. They are giving it ideas, patterns of emotion and thought, standards on which to base future choices. A child cannot make up its own mind with nothing to work on. It has to see how people behave. For this, it watches other children, and people in the movies, and characters in books; but the people who bulk largest and whose acts have most authority, in the time when its formless mind is being shaped, are its mother and its father. Enormous in size, terrible in strength, unbelievably clever, all-seeing and all-knowing, frightful in anger, miraculously bountiful, unpredictable as a cyclone, cruel even in kindness, brave and impressive, mostly incomprehensible even when they speak, a child's mother and father are its original King and Queen, Ogre and

Witch, Fairy and Giant, Mother-Goddess and Saviour-God. It obeys them and makes itself to suit them, it watches them to copy them, and, often without knowing it, it becomes them—or else it becomes an opposite of them in which their power is still expressed.

Whatever the father does, his child will learn from him. It is far better then for him to decide what to teach it, and how. As he does so, he will be giving up some part of his own personality, and some of his time and energy. But afterwards, when the results begin to show, he will be astonished to see that the sacrifice is repaid: his character (when he was perhaps becoming a little tired of its inadequacies) reappears with new strength and new originality in his child. Then he will really be able to say that he made it, and that he is its father.

It would be interesting to write a book on the fathers of great men: those who educated their sons by neglecting them, those who educated their sons by bullying and thwarting them, those who educated their sons by being their friends. These all taught their sons something about the world, for the world gives us all these treatments. It would be interesting, too, to write a book on the last of these three groups. It would not mention the fathers who taught their sons badly, like Chesterfield, and Cicero, and Pope Alexander VI (Borgia), and Coleridge. It would spend some time on those families in which many talents have been kept flowing through several generations, not only by heredity, but by the activity of successive fathers maintaining a tradition of excellence in their sons: the Bachs, the Medici, the Este, the Churchills, the Adamses, the Lowells, the Coelhos, the Montmorencys. It would study the psychological links between brilliant well-taught sons and their fathers, so often based on rivalry and conflict, acknowledged or unknown; sometimes built on genuine selfless affection and forming part of a rich happy family life; occasionally expressing the father's bitter frustration, which the son *must* grow up to compensate, to avenge. Here we can point out only a few of the fathers whose sons, through their teaching, became great and famous.

The first group looks at us, out of the picture-frames, with a steady, rather frowning gaze, firm lips, neat clothes, and an expression of cold competence. Their sons sometimes stand near them, looking much more like diminutive copies of their fathers than the independent geniuses we know from their own later portraits, wearing similar clothes, and ready to perform in the same way as their parent-teacher. These are the professional fathers who had talented sons and taught them their specialty. Out of a hundred thousand such families only one reaches eminence—but that is rather good odds compared with Nature's usual wild gamble in the game of birth and survival. Usually the fathers had no thought of training world-famous artists whom future generations must admire. They thought merely of giving their children a good living by starting them early in a profession; and sometimes of training an assistant who could take some of the work off their own shoulders.

A number of these fathers are musicians. For music is a language, and no one can be fluent in it, far less write works of art, unless he begins to learn it early. Mozart's father was a musician with a considerable reputation. Both his daughter and his little son took to music under his tuition so well that he also became their manager. He taught them so kindly and efficiently that the boy was writing sonatas at the age of seven and operas at the age of twelve, that he not only played the harpsichord exquisitely but toured Europe giving infant-prodigy concerts, that instead of becoming bored with the whole business (like so many child virtuosi) and composing facile but empty pieces, he continued throughout his life to write sweeter and richer and nobler music. Even in his hours of personal tragedy, it speaks with an angelic serenity that is a fine tribute to the father who taught him that art is an infallible consolation for the worst of life, and the very voice of the best.

Not all musical fathers formed the character of their sons so well. Beethoven's father was a brutal drunken beast. The boy had to go to the bars and pick him up when he was too drunk to get home, then to help him through the streets past the censorious looks of the other boys' parents, then to get him into the house and if possible dodge the kicks and slaps with which his father rewarded him. If Beethoven saw the world afterwards as a society in which life was possible only through tremendous exercise of will-power, if he admired heroes who rebelled against their powerful masters (Fidelio, Coriolanus, Prometheus), if his own manners were coarse and violent, and if he ruined his own and his adoptive son's life by giving the boy too much care and love, he learnt all this from the sot who shut him in the cellar when he was a boy and whom he had to rescue from the police when he was a young man. Still, his father did teach Beethoven music. He taught him to play the violin and the clavier beginning at four, and when at nine he could learn no more from his father, the man was wise enough to hand him on to better teachers; and he gave him much of the animal energy and drive which had been perverted and drowned in himself.

Bach was himself the grandson of a competent musician, and the brother and the cousin and the great-grandson. The Bachs had all been musicians for three generations or more. He was well taught himself by his elder brother, and he taught his own children very well. We still have a little book of progressively arranged first exercises that he wrote out for his son Wilhelm Friedemann, and another little clavier book he made for his young second wife. Of his twenty children, five became competent musicians, and three showed superior talent. You can see his interest in teaching coming out in several of his best works. For instance, the Forty-eight Preludes and Fugues, two each in every major and minor key throughout the twelve-note scale, are conceived and described as exercises to help musicians to grow familiar with all the possibilities of the new keyboard instrument. As he said himself, "I have had to work hard: anyone else who works as hard will get as far ahead." If Bach has a fault, it is occasional dryness and solemnity. Therefore he had one son who was a wonderful improviser and ruined his life with drink.

One could go through the other professions in the same way, noticing that the chief interest of professional fathers is not to build character but to build technique. This is one of the main reasons for what is sometimes called "the instability of genius." Many an artistic father will teach his son how to plan a quartet, but not how to control his expenses; how to choose words, but not how to avoid drugs. One peculiar example of this we have already met. Alexander the Great was an amazingly fine soldier and statesman. By the age of twenty-five he had mastered complex problems of supply and tactics, conquest and administration, propaganda and morale, which taken separately would need years to study. This was because he was his father's pupil. King Philip of Macedonia came of an astute and ruthless family, which had climbed to power among the north Greek highland clans over the bodies of many opponents. Philip learned "the hard way" how to divide his enemies and lie to them, when to attack them and when to make peace with them and when to invite them to a conference, how to keep an army in good training when it was not fighting, how to study the opponent's tactics and outthink him, where to get money and how to spend it, what to do and what to delegate. The young prince rode with him, fought under him, became his aide and his lieutenant and leader of his best troops, heard him explain his problems and argued about them, even, in defense of his mother, quarreled with him. Alexander's achievement was improbable enough. It would have been impossible without his father's teaching. But Philip also taught him his personal

failings, cruelty and debauchery and vanity, a brutal streak which we
sometimes see in the horns Alexander wears when he is pictured as a
god. Aristotle, his other teacher, tried to counteract it but could not
quite outweigh his father's influence.

The second group of fathers who taught their sons are quite different
from these competent technicians. We do not know their faces as we
know the faces of Bach or the elder Mozart. They do not appear in
portraits with their sons. They are neglected in biographies. Quite often
they would have been well content with this, for they were happy men
whose life was its own reward. They are the fathers who taught their
sons well because they themselves were overflowing with ideas. With
no idea of training their sons to any special profession, they simply
wanted to share with them the wisdom and beauty achieved by the
human race. They enjoyed culture themselves. They would not deny
it to their sons any more than a passionate Alpinist would forbid his
son to climb hills. Sometimes we see them saying to the boy: "I missed
this happiness until I was about thirty, because nobody told me of it.
Let me show it to you." Sometimes they tried terribly hard to teach
their sons one set of lessons, which the boys rejected; and yet the lessons which the boys finally learnt were also learnt indirectly from their
fathers. There is a fine biography which shows the beginnings of this,
Edmund Gosse's *Father and Son*. Gosse was the only child of a rather
staid and elderly Victorian couple who belonged to a very pious, very
limited religious sect. But they were charming people, who loved each
other and their son very dearly. The mother was a writer in a small
way. The father was a biologist, whose profession was to study, describe,
and teach the public about the animal life of England, and particularly the fish and shellfish of the coastal waters. The two parents made
little Gosse completely a part of their lives. He was even inducted into
their tiny church at an age which would have been impossible for
other children, because he had learnt so much about its doctrines. He
really lived almost wholly on their level. There is a delicious account
of how he went to a children's party where the other boys and girls
recited *Casabianca* and similar "sweet stanzas." When he was asked if
he could say any poetry, he stepped out quite cheerfully and began a
passage of stern baroque moralization from one of the devout works
his family admired. It was Blair's elegy *The Grave*. Off went Gosse,
aged twelve:

> If death were nothing, and nought after death, —
> If when men died at once they ceased to be, —

Returning to the barren womb of Nothing
Whence first they sprung, then might the debauchee . . .

At this point his hostess said: "Thank you, dear, that will do. We won't ask you to repeat any more," and, to Gosse's inexpressible surprise, stopped his recitation.

Now, what Gosse's father tried to teach him was (a) the religious beliefs of the Plymouth Brethren, and (b) marine biology. The boy drew hundreds of specimens for his father, and colored them with the bold simple tints of a primitive or a scientist; he even discovered a new species of mollusk. In his book he describes with great delight the long hours he spent with his father looking into the rocky pools of the Cornish coast and learning the habits and appearance of tiny but beautiful creatures living in a different element from ours. You will note, though, that in spite of the grim limitations of the family's life, literature was taken very seriously. The mother wrote; all read—not trash, but good though stodgy books; and the father had once, before giving up "profane things," known and loved even better literature. Gosse tells how once his father, hearing him at his first Latin lessons, took down his own favorite Vergil and read a few lines—their melody was so exquisite, even without meaning, that they enchanted the boy: he learnt them off by heart for sheer delight. As Gosse grew up, he went through the usual struggle to free himself of his father's influence— more severe in his case because they loved each other genuinely. After a painful break, he became something his father could scarcely have guessed, and would not have approved: the leading literary critic in England, a dandy, and a snob. Yet he was a complete personality. The best and the worst in him flowed from his father's teaching. His industrious habits, his refinement of taste, his eager sincerity, his admiration for beauty, his love for literature itself were his father's lessons; his worldliness and distrust of religion and epicureanism were reverse products of his father's teaching. Proust could have written an amusing page comparing, in one single sentence as fluid and iridescent as those seaweed fringes through which the biologist's apprentice once conducted his minute safaris, the bright crowded rooms of his home, bustling with visitors, whether familiar neighbors or bewildered strangers washed up by the tide of success, to the rich pools in which he had once entertained and examined his favorite curiosities; the poets and prosateurs whom, after discovering, he explained, with equal enthusiasm whether they were small, obscure, and difficult like shy rock insects or large, opulent, and insubstantial as anemones and nautili, to the

biological specimens collected by his father and himself through many
an exciting morning and drawn and colored as brightly as life through
many a laborious evening; and the formidably large output of books
which he poured out through his critical career to the illustrated catalogues of fauna which his father, with scientific completeness, filled up
year after year, rather than to the bolder, more cohesive work of a constructive critic of literature.

In spite of Gosse's tribute to his father, their relationship was rather
sad. A much gayer one was that between Robert Browning and his
father. Obviously his father taught him an energetic attack on life's
problems; gaiety and optimism; versatility; open-mindedness; much
else. But in a fine little poem written when he was about seventy-five he
crystallizes all his debts into gratitude to his father for teaching him
Greek—and poetry in general. When he was five, he says, he saw his
father reading and asked him what he was reading about. Looking up
from his Homer, his father said: "The siege of Troy." "What's a siege?"
said the little boy, "and what is Troy?" Now, at this point most fathers
would reply: "Troy is a city in Asia, now run off and play with your
train." Browning's father was different. He leapt up and began to
build Troy, there in the living-room. He built a city of tables and chairs.
On top he put an armchair for a throne and popped little Robert into
it. "There now," he said, "that's Troy, and you're King Priam, and
let me see, here's Helen of Troy, beautiful and sleek," and he pointed
to the cat beneath the footstool. "Outside, you know the two big dogs
in the yard, always trying to get in and catch Helen? They are the
fighting kings, Agamemnon and Menelaus, and they are making a
siege of Troy so as to capture Helen." And so he told the child as much
of the story as could interest him, in just the terms he could understand.
Sometimes I laugh when I read the poem, and think of the boy's delight
and astonishment at his cheerful energetic father jumping up and
slamming the book and piling an armchair on top of a table and pop-
ping him into the chair—like a magician in a fairy-story, changing him
into a king and the familiar room into a city with a siege. Browning
goes on to say that later, when he was seven or eight, his father gave
him a translation of the *Iliad* to read, encouraging him (as soon as he
could) to start it in Greek. And he judges his father a wise teacher for
giving him not only an amusement for a day but a possession for all his
lifetime, and choosing the right stimulus for each age in his growth.

Tennyson's father was a less happy and successful man. We hear
that he taught his son carefully but badly. He made him learn off by

heart all the lyric poems of Horace, in Latin, with all their complex meters and difficult ideas. The result was exactly the same as was produced on Byron ("Then farewell, Horace—whom I hated so, Not for thy faults, but mine"), on Swinburne, on Kipling, and on many others. It was a ridiculous and cruel "overdose." None but a great poet like Horace could have retained any appeal after it wore off. Years later Tennyson said that, although it was the wrong system, he was grateful for knowing Horace—the poet whose subtle art of word-placing and high sense of duty are often like his own.

Making the boy learn his poems *by heart* was the mistake. At most that might have been made tolerable as a game with other boys: not all alone. Pitt, the statesman who organized the resistence to Napoleon, was well educated by his father, who got him to translate passages from the great orators of the past, aloud, and at sight. That was not done as a task, however. It was done as a competition, a display in which his father was both trainer, rival, and audience. It was to his training that his friends attributed those amazing powers of oratory which he developed so early, which contained such a wealth of vivid imagery and powerful phrases, and which astonished, delighted, overpowered even his most durable opponents. That was not only a training in languages: it was a training in oratory, in the command of ideas, in greatness of soul.

I wonder how much the word "heredity" really means. Physically it probably means a lot. Mentally and spiritually, what do we inherit? Does it make any sense to say "Your son has inherited your knack of handling machines" or "Your daughter inherits your love of sports"? Is it not truer to say "You have taught your son to handle machines" by constant example, stimulation, and practice, and "You have taught your girl to love sports" by praising her golf-swing and giving her a new tennis racket for her birthday and chatting to her about games and taking her to matches? Do we use the words "inherit" and "heredity" to cover up our feeling that parents ought to think very carefully about how and what to teach their children, although most of them do not? Do we wish to imply that it will be all right without planning, that what we wish our children to learn will get into them somehow, through their pores perhaps? If so, we are wrong. We know that the world is full of people who are unhappy because they are vague and confused. Yet we often miss the priceless chance of teaching our own children something sure and reliable. The commonest answer to this charge is that we don't know ourselves what is sure and reliable. But that is not true. By the time we have reached the age of thirty-five or forty, and our children are becoming old enough to be taught the difficult questions, we have found answers which satisfy us as a working basis. Good. Let us teach them to our children. They will criticize them, attack them, and discard them, for a time at least. Good. We have done our duty. We have given them a basis to work on for themselves. They can come back to it, or find something better. They can accuse us of teaching them wrongly (although usually not of deliberately cheating them), and of trying to thrust our opinions down their throats (however gently we teach them, they will say that); but they cannot say we neglected them, wasting forty years of our own experience and fifteen years of their lives. Juvenile courts and mental homes are full of youngsters who were taught nothing useful by their fathers and mothers. It is not that they were badly brought up. They were not really brought up at all. They were never told how to behave. School meant practically nothing to them. The other children whom they knew were equally ignorant. The movies taught them that life meant excitement and daring. Their fathers never told the boys how to control their powers and arrange their lives. Their mothers told the girls nothing about the real pleasures and satisfactions of life. Nothing. When we look at the pouched and bestial face of such a boy or girl, ruined at seventeen, and instinctively feel that he or she looks worse than a savage, we are right. A Sudanese tribesman, a Jivaro Indian, a Borneo highlander trains his children far more purposefully and far more successfully than many fathers in the mightiest cities of the civilized world.

Questions and Suggestions

1. What is Highet's estimate of the success of the modern family in educating its children?
2. Study the organization of this portion of a much longer essay. State the central purpose.
3. If you outline this selection, how many major divisions do you find?
4. Examine Highet's use of detailed examples.
5. Many of Highet's sentences are worthy of close analysis. Pay attention to his use of series, parallel constructions, and sharp contrasts.
6. To become better acquainted with your library and to see why Highet says these men taught their own children poorly, consult the appropriate works of Chesterfield, Cicero, and Coleridge.

7. If you master the diction of this essay, you should increase your vocabulary considerably. Learn to use the following words correctly: *existentialist, ogre, virtuosi, facile, clavier, fugue, stodgy, epicureanism, safaris, prosateur, anemones, nautili, bestial.* Use the orthographical section of your dictionary to find the rules for the proper construction of plurals. Who were *Coriolanus, Prometheus, Proust?* Who are the *Jivaro Indians?*

Ideas for Writing

1. Show how your family takes literature seriously, or the converse.
2. Use one or two related episodes that will explain how your father or mother cheated you by being too busy to be a teacher-parent.
3. Recall what the memorizing of poetry did for you.
4. Point out aspects of a friend's life that show how he has been damaged by mentally lazy parents.
5. Why were your parents unable to attend college? If they have degrees, how much impact has the additional education had upon their lives and interests?
6. Have you found your parents' advice valuable?
7. Equate Mrs. Bridge, Mr. Baldwin, or Mrs. Lee with one of the individuals briefly portrayed in this essay.

part two ❧ *Seeing ourselves and others*

OP THE RIGGING

ERIC NEWBY

Shortly after leaving preparatory school, Eric Newby (1919–), who was born in London, went to work for an advertising agency. Tired of that atmosphere, he wrote to Gustav Erikson, a Finn, for a place as an apprentice seaman on one of his grain ships. Accepted, Newby describes that voyage in *The Last Grain Race.* His experiences at sea gave him some preparation for his war-time duties as a member of the Special Boat Service. Captured when he and five companions tried to rejoin the submarine from which they had landed to attack a German airfield in Sicily, Newby eventually married the girl who helped him escape from a prisoner of war camp. Since then has he has explored remote parts of Afghanistan, describing his experiences in *A Short Walk in the Hindu Kush,* and has became a member of an English publishing firm.

Somewhere on the deck a whistle blew. One by one the occupants of the starboard fo'c'sle went out to continue their work and
soon the sounds of hammering proceeded from the portside of the ship
where most of them were over the side chipping rust and painting.

Because Vytautas, the Lithuanian, had been watchman all night, he
did not go with them. He advised me to get into my working clothes
and report my arrival to the Mate. First he helped me stow my trunk
in a convenient space behind the fo'c'sle door. Gingerly I put on my
navy blue dungarees, which seemed stiff and unprofessional compared
with the faded blue overalls worn by most of the boys.

"Do not leave anything in the fo'c'sle," said Vytautas in his rather
oriental singsong. "These stevedores are thieves. At sea we are all right.
Here . . . nobody is good."

I asked him whether he had just joined the ship, but he replied that
this was his second voyage. *Moshulu* had been on the timber run from
Finland to Lourenço Marques in Portuguese East Africa in 1937 before
going to Australia for her grain cargo. I was glad; at least he was not
leaving, as many of the others were. I had already begun to cling to
any acquaintance as a drowning man clutches at a straw.

It so happened that I met not the First Mate but the Second, since
everything was in a state of flux: some members of the crew were
signing off and returning to Mariehamn, others arriving to take their
place. The old Captain, Boman, who had commanded her since he
joined the Erikson fleet, was going home and being replaced by Captain
Sjögren, who was coming from the *Archibald Russell.*

The Second Mate was thin, watery-eyed, and bad-tempered. At sea
he was to prove better than he looked to me this morning. He did not
like ports and he did not like to see the ship in her present state. My
arrival did not seem propitious, and after dressing me down for not
reporting aft directly I had come on board, he suddenly shot at me,
"Even been aloft before?"

"No, sir."

We were standing amidships by the mainmast. He pointed to the
lower main shrouds which supported the mast and said simply, "Op
you go then." I could scarcely believe my ears. I had imagined that I
should be allowed at least a day or two to become used to the ship and
the feel of things, but this was my introduction to discipline. I looked
at the Mate. He had a nasty glint in his eye and I decided I was more
afraid of him than of the rigging. If I was killed it would be his fault,
not mine, I said to myself with little satisfaction. Nevertheless I asked
him if I could change my shoes, which had slippery soles.

"Change your shoes? Op the rigging." He was becoming impatient.

At this time *Moshulu* was the greatest sailing ship in commission, and probably the tallest. Her mainmast cap was 198 feet above the keel. I started towards the main rigging on the starboard side nearest the quay, but was brought back by a cry from the Mate.

"Babord, portside. If you fall you may fall in the dock. When we're at sea you will always use the weather rigging, that's the side from which the wind blows. Never the lee rigging. And when I give you an order you repeat it."

"Op the rigging," I said.

The first part of the climb seemed easy enough. The lower main shrouds supporting the mast were of heavy wire made from plough steel and the first five ratlines were iron bars seized across four shrouds to make a kind of ladder that several men could climb at once. Above them the ratlines were wooden bars seized to the two centre shrouds only, the space for the feet becoming narrower as they converged at the "top," 80 feet up, where it was difficult to insert a foot as large as mine in the ratlines at all. Before reaching this point, however, I came abreast of the main yard. It was of tapered steel, 97 feet from arm to arm, 2½ feet in diameter at the centre, and weighed over 5 tons. It was trussed to the mainmast by an iron axle and preventer chain, which allowed it to be swung horizontally from side to side by means of tackle to the yardarms—an operation known as "bracing."

Above me was the top, a roughly semicircular platform with gratings in it. This was braced to the mast by steel struts called futtock shrouds. To get to the top I had to climb outwards on the rope ratlines seized to the futtock shrouds. There was a hole in the top, which it was considered unsporting to use. I only did so once for the experience and cut my ear badly on a sharp projection which was probably put there as a deterrent. I found difficulty in reaching the top this first time and remained transfixed, my back nearly parallel with the deck below, while I felt for a rope ratline with one foot. I found it at last and heaved myself, nearly sick with apprehension, onto the platform, where I stood for a moment, my heart thumping. There was only a moment's respite, in which I noticed that the mainmast and the topmast were in one piece—not doubled as in most sailing ships—before the dreadful voice of the Mate came rasping up at me.

"Get on op."

The next part was nearly 50 feet of rope ratline seized to the topmast shrouds. Nearly vertical, they swayed violently as I went aloft; many of them were rotten and one broke underfoot when I was at the level of the topsail yards. Again the voice from the deck.

"If you want to live, hold on to those shrouds and leave the bloody ratlines alone."

The lower topsail yard was slung from an iron crane but the upper topsail yard above it was attached to a track on the foreside of the topmast, allowing the yard to be raised by means of a halliard and lifts more than 25 feet to the level of the crosstrees. The crosstrees formed an open frame of steel girdering about 130 feet up, at the heel of the topgallant mast. Originally the topsail had been a single sail, but to make it easier for the reduced crews to take in sail, it had been divided into two. At the moment the upper topsail yard was in its lowered position, immediately on top of the lower topsail yard. The crosstrees seemed flimsy when I reached them, two long arms extended aft from the triangle, spreading the backstays of the royal mast, the highest mast of all. I stood gingerly on this slippery construction; the soles of my shoes were like glass; all Belfast spread out below. I looked between my legs down to a deck as thin as a ruler and nearly fell from sheer panic.

"Op to the royal yard," came the imperious voice, fainter now.

Another forty feet or so of trembling topgallant shroud, past the lower and upper topgallant yards, the upper one, like the upper topsail yard, movable on its greased track. The ratlines were very narrow now and ceased altogether just below the level of the royal yard.

I was pretty well all in emotionally and physically, but the by now expected cry of "Out on the yard" helped me to heave myself on to it. In doing so I covered myself with grease from the mast track on which the royal yard moved up and down. It was 51 feet long and thinner than those below it. As on all the other yards, an iron rail ran along the top. This was the jackstay, to which the sail was bent.

In cadet training ships this rail would have had another parallel to it to hold on to, since, with the sail bent to the forward jackstay, there was little or no handhold. *Moshulu* had not been built for cadets, and this refinement was lacking. With no sails bent what I had to do was easy, but I did not appreciate my good fortune at the time. Underneath the yard was a wire rope that extended the length of it and was supported halfway between the mast and either yardarm by vertical stirrups. This footrope was called the "horse." When I ventured out on it I found it slippery as well as slack so that both feet skidded in opposite directions, leaving me like a dancer about to do the splits, hanging on grimly to the jackstay.

"Out. Right out to the yardarm," came the Mate's voice, fainter still. I hated him at this moment. There were none of the "joosts" and "ploddys" of the stylized Scandinavian to make me feel superior to this grim officer. He spoke excellent English.

Somehow I reached the yardarm. I tried to rest my stomach on it, and stick my legs out behind me but I was too tall; the footrope came up very close to the yard at this point, where it was shackled to the brace pendant, and my knees reached to the place on the yard where the riggers had intended my stomach to be, so that I had the sensation of pitching over it. Fortunately there was a lift shackled to the yardarm band, a wire tackle which supported the yard in its lowered position, and to this I clung while I looked about me.

What I saw was very impressive and disagreeable. By now I had forgotten what the Mate had said about falling into the dock. I was right out at the starboard yardarm, 160 feet above the sheds into which *Moshulu's* 62,000 sacks of grain were being unloaded. The rooftops of these sheds were glass, and I remember wondering what would happen if I fell. Would I avoid being cut to pieces by the maze of wires below, or miss them and make either a large expensive crater in the roof or a smaller one shaped like me? I also wondered what kind of technique the ambulance men employed to scoop up what was left of people who fell from such heights. I tried to dismiss these melancholy thoughts but the beetle-like figures on the dock below that were stevedores only accentuated my remoteness. The distant prospect was more supportable: a tremendous panorama beyond the city to the Antrim hills and far up the Belfast Lough to the sea.

"Orlright," called the Mate. "Come in to the mast." I did so with alacrity, but was not pleased when he told me to go to the cap on the very top of the mast. I knew that with these blasted shoes I could never climb the bare pole, so I took them off, and my socks too, and wedged them under the jackstay.

There were two or three very rotten ratlines seized across the royal backstays. The lowest broke under my weight so I used the backstays alone to climb up to the level of the royal halliard sheave to which the yard was raised when sail was set. And above this nothing. Only six feet of bare pole to the cap. I was past caring whether I fell or not.

I embraced the royal mast and shinned up. The wind blew my hair over my nose and made me want to sneeze. I stretched out my arm and grasped the round hardwood cap 198 feet above the keel and was surprised to find it was not loose, or full of chocolate creams as a prize. Now the bloody man below me was telling me to sit on it, but I ignored him. I could think of no emergency that would make it necessary. So I slid down to the royal halliard and to the yard again.

"You can come down now," shouted the Mate. I did. It was worse than going up and more agonizing because I was barefoot, with my shoes stuffed inside my shirt.

"You were a fool to take your shoes off," said the Mate when I reached the deck. "Now you can learn to clean the lavatories."

Since that day I have been aloft in high rigging many hundreds of times and in every kind of weather, but I still get that cold feeling in the pit of the stomach when I think of the first morning out on the royal yard with the sheds of the York Dock below.

Questions and Suggestions

1. Why does the Second Mate of the S.V. *Moshulu* treat Newby, fresh from the office of an advertising agency, as he does?
2. Why is it fortunate that Newby did not suffer from acrophobia? Does he use any details to make the hazardous climb clear to the reader?
3. Does Newby mean that he really was surprised not to find a prize on the cap of the royal mast?
4. This essay, by necessity, contains a number of technical terms; if by their context they are not completely clear, consult your dictionary. To get an even clearer visual image of Newby's introduction to climbing the rigging, you might study the line drawing of a full-rigged sailing vessel that accompanies the word *sail* in your dictionary.

Ideas for Writing

1. Were you ever introduced to a new job and given no time to get adjusted?
2. Was your physical courage ever tested?
3. Organize the reasons why you would or would not want to be a construction worker on a skyscraper, a window-washer in Manhattan, a sailor, an airline hostess, a stunt performer for films, an astronaut, or an aerial artist in the circus.
4. Do you suffer from agoraphobia, claustrophobia, hydrophobia, photophobia, or pyrophobia? Do you know anyone who does? How has the fear affected your or his life?
5. Can you record your reaction, as Edmund Wilson does in his

description of Mlle. Leitzel, the famous circus aerialist, to "the spectacle of any human aptitude carried to its extreme unpredictable limit"?

6. From John Masefield's *Sard Harker,* Richard H. Dana's *Two Years before the Mast,* Herman Melville's *Omoo* or *Moby Dick,* Joseph Conrad's *The Nigger of the "Narcissus,"* Ernest Shackleton's *South,* or Basil Lubbock's *Round the Horn before the Mast,* find a passage which you can contrast with Newby's.

7. What difficulty did you have in acquainting yourself with some of the technical terms used on a particular job?

ASSIGNMENT WITH AN OCTOPUS

SIR ARTHUR GRIMBLE

In 1914, Arthur Grimble (1889–1956), who was born in Hong Kong, entered the British Colonial Service as a Cadet and sailed for the Gilbert and Ellice Islands. Three years later, as the "young man of Matang," or a European, he was made District Officer of the islands, having proved his ability as a leader. Grimble remained in the foreign service until his retirement in 1948. The author of some verses and ethnographical papers dealing with the Gilbertese, he established himself as a writer and lecturer only during the last years of his life.

I certainly should never have ventured out alone for pure sport, armed with nothing but a knife, to fight a tiger shark in its own element. I am as little ashamed of that degree of discretion as the big-game hunter who takes care not to attack a rhinoceros with a shotgun. The fear I had for the larger kinds of octopus was quite different. It was a blind fear, sick with disgust, unreasoned as a child's horror of darkness. Victor Hugo was the man who first brought it up to the level of my conscious thought. I still remember vividly the impression left on me as a boy of fourteen by that account in *Les Travailleurs de la*

Mer of Gilliatt's fight with the monster that caught him among the rocks of the Douvres. For years after reading it, I tortured myself with wondering however I could behave with decent courage if faced with a giant at once so strong and so loathsome. My commonest nightmare of the period was of an octopus-like Presence poised motionless behind me, towards which I dared not turn, from which my limbs were too frozen to escape. But that phase did pass before I left school, and the Thing lay dormant inside me until a day at Tarawa.

Before I reached Tarawa, however, chance gave me a swift glimpse of what a biggish octopus could do to a man. I was wading at low tide one calm evening on the lip of the reef at Ocean Island when a Baanaban villager, back from fishing, brought his canoe to land within twenty yards of where I stood. There was no more than a show of breaking seas, but the water was only knee-deep, and this obliged the fisherman to slide overboard and handle his lightened craft over the jagged edge. But no sooner were his feet upon the reef than he seemed to be tied to where he stood. The canoe was washed shorewards ahead of him, while he stood with legs braced tugging desperately away from something. I had just time to see a tapering, greyish-yellow rope curled around his right wrist before he broke away from it. He fell sprawling into the shallow water; the tapered rope flicked writhing back into the foam at the reef's edge. The fisherman picked himself up and nursed his right arm. I had reached him by then. The octopus had caught him with only the tip of one tentacle, but the terrible hold of the few suckers on his wrist had torn the skin whole from it as he wrenched himself adrift.

This is not to say that all the varieties of octopus known to the Gilbertese are dangerous to man. Some of them are mere midgets, and very beautiful. Lying face-down on a canoe anchored over rocks and sand in Tarawa lagoon I sometimes used to watch for the smaller kinds through a water glass.

The smallest I saw could have been comfortably spread on the lid of a cigarette tin. I noticed that the colours of all the little ones varied very much according to where they were crawling, from the mottled rust-red and brown of coral rock to the clear gold and orange-brown of sunlit sand speckled with seaweed. From the height of my top window, most of them looked as flat as starfish slithering over the bottom, but there was one minute creature that had a habit of standing on its toes. It would constrict its tentacles into a kind of neck where they joined the head and, with its body so raised, would jig up and down

rather like a dancing frog. But what appealed most to my wonder was
the way they all swam. A dozen sprawling, lacelike shapes would
suddenly gather themselves into stream lines and shoot upwards, jet-
propelled by the marvellous syphon in their heads, like a display of
fairy water rockets. At the top of their flight, they seemed to explode;
their tails of trailed tentacles burst outwards into shimmering points
around their tiny bodies, and they sank like drifting gossamer stars
back to the sea floor again.

The female octopus anchors her eggs to stalks of weed and coral
under water. It seems to be a moot point whether she broods in their
neighbourhood or not, but I once saw what I took to be a mother out
for exercise with five babies. She had a body about the size of a tennis
ball and tentacles perhaps a foot long. The length of the small ones,
streamlined for swimming, was not more than five inches over all.
They were cruising around a coral pinnacle in four feet of water. The
big one led, the babies followed six inches behind, in what seemed to
be an ordered formation: they were grouped, as it were, around the
base of a cone whereof she was the forward-pointing apex.

They cruised around the pinnacle for half a minute or more, and
then went down to some small rocks at its base. While the little ones
sprawled over the bottom, the mother remained poised above them. It
looked to my inexpert eye exactly as if she was mounting guard over her
young. And at that point a big trevally was obliging enough to become
the villain of a family drama for my benefit. He must have been watching the little group from deeper water. As the mother hovered there,
he came in at her like a blue streak. But she avoided him somehow;
he flashed by and turned to dart in again, only to see a black cloud of
squirted ink where the octopus had been. (Incidentally, that was the
only time I ever saw an octopus discharge its ink sac.) The trevally
swerved aside, fetched a full circle and came very slowly back to the
edge of the black cloud, while the mother and her family were escaping
towards the shallows on the other side. He loitered around for a while,
then seemed to take fright and flicked away at speed into the deep water.

The old navigators of the Gilberts used to talk with fear of a gigantic
octopus that inhabited the seas between Samoa and the Ellice Islands.
They said its tentacles were three spans long and thicker at the base
than the body of a full-grown man—a scale of measurements not out
of keeping with what is known of the atrocious monster called *Octopus
apollyon*. There were some who stated that this foul fiend of the ocean
was also to be found in the waters between Onotoa, Tamana and Arorae

in the Southern Gilberts. But I never came across a man who had seen one, and the biggest of the octopus breed I ever saw with my own eyes had tentacles only a little over six feet long. It was a member of the clan *Octopus vulgaris*, which swarms in all the lagoons. An average specimen of this variety is a dwarf beside *Octopus apollyon*: laid out flat, it has a total spread of no more than nine or ten feet; but it is a wicked-looking piece of work, even in death, with those disgusting suckers studding its arms and bulging, filmed eyes staring out of the mottled gorgon face.

Possibly, if you can watch objectively, the sight of *Octopus vulgaris* searching for crabs and crayfish on the floor of the lagoon may move you to something like admiration. You cannot usually see the dreadful eyes from a water glass straight above its feeding ground, and your feeling for crustaceans is too impersonal for horror at their fate between pouncing suckers and jaws. There is real beauty in the rich change of its colours as it moves from shadow to sunlight, and the gliding ease of its arms as they reach and flicker over the rough rocks fascinates the eye with its deadly grace. You feel that if only the creature would stick to its grubbing on the bottom, the shocking ugliness of its shape might even win your sympathy, as for some poor Caliban in the enchanted garden of the lagoon. But it is no honest grubber in the open. For every one of its kind that you see crawling below you, there are a dozen skulking in recesses of the reef that falls away like a cliff from the edge where you stand watching. When *Octopus vulgaris* has eaten its fill of the teeming crabs and crayfish, it seeks a dark cleft in the coral face, and anchors itself there with a few of the large suckers nearest to its body. Thus shielded from attack in the rear, with tentacles gathered to pounce, it squats glaring from the shadows, alert for anything alive to swim within striking distance. It can hurl one or all of those whiplashes forward with the speed of dark lightning, and once its scores of suckers, rimmed with hooks for grip on slippery skins, are clamped about their prey, nothing but the brute's death will break their awful hold.

But that very quality of the octopus that most horrifies the imagination—its relentless tenacity—becomes its undoing when hungry man steps into the picture. The Gilbertese happen to value certain parts of it as food, and their method of fighting it is coolly based upon the one fact that its arms never change their grip. They hunt for it in pairs. One man acts as the bait, his partner as the killer. First, they swim eyes-under at low tide just off the reef, and search the crannies of the submarine cliff for sight of any tentacle that may flicker out for a catch.

When they have placed their quarry, they land on the reef for the next stage. The human bait starts the real game. He dives and tempts the lurking brute by swimming a few strokes in front of its cranny, at first a little beyond striking range. Then he turns and makes straight for the cranny, to give himself into the embrace of those waiting arms. Sometimes nothing happens. The beast will not always respond to the lure. But usually it strikes.

The partner on the reef above stares down through the pellucid water, waiting for his moment. His teeth are his only weapon. His killing efficiency depends on his avoiding every one of those strangling arms. He must wait until his partner's body has been drawn right up to the entrance of the cleft. The monster inside is groping then with its horny mouth against the victim's flesh, and sees nothing beyond it. That point is reached in a matter of no more than thirty seconds after the decoy has plunged. The killer dives, lays hold of his pinioned friend at arm's length, and jerks him away from the cleft; the octopus is torn adrift from the anchorage of its proximal suckers, and clamps itself the more fiercely to its prey. In the same second, the human bait gives a kick which brings him, with quarry annexed, to the surface. He turns on his back, still holding his breath for better buoyancy, and this exposes the body of the beast for the kill. The killer closes in, grasps the evil head from behind, and wrenches it away from its meal. Turning the face up towards himself, he plunges his teeth between the bulging eyes, and bites down and in with all his strength. That is the end of it. It dies on the instant; the suckers release their hold; the arms fall away; the two fishers paddle with whoops of delighted laughter to the reef, where they string the catch to a pole before going to rout out the next one.

Any two boys of seventeen, any day of the week, will go out and get you half a dozen octopus like that for the mere fun of it. Here lies the whole point of this story. The hunt is, in the most literal sense, nothing but child's play to the Gilbertese.

As I was standing one day at the end of a jetty in Tarawa lagoon, I saw two boys from the near village shouldering a string of octopus slung on a pole between them. I started to wade out in their direction, but before I hailed them they had stopped, planted the carrying-pole upright in a fissure and, leaving it there, swum off the edge for a while with faces submerged, evidently searching for something under water. I had been only a few months at Tarawa, and that was my first near view of an octopus hunt. I watched every stage of it from the dive of the human bait to the landing of the dead catch. When it was over, I went up to them. I could hardly believe that in those few seconds, with no more than a frivolous-looking splash or two on the surface, they could have found, caught and killed the creature they were now stringing up before my eyes. They explained the amusing simplicity of the thing.

"There's only one trick the decoy-man must never forget," they said, "and that's not difficult to remember. If he is not wearing the water spectacles of the Men of Matang, he must cover his eyes with a hand as he comes close to the *kika* [octopus], or the suckers might blind him." It appeared that the ultimate fate of the eyes was not the thing to worry about; the immediate point was that the sudden pain of a sucker clamping itself to an eyeball might cause the bait to expel his breath and inhale sea water; that would spoil his buoyancy, and he would fail then to give his friend the best chance of a kill.

Then they began whispering together. I knew in a curdling flash what they were saying to each other. Before they turned to speak to me again, a horrified conviction was upon me. My damnable curiosity had led me into a trap from which there was no escape. They were going to propose that I should take a turn at being the bait myself, just to see how delightfully easy it was. And that is precisely what they did. It did not even occur to them that I might not leap at the offer. I was already known as a young Man of Matang who liked swimming, and fishing, and laughing with the villagers; I had just shown an interest in this particular form of hunting; naturally, I should enjoy the fun of it as much as they did. Without even waiting for my answer, they gleefully ducked off the edge of the reef to look for another octopus—a fine fat one—*mine*. Left standing there alone, I had another of those visions. . . .

It was dusk in the village. The fishers were home, I saw the cooking fires glowing orange-red between the brown lodges. There was laughter and shouted talk as the women prepared the evening meal. But the laughter was hard with scorn. "What?" they were saying. "Afraid of a *kika*? The young Man of Matang? Why, even our boys are not afraid of a *kika!*" A curtain went down and rose again on the residency; the Old Man was talking. "A leader? You? The man who funked a schoolboy game? We don't leave your sort in charge of districts." The scene flashed to my uncles. "Returned empty," they said. "We always knew you hadn't got it in you. Returned empty. . . ."

Of course it was all overdrawn, but one fact was beyond doubt:

the Gilbertese reserved all their most ribald humour for physical cowardice. No man gets himself passed for a leader anywhere by becoming the butt of that kind of wit. I decided I would rather face the octopus.

I was dressed in khaki slacks, canvas shoes and a short-armed singlet. I took off the shoes and made up my mind to shed the singlet if told to do so; but I was wildly determined to stick to my trousers throughout. Dead or alive, said a voice within me, an official minus his pants is a preposterous object, and I felt I could not face that extra horror. However, nobody asked me to remove anything.

I hope I did not look as yellow as I felt when I stood to take the plunge; I have never been so sick with funk before or since. "Remember, one hand for your eyes," said someone from a thousand miles off, and I dived.

I do not suppose it is really true that the eyes of an octopus shine in the dark; besides, it was clear daylight only six feet down in the limpid water; but I could have sworn the brute's eyes burned at me as I turned in towards his cranny. That dark glow—whatever may have been its origin—was the last thing I saw as I blacked out with my left hand and rose into his clutches. Then, I remember chiefly a dreadful sliminess with a herculean power behind it. Something whipped round my left forearm and the back of my neck, binding the two together. In the same flash, another something slapped itself high on my forehead, and I felt it crawling down inside the back of my singlet. My impulse was to tear at it with my right hand, but I felt the whole of that arm pinioned to my ribs. In most emergencies the mind works with crystal-clear impersonality. This was not even an emergency, for I knew myself perfectly safe. But my boyhood nightmare was upon me. When I felt the swift constriction of those disgusting arms jerk my head and shoulders in towards the reef, my mind went blank of every thought save the beastliness of contact with that squat head. A mouth began to nuzzle below my throat, at the junction of the collar bones. I forgot there was anyone to save me. Yet something still directed me to hold my breath.

I was awakened from my cowardly trance by a quick, strong pull on my shoulders, back from the cranny. The cables around me tightened painfully, but I knew I was adrift from the reef. I gave a kick, rose to the surface and turned on my back with the brute sticking out of my chest like a tumour. My mouth was smothered by some flabby moving horror. The suckers felt like hot rings pulling at my skin. It was only two seconds, I suppose, from then to the attack of my deliverer, but it seemed like a century of nausea.

My friend came up between me and the reef. He pounced, pulled, bit down, and the thing was over—for everyone but me. At the sudden relaxation of the tentacles, I let out a great breath, sank, and drew in the next under water. It took the united help of both boys to get me, coughing, heaving and pretending to join in their delighted laughter, back to the reef. I had to submit there to a kind of war dance around me, in which the dead beast was slung whizzing past my head from one to the other. I had a chance to observe then that it was not by any stretch of fancy a giant, but just plain average. That took the bulge out of my budding self-esteem. I left hurriedly for the cover of the jetty, and was sick.

Questions and Suggestions

1. Although in this essay Grimble recalls episodes that took place almost thirty-five years earlier, how does he create a sense of immediacy? What does he tell you about the arts of observation, selection, and memory?

2. Why is this essay more interesting than the one Grimble might have written the day after his adventure?

3. What are some of the ways in which he gives unity to the essay? How many major divisions do you find? What are the transitional devices?

4. In various parts of this essay Grimble describes processes. What are they?

5. Why are the references to *Caliban* and *Victor Hugo* successful?

Ideas for Writing

1. Recall a nightmare that formerly haunted your waking hours. Your paper will have more meaning if you can explain some of the reasons why the dream came to be fixed in your mind.

2. If you are a swimmer, you might center a paper around the pleasures or terrors of the aqua-lung. If a deep-sea fisherman, you might tell how you landed your biggest catch.

3. Imagine a Gilbert Islander's reaction to a drag race, the Indianapolis speedway, the Daytona races, quarter-midget racing, football, basketball, golf, or boxing.

4. Discuss a dangerous sport that we take for granted.

5. One of your acquaintances may have a strange or daring occupation: alligator wrestler, snake charmer, feeder at an

oceanrama, tattooist, sword swallower, city policeman, private detective, tunnel guard, steeple-jack, or deep-sea diver. In *New York,* by Meyer Berger, and in *New York—A Serendipiter's Journey,* by Gay Talese, you will find a number of familiar essays and vignettes dealing with the strange occupations of many New Yorkers.

A FEW DROPS OF PHENOMENOLOGY

JOSÉ ORTEGA y GASSET

José Ortega y Gasset (1883–1955), who was born in Madrid, was still quite young when he received his Ph.D. in philosophy from the University of Madrid. Perhaps the most influential professor of philosophy in Spain, and the editor of numerous magazines and journals, he verbally fought against the Spanish monarchy. Knowing that the Civil War offered no solution to Spanish problems, he left Spain when it broke out, remaining an exile in France, South America, and Portugal until 1949. His book that is best known to Americans is *The Revolt of the Masses.*

A great man is dying. His wife is by his bedside. A doctor takes the dying man's pulse. In the background two more persons are discovered: a reporter who is present for professional reasons, and a painter whom mere chance has brought here. Wife, doctor, reporter, and painter witness one and the same event. Nonetheless, this identical event—a man's death—impresses each of them in a different way. So different indeed that the several aspects have hardly anything in common. What this scene means to the wife who is all grief has so little to do with what it means to the painter who looks on impassively that it seems doubtful whether the two can be said to be present at the same event.

It thus becomes clear that one and the same reality may split up into

From *The Dehumanization of Art and Other Writings on Art and Culture,* Willard R. Trask, tr. Copyright 1948 by Princeton University Press. Reprinted by permission of the publishers.

many diverse realities when it is beheld from different points of view. And we cannot help asking ourselves: Which of all these realities must then be regarded as the real and authentic one? The answer, no matter how we decide, cannot but be arbitrary. Any preference can be founded on caprice only. All these realities are equivalent, each being authentic for its corresponding point of view. All we can do is to classify the points of view and to determine which among them seems, in a practical way, most normal or most spontaneous. Thus we arrive at a conception of reality that is by no means absolute, but at least practical and normative.

As for the points of view of the four persons present at the death-bed, the clearest means of distinguishing them is by measuring one of their dimensions, namely the emotional distance between each person and the event they all witness. For the wife of the dying man the distance shrinks to almost nothing. What is happening so tortures her soul and absorbs her mind that it becomes one with her person. Or to put it inversely, the wife is drawn into the scene, she is part of it. A thing can be seen, an event can be observed, only when we have separated it from ourselves and it has ceased to form a living part of our being. Thus the wife is not present at the scene, she is in it. She does not behold it, she "lives" it.

The doctor is several degrees removed. To him this is a professional case. He is not drawn into the event with the frantic and blinding anxiety of the poor woman. However it is his bounden duty as a doctor to take a serious interest, he carries responsibility, perhaps his professional honor is at stake. Hence he too, albeit in a less integral and less intimate way, takes part in the event. He is involved in it not with his heart but with the professional portion of his self. He too "lives" the scene although with an agitation originating not in the emotional center, but in the professional surface, of his existence.

When we now put ourselves in the place of the reporter we realize that we have traveled a long distance away from the tragic event. So far indeed that we have lost all emotional contact with it. The reporter, like the doctor, has been brought here for professional reasons and not out of a spontaneous human interest. But while the doctor's profession requires him to interfere, the reporter's requires him precisely to stay aloof; he has to confine himself to observing. To him the event is a mere scene, a pure spectacle on which he is expected to report in his newspaper column. He takes no feeling part in what is happening here, he is emotionally free, an outsider. He does not "live" the scene, he observes it. Yet he observes it with a view to telling his readers about it. He wants to interest them, to move them, and if possible to make them weep as though they each had been the dying man's best friend. From his schooldays he remembers Horace's recipe: *"Si vis me flere dolendum est primum ipsi tibi"*—if you want me to weep you must first grieve yourself.

Obedient to Horace the reporter is anxious to pretend emotion, hoping that it will benefit his literary performance. If he does not "live" the scene he at least pretends to "live" it.

The painter, in fine, completely unconcerned, does nothing but keep his eyes open. What is happening here is none of his business; he is, as it were, a hundred miles removed from it. His is a purely perceptive attitude; indeed, he fails to perceive the event in its entirety. The tragic inner meaning escapes his attention which is directed exclusively toward the visual part—color values, lights, and shadows. In the painter we find a maximum of distance and a minimum of feeling intervention.

The inevitable dullness of this analysis will, I hope, be excused if it now enables us to speak in a clear and precise way of a scale of emotional distances between ourselves and reality. In this scale, the degree of closeness is equivalent to the degree of feeling participation; the degree of remoteness, on the other hand, marks the degree to which we have freed ourselves from the real event, thus objectifying it and turning it into a theme of pure observation. At one end of the scale the world—persons, things, situations—is given to us in the aspect of "lived" reality; at the other end we see everything in the aspect of "observed" reality.

At this point we must make a remark that is essential in aesthetics and without which neither old art nor new art can be satisfactorily analyzed. Among the diverse aspects of reality we find one from which all the others derive and which they all presuppose: "lived" reality. If nobody had ever "lived" in pure and frantic abandonment a man's death, the doctor would not bother, the readers would not understand the reporter's pathos, and the canvas on which the painter limned a person on a bed surrounded by mourning figures would be meaningless. The same holds for any object, be it a person, a thing, or a situation. The primal aspect of an apple is that in which I see it when I am about to eat it. All its other possible forms—when it appears, for instance, in a Baroque ornament, or on a still life of Cézanne's, or in the eternal metaphor of a girl's apple cheeks—preserve more or less that original aspect. A painting or a poem without any vestiges of "lived" forms would be unintelligible, i.e., nothing—as a discourse is nothing whose every word is emptied of its customary meaning.

That is to say, in the scale of realities "lived" reality holds a peculiar primacy which compels us to regard it as "the" reality. Instead of "lived" reality we may say "human" reality. The painter who impassively witnesses the death scene appears "inhuman." In other words, the human point of view is that in which we "live" situations, persons, things. And, vice versa, realities—a woman, a countryside, an event—are human when they present the aspect in which they are usually "lived."

As an example, the importance of which will appear later, let us mention that among the realities which constitute the world are our ideas. We use our ideas in a "human" way when we employ them for thinking things. Thinking of Napoleon, for example, we are normally concerned with the great man of that name. A psychologist, on the other hand, adopts an unusual, "inhuman" attitude when he forgets about Napoleon and, prying into his own mind, tries to analyze his idea of Napoleon as such idea. His perspective is the opposite of that prevailing in spontaneous life. The idea, instead of functioning as the means to think an object with, is itself made the object and the aim of thinking.

Questions and Suggestions

1. Explain why Ortega y Gasset says that the wife is not really present at her husband's death. Paraphrase the paragraphs that explain not only the reporter's relationship to the deathbed scene but also his own responsibilities.

2. What does the author mean by the "scale of emotional distances between ourselves and reality"? In answering this question, use at least one example from your own experience.

3. What attitude does Ortega y Gasset take toward abstractions in poetry and painting? Why does he find this approach necessary?

4. What are the major divisions of the essay?

5. From the context and your dictionary, what is the definition of *arbitrary, caprice, aesthetics, pathos, limned,* and *Baroque?* How does the author use the words *tragic* and *inhuman?* Who were *Horace* and *Cézanne?*

Ideas for Writing

1. Who are you? Use examples that will clarify how you are one person for each of your parents, another for friends your own age, older friends, friends away from home, members of the other sex, your minister, teacher, and your boss.

2. Recreate a single episode, such as a death in the family, a
    marriage, a mid-term test, or a home-coming, but use the
    points of view of several people who are involved. If you find
    it difficult to make the transition, from one person to the next,
    divide your paper into several parts; in fact, you might use
    this topic for several assignments, limiting each account to a
    single point of view. Ryunosuke Akutagawa's "In a Grove,"
    found in the collection of stories entitled *Rashomon,* is told
    from seven points of view, each clearly titled to show who
    the speaker is.

3. Describe one person as seen from several imaginary points of
    view, such as the town loafer or drunk as seen by a merchant,
    a child, a mother, or a newcomer to the area; the dentist as
    seen by his assistant, another dentist, or a patient; the waitress
    as seen by another waitress, the cook, or a customer; or a
    professor as seen by several students.

4. Contrast a rural face with a city one, or a sloppily dressed
    student with one who is finically attired.

5. Why did two friends who were "going steady" break up?
    Consider both sides.

THE PATENTED GATE AND THE MEAN HAMBURGER

ROBERT PENN WARREN

Poet, novelist, short story writer, essayist, dramatist, critic, editor,
biographer, and celebrated teacher, Robert Penn Warren (1905–)
was born in Todd County, Kentucky. He received his education
at Vanderbilt, California, Yale, and Oxford, where he was a
Rhodes Scholar. He has taught and lectured at a number of colleges and universities. He and Cleanth Brooks founded the distinguished literary quarterly, *The Southern Review;* in addition,
they have been the co-authors of several influential college texts.
The recipient of many honors, Mr. Warren received the Pulitzer
Prize for his third novel, *All the King's Men.* His wife, Eleanor
Clark, is also a novelist.

You have seen him a thousand times. You have seen him standing on the street corner on Saturday afternoon, in the little county-seat towns. He wears blue jean pants, or overalls washed to a pale pastel blue like the color of sky after a shower in spring, but because it is Saturday he has on a wool coat, an old one, perhaps the coat left from the suit he got married in a long time back. His long wrist bones hang out from the sleeves of the coat, the tendons showing along the bone like the dry twist of grapevine still corded on the stove-length of a hickory sapling you would find in his wood box beside his cookstove among the split chunks of gum and red oak. The big hands, with the knotted, cracked joints and the square, horn-thick nails, hang loose off the wrist bone like clumsy, home-made tools hung on the wall of a shed after work. If it is summer, he wears a straw hat with a wide brim, the straw fraying loose around the edge. If it is winter, he wears a felt hat, black once, but now weathered with streaks of dark gray and dull purple in the sunlight. His face is long and bony, the jawbone long under the drawn-in cheeks. The flesh along the jawbone is nicked in a couple of places where the unaccustomed razor has been drawn over the leather-coarse skin. A tiny bit of blood crusts brown where the nick is. The color of the face is red, a dull red like the red clay mud or clay dust which clings to the bottom of his pants and to the cast-iron-looking brogans on his feet, or a red like the color of a piece of hewed cedar which has been left in the weather. The face does not look alive. It seems to be molded from the clay or hewed from the cedar. When the jaw moves, once, with its deliberate, massive motion on the quid of to-bacco, you are still not convinced. That motion is but the cunning triumph of a mechanism concealed within.

But you see the eyes. You see that the eyes are alive. They are pale blue or gray, set back under the deep brows and thorny eyebrows. They are not wide, but are squinched up like eyes accustomed to wind or sun or to measuring the stroke of the ax or to fixing the object over the rifle sights. When you pass, you see that the eyes are alive and are warily and dispassionately estimating you from the ambush of the thorny brows. Then you pass on, and he stands there in that stillness which is his gift.

With him may be standing two or three others like himself, but they are still, too. They do not talk. The young men, who will be like these men when they get to be fifty or sixty, are down at the beer parlor, carousing and laughing with a high, whickering laugh. But the men on the corner are long past all that. They are past many things. They have endured and will endure in their silence and wisdom. They will stand on the street corner and reject the world which passes under their level gaze as a rabble passes under the guns of a rocky citadel around whose base a slatternly town has assembled.

I had seen Jeff York a thousand times, or near, standing like that on the street corner in town, while the people flowed past him, under the distant and wary and dispassionate eyes in ambush. He would be waiting for his wife and the three tow-headed children who were walking around the town looking into store windows and at the people. After a while they would come back to him, and then, wordlessly, he would lead them to the store where they always did their trading. He would go first, marching with a steady bent-kneed stride, setting the cast-iron brogans down deliberately on the cement; then his wife, a small woman with covert, sidewise, curious glances for the world, would follow, and behind her the towheads bunched together in a dazed, glory-struck way. In the store, when their turn came, Jeff York would move to the counter, accept the clerk's greeting, and then bend down from his height to catch the whispered directions of his wife. He would straighten up and say, "Gimme a sack of flahr, if'n you please." Then when the sack of flour had been brought, he would lean again to his wife for the next item. When the stuff had all been bought and paid for with the grease-thick, wadded dollar bills which he took from an old leather coin purse with a metal catch to it, he would heave it all together into his arms and march out, his wife and towheads behind him and his eyes fixed level over the heads of the crowd. He would march down the street and around to the hitching lot where the wagons were, and put his stuff into his wagon and cover it with an old quilt to wait till he got ready to drive out to his place.

For Jeff York had a place. That was what made him different from the other men who looked like him and with whom he stood on the street corner on Saturday afternoon. They were croppers, but he, Jeff York, had a place. But he stood with them because his father had stood with their fathers and his grandfathers with their grandfathers, or with men like their fathers and grandfathers, in other towns, in settlements in the mountains, in towns beyond the mountains. They were the great-great-great-grandsons of men who, half woodsmen and half farmers, had been shoved into the sand hills, into the limestone hills, into the barrens, two hundred, two hundred and fifty years before and had learned there the way to grabble a life out of the sand and the stone. And when the soil had leached away into the sand or burnt off the stone, they went on west, walking with the bent-kneed stride over the mountains, their eyes squinching warily in the gaunt faces, the rifle over the crooked arm, hunting a new place.

But there was a curse on them. They only knew the life they knew, and that life did not belong to the fat bottom lands, where the cane was head-tall, and to the grassy meadows and the rich swale. So they passed those places by and hunted for the place which was like home and where they could pick up the old life, with the same feel in the bones and the squirrel's bark sounding the same after first light. They had walked a long way, to the sand hills of Alabama, to the red country of North Mississippi and Louisiana, to the Barrens of Tennessee, to the Knobs of Kentucky and the scrub country of West Kentucky, to the Ozarks. Some of them had stopped in Cobb County, Tennessee, in the hilly eastern part of the county, and had built their cabins and dug up the ground for the corn patch. But the land had washed away there, too, and in the end they had come down out of the high land into the bottoms—for half of Cobb County is a rich, swelling country— where the corn was good and the tobacco unfurled a leaf like a yard of green velvet and the white houses stood among the cedars and tulip trees and maples. But they were not to live in the white houses with the limestone chimneys set strong at the end of each gable. No, they were to live in the shacks on the back of the farms, or in cabins not much different from the cabins they had once lived in two hundred years before over the mountains or, later, in the hills of Cobb County. But the shacks and the cabins now stood on somebody else's ground, and the curse which they had brought with them over the mountain trail, more precious than the bullet mold or grandma's quilt, the curse which was the very feeling in the bones and the habit in the hand, had come full circle.

Jeff York was one of those men, but he had broken the curse. It had taken him more than thirty years to do it, from the time when he was nothing but a big boy until he was fifty. It had taken him from sun to sun, year in and year out, and all the sweat in his body, and all the power of rejection he could muster, until the very act of rejection had become a kind of pleasure, a dark, secret, savage dissipation, like an obsessing vice. But those years had given him his place, sixty acres with a house and barn.

When he bought the place, it was not very good. The land was run-down from years of neglect and abuse. But Jeff York put brush in the gullies to stop the wash and planted clover on the run-down fields.

He mended the fences, rod by rod. He patched the roof on the little house and propped up the porch, buying the lumber and shingles almost piece by piece and one by one as he could spare the sweat-bright and grease-slick quarters and half-dollars out of his leather purse. Then he painted the house. He painted it white, for he knew that that was the color you painted a house sitting back from the road with its couple of maples, beyond the clover field.

Last, he put up the gate. It was a patented gate, the kind you can ride up to and open by pulling on a pull rope without getting off your horse or out of your buggy or wagon. It had a high pair of posts, well braced and with a high crossbar between, and the bars for the opening mechanism extending on each side. It was painted white, too. Jeff was even prouder of the gate than he was of the place. Lewis Simmons, who lived next to Jeff's place, swore he had seen Jeff come out after dark on a mule and ride in and out of that gate, back and forth, just for the pleasure of pulling on the rope and making the mechanism work. The gate was the seal Jeff York had put on all the years of sweat and rejection. He could sit on his porch on a Sunday afternoon in summer, before milking time, and look down the rise, down the winding dirt track, to the white gate beyond the clover, and know what he needed to know about all the years passed.

Meanwhile Jeff York had married and had had the three towheads. His wife was twenty years or so younger than he, a small, dark woman, who walked with her head bowed a little and from that humble and unprovoking posture stole sidewise, secret glances at the world from eyes which were brown or black—you never could tell which because you never remembered having looked her straight in the eye—and which were surprisingly bright in that sidewise, secret flicker, like the eyes of a small, cunning bird which surprise you from the brush. When they came to town she moved along the street, with a child in her arms or later with the three trailing behind her, and stole her looks at the world. She wore a calico dress, dun-colored, which hung loose to conceal whatever shape her thin body had, and in winter over the dress a brown wool coat with a scrap of fur at the collar which looked like some tattered growth of fungus feeding on old wood. She wore black high-heeled shoes, slippers of some kind, which she kept polished and which surprised you under that dress and coat. In the slippers she moved with a slightly limping, stealthy gait, almost sliding them along the pavement, as though she had not fully mastered the complicated trick required to use them properly. You knew that she wore them only when she came to town, that she carried them wrapped up in a piece of newspaper until their wagon had reached the first house on the outskirts of town, and that, on the way back, at the same point, she would take them off and wrap them up again and hold the bundle in her lap until she got home. If the weather happened to be bad, or if it was winter, she would have a pair of old brogans under the wagon seat.

It was not that Jeff York was a hard man and kept his wife in clothes that were as bad as those worn by the poorest of the women of the croppers. In fact, some of the cropper women, poor or not, black or white, managed to buy dresses with some color in them and proper hats, and went to the moving picture show on Saturday afternoon. But Jeff still owed a little money on his place, less than two hundred dollars, which he had had to borrow to rebuild his barn after it was struck by lightning. He had, in fact, never been entirely out of debt. He had lost a mule which had got out on the highway and been hit by a truck. That had set him back. One of his towheads had been sickly for a couple of winters. He had not been in deep, but he was not a man, with all those years of rejection behind him, to forget the meaning of those years. He was good enough to his family. Nobody ever said the contrary. But he was good to them in terms of all the years he had lived through. He did what he could afford. He bought the towheads a ten-cent bag of colored candy every Saturday afternoon for them to suck on during the ride home in the wagon, and the last thing before they left town, he always took the lot of them over to the dogwagon to get hamburgers and orange pop.

The towheads were crazy about hamburgers. And so was his wife, for that matter. You could tell it, even if she didn't say anything, for she would lift her bowed-forward head a little, and her face would brighten, and she would run her tongue out to wet her lips just as the plate with the hamburger would be set on the counter before her. But all those folks, like Jeff York and his family, like hamburgers, with pickle and onions and mustard and tomato catsup, the whole works. It is something different. They stay out in the country and eat hog-meat, when they can get it, and greens and corn bread and potatoes, and nothing but a pinch of salt to brighten it on the tongue, and when they get to town and get hold of beef and wheat bread and all the stuff to jack up the flavor, they have to swallow to keep the mouth from flooding before they even take the first bite.

So the last thing every Saturday, Jeff York would take his family over to Slick Hardin's *Dew Drop Inn Diner* and give them the treat. The diner was built like a railway coach, but it was set on a concrete foundation on a lot just off the main street of town. At each end the concrete was painted to show wheels. Slick Hardin kept the grass just in front of the place pretty well mowed and one or two summers he even had a couple of flower beds in the middle of that shirttail-size lawn. Slick had a good business. For a few years he had been a prelim fighter over in Nashville and had got his name in the papers a few times. So he was a kind of hero, with the air of romance about him. He had been born, however, right in town and, as soon as he had found out he wasn't ever going to be good enough to be a real fighter, he had come back home and started the dogwagon, the first one ever in town. He was a slick-skinned fellow, about thirty-five, prematurely bald, with his head slick all over. He had big eyes, pale blue and slick looking like agates. When he said something that he thought smart, he would roll his eyes around, slick in his head like marbles, to see who was laughing. Then he'd wink. He had done very well with his business, for despite the fact that he had picked up city ways and a lot of city talk, he still remembered enough to deal with the country people, and they were the ones who brought the dimes in. People who lived right there in town, except for school kids in the afternoon and the young toughs from the pool room or men on the night shift down at the railroad, didn't often get around to the dogwagon.

Slick Hardin was perhaps trying to be smart when he said what he did to Mrs. York. Perhaps he had forgotten, just for that moment, that people like Jeff York and his wife didn't like to be kidded, at least not in that way. He said what he did, and then grinned and rolled his eyes around to see if some of the other people present were thinking it was funny.

Mrs. York was sitting on a stool in front of the counter, flanked on one side by Jeff York and on the other by the three towheads. She had just sat down to wait for the hamburger—there were several orders in ahead of the York order—and had been watching in her sidewise fashion every move of Slick Hardin's hands as he patted the pink meat onto the hot slab and wiped the split buns over the greasy iron to make them ready to receive it. She always watched him like that, and when the hamburger was set before her she would wet her lips with her tongue.

That day Slick set the hamburger down in front of Mrs. York, and said, "Anybody likes hamburger much as you, Mrs. York, ought to git him a hamburger stand."

Mrs. York flushed up, and didn't say anything, staring at her plate. Slick rolled his eyes to see how it was going over, and somebody down the counter snickered. Slick looked back at the Yorks, and if he had not been so encouraged by the snicker he might, when he saw Jeff York's face, have hesitated before going on with his kidding. People like Jeff York are touchous, and they are especially touchous about the women-folks, and you do not make jokes with or about their womenfolks unless it is perfectly plain that the joke is a very special kind of friendly joke. The snicker down the counter had defined the joke as not entirely friendly. Jeff was looking at Slick, and something was growing slowly in that hewed-cedar face, and back in the gray eyes in the ambush of thorny brows.

But Slick did not notice. The snicker had encouraged him, and so he said, "Yeah, if I liked them hamburgers much as you, I'd buy me a hamburger stand. Fact, I'm selling this one. You want to buy it?"

There was another snicker, louder, and Jeff York, whose hamburger had been about half way to his mouth for another bite, laid it down deliberately on his plate. But whatever might have happened at that moment did not happen. It did not happen because Mrs. York lifted her flushed face, looked straight at Slick Hardin, swallowed hard to get down a piece of the hamburger or to master her nerve, and said in a sharp, strained voice, "You sellen this place?"

There was complete silence. Nobody had expected her to say any-thing. The chances were she had never said a word in that diner in the couple of hundred times she had been in it. She had come in with Jeff York and, when a stool had come vacant, had sat down, and Jeff had said, "Gimme five hamburgers, if'n you please, and make 'em well done, and five bottles of orange pop." Then, after the eating was over, he had always laid down seventy-five cents on the counter— that is, after there were five hamburger-eaters in the family—and walked out, putting his brogans down slow, and his wife and kids following without a word. But now she spoke up and asked the ques-tion, in that strained, artificial voice, and everybody, including her husband, looked at her with surprise.

As soon as he could take it in, Slick Hardin replied, "Yeah, I'm selling it."

She swallowed hard again, but this time it could not have been hamburger, and demanded, "What you asken fer hit?"

Slick looked at her in the new silence, half shrugged, a little con-temptuously, and said, "Fourteen hundred and fifty dollars."

She looked back at him, while the blood ebbed from her face. "Hit's a lot of money," she said in a flat tone, and returned her gaze to the hamburger on her plate.

"Lady," Slick said defensively, "I got that much money tied up here. Look at that there stove. It is a *Heat Master* and they cost. Them coffee urns, now. Money can't buy no better. And this here lot, lady, the diner sets on. Anybody knows I got that much money tied up here. I got more. This lot cost me more'n . . ." He suddenly realized that she was not listening to him. And he must have realized, too, that she didn't have a dime in the world and couldn't buy his diner, and that he was making a fool of himself, defending his price. He stopped abruptly, shrugged his shoulders, and then swung his wide gaze down the counter to pick out somebody to wink to.

But before he got the wink off, Jeff York had said, "Mr. Hardin." Slick looked at him and asked, "Yeah?"

"She didn't mean no harm," Jeff York said. "She didn't mean to be messen in yore business."

Slick shrugged. "Ain't no skin off my nose," he said. "Ain't no secret I'm selling out. My price ain't no secret neither."

Mrs. York bowed her head over her plate. She was chewing a mouthful of her hamburger with a slow, abstracted motion of her jaw, and you knew that it was flavorless on her tongue.

That was, of course, on a Saturday. On Thursday afternoon of the next week Slick was in the diner alone. It was the slack time, right in the middle of the afternoon. Slick, as he told it later, was wiping off the stove and wasn't noticing. He was sort of whistling to himself, he said. He had a way of whistling soft through his teeth. But he wasn't whistling loud, he said, not so loud he wouldn't have heard the door open or the steps if she hadn't come gum-shoeing in on him to stand there waiting in the middle of the floor until he turned round and was so surprised he nearly had heart failure. He had thought he was there alone, and there she was, watching every move he was making, like a cat watching a goldfish swim in a bowl.

"Howdy-do," he said, when he got his breath back.

"This place still fer sale?" she asked him.

"Yeah, lady," he said.

"What you asken fer hit?"

"Lady, I done told you," Slick replied, "fourteen hundred and fifty dollars."

"Hit's a heap of money," she said.

Slick started to tell her how much money he had tied up there, but before he had got going, she had turned and slipped out of the door.

"Yeah," Slick said later to the men who came into the diner, "me like a fool starting to tell her how much money I got tied up here when I knowed she didn't have a dime. That woman's crazy. She must walked that five or six miles in here just to ask me something she already knowed the answer to. And then turned right round and walked out. But I am selling me this place. I'm tired of slinging hash to them hicks. I got me some connections over in Nashville and I'm gonna open me a place over there. A cigar stand and about three pool tables and maybe some beer. I'll have me a sort of club in the back. You know, membership cards to git in, where the boys will play a little game. Just sociable. I got good connections over in Nashville. I'm selling this place. But that woman, she ain't got a dime. She ain't gonna buy it."

But she did.

On Saturday Jeff York led his family over to the diner. They ate hamburgers without a word and marched out. After they had gone, Slick said, "Looks like she ain't going to make the invest-mint. Gonna buy a block of bank stock instead." Then he rolled his eyes, located a brother down the counter, and winked.

It was almost the end of the next week before it happened. What had been going on inside the white house out on Jeff York's place nobody knew or was to know. Perhaps she just starved him out, just not doing the cooking or burning everything. Perhaps she just quit attending to the children properly and he had to come back tired from work and take care of them. Perhaps she just lay in bed at night and talked and talked to him, asking him to buy it, nagging him all night long, while he would fall asleep and then wake up with a start to hear her voice still going on. Or perhaps she just turned her face away from him and wouldn't let him touch her. He was a lot older than she, and she was probably the only woman he had ever had. He had been too ridden by his dream and his passion for rejection during all the years before to lay even a finger on a woman. So she had him there. Because he was a lot older and because he had never had another woman. But perhaps she used none of these methods. She was a small, dark, cunning woman, with a sidewise look from her lowered face, and she could have thought up ways of her own, no doubt.

Whatever she thought up, it worked. On Friday morning Jeff York went to the bank. He wanted to mortgage his place, he told Todd Sullivan, the president. He wanted fourteen hundred and fifty dollars, he said. Todd Sullivan would not let him have it. He already owed the bank one hundred and sixty dollars and the best he could get on a mortgage was eleven hundred dollars. That was in 1935 and then farmland wasn't worth much and half the land in the country was mortgaged anyway. Jeff York sat in the chair by Todd Sullivan's desk and didn't say anything. Eleven hundred dollars would not do him any good. Take off the hundred and sixty he owed and it wouldn't be but a little over nine hundred dollars clear to him. He sat there quietly for a minute, apparently turning that fact over in his head. Then Todd Sullivan asked him, "How much you say you need?"

Jeff York told him.

"What you want it for?" Todd Sullivan asked.

He told him that.

"I tell you," Todd Sullivan said, "I don't want to stand in the way of a man bettering himself. Never did. That diner ought to be a good proposition, all right, and I don't want to stand in your way if you want to come to town and better yourself. It will be a step up from that farm for you, and I like a man has got ambition. The bank can't lend you the money, not on that piece of property. But I tell you what I'll do. I'll buy your place. I got me some walking horses I'm keeping out on my father's place. But I could use me a little place of my own. For my horses. I'll give you seventeen hundred for it. Cash."

Jeff York did not say anything to that. He looked slow at Todd Sullivan as though he did not understand.

"Seventeen hundred," the banker repeated. "That's a good figure. For these times."

Jeff was not looking at him now. He was looking out the window, across the alleyway—Todd Sullivan's office was in the back of the bank. The banker, telling about it later when the doings of Jeff York had become for a moment a matter of interest, said, "I thought he hadn't even heard me. He looked like he was half asleep or something. I coughed to sort of wake him up. You know the way you do. I didn't want to rush him. You can't rush those people, you know. But I couldn't sit there all day. I had offered him a fair price."

It was, as a matter of fact, a fair price for the times, when the bottom was out of everything in the section.

Jeff York took it. He took the seventeen hundred dollars and bought the dogwagon with it, and rented a little house on the edge of town and moved in with his wife and the towheads. The first day after they

got settled, Jeff York and his wife went over to the diner to get instruc-
tions from Slick about running the place. He showed Mrs. York all
about how to work the coffee machine and the stove, and how to make
up the sandwiches, and how to clean the place up after herself. She
fried up hamburgers for all of them, herself, her husband, and Slick
Hardin, for practice, and they ate the hamburgers while a couple of
hangers-on watched them. "Lady," Slick said, for he had money in his
pocket and was heading out for Nashville on the seven o'clock train
that night, and was feeling expansive, "lady, you sure fling a mean
hamburger."

He wiped the last crumbs and mustard off his lips, got his valise
from behind the door, and said, "Lady, git in there and pitch. I hope
you make a million hamburgers." Then he stepped out into the bright
fall sunshine and walked away whistling up the street, whistling
through his teeth and rolling his eyes as though there were somebody
to wink to. That was the last anybody in town ever saw of Slick Hardin.

The next day, Jeff York worked all day down at the diner. He was
scrubbing up the place inside and cleaning up the trash which had
accumulated behind it. He burned all the trash. Then he gave the
place a good coat of paint outside, white paint. That took him two
days. Then he touched up the counter inside with varnish. He
straightened up the sign out front, which had begun to sag a little.
He had that place looking spick and span.

Then on the fifth day after they got settled—it was Sunday—he
took a walk in the country. It was along toward sun when he started
out, not late, as a matter of fact, for by October the days are shortening
up. He walked out the Curtisville pike and out the cut-off leading to his
farm. When he entered the cut-off, about a mile from his own place,
it was still light enough for the Bowdoins, who had a filling station at
the corner, to see him plain when he passed.

The next time anybody saw him was on Monday morning about
six o'clock. A man taking milk into town saw him. He was hanging
from the main cross bar of the white patented gate. He had jumped off
the gate. But he had propped the thing open so there wouldn't be any
chance of clambering back up on it if his neck didn't break when he
jumped and he should happen to change his mind.

But that was an unnecessary precaution, as it developed. Dr. Stauffer
said that his neck was broken very clean. "A man who can break a neck
as clean as that could make a living at it," Dr. Stauffer said. And added,
"If he's damned sure it ain't ever his own neck."

Mrs. York was much cut up by her husband's death. People were sympathetic and helpful, and out of a mixture of sympathy and curiosity she got a good starting trade at the diner. And the trade kept right on. She got so she didn't hang her head and look sidewise at you and the world. She would look straight at you. She got so she could walk in high heels without giving the impression that it was a trick she was learning. She wasn't a bad-looking woman, as a matter of fact, once she had caught on how to fix herself up a little. The railroad men and the pool hall gang liked to hang out there and kid with her. Also, they said, she flung a mean hamburger.

Questions and Suggestions

1. Who is the narrator? Who is the *you* whom he addresses in the opening paragraphs?
2. Is his account rich in figures of speech?
3. Where in the story does Warren stop using the method of summary narrative? Does he return to it?
4. What does the scene in the grocery store foretell? Does Ortega y Gasset's expression "emotional distance" apply to the relationship between the narrator and Jeff York? How sympathetic is the speaker to Mrs. York, to Slick Harden?
5. What is the curse from which York escaped? Why does he commit suicide? Why did he choose to use the patented gate?
6. The narrator could not be present to know how Mrs. York convinced her husband that he should sell the farm. How does Warren solve that problem for the reader?

Ideas for Writing

1. An account of a family with whom you are familiar who gave up a good life for a shoddy substitute. Try using more similes and metaphors than you normally use.
2. If you have ever lived in a small town, describe the crowd that gathers around the courthouse or loiters on a favorite street, especially on Saturdays.
3. Contrast the York family with the one in William Faulkner's famous story "Barn Burning."
4. In Flannery O'Connor's "Good Country People," a story that appears in *A Good Man Is Hard to Find*, Mrs. Hopewell claims that " 'good country people are the salt of the earth' " and that " 'there aren't enough good country people in the world.' " In the story her statements assume an ironic twist. She makes them to a complete charlatan—a Bible salesman

who looks as if he has come straight from a farm. She assumes that he is simple and good, but he cruelly outsmarts all the people he meets. Can you explain your own realistic or romantic concept of country folk?

5. Perhaps you know a rich man who gives the appearance of being poor. How does he achieve the effect? Perhaps you know a family that shows the effects of poverty that has existed over several generations, or you may be well acquainted with a husband and wife whose goals are not the same.

A QUICK SKETCH OF VAN DYCK

EUGÈNE FROMENTIN

Sainte-Beuve, the famous French critic, praised Samuel-Auguste-Eugène Fromentin (1820–1876) for being a "fine artist," both as a writer and as a painter. Born in La Rochelle, France, Fromentin first studied law but later turned to painting, finding his greatest interest in North African scenes. His canvases no longer receive great praise, but his book, *Les Maîtres d'autrefois*, which has as its subtitle in English, *Dutch and Flemish Painting from Van Eyck to Rembrandt*, has become a classic. Fromentin visited churches, museums, and private galleries in Belgium and Holland in 1875; his journals first appeared in 1876 in the *Revue des Deux-Mondes*.

This is what I should imagine a portrait of Van Dyck to be like, in a rough sketch, with unblended crayon strokes.

A young prince of royal blood, with everything in his favour— beauty, elegance, magnificent parts, precocious genius, unique education, and with all the chance happenings of fortunate birth before him; petted by his master, already himself a master among his schoolfellows, admired everywhere, invited everywhere, welcomed everywhere, abroad even more than in his own country; the equal of the greatest lords, the favourite and friend of kings; entering thus, at one

From "Van Dyck," in *The Masters of Past Time*, Andrew Boyle, tr. Reprinted by permission of E. P. Dutton & Co., Inc., and J. M. Dent & Sons, Ltd.

stroke, into possession of all the most desirable things of this earth—
talent, fame, honours, luxury, love, adventure; ever young, even in
his mature years; never wise, even in his last years; a libertine, a gambler, greedy, prodigal, wasteful, playing the devil, and, as they would
have said in his time, selling his soul to the devil for guineas, and
then throwing them away open-handed, for horses, display, feasts,
ruinous gallantries; enamoured of his art in the highest degree, yet
sacrificing it to less noble passions, to less faithful amours, to less
fortunate attachments; charming, of strong race, of slender, elegant
stature, as happens in the second remove of great races; of a constitution already less virile, rather delicate, in fact; with the air of a
Don Juan rather than of a hero, with a tinge of melancholy and an
undertone of sadness underlying all the gaiety of his life, the im-
pressionableness of a heart easily smitten, and that something of dis-
illusionment proper to those whose hearts are too easily smitten; a
nature inflammable rather than burning; at bottom, more sensuality
than real fire, less transport than unrestraint; less capable of grasping
things than of allowing himself to be seized by them and of abandoning
himself to them; a man delightful in his own attractiveness and sensible to all other attractiveness, devoured by that which is most consum-
ing in this world—the muse and women; having abused everything—
his charms, his health, his dignity, his talent; overwhelmed with needs,
worn out by pleasure, drained of resources; an insatiable being who
ended, they say, by keeping low company with Italian rascals and by
seeking surreptitiously the Philosopher's Stone; an adventurer at his
last resources, who married, by command so to speak, a charming,
high-born lady, at a time when he had little to offer her—not much
strength, not much money, no longer any great charm nor very certain
life; the wreck of a man who, up to his last hour, had the good fortune
—the most extraordinary of all—to keep his greatness when he painted;
in short, a scamp, adored, decried, slandered later on, at bottom better
than he was reputed to be, and a man who gained pardon for all his
faults by a supreme gift, one of the forms of genius—grace; to put
it plainly—a Prince of Wales dying as soon as the throne was empty,
and who was not to reign.

Questions and Suggestions

    1. Use a standard rhetoric to define balanced and periodic
        sentences, antithesis, parallelism, climax, and chiasmus. Be
        able to explain which of these devices Fromentin uses.

2. When are you first aware that the portrait of Van Dyke will not be entirely favorable? Does Fromentin seem at all anxious to persuade his readers to agree with his attitude toward the painter?

3. Are the comparisons that Fromentin uses equally effective or are some better than others?

4. How interested was he in specific facts?

5. In one edition of this selection, a colon rather than a period is used at the end of the first sentence. Which do you prefer?

Ideas for Writing

1. Without giving up after a first try, attempt a theme, about the length of Fromentin's paragraph, wherein you briefly focus your attention on the physical, financial, mental, moral, and social characteristics of a friend. You might do your best work with a person who, at least according to your judgment, has failed to achieve his potential. Definitely try to make greater use of antithesis than is normal in your work and yet aim toward compactness. Such a paper would also be more successful if you build to a climax.

2. Discuss why you respect a certain artist, iconoclast, or "beatnick," even if his behavior, dress, or ideas at times seem bizarre.

3. Contrast this portrait of Van Dyke with the one you find in the *Encyclopaedia Britannica* or any other reputable reference work. Do the purposes of the authors vary?

HOW EINSTEIN CAME TO PRINCETON

JOHN A. LAMPE

John A. Lampe, D.D. (1911–) graduated from Knox College the same year that he met Einstein. He served pastorates in Ohio and Illinois before becoming the senior minister of the Carmel Presbyterian Church in Glenside, Pennsylvania, a suburb of Philadelphia.

I was not the one who recruited the late Albert Einstein for the faculty of the Institute for Advanced Study. But I like to believe it was I, as a broke and lonely student at Princeton, who made him welcome to the real America. Certainly I was first to share with him the delicious mysteries of an ice-cream cone and dime-store shopping. Those simple pleasures so absorbed the utterly simple and unpretentious human behind his towering genius that neither he nor I felt required to speak a word.

The year was 1933, and the month October. I was a divinity student at the Princeton Seminary. The newspapers had been full of headlines reporting the flight of the famous scientist from Germany. As a member of a minority he felt the full scorn and hate of a vengeful political party in his own country. Seeking a place of peace where he could quietly pursue his studies, he chose haven here. After he was safely on board a transatlantic ship the papers began to make ever larger headlines of his coming.

At last the 17th of October dawned, the day when the ship was to reach the Port of New York. Public excitement had been whipped to frenzy of such pitch that even the quiet town of Princeton had become infected. Every student with sufficient cash and class-cuts left in his school schedule, vanished from the village, and headed for the pier where Einstein was due to set foot on American soil.

As usual in those Depression days, I was low on cash. Besides, I lacked the allowable class-cuts to make the trip. So, on the day Einstein came to America I felt very much alone and quite forlorn. The newness of school had worn off, the burden of strange lessons was bearing down, my family was in St. Louis, and my favorite girl was in California. I wandered up Nassau Street, in the center of the business district, to the Baltimore, an ice cream shop which we all called "The Balt."

"The Balt" had a special ice-cream cone which almost all students automatically bought to nibble while they made up their minds which of more choice sodas or sundaes they would order. This delightful treat consisted simply of vanilla ice cream in a cone which the waitress dipped into a huge bowl of chocolate dragées.

Without thinking too much about the matter I ordered this confection and turned to observe the street outside as my order was being filled. At that moment a very short, dumpy, little man wearing a nondescript grey sweater and baggy trousers passed the window, looked in, and opened the door. His long grey hair, flowing free toward the back of his head, was a familiar sight already because of the news photographers.

Einstein!

Einstein's boat was not yet at the pier in New York. Yet Einstein walked through the doorway just as the waitress behind the counter handed me my special ice-cream cone!

The great man looked at the cone, smiled at me, turned to the girl, and pointed his thumb first at the cone and then at himself.

I wish I could say that I had the generosity or presence of mind to pay for Einstein's first typically American treat. But that would not be the truth. When the waitress handed his cone over the counter Einstein gave her a coin and she made change, muttering something like "This one goes in my memory book."

Einstein and I stood there together, then, nibbling our ice-cream cones and looking out the window into Nassau Street. Neither of us said anything. We finished the cones about the same instant and I think I held the door for him as he stepped out.

Outside "The Balt" we stood together momentarily, still not saying a word. Then, as though we were reading each other's minds, we walked up the street together to the dime store. We went into the store together and stopped side by side in front of the counter containing school supplies. Pencils could be had for a penny each in those days, and I bought one. I also bought an eraser. Einstein was in the act of picking out a pencil that he particularly liked when the two of us were suddenly pinned against the counter by a mob of students.

From the looks of them I took them all to be undergraduates on the Princeton campus. Eight score lads were jammed in the narrow aisles of that store. No one could move. Everyone was pressing as close as he could to the counter, trying to see Einstein.

Where had they come from? How had they arrived so fast? I couldn't recall having seen five students in any direction as we walked the few steps from "The Balt" to the dime store. The gang just appeared out of nowhere, as though in psychic response to the great man who had appeared out of nowhere.

Trapped against the counter, unable to move or even to finish buying the pencil he had chosen, Einstein looked as calm and undisturbed as though this kind of thing happened to him every day.

There must have been someone who did not share his aplomb. Perhaps the manager of the store grew worried about the size of the crowd. Somehow word reached the village police force, and several policemen appeared and shouldered through the mob to escort Einstein away. The students immediately closed in behind the police, and I did not reach the sidewalk with my new pencil and eraser until everyone else had gone. My new friend was nowhere in sight by the time I got out of the store.

That evening, at suppertime, my fellows at the Seminary came straggling home from New York. Disappointment showed large on their faces. They reported that they had stood on the pier and scrutinized each person who came off the ship. No one had seen Albert Einstein. They reported that jostling mobs had stormed the area for a glimpse of the famous scientist. But no one had seen him at all. Everyone was baffled.

When I spoke up and said that Einstein and I had eaten ice-cream cones together at "The Balt" that afternoon and shopped at the five-and-ten for pencils and erasers, I was hooted down as a man unworthy of the cloth.

Next morning *The New York Times* explained everything. Einstein had been taken off the liner at the Battery and was met there by two trustees of the Institute for Advanced Study, who drove him to Princeton. The official Welcoming Committee and an attendant throng had waited in vain at the 23rd Street pier in Manhattan, innocent of what was happening.

The *Times* reported that in the late afternoon of that day Einstein accompanied Dr. Walter Mayer in a walk from the Peacock Inn to the center of Princeton to buy a newspaper. The *Times* did not know it, but that walk with Dr. Mayer was Einstein's second walk uptown. The first one was taken alone. Einstein must have gone directly to the home that had been secured for him in the town, changed into comfortable old clothes, and gone out to explore his new environment. It was bright daylight—probably not before 2 p.m. and not later than 4— when he looked into the window at "The Balt" and saw my ice-cream cone.

Almost every day of that school year I passed Einstein on the Seminary campus as he walked from his home to the campus of the Institute for Advanced Study. Other students who spoke German sometimes conversed with him. Not knowing German, I could only nod and call "Hello!" But I always felt I knew him much better than the other fellows did. He seemed to say so, too, in the way he always smiled.

Questions and Suggestions

1. What is the purpose of Lampe's first three paragraphs?
2. Why does he conclude his essay with the explanation paraphrased from *The New York Times*?
3. Why did Einstein come to America? What did he do at the Institute for Advanced Study? If necessary, consult the index to *The New York Times* and *The Reader's Guide to Periodical Literature* for more information concerning Einstein's reasons for leaving Europe, his activities at Princeton, and his ideas about the development of atomic weapons.
4. What purpose does the waitress' comment serve? If it reveals something of her nature, does it also hint at levels of cultural interests that exist in America? What would Ortega y Gasset think of her?
5. Why does Lampe believe that he "knew him much better than the other fellows did"? How true is this remark?
6. Do you know the meaning of *psychic* and *aplomb?*

Ideas for Writing

1. Recall an experience that you have had with one of your professors outside of the classroom, showing how he appeared more human than he had seemed before, or remained much the same as he was in the lecture hall.
2. Describe the arrival of a personage into your community and some of the local reactions.
3. Point out the differences in cultural interests among a group of your acquaintances.
4. Using examples, contrast or compare the interests of your student body with those of the undergraduates who crowded into the store to see Einstein.
5. Why was Einstein one of the most influential scientists of the twentieth century?

WALT WHITMAN

LOGAN PEARSALL SMITH

Logan Pearsall Smith (1865–1946) was born in Millville, New Jersey. After he had studied at Haverford and Harvard, Smith, finding himself financially independent, decided to move to England and join the other members of his family who had already

From *Unforgotten Years.* Reprinted by permission of John Russell.

established residence there. One of his sisters was Bertrand Russell's first wife, and the other became Mrs. Bernard Berenson. Smith studied at Balliol and in 1913 became a naturalized British subject. A precisionist with words and one who always wrote mellifluously, he is chiefly remembered as an essayist.

This was the point at which I had arrived when, in 1882, returning home again for the Easter holidays, I was told important news by my sister Mary, when she too arrived for her holidays from Smith College (for the ban on the college education of girls was now removed). There was a poet, she informed me and the rest of our family, a great American poet and prophet,—though most Americans were not at all aware of his greatness,—now living in poverty and neglect among us in America, living actually not far from our neighborhood, and it was her purpose, she informed us, to go without delay and offer him a due tribute of praise and admiration. How had she heard of this poet? her perturbed relatives inquired. A lady lecturer, she replied, had come from Boston to Smith College, and had praised his works, which she had herself immediately ordered from Boston, and which had revealed to her a message of tremendous import, and the purpose of her intended visit was to discuss this message. Consternation fell upon us all, and my father at once forbade it. He vaguely knew the name of the poet, which was by no means a name of good repute in Philadelphia; the district in which he lived was a district not visited by people who respected their own position; no daughter of his, he peremptorily declared, should, while she lived under his roof, be allowed to take so unseemly a step.

My father's refusal to permit this indecorum, though impressive as the poor man could make it, had no effect whatsoever upon my sister. She thought of going, she said, on the following Thursday; and my father, being in his heart well aware of the powerlessness of American parents in their dealings with their daughters, and convinced, as he was, that if my sister meant to go on Thursday, on Thursday she would go, wisely, if unheroically, decided that the best thing under the circumstances was for him to accompany her, and thus lend an air of propriety to the visit. I was invited to join the party, and so on Thursday afternoon, off we started from our home in Germantown, behind my father's fine pair of horses. We flashed along through Fairmount Park, we drove across Philadelphia, we embarked in the ferry and crossed the Delaware, and dashed up before the little two-story wooden house in Camden to which we had been directed. An elderly woman who answered the doorbell ushered us into a little parlor and shouted upstairs, "Walt, here's some carriage folk come to see you." We heard a stirring above us as of a slow and unwieldy person, and soon through the open door we saw two large feet in carpet slippers slowly descending the stairs, and then the bulky form of the old man appeared before us. Walt Whitman greeted us with friendly simplicity; he had no notion who we were, and we had no introduction to him, but the unannounced appearance of these "carriage folk" from across the river— this portly and opulent-looking gentleman with his tall son and beautiful tall daughter—did not seem to surprise him in the least. My sister informed him that our name was Smith, that she had read his *Leaves of Grass,* and had come to express her immense admiration for that volume, and this explanation was received with great complacency; we were all invited to follow him upstairs to his den, where we sat down on what chairs could be hastily provided, and were soon engaged in lively talk.

My father, who at first held himself aloof in the most disapproving manner, soon, to the surprise of my sister and myself, began to join in this friendly conversation, and we were still more surprised, when we got up to take our departure, to hear our impulsive parent invite the object of his grave disapprobation to drive back with us to Germantown and spend the night. The afternoon was, he urged, a fine one, the drive across the Park would be pleasant, and it would be a pity to bring to a premature end so agreeable a confabulation. "No, Mr. Smith, I think I won't come," the poet answered; but when he had hobbled to the window and seen, waiting in the street outside, my father's equipage, he said that he thought he might as well come after all, and, hastily putting a nightshirt and a few other objects in a little bag, he hobbled downstairs and we all drove off together. It was, as my father had said, a pleasant afternoon; we crossed again the ferry, we drove through Philadelphia and through the Park to our home in Germantown, where Walt Whitman remained with us for a month, and whither he would often afterwards return. He became indeed a familiar and friendly inmate of the house, whose genial presence, even when we did not see him, could hardly pass unnoticed, for he had the habit of singing "Old Jim Crow" when not occupied in conversation, and his loud and cheerful voice could be heard echoing every morning from the bathroom or the water closet. His arrivals were always unannounced; he would appear when he liked, stay as long as he liked; and then one morning we would find at breakfast a penciled note to say that he had departed early, having had for the present enough of our society.

The reputation which the author of the *Leaves of Grass* had acquired by that daring and not decent publication was a dubious one in America at that time; this reputation had reached our Quaker suburb, and our neighbors and relations avoided our house, and forbade their children to visit it, when it was known that Walt Whitman was staying with us. There was, indeed, a grave charge which could have been brought against him, and which would have greatly shocked us all, if we had known (as we fortunately did not) anything about it. There can be no doubt, I fear, that from his boyhood Walt Whitman had associated with Hicksite Quakers, that his father and mother had been followers of this prophet, and that he himself had in his youth heard him preach. Indeed, in his old age he wrote a eulogy of this aged Quaker in which he described the long life of piety and benevolence of the saintly old man, and quoted without the least disapproval his doctrine that true religion consisted, not in sermons and ceremonials, but in spirituality, purity, and the love of God and man.

This eulogy of Elias Hicks was written perhaps by the naughty old poet while he was staying under our roof. But, as I say, one's sense of wrong grows weaker with the years, and the other day I read Walt Whitman's account of Elias Hicks with no overwhelming moral condemnation. Indeed it was difficult at any time for anyone to retain a prejudice against Walt Whitman for long. His manners were grand and primeval, like those of the old patriarchs and bards in a picture of Blake's; he treated all people with the same politeness, and only on one occasion did we notice in him any sense of times and occasions and the demands of social etiquette. He had arrived on a visit in a knitted vest, and, when told that a number of people were coming that evening to dinner, the thought occurred to him that probably he ought to put on a coat for the occasion, and after some meditation he appeared at dinner time a consummate man of the world in his overcoat, thus sacrificing his comfort, for the night was hot, to the demands of the occasion.

Almost every afternoon my father would take Walt Whitman driving in the Park; it was an unfailing interest to them to drive as close as they could behind buggies in which pairs of lovers were seated, and observe the degree of slope towards each other, or "buggy-angle," as they called it, of these couples; and if ever they saw this angle of approximation narrowed to an embrace, my father and Walt Whitman, who had ever honored that joy-giving power of nature symbolized under the name of Venus, would return home with happy hearts.

My acquaintanceship with this great and famous poet,—for Walt Whitman had already become famous in England, and his glory had flashed back across the Atlantic to Boston, and thence, as I have described, to where we sat in Germantown in darkness,—the familiar presence of this poet in our house, must have had an influence upon me which was more powerful than anything that I was aware of at the time. He was, as John Burroughs has well described him, "large and picturesque of figure, slow of movement, tolerant, receptive, democratic and full of charity and good will towards all. His life was a poet's life from first to last—free, unworldly, unhurried, unconventional, unselfish, and was contentedly and joyously lived." He was already old and half-paralyzed when we made his acquaintance, but of the disabilities of age he never spoke, although their shadows are not absent from his poems of this period. In one of these, for instance, "Queries to My Seventieth Year," which was written just when we came to know him, he thus addresses the oncoming year: —

> Approaching, nearing, curious,
> Thou dim, uncertain spectre—bringest thou life or death?
> Strength, weakness, blindness, more paralysis and heavier?
> Or placid skies and sun? Wilt stir the waters yet?
> Or haply cut me short for good? Or leave me here as now,
> Dull, parrot-like and old, with crack'd voice harping, screeching?

It was, however, the calm serenity of age, its placid skies and sun, which diffused about him that atmosphere of peace and leisure which made his companionship so genial, and our endless conversations with him so great a pleasure. He was fond of talking with young people, and would listen with the utmost good nature to our crude notions; and when he was not with us, my sisters and I would often visit him in Camden, where on summer days we would find him seated at his window, fanning himself with a large palm-leaf fan, and gazing out on the lazy sunshine that filled his little street. Not infrequently during our visits he would recognize some workingman of his acquaintance as he passed, and call out, "Come up, Bill, and meet some friends of mine," and the workingman would come in, or the passing postman, or the driver of an express wagon, and we would all share an improvised meal together.

The floor of the room upstairs in which he lived was covered to the depth of a foot or so with a sea of papers, and now and then he would stir this pool with his stick and fish up a letter from an English admirer—Tennyson perhaps, or Symonds, or Edward Dowden—or some newspaper article about "the Good Grey Poet." Walt Whitman, who had been himself so long a newspaper writer, was curiously fond of newspaper publicity; his floor was strewn with press cuttings in which his name was mentioned, and he would even, I believe, now and then, write anonymous articles about himself for insertion in the local papers. Otherwise he was quite free from literary vanity, and never spoke of his writings unless we questioned him. Then, however, he would answer with great simplicity and frankness.

My sister Mary (whom he called his "bright, particular star") recalls how once, when she was on the Camden ferry, she saw an Englishman also on the boat. He must, she rightly concluded, be on a pilgrimage like herself to visit Walt Whitman, for how otherwise account for the presence of that Englishman? She, therefore, accosted the correct and dapper figure, who confessed, with some surprise, that this was in fact his purpose. My sister offered to show him the way to Walt Whitman's house, and they proceeded thither, to find, however, that the door was locked and they could get no answer to their knockings. "I'm sure he's upstairs," my sister said; "he always is, so the best thing is for me to boost you up to the window, which you can open, and then come down and let me in." Edmund Gosse (for the Englishman was Edmund Gosse) seemed considerably surprised, my sister says, by the unconventionality of this proposal, but as he had come a long way to visit Walt Whitman, and did not wish to be baffled in his object, he finally allowed my sister to boost him up; and then he descended to open the front door to her, and they found Walt Whitman as usual in his study, and their visit was a satisfactory one in every way. It is only fair, however, to add that when, thirty or forty years after, I arranged for Mrs. Berenson and Sir Edmund Gosse to meet at luncheon, the latter, though admitting that he had met my sister at Walt Whitman's, angrily denied the boosting and his informal entrance. Knowing both Gosse and my sister to be endowed with more picturesque than accurate memories, I have never been able to decide which of them was telling the truth.

I remember once speaking to Walt Whitman about his poem, "With husky-haughty lips, O sea!" which had just been published, and he told me, sitting one summer evening on our porch in Germantown, of the way he had come to write it; how always, from the days of his boyhood on the Long Island coasts, he had tried and tried again to seize the meaning which the voice of the ocean was always whispering in his ears; how often by day, and more often by night, he had sat or lain amid the sandhills on its margin, listening in a kind of torment of attention to the great voice—some voice—in what words could he best describe it?

> . . . some voice, in huge monotonous rage, of freedom-lover pent,
> Some vast heart, like a planet's, chain'd and chafing in those breakers.

This notion of receptivity to experience, and of a complete surrender to it, combined with a patient effort to grasp its deepest meaning and to embody that meaning in significant words—this account of the old man's poetic method, as he told it one summer evening, was deeply impressive to his boyish listener, although that listener had then no thought of attempting to coin his own experience into enduring metal. To melt material sand into salable glass bottles—this, he believed, was to be his destiny; and the idea that all such massy unmetaphorical gold might be gladly bartered—as Walt Whitman would gladly have bartered it—for the ability to embody in words some one of Nature's aspects,—the sea's voice, for instance, or the breath of its salt fragrance, or even, as he himself had said, "the undulation of one wave,"—the idea of so mad a preference would have seemed to his youthful listener at that date fantastic indeed.

Thus I listened to the impressive talk of the old poet, and though I had no notion of following his example, the effect upon me of his poems, as I read and reread that strange volume, the *Leaves of Grass*—how can I adequately describe it? There are books which come to us like revelations, which, as Emerson says, "take rank in our lives with parents and lovers and passionate experiences," and to come on such a book to which one can yield oneself in absolute surrender—there is no intellectual enjoyment, I believe, no joy of the mind greater in youth than this. Books of this kind should be contemporary books, written by the living for the living; and should present us with a picture of life as we ourselves know it and feel it. And they should above all reveal us to ourselves, should hold up a looking glass before our eyes in which we see our own faces. Much that was suppressed in the young people of my generation found a frank avowal in the *Leaves of Grass;* feelings and affections for each other, which we had been ashamed of, thoughts which we had hidden as unutterable, we found printed in its pages, discovering that they were not, as we had believed, the thoughts and feelings of young, guilty, half-crazy goblins, but portions of the Kingdom of Truth and the sane experience of mankind. It was above all Walt Whitman's rejoicing in his flesh and blood,—

"there is so much of me," he sang, "and all so luscious,"—his delight
in his own body and the bodies of his friends, which seemed a revelation and gave the *Leaves of Grass* so strong a hold upon a generation
born of puritans who had ignored, or treated as shameful, those habita-
tions of the spirit. Then, too, Walt Whitman's affection for his fellow
human beings,—for he was one of those rare spirits who really love
the human race,—his feeling that all men and women, of whatever
race or class and in whatever state of degradation, were all of them
not worthless and of no account, but lovable and mysterious and divine—this seemed to fill for us the many-peopled world with innumerable creatures, all dear and infinitely precious. These were the streams
of life which flowed from that fountain; and catching also from its
pages the fervor of his exultant pride in Democracy, in America and
the age we lived in, and moved also by the splendid passages here and
there of great poetry, it is no wonder that we came to regard as a sacred
book the vast printed chaos of the *Leaves of Grass*. It gave us ears, it
gave us eyes, it revealed to us the miracle of our own existence, and for
me, at least, with my meager ideals of borrowed culture, it seemed to
open a great shining window in my narrow house of life.

Questions and Suggestions

1. In the opening pages of this essay, which are not included in
   your text, Smith recalls the intellectual changes that were
   gradually taking place within himself. Throughout his youth
   he had expected to enter his family's glass-making establishment, but through the influence of a sister, much more than
   from his classes at Haverford, he came to know the "fashionable prophets of the day, Carlyle and Emerson and Ruskin."
   After studying their works, Smith developed an interest in
   poets and poetry. He also came to recognize that young women
   were gradually becoming emancipated and that European cultural influences were reaching America. Eventually he turned
   from the family business and concerned himself with belles-
   lettres.

2. How much do you know about the "fashionable prophets" of
   our day? Are you conscious that your interests are broadening,
   or is college failing to give you the stimulation you want and
   need?

3. What does Smith mean in the last sentence by the expression
   "borrowed culture"?

4. What impression do you get of Smith's father, the relatives
   outside the immediate household, and Whitman?

5. What do you learn concerning Whitman's idiosyncrasies? Do they seem to have been natural or posed?

6. Look at facsimile editions of Blake's work and see for yourself what his *bards* are like. See what you can learn concerning *Elias Hicks*. What was the "grave charge" against Whitman "which would have greatly shocked" the Smiths? Who were *Bernard Berenson* and *Edmund Gosse*? Read as much of *Leaves of Grass* as you can and determine why the book appeared "daring and not decent." Do you think that moral concepts change?

Ideas for Writing

1. Discuss a book that was as important for you as *Leaves of Grass* was for Smith.

2. Describe a friend who seems to find order in chaos, perhaps paying particular attention to the room in which he centers his life. Re-read the description of Whitman's room before you begin.

3. Recall the effect of fame or even temporary glory upon one of your associates.

4. Contrast this portrait of Whitman with the one D. H. Lawrence creates in "Whitman," an essay included in *Studies in Classic American Literature,* or the one in Charles Algernon Swinburne's long poem "To Walt Whitman in America," or the one in Edward Dowden's "The Poetry of Democracy: Walt Whitman," in *Studies in Literature: 1789–1877.*

5. Have you ever visited a celebrated individual?

6. Recall how you felt as a child when you were embarrassed by the dress or the habits of a visitor in your home.

GRACE

ELIZABETH BOWEN

Of Anglo-Irish origins, Elizabeth Dorothea Cole Bowen (1899–) is a writer of authority and distinction. Born in Ireland, she received her formal education in England. From the first, her work, whether in the form of the short story, novel, essay, or social

From *Collected Impressions.* Copyright 1950. Reprinted by permission of Alfred A. Knopf, Inc. and Longmans, Green & Co., Ltd.

history, has received acclaim. Dividing her time between London
and Bowen's Court, her ancestral home, Miss Bowen also finds
opportunities for travel, having visited America a number of
times. In the "Foreword" to *Collected Impressions,* she states
that upon re-reading her book reviews, she found that she had
"written best, because most happily, about books whose claim was
their subject rather than their style," adding the additional idea
that biographies often served as "annexes to experience in actual
life."

Selection is always present in any act of the memory; it cannot but be continuously present in the attempt to re-create one's own
life. One cannot surprise one's past: the very quickest look back makes
everything fall into order—if only into a momentary order, the order
of a mood. The long look back compels one's years into form. This
may be because before any deliberate retrospection starts one has already
rejected, with an unconscious violence, what is untoward, what might
not fit in the pattern. For that pattern, whatever may be its nature, is
an intimate part of one's self-esteem, and one's idea of survival is
closely bound up in it. Having always in view the pattern one must not
lose, one's sense of relevance, in reviewing one's own life, becomes as
strict, as immovable as a law of art. Ultimately, one's own emotional
taste must be the censor of memory. Thus the memoir, the reminiscence takes its place half-way [between] æsthetics and pathology.

When a writer writes his own life the wish to give form is doubled;
the wish is conscious as well as necessitous. His past is to serve his
book; it is no more than so much matter. He is not strange to himself;
he has lived in his own presence; he can write of himself with a cold
familiarity. He looks back at a life lived entirely consciously; there is
no question, here, of harvesting naïve and unknowing years. Before he
could hold a pen, perhaps, he has been Trigorin, secreting prose round
moments even while they were living. To an extent, he has made his
experience. He has noted life from an angle; what he has not noted
does not, for him, exist. His very pains and pleasures have been largely
selected, even at times when they seemed most deeply felt. Scenes had
a memory-value even while they were lived. Disciplined, automatic,
his memory works to plan. The writer's memory is like a tidy cupboard:
he knows exactly what he will find inside. What he cannot assimilate,
he has already rejected. He has thrown out all bulky untoward objects,
objects on which the cupboard might not shut.

Mr. Logan Pearsall Smith wrote his reminiscences during a cruise
on Mrs. Wharton's yacht. On this cruise, nothing untoward happened,
except a misunderstanding with the skipper about a boat, and a rather
vigorous argument about peonies. He has titled those reminiscences
with what seems, at the first glance, a happy banality. *Unforgotten
Years* could be a sort of generic title for memoirs; it epitomizes the
names of a hundred volumes, very often of social interest only, that
sit in libraries on the memoir shelves. At the first glance, it seems odd
that such a title should not already have been hit on—by some lady of
fashion at her wobbly, frail *escritoire*. It could be no more than nos-
talgic, ambiguous, mellow, safe. But that this choice should have been
Mr. Pearsall Smith's gives the title a sinister exactitude. There is no
ambiguity here. He knows that years' survival is more than a touching
accident. Years do not stand in the memory by sheer virtue of having
been once lived. Years are turned away or recalled exactly as one
wishes. Those years one accepts are the unforgotten years.

An intensive censorship of experience underlies Mr. Pearsall Smith's
perfected prose. No dust has collected on the years, the moments that
were once so analytically lived; they are in perfect condition, ready to
be assembled into what is, for a memoir, a faultless form. His style
shows his distinguished wilful precision; it has no rough matter to cope
with, for nothing that he records as having happened has not already
been assimilated by him. From seven (when he attained the state of
sanctification) he undeviatingly chose his experience. He was the child
of a Philadelphian Quaker household dominated by a magnificent,
zealous faith. In such a household, life was a crucible. As a very small
child, Mr. Pearsall Smith was agonizedly conscious of the untoward.
There was much that he did not like; he was 'a gorilla for screaming.'
When he was four, the reconciliation, at first in itself painful, began.
Two little girls prayed aloud for him in his presence, prayed that he
might be given a new heart. Between four and seven his struggles
intensified.

> In vain were his efforts to keep good by the force of his own
> will alone; and it was only after three years of spiritual struggle
> . . . that he renounced these Pelagian attempts to conquer Sin and
> Satan by his own carnal struggles, and realised that only by Grace,
> and unmerited Grace alone, and by no 'deadly doing' could he
> attain the conquest that he sought.

By seven, he had won through.

> I may do, I have undoubtedly done, things that were foolish,
> tactless and dishonest, and what the world would consider wrong,

but since I attained the state of Sanctification at the age of seven
I have never felt the slightest twinge of conscience, never experienced for a moment the sense of sin.

These passages from the early life are important because they explain,
I think, Mr. Pearsall Smith's persisting attitude to life—an attitude,
above all, of immunity. His taste, his nature, his gifts, his suscepti-
bilities seem to have been able to ripen and to perfect themselves inside
a small, separate and unthreatened world. There can have been no
more upheavals; his piety has veered quietly from religion to art. Those
delicious sensations that surrounded religious experience surround
æsthetic experience. He belongs to the generation of the Chosen—and
how far the Chosen are from us now—their leisure, their grace, their
subtleties and, above all, their immunity. They enjoyed Grace—Grace
tempered with irony.

And what a prose Grace produced! Emerson was the earliest influence, then came Pater, then the nobler aspects of Flaubert. (Were
the passages about the sweating and the hysterics also copied into Mr.
Pearsall Smith's commonplace book?) And there was always Sir
Thomas Browne. Over all this book about inner experience there ex-
tends a levelling irony. He writes—this perfected prose, adamant,
unechoing, unevocative, prose like a fortification, prose without any
belfry to hold a bat. In this prose are embedded once-living creatures
and moments. As though overtaken by lava, forever immobilized,
scenes, gestures, hopes, fears, illusions, traditions, fanaticisms are here
to be marvelled at. Philadelphia, the Quaker traditions, Evangelical
English house parties, Harvard, Balliol, Paris, the house in Sussex with
its terrace and talks . . . Walt Whitman and Mrs. Wharton. . . .

Mr. Pearsall Smith writes best—that is to say, most feelingly—in
the early chapters, in which his lovely, dignified and unaccountable
mother appears, and in the last chapter but one, about manuscript-
hunting—a chapter the sportsman dominates. The rest of *Unforgotten
Years* reads like an ordered dream, a dream explored to its limits, with
no cold shadow of to-morrow morning ahead.

Questions and Suggestions

1. When we recall our past experiences, why is the principle of
   selection that we use likely to differ from that of the novelist
   as he chooses events for a fictional portrayal of life?
2. Why, right after the account of Smith's early crisis, do the
   terms *chosen* and *grace* seem appropriate in Miss Bowen's
   description of his maturity?

3. What do the subjects about which Smith argued, while aboard the yacht, tell you of the man?

4. Contrast Smith and Whitman—especially in terms of how each viewed the world. Draw a similar contrast between Smith and Laurie Lee, noting also any difference in style (*e.g.*, diction, imagery, or sentence structure).

5. Which paragraphs have expressed topic sentences, which implied?

6. What does Miss Bowen mean when she states that Smith's prose was "without any belfry to hold a bat"?

7. Who are *Mrs. Wharton, Pater, Flaubert,* and *Sir Thomas Browne?* What is the meaning of *banality, generic, epitomizes, escritoire,* and *adamant?*

Ideas for Writing

1. Speculate on the current aptness of Elizabeth Bowen's lament, "how far the Chosen are from us now." Listening to or reading Winston Churchill's speech, "Dunkirk: Address to Commons, June 4, 1940," may give you perspective on this statement.

2. Describe your own childhood memories of "those delicious sensations that surrounded religious experience."

3. Imagine the type of autobiography that one of your parents might write.

4. Contrast Smith's world with that of a teacher, minister, or public official whom you know personally.

5. To test Elizabeth Bowen's point that reminiscence recreates past experiences in an orderly manner, examine your own "unforgotten years." Do you also have "forgotten years," as she would expect?

THIS MASS OF MEN

WALT WHITMAN

Walt Whitman (1819–1892), a great innovator of poetic forms and one whose poetry and prose were to have an enormous influence on succeeding generations, was born at West Hills, near Huntington, Long Island. As a young man he worked on the staffs

From *Democratic Vistas, And Other Papers,* London, 1888. The title of this selection has been added by the editors.

of several newspapers and magazines. In 1855, he published the
first edition of *Leaves of Grass*. When Smith went to visit Whitman, the poet was still being sought out by more Europeans than
Americans. In 1888, when he published *Democratic Vistas*, Whitman was convinced, whatever claims others might make for
politics, that "Literature—a new, superb, democratic literature—
is to be the medicine and lever, and (with Art) the chief influence
in modern civilization."

Huge and mighty are our days, our republican lands—and
most in their rapid shiftings, their changes, all in the interest of the
cause. As I write this particular passage, (November, 1868,) the din
of disputation rages around me. Acrid the temper of the parties, vital
the pending questions. Congress convenes; the President sends his
message; reconstruction is still in abeyance; the nomination and the
contest for the twenty-first Presidentiad draw close, with loudest threat
and bustle. Of these, and all the like of these, the eventuations I know
not; but well I know that behind them, and whatever their eventuations, the vital things remain safe and certain, and all the needed work
goes on. Time, with soon or later superciliousness, disposes of Presi-
dents, Congressmen, party platforms, and such. Anon, it clears the
stage of each and any mortal shred that thinks itself so potent to its
day; and at and after which, (with precious, golden exceptions once
or twice in a century,) all that relates to sir potency is flung to
moulder in a burial-vault, and no one bothers himself the least bit
about it afterward. But the People ever remain, tendencies continue,
and all the idiocratic transfers in unbroken chain go on.

In a few years the dominion-heart of America will be far inland, toward the West. Our future national capital may not be where the
present one is. It is possible, nay likely, that in less than fifty years, it
will migrate a thousand or two miles, will be re-founded, and every
thing belonging to it made on a different plan, original, far more superb.
The main social, political, spine-character of the States will probably
run along the Ohio, Missouri and Mississippi rivers, and west and north
of them, including Canada. Those regions, with the group of powerful
brothers toward the Pacific, (destined to the mastership of that sea and
its countless paradises of islands,) will compact and settle the traits of
America, with all the old retain'd, but more expanded, grafted on newer,
hardier, purely native stock. A giant growth, composite from the rest,
getting their contribution, absorbing it, to make it more illustrious. From

the north, intellect, the sun of things, also the idea of unswayable justice, anchor amid the last, the wildest tempests. From the south the living soul, the animus of good and bad, haughtily admitting no demonstration but its own. While from the west itself comes solid personality, with blood and brawn, and the deep quality of all-accepting fusion.

Political democracy, as it exists and practically works in America, with all its threatening evils, supplies a training-school for making first-class men. It is life's gymnasium, not of good only, but of all. We try often, though we fall back often. A brave delight, fit for freedom's athletes, fills these arenas, and fully satisfies, out of the action in them, irrespective of success. Whatever we do not attain, we at any rate attain the experiences of the fight, the hardening of the strong campaign, and throb with currents of attempt at least. Time is ample. Let the victors come after us. Not for nothing does evil play its part among us. Judging from the main portions of the history of the world, so far, justice is always in jeopardy, peace walks amid hourly pit-falls, and of slavery, misery, meanness, the craft of tyrants and the credulity of the populace, in some of their protean forms, no voice can at any time say, They are not. The clouds break a little, and the sun shines out—but soon and certain the lowering darkness falls again, as if to last forever. Yet is there an immortal courage and prophecy in every sane soul that cannot, must not, under any circumstances, capitulate. *Vive,* the attack—the perennial assault! *Vive,* the unpopular cause—the spirit that audaciously aims—the never-abandon'd efforts, pursued the same amid opposing proofs and precedents.

Once, before the war, (Alas! I dare not say how many times the mood has come!) I, too, was fill'd with doubt and gloom. A foreigner, an acute and good man, had impressively said to me, that day—putting in form, indeed, my own observations: "I have travel'd much in the United States, and watch'd their politicians, and listen'd to the speeches of the candidates, and read the journals, and gone into the public houses, and heard the unguarded talk of men. And I have found your vaunted America honey-comb'd from top to toe with infidelism, even to itself and its own programme. I have mark'd the brazen hell-faces of secession and slavery gazing defiantly from all the windows and door-ways. I have everywhere found, primarily, thieves and scalliwags arranging the nominations to offices, and sometimes filling the offices themselves. I have found the north just as full of bad stuff as the south. Of the holders of public office in the Nation or the States or their municipalities, I have found that not one in a hundred has been chosen by any spontaneous selection of the outsiders, the people, but all have been nominated and put through by little or large caucuses of the politicians, and have got in by corrupt rings and electioneering, not capacity or desert. I have noticed how the millions of sturdy farmers and mechanics are thus the helpless supple-jacks of comparatively few politicians. And I have noticed more and more, the alarming spectacle of parties usurping the government, and openly and shamelessly wielding it for party purposes."

Sad, serious, deep truths. Yet are there other, still deeper, amply confronting, dominating truths. Over those politicians and great and little rings, and over all their insolence and wiles, and over the powerfulest parties, looms a power, too sluggish maybe, but ever holding decisions and decrees in hand, ready, with stern process, to execute them as soon as plainly needed—and at times, indeed, summarily crushing to atoms the mightiest parties, even in the hour of their pride.

In saner hours far different are the amounts of these things from what, at first sight, they appear. Though it is no doubt important who is elected governor, mayor, or legislator (and full of dismay when incompetent or vile ones get elected, as they sometimes do), there are other, quieter contingencies, infinitely more important. Shams, &c., will always be the show, like ocean's scum; enough, if waters deep and clear make up the rest. Enough, that while the piled embroider'd shoddy gaud and fraud spreads to the superficial eye, the hidden warp and weft are genuine, and will wear forever. Enough, in short, that the race, the land which could raise such as the late rebellion, could also put it down.

The average man of a land at last only is important. He, in these States, remains immortal owner and boss, deriving good uses, somehow, out of any sort of servant in office, even the basest; (certain universal requisites, and their settled regularity and protection, being first secured,) a nation like ours, in a sort of geological formation state, trying continually new experiments, choosing new delegations, is not served by the best men only, but sometimes more by those that provoke it—by the combats they arouse. Thus national rage, fury, discussion, &c., better than content. Thus, also, the warning signals, invaluable for after times.

What is more dramatic than the spectacle we have seen repeated, and doubtless long shall see—the popular judgment taking the successful candidates on trial in the offices—standing off, as it were, and observing them and their doings for a while, and always giving, finally, the fit, exactly due reward? I think, after all, the sublimest part of political history, and its culmination, is currently issuing from the American people. I know nothing grander, better exercise, better digestion, more positive proof of the past, the triumphant result of faith in human kind, than a well-contested American national election.

Then still the thought returns, (like the thread-passage in overtures,) giving the key and echo to these pages. When I pass to and fro, different latitudes, different seasons, beholding the crowds of the great cities, New York, Boston, Philadelphia, Cincinnati, Chicago, St. Louis, San Francisco, New Orleans, Baltimore—when I mix with these interminable swarms of alert, turbulent, good-natured, independent citizens, mechanics, clerks, young persons—at the idea of this mass of men, so fresh and free, so loving and so proud, a singular awe falls upon me. I feel, with dejection and amazement, that among our geniuses and talented writers or speakers, few or none have yet really spoken to this people, created a single image-making work for them, or absorb'd the central spirit and the idiosyncrasies which are theirs—and which, thus, in highest ranges, so far remain entirely uncelebrated, unexpress'd.

Questions and Suggestions

1. In this essay Whitman tends to be general rather than specific, apocalyptic rather than realistic. Does his optimistic belief that "the vital things remain safe and certain" and that man will steadily progress appear to be as valid now as it was in 1888?

2. Whitman also claims "Time is ample." Is this statement still true?

3. Do you agree that the "average man . . . only is important"?

4. If in national affairs the "warp and weft are genuine," do you believe that they "will wear forever"? Does Time always dispose of political leaders and their acts as completely as Whitman affirms?

5. Do you agree with his generalizations concerning the regions of America?

6. Which of the paragraphs have stated topic sentences?

7. The Romans spoke of the Mediterranean Sea as *mare nostrum*, "our sea." Does Whitman at any point in the essay remind you of them?

Ideas for Writing

1. What parts do people actually play in local and national elections?

2. Can you cite any specific examples of non-democratic restrictions on registration and voting that are in effect in your community?

3. Discuss the spoils system as you have encountered it at the municipal or state level.

4. Explain why the citizen is, or is not, the "immortal owner and boss" of politicians. For subsequent accounts that show how politicians disregarded Whitman's ideals, read Margaret Leech's *In the Days of McKinley* and William R. Manchester's novel, *City of Anger,* that deals with political corruption in a northern city.

5. What respect do you have for the local and campus policemen, sheriffs, and their deputies?

6. Campus politics: a training ground.

7. What advice would you give to the potential president of a campus organization?

8. Is there a belief or an unpopular cause in which you will "not, under any circustances, capitulate"?

9. Is gerrymandering practiced in your area? For an example of an unsuccessful attempt to control voter registration, read Bernard Taper's "Gomillion Versus Lightfoot" in *The New Yorker,* June 10 and June 17, 1961.

part three ✕ *The realms of place*

THROUGH THE SAND AFOOT

JOHN MUIR

In *The Story of My Boyhood and Youth,* John Muir (1838–1914), naturalist and father of our national parks, vividly recalls his early years in Dunbar, Scotland, and his formative years in Wisconsin. For four years Muir studied at the University of Wisconsin. In 1868, already a wanderer, he sailed from New York for California, carrying one of his favorite books, the first volume of Emerson's *Prose Works.* He lived and worked in Yosemite Valley until 1873, when he left the Valley, to settle in Oakland. City life, however, did not agree with him, and one day he returned to the Valley, describing the trip in a long letter to Mrs. Carr, one of his most helpful friends.

Here again are pine trees, and the wind, and living rock and water! I've met two of my ouzels on one of the pebble ripples of the

From William Frederic Bade, *The Life and Letters of John Muir,* Vol. II. Copyright 1952 by John Muir Hanna. Reprinted by permission of Houghton Mifflin Company. The title of this selection has been added by the editors.

river where I used to be with them. Most of the meadow gardens are disenchanted and dead, yet I found a few mint spikes and asters and brave, sunful goldenrods and a patch of the tiny Mimulus that has two spots on each lip. The fragrance and the color and the form, and the whole spiritual expression of goldenrods are hopeful and strength-giving beyond any other flowers that I know. A single spike is sufficient to heal unbelief and melancholy.

On leaving Oakland I was so excited over my escape that, of course, I forgot and left all the accounts I was to collect. No wonder, and no matter. I'm beneath that grand old pine that I have heard so often in storms both at night and in the day. It sings grandly now, every needle sun-thrilled and shining and responding tunefully to the azure wind.

When I left I was in a dreamy exhausted daze. Yet from mere habit or instinct I tried to observe and study. From the car window I watched the gradual transitions from muddy water, spongy tule, marsh and level field as we shot up the San Jose Valley, and marked as best I could the forms of the stream cañons as they opened to the plain and the outlines of the undulating hillocks and headlands between. Interest increased at every mile, until it seemed unbearable to be thrust so flyingly onward even towards the blessed Sierras. I will study them yet, free from time and wheels. When we turned suddenly and dashed into the narrow mouth of the Livermore pass I was looking out of the right side of the car. The window was closed on account of the cinders and smoke from the locomotive. All at once my eyes clasped a big hard rock not a hundred yards away, every line of which is as strictly and outspokenly glacial as any of the most alphabetic of the high and young Sierra. That one sure glacial word thrilled and overjoyed me more than you will ever believe. Town smokes and shadows had not dimmed my vision, for I had passed this glacial rock twice before without reading its meaning.

As we proceeded, the general glacialness of the range became more and more apparent, until we reached Pleasanton where once there was a grand *mer de glace*. Here the red sun went down in a cloudless glow and I leaned back, happy and weary and possessed with a lifeful of noble problems.

At Lathrop we suppered and changed cars. The last of the daylight had long faded and I sauntered away from the din while the baggage was being transferred. The young moon hung like a sickle above the shorn wheat fields, Ursa Major pictured the northern sky, the Milky Way curved sublimely through the broadcast stars like some grand celestial moraine with planets for boulders, and the whole night shone resplendent, adorned with that calm imperishable beauty which it has worn unchanged from the beginning.

I slept at Turlock and next morning faced the Sierra and set out through the sand afoot. The freedom I felt was exhilarating, and the burning heat and thirst and faintness could not make it less. Before I had walked ten miles I was wearied and footsore, but it was real earnest work and I liked it. Any kind of simple natural destruction is preferable to the numb, dumb, apathetic deaths of a town.

Heavy wagon loads of wheat had been hauled along the road and the wheels had sunk deep and left smooth beveled furrows in the sand. Upon the smooth slopes of these sand furrows I soon observed a most beautiful and varied embroidery, evidently tracks of some kind. At first I thought of mice, but soon saw they were too light and delicate for mice. Then a tiny lizard darted into the stubble ahead of me, and I carefully examined the track he made, but it was entirely unlike the fine print embroidery I was studying. However, I knew that he might make very different tracks if walking leisurely. Therefore I determined to catch one and experiment. I found out in Florida that lizards, however swift, are short-winded, so I gave chase and soon captured a tiny gray fellow and carried him to a smooth sand-bed where he could embroider without getting away into grass tufts or holes. He was so wearied that he couldn't skim and was compelled to walk, and I was excited with delight in seeing an exquisitely beautiful strip of embroidery about five-eighths of an inch wide, drawn out in flowing curves behind him as from a loom. The riddle was solved. I knew that mountain boulders moved in music; so also do lizards, and their written music, printed by their feet, moved so swiftly as to be invisible, covers the hot sands with beauty wherever they go.

But my sand embroidery lesson was by no means done. I speedily discovered a yet more delicate pattern on the sands, woven into that of the lizard. I examined the strange combination of bars and dots. No five-toed lizard had printed that music. I watched narrowly down on my knees, following the strange and beautiful pattern along the wheel furrows and out into the stubble. Occasionally the pattern would suddenly end in a shallow pit half an inch across and an eighth of an inch deep. I was fairly puzzled, picked up my bundle, and trudged discontentedly away, but my eyes were hungrily awake and I watched all the ground. At length a gray grasshopper rattled and flew up, and the truth flashed upon me that he was the complementary embroiderer of the lizard. Then followed long careful observation, but I never could see the grasshopper until he jumped, and after he alighted he invariably stood watching me with his legs set ready for another jump in case of danger. Nevertheless I soon made sure that he was my man, for I found that in jumping he made the shallow pits I had observed at the termination of the pattern I was studying. But no matter how patiently I waited he wouldn't *walk* while I was sufficiently near to observe. They are so nearly the color of the sand. I therefore caught one and lifted his wing covers and cut off about half of each wing with my penknife, and carried him to a favorable place on the sand. At first he did nothing but jump and make dimples, but soon became weary and *walked* in common rhythm with all his six legs, and my interest you may guess while I watched the embroidery—the written music laid down in a beautiful ribbon-like strip behind. I glowed with wild joy as if I had found a new glacier—copied specimens of the precious fabric into my notebook, and strode away with my own feet sinking with a dull craunch, craunch, craunch in the hot gray sand, glad to believe that the dark and cloudy vicissitudes of the Oakland period had not dimmed my vision in the least. Surely Mother Nature pitied the poor boy and showed him pictures.

Happen what would, fever, thirst, or sunstroke, my joy for that day was complete. Yet I was to receive still more. A train of curving tracks with a line in the middle next fixed my attention, and almost before I had time to make a guess concerning their author, a small hawk came shooting down vertically out of the sky a few steps ahead of me and picked up something in his talons. After rising thirty or forty feet overhead, he dropped it by the roadside as if to show me what it was. I ran forward and found a little bunchy field mouse and at once suspected him of being embroiderer number three. After an exciting chase through stubble heaps and weed thickets I wearied and captured him without being bitten and turned him free to make his mark in a favorable sand bed. He also embroidered better than he knew, and at once claimed the authorship of the new track work.

I soon learned to distinguish the pretty sparrow track from that of the magpie and lark with their three delicate branches and the straight scratch behind made by the back-curving claw, dragged loosely like a spur of a Mexican vaquero. The cushioned elastic feet of the hare frequently were seen mixed with the pattering scratchy prints of the squirrels. I was now wholly trackful. I fancied I could see the air whirling in dimpled eddies from sparrow and lark wings. Earthquake boulders descending in a song of curves, snowflakes glinting songfully hither and thither. "The water in music the oar forsakes." The air in music the wing forsakes. All things move in music and write it. The mouse, lizard, and grasshopper sing together on the Turlock sands, sing with the morning stars.

Questions and Suggestions

1. Muir wrote this letter, only a portion of which is reprinted here, from Yosemite Valley, in September, 1874. How does he reveal his belief in the significance of the universe?
2. What does he mean by the idea, "All things move in music and write it"?
3. Explain how you know Muir was a careful observer.
4. What does he mean by the rock being "as strictly and outspokenly glacial as any of the most alphabetic of the high and young Sierra"?
5. How does the time element function in the letter?
6. Do you know the meaning of *tule, Mimulus, moraine,* and *mer de glace?* How do you pronounce *ouzels?*

Ideas for Writing

1. Describe the movements of a fly against a windowpane, or look at a patch of earth and record what you see.
2. After studying your hands carefully, describe them in such a way that the reader will know that they belong to you and not to someone else.
3. What do you see when you observe a flight of geese, the swoop of a hawk, or birds at a feeder? See what Tennyson accomplished in "The Eagle" with only six lines.
4. Describe your reactions to open spaces as against the confinement of towns and cities.
5. For additional ideas, study Thoreau's description of the battle of the black and red ants in chapter 12, "Brute Neighbors," of *Walden.*

THE AVALANCHE

F. S. SMYTHE

Born in Maidstone, England, Francis Sydney Smythe (1900–1949) studied at the Faraday House Engineering College, served

briefly in the Royal Air Force, and in 1930 became a member of
the International Kangchenjunga Expedition. Mt. Kangchenjunga,
almost due north of Darjeeling but south of Tibet, rises 28,156
feet, virtually on the boundary between Nepal and Sikkim. Smythe
served on several subsequent Himalayan expeditions, as well as
taking part in climbs in the Swiss Alps and the Canadian Rockies.
He was the author of one novel and many books dealing with
mountaineering and skiing.

I lay long in my tent that evening writing, and it was nearly
midnight before I blew out the candle, and composed myself to sleep.
But sleep would not come. I was quite comfortable, my digestive organs
were in good order, and acclimatisation had reduced my pulse-rate to
nearly normal. The night was curiously warm, in fact, the warmest
night we had had since we arrived at the Base Camp. Now and again
came the long-drawn-out thunder of avalanches.

Perhaps it was the atmosphere, or maybe some trick of the imagination, but the sound of the avalanches seemed dull and muffled. It was
as though Kangchenjunga was choking with suppressed wrath. My
body was ready for sleep, but my mind was not. It was troubled and
restless, groping in a catacomb of doubt and fear. I have known fear
before on a mountain, but that was fear of a different nature, sharp
and sudden in the face of an immediate danger, but I have never known
what it was to lie awake before a climb tortured by the devils of mis-
giving.

Some people may call this a premonition, but I do not think it can
be so defined. Premonition of danger is, after all, an anticipation of
danger, where, theoretically, danger ought not to exist. That danger
existed in this case cannot be denied. The mind had brooded over it
consciously and subconsciously to the detriment of the nerves, and these
had become temporarily unstrung. That is a more logical explanation
than the acceptance of the premonition theory, which is more dependent
upon a belief in psychical phenomena.

When, at last, I fell asleep, I was troubled with terrible dreams.
These dreams were not dreams of personal danger, but of danger to
the porters. They were always getting into an impossible position, and
would turn to me appealingly for help. But I was unable to help. After-

From *The Kangchenjunga Adventure*. Reprinted by permission of
Christy & Moore, Ltd.

wards, Wood Johnson told me he used frequently to dream this too. Possibly it was due to an innate sense of responsibility. Others on Himalayan expeditions have probably experienced the same sort of dreams. It was a bad night.

I crawled out of my tent the next morning, dull, heavy, and unrefreshed. I looked at the ice wall, and the weary track leading up through the snow to it, with loathing. Neither mentally nor physically did I feel fit to start.

The morning was ominously warm and a steamy heat beat down through sluggish mists. The sun was obscured, but for the first time on the mountain we were able to sit outside and keep reasonably warm without its rays on us.

It was decided that the scheme arranged the previous day should be adhered to. All except the cook and myself were to leave and try to establish Camp Three on the terrace.

Schneider, with his usual boundless energy, was the first to leave. He was accompanied by his servant, "Satan" Chettan, who was carrying a considerable load.

There was no porter in the expedition of a finer physique than "Satan," and I remember watching him swing on his load with effortless ease, and start off in the wake of his master, his legs propelling him uphill in shambling, powerful strides, the gait of a born hillman and mountaineer.

Duvanel and three porters carrying cinematograph apparatus came next, as the former wished to obtain "shots" of the last party, which consisted of Hoerlin, Wieland, and eight porters carrying heavy loads. For a while I sat on a packing-case, watching them as they slowly plodded up the slopes of soft snow; then I adjourned to my tent in order to write some letters.

Perhaps half an hour later I was startled by a tremendous roar. Two thoughts flashed through my mind. Firstly, that only an exceptionally large ice avalanche falling close at hand could make such a din, and secondly, with a sudden clutch of horror at my heart, that the noise came, not from the usual direction of Kangchenjunga's face, but from the ice wall!

I dashed outside. What I saw is indelibly engraved on my memory.

An enormous portion of the ice wall had collapsed. Huge masses of ice as high as cathedrals, were still toppling to destruction; billowing clouds of snow spray were rushing upwards and outwards in the van of a huge avalanche. On the slope below was the party, mere black dots, strung out in a straggling line. They were not moving. For an instant, during which I suppose my brain must have been stunned, the scene was stamped on my mind like a still photograph, or perhaps a more apt comparison would be a ciné-film that has jammed for a fraction of a second. Then everything jerked on again. I remember feeling no surprise; it was almost like a fantastic solution to something that had been puzzling me.

Now the dots were moving, moving to the left; they were running, but how slowly, how uselessly before the reeling clouds of death that had already far outflanked them. The next moment the avalanche had swept down upon them; they were engulfed and blotted out like insects beneath a tidal wave.

In the tent I had been conscious of noise, but now I was no longer aware of it. The clouds of snow swept nearer. At first they had seemed to move slowly, but now they were shooting forwards with incredible velocity. Vicious tongues of ice licked out under them. Here and there solitary blocks broke free from the pall; behind them I caught a glimpse of a confused jumble of ice blocks, grinding together like the boulders in a stream bed caught up by the flood waters of a cloudburst.

The thought of personal danger had not occurred to me at first, but now, suddenly, came the realisation that the avalanche might sweep the camp away. I glanced round for the cook—he was standing outside the cooking tent—and yelled to him to run for it.

I had stood and watched the avalanche like one rooted to the spot in a nightmare. Running was nightmarish too. The feet sank deeply into the snow; at the height (20,000 feet) every step was an effort. We floundered along for perhaps twenty yards, then heart and lungs gave out, and neither of us could continue. We looked round; the avalanche was stopping two hundred yards away. Though I had not been conscious of any noise after the initial roar, I was paradoxically conscious of it ceasing.

The avalanche stopped; only the clouds of snow, driven by the wind displaced by the falling masses, writhed far into the air. There no sign of my companions. I turned to the cook: "They are all killed, but we must do what we can." We retraced our steps to the camp, seized ice-axes, and set out for the scene of the disaster. We tried to move quickly, but it was impossible at the altitude; it was better to go slowly and steadily, and how slow this was.

The clouds of snow began to settle, the veil thinned. It was a terrible moment. I expected to see no sign of the party. Then, to my immense relief, I saw dimly a figure away to the left, and then some more figures. We toiled upwards, skirting the edge of the avalanche; it was sharply defined, and the ice blocks were piled several feet high. Beyond it the snow was untouched, save where it had been scored by solitary blocks flung forwards from the main mass of ice.

Two hundred yards from the camp the track vanished beneath the debris of the avalanche. We reached a little group of porters. They were standing stupidly, without moving or speaking, on the edge of the debris, all save one, who was probing energetically with an ice-axe between the ice blocks. It was Nemu. I asked him what he was doing, whether there was a man buried there, and he replied, "Load, sahib, I look for load." In order to run and escape from the avalanche he had dropped his load, and this was seriously worrying him. Who were alive and who were dead did not concern him; he had dropped his load, and a load entrusted to him by the sahibs.

I counted the party, two were missing. Hoerlin, Wieland, and Duvanel I could see above me. The missing ones were Schneider and Chettan. Two hundred feet higher I saw Wieland approaching something sticking out between the ice blocks. It was Chettan's hand. By the time I had climbed up he had been dug out. He was dead, having been carried down at least three hundred feet, and crushed in the torrent of ice blocks. His head was severely injured, but as a forlorn hope we administered artificial respiration for over an hour. In the middle of it Schneider reappeared. He had had a marvellous escape. He had actually been under the ice wall when it came down. He said: "I heard a crack; then down it came, huge masses of ice from hundreds of feet above. I thought I was dead, but I ran to the left, and the avalanche missed me by five metres." Chettan had been too far behind Schneider to save himself.

The remainder of the party had amazing luck. They had been on the track where it ran farthest to the left. Had they been ten minutes earlier or later, nothing could have saved them. Even so, they had had to run for their lives, and the track was swept almost from end to end. Duvanel told me that when he saw it coming, the thought of being able to escape never even occurred to him. But, like the others, he had run to the left, as it seemed better to be killed *doing something* than waiting for apparently certain death. So narrow had been the escape of the main body of the porters that some of them had actually been bruised by blocks of ice on the edge of the avalanche. The escape of the party can only be called a miracle of the mountains.

The portion of the wall that had fallen had been that outlined by the crack noted by Hoerlin and Schneider the previous day. In falling it swept the route on the ice wall diagonally, completely obliterating the lower part of the route that Wieland and I had made, destroying the snow bridge over the crevasse, and the ice hump under which we had sat. In fact, the topography of the route we had made at the expense of so much labour had been altered completely. The area of snow slopes covered by the debris must have been nearly a mile square, and the avalanche can scarcely have weighed less than a million tons.

We returned to camp, two of the porters taking turns at carrying Chettan. According to those who had been highest, another crack had opened up above the ice wall, and there was a strong possibility of another avalanche, possibly greater even than the first, which might conceivably sweep away the camp. It was advisable to retire to Camp One with all speed. But before doing so we buried Chettan.

It was a simple, yet impressive ceremony. A hole was dug in the snow, and the body, dressed as it was in climbing clothes, laid within with folded arms. A handful of rice was roasted by the porters, and this was scattered over the body to the accompaniment of muttered prayers. We stood round with bared heads. Then someone gave an order, and snow was quickly shovelled into the grave. As this was done the mists dispersed, and the sun shone through for a few instants. Almost one could see the brave soul winging its way over the mountains. We drove in an ice-axe to mark the spot, and silently turned away. We had lost not a porter, but a valued friend. We left him buried amid one of the grandest mountain cirques in the world.

So died a genuine lover of the mountains, a real adventurer at heart, and one whom members of several Himalayan expeditions will mourn.

We descended to Camp One in a wet and soaking snowstorm, that later developed into a blizzard. Word was sent down to the Base Camp of the disaster, requesting that Professor Dyhrenfurth and Kurz should come up and discuss matters.

Wind was howling, and snow lashing the tents, as we ate supper and crept miserably into our sleeping-bags.

Questions and Suggestions

1. Why does the author claim that his fear of danger was on this occasion not a "premonition"?
2. Smythe was not only a famous mountain climber, but on this expedition he also served as special correspondent and photog-

rapher to *The* (London) *Times*. What is his intention in this essay?

3. How successful are his similes, metaphors, and comparisons?
4. What comment can you make about the construction of the paragraphs?
5. What is the meaning of *catacomb, paradoxically, sahibs, crevasse,* and *cirques?*
6. If you do not know why the Sherpas sprinkled rice into Chettan's grave, consult volume 3, *Taboo and the Perils of the Soul* in Sir James Frazer's *The Golden Bough.*

Ideas for Writing

1. "Satan" Chettan, the most experienced of the Himalayan porters on the expedition, came from a financially impoverished background. Have you noticed that members of poor families often have better physical attributes than those who have led easy lives? Herb Elliott, the Australian miler, recently stated in his autobiography, *The Golden Mile,* that Americans suffer because of their "soft, synthetic" way of life, that we are not hardy enough. After looking at the students around you, evaluate their physical qualities.
2. Contrast Smythe's prose with any episode in Vivian Fuchs' and Edmund Hillary's *The Crossing of Antarctica,* or compare this description of an avalanche with the one you find in "Below 26,000 Feet" in Hermann Buhl's *Nanga Parbat Pilgrimage.*
3. You might try a narrative episode which recreates the time when you too just escaped sudden death.
4. Can you recall the time when you had a foreboding of some dire event and how you felt as you waited for it to take place?
5. Why do you believe in extra-sensory perception?
6. Are there any objects or customs that have a symbolic value for you or other members of our society?

THE CITY OF MAGNIFICENT INTENTIONS

CHARLES DICKENS

The most popular author of his time, Charles Dickens (1812–1870), who was born near Portsmouth, England, made his first visit to America in 1842. Save for the fact that in some of his lectures he favored the introduction of an international copyright law, he was enthusiastically received. *American Notes* appeared in October 1842, shortly after his return home. Popular in England, the book produced violent reactions among many Americans who claimed he had viewed the country "with ill-nature, animosity, or partisanship." Dickens, an outspoken abolitionist, came to distrust a number of "influences and tendencies" which he had noticed during his travels. It was not until 1867 that he made his second lecture tour. By that time Americans had forgotten most of their former resentments.

We reached Washington at about half-past six that evening, and had upon the way a beautiful view of the Capitol, which is a fine building of the Corinthian order, placed upon a noble and commanding eminence. Arrived at the hotel; I saw no more of the place that night; being very tired, and glad to get to bed.

Breakfast over next morning, I walk about the streets for an hour or two, and, coming home, throw up the window in the front and back, and look out. Here is Washington, fresh in my mind and under my eye.

Take the worst parts of the City Road and Pentonville, or the straggling outskirts of Paris, where the houses are smallest, preserving all their oddities, but especially the small shops and dwellings, occupied in Pentonville (but not in Washington) by furniture-brokers, keepers of poor eating-houses, and fanciers of birds. Burn the whole down; build it up again in wood and plaster; widen it a little; throw in part of St. John's Wood; put green blinds outside all the private houses, with a red curtain and a white one in every window; plough up all the roads; plant a great deal of coarse turf in every place where it ought *not* to be; erect three handsome buildings in stone and marble, anywhere, but the more entirely out of everybody's way the better; call one the Post Office, one the Patent Office, and one the Treasury; make it scorching hot in the morning, and freezing cold in the afternoon, with an occasional tornado of wind and dust; leave a brick-field without the bricks, in all central places where a street may naturally be expected: and that's Washington.

The hotel in which we live, is a long row of small houses fronting on the street, and opening at the back upon a common yard, in which

From *American Notes For General Circulation,* London, 1850. The title of this selection has been added by the editors.

hangs a great triangle. Whenever a servant is wanted, somebody beats on this triangle from one stroke up to seven, according to the number of the house in which his presence is required; and as all the servants are always being wanted, and none of them ever come, this enlivening engine is in full performance the whole day through. Clothes are drying in this same yard; female slaves, with cotton handkerchiefs twisted round their heads, are running to and fro on the hotel business; black waiters cross and recross with dishes in their hands; two great dogs are playing upon a mound of loose bricks in the centre of the little square; a pig is turning up his stomach to the sun, and grunting "that's comfortable!"; and neither the men, nor the women, nor the dogs, nor the pig, nor any created creature takes the smallest notice of the triangle, which is tingling madly all the time.

I walk to the front window, and look across the road upon a long, straggling row of houses, one story high, terminating, nearly opposite, but a little to the left, in a melancholy piece of waste ground with frowzy grass, which looks like a small piece of country that has taken to drinking, and has quite lost itself. Standing anyhow and all wrong, upon this open space, like something meteoric that has fallen down from the moon, is an odd, lop-sided, one-eyed kind of wooden building, that looks like a church, with a flag-staff as long as itself sticking out of a steeple something larger than a tea-chest. Under the window, is a small stand of coaches, whose slave-drivers are sunning themselves on the steps of our door, and talking idly together. The three most obtrusive houses near at hand, are the three meanest. On one—a shop, which never has anything in the window, and never has the door open —is painted in large characters, "The City Lunch." At another, which looks like the backway to somewhere else, but is an independent building in itself, oysters are procurable in every style. At the third, which is a very, very little tailor's shop, pants are fixed to order; or, in other words, pantaloons are made to measure. And that is our street in Washington.

It is sometimes called the City of Magnificent Distances, but it might with greater propriety be termed the City of Magnificent Intentions; for it is only on taking a bird's-eye view of it from the top of the Capitol, that one can at all comprehend the vast designs of its projector, an aspiring Frenchman. Spacious avenues, that begin in nothing, and lead nowhere; streets, mile-long, that only want houses, roads, and inhabitants; public buildings that need but a public to be complete; and ornaments of great thoroughfares, which only lack great thoroughfares to ornament—are its leading features. One might fancy the season over, and most of the houses gone out of town for ever with their masters. To the admirers of cities it is a Barmecide Feast; a pleasant field for the imagination to rove in; a monument raised to a deceased project, with not even a legible inscription to record its departed greatness.

Such as it is, it is likely to remain. It was originally chosen for the seat of Government, as a means of averting the conflicting jealousies and interests of the different States; and very probably, too, as being remote from mobs; a consideration not to be slighted, even in America. It has no trade or commerce of its own: having little or no population beyond the President and his establishment; the members of the legislature who reside there during the session; the Government clerks and officers employed in the various departments; the keepers of the hotels and boarding-houses; and the tradesmen who supply their tables. It is very unhealthy. Few people would live in Washington, I take it, who were not obliged to reside there; and the tides of emigration and speculation, those rapid and regardless currents, are little likely to flow at any time towards such dull and sluggish water.

Questions and Suggestions

1. When Dickens compares parts of Washington with City Road, Pentonville, and St. John's Wood, he uses London references that a majority of his English readers would automatically know. Only one term should cause you any difficulty—*Barmecide Feast*, which Dickens, in part, explains by the context, and which he would expect any reader of *The Arabian Nights* to know. What does it mean?

2. What tone does Dickens use in his discussion?

3. Does he draw any false conclusions?

4. How successful is the second sentence of the second paragraph? Compare or contrast this sentence with the one that Fromentin uses to introduce his sketch of Van Dyke.

Ideas for Writing

1. Describe the approaches to a city which you know quite well. What impression would a traveler receive?

2. Study the façades of the buildings on one city block. What do you find?

3. How effective are the neon signs in one area of the city?

4. What impression did Washington make on you during your first visit?

5. Set forth and explain some advantages to be found in the compactness of cities.

6. Record the effects of city-planning with which you are acquainted.
7. Comment on the persistent destruction of the countryside.
8. Explain how a city or town has managed to keep some of its architectural values, or why it was willing to destroy the old for the new.
9. Compare Dickens's account with one in Noah Brooks's *Washington in Lincoln's Time*. Brooks, Lincoln's favorite newspaper reporter, was particularly concerned with politics.

WASHINGTON

SIMONE DE BEAUVOIR

The French, much more than Americans, make national celebrities out of their artists and savants. When Simone de Beauvoir (1908–) lectured in America in 1947, she was already well known internationally, not only as a novelist but also as the second most important existentialist philosopher. Born in Paris, Mlle. de Beauvoir received her Ph.D. in philosophy from the Sorbonne. A number of her books have been translated into English and, in general, have received most favorable reviews. However, the journal of her visit received more unfavorable than favorable criticism.

February 14th

At New London I just had time to dine beside the sea before giving my lecture, and I took the night train for Washington, where I had another lecture to give. It was the first city in America that I saw after New York; I knew nobody and would only spend a day and a half in traveling. Just when I was beginning to settle down in America, I had become a tourist again.

The hotel in which I got a room was at the top of the city, on the edge of a park larger than the Bois de Boulogne. From my window I saw tennis courts and a large garden. It was like being in some

From *America Day by Day*, Patrick Dudley, tr. Copyright 1953 by Grove Press, Inc. Reprinted by permission of Grove Press, Inc., and Librairie Gallimard.

watering place. There was a radio which one could listen to for hours on end by dropping fifty cents into a slot. What to do with myself? I know how to wander around a European town, but in America it's different.

I had to take the plunge. I went downstairs and took a taxi. The avenues lined with quiet villas, smart and discreet shopfronts, did not resemble those of New York in any way. The houses were of brick. There were few cars and few pedestrians: it was a country town. The taxi turned into a wide boulevard lined with monuments, which had the whiteness of marble: perhaps they were marble. At all events, the style was Greco-Roman. Far away, the Capitol stood out, just as I had often seen it in movies. I hesitated. To gain time before leaping into the unknown, I decided to go to the National Gallery. It, too, is Greco-Roman in style. Nor does the interior fall short of the façade. With its enormous marble colonnades, flight of steps, plaques and green plants, this museum derives in style from a mausoleum and a Turkish bath. The richness of the collections bewildered me. Yet there was something restful in finding oneself again in the serene, international world of pictures: I could believe that I was back in the Louvre, the Prado, the Uffizi; the old world closed in on the new; they have but a single past. I was astonished when I emerged to find myself back in Washington again.

I am a conscientious tourist. I lunched in the business section: an ugly, dreary district where geometry does not reach to grand proportions but merely induces boredom. Then I went to the Capitol. Thousands of Americans from every part of the country make this pilgrimage. As with all public monuments, they measure the height of the cupola with their eyes and halt before the statues; the most courageous climb to the top of the dome by a labyrinth of stairs and iron ladders. They all glance timidly at the great Hall of Congress, half empty now at the beginning of the afternoon session. Guides explain the past and also the present, but I was content with merely a superficial survey. With its corridors, halls, underground passages, terraces, staircases, monuments, colonnades and galleries, the Capitol is just as boring as the Pantheon or the Chamber of Deputies. And the green esplanade which stretches as far as the obelisk, erected in memory of Washington, is even more depressing than the Champs de Mars. In spite of the gentle light and the freshness of the lawn, it looked like a torrid desert: from their marble façades the buildings still reflected the tired heat of the fierce summer.

I fled these official splendors, turned to the left and went down to the quays that smelled of tar and fish. The Potomac—a fabulous name. No doubt, for me, of course, some of its poetry comes from Cocteau's book, and its Mortimers and Eugenes. And then, there is the barbarous sonority of the old Indian names; this savageness takes one quite by surprise in Washington, where the conquest of nature by diplomacy, politics and monuments to the dead tends to assert itself. The Potomac was frozen over. Ships, yachts and rowing boats were held fast in the ice. I followed the river bank. Children amused themselves by throwing heavy stones onto the shining surface, which sometimes resisted the shock, and then again would crack under it. Parks and green banks marked the course of the river, which bends and broadens into a lake. It is very wide, and the wooded hills on the far bank appear distant. At no great distance, however, on a green islet, I caught sight of colonnades with the whiteness of marble: Jefferson's memorial. So much ugliness is confusing in a country of skyscrapers, but if one sits on the step and turns one's back on that city where history is petrified in boredom, one can contemplate a sight worthy of the memories it recalls. It is a great Nordic river, gleaming with a solid brilliance under a southern sky in the midst of spring meadows. For Washington is already the South for most New Yorkers, and I, too, felt a presentiment of the South in the unexpected heat after the snows of Central Park; it was wonderful to be sitting in the sun beside the frozen water under a brilliant blue sky. . . .

February 15th

Setting off on foot through Washington this morning seemed without purpose: the very dimensions of American cities discourage one. I wanted to take refuge in some corner with a book and pretend that I was not on a journey. But I reckoned without the indefatigable kindness of Americans: two old ladies phoned me to suggest driving me around the city. Half an hour later we had already started. We went down a hill and followed the bottom of a ravine: this park was a bit of the country, not artificial, but wooded, hilly and crossed by rivers bordered by huge rocks: it reminded me of a part of Brittany near Huelgoat. The graves of an old cemetery have been laid out on different levels in the middle of the woods. We reached a prosperous-looking residential district, and once again I was amazed to find, in reality, what I had long taken for a studio set in the movies. I recognized, along the empty sidewalks, those white gates opening into flower gardens and those white houses, inviting but monotonous.

I was surprised to find myself suddenly in the heart of an old Dutch town: the streets were paved with small cobbles; they were trim and narrow. The old houses were painted red or white, and under the paint one could trace the tiny rectangular bricks. It was Georgetown, the oldest quarter in Washington. On the façades one reads the dates: 1776, 1780. The little windows, terraces, pointed roofs and wrought-iron work reminded me of those doll houses in the villages of the Zuyder Zee. A few miles further on we found ourselves in the quiet streets of an English village, with cottages decorated with flowering geraniums, broad thatched roofs. I never expected to find so near Washington the picturesqueness of Europe, and I thought, with pleasure, that America had many more unexpected delights in store for me.

We crossed the Potomac and entered Arlington Cemetery. It is a splendid park, where those who have deserved special honors are buried. They have not failed to erect a hideous monument at the top of the hill, from which, by the way, you get a striking view of Washington and the Potomac. But nothing disfigures the green lawns and the twisting alleys. The tombs are white stones, vertical and bearing only a name. There are neither inscriptions, wreaths nor flowers: the trees and the sky are enough to honor the dead, and the stones are widely spaced, swamped by green lawns. Each dead hero reigns over a wide space, and it looks as if the choice of site has been prompted by personal considerations; there is no symmetry, no single design for the whole; no doubt, the shade of this particular tree was agreeable to this dead man, the bareness of that hill to that one.

People do not talk willingly of death in America. True, I often caught sight of neon signs illuminating the night with the words: Funeral Home. But the name is supposed to be comforting: from the outside, they look like bars or cabarets. I had read the words on posters. *Funeral Home: Reception Rooms, Children's Playrooms, Cloakroom, Low Prices.* It is there that, prior to burial, the dead man gives his last party: his face is exposed, made up in glaring colors, and he wears a gardenia or an orchid in his buttonhole. His friends all come to greet him for the last time. As for me, these engaging "Homes," wedged between bars and drugstores, give me the creeps: I always expect to see some zombie or vampire emerge from them; the truth of death is vainly denied, but in the cemeteries it is revealed, and it is this which gives their funeral parks an unexpected charm. All of a sudden, in this country where health and happiness are guaranteed by the most modern processes, you discover death, and life recovers a dimension it had lost in trying to conform to the lines suggested by advertisements for Quaker Oats.

On Broadway, despite the weighty skyscrapers, in Queens, despite the dreary uniformity of the working class sections, and at Arlington, despite the marble serenity of the Capitol, the cemeteries remind you that each life is individual and everyman is finite in himself; they remind you that life is carnal, and that even conditioned air is breathed through the lungs. Returning to dust, man shows that he is not a machine; he is flesh, and real blood runs in his veins. In America, it is the graves that affirm man's humanity most authoritatively. I do not know if Americans are sensitive to this or if they feel more tenderly than they admit about that sleep which will give them rest from their breathless business of life: the fact is, their cemeteries have more character than their cities. Among these headstones half sunk into the ground, one finally escapes from the trivialities of daily life.

Questions and Suggestions

1. What similarities do you find in this essay and "The City of Magnificent Intentions"?
2. How does the tone of this essay differ from that of Dickens's account?
3. What does Mlle. de Beauvoir think of the National Gallery? Why does she find "so much ugliness" and "boredom" in Washington? What does she consider ugly and boring?
4. Explain why you agree or disagree with the author that American "cemeteries have more character than their cities."
5. Consider the validity of some of the generalizations that you find in this essay.
6. What is the meaning of *Bois de Boulogne, watering place, Greco-Roman, Louvre, Prado, Uffizi, Pantheon, Chamber of Deputies, obelisk, Champs de Mars,* and *Nordic?*

Ideas for Writing

1. For an American's view of Washington, read Edmund Wilson's essays that deal with the city as it was between 1932 and 1934, in *The American Earthquake.*
2. What reasons can you give for not walking much in the American community that you know best?
3. Explain how "the truth of death is vainly denied" in the funeral services that you have attended. Consult the description of the funeral in Eudora Welty's *The Ponder Heart.*

4. Give examples of hasty generalizations that proved to be incorrect.

5. As a visitor for a brief time in a large American city or one abroad, what impressed you the most, favorably or unfavorably? If you felt overwhelmed, compare your reactions with Theodore Dreiser's account of "Sister Carrie's" feelings as she first came to Chicago from a small town in Wisconsin.

SOPHIATOWN

TREVOR HUDDLESTON

For years Trevor Huddleston (1913–) has been disturbed by the conflict between Christian duty and duty to the State. British by birth, Father Huddleston was appointed priest to the Anglican Missions in the suburbs of Johannesburg in 1943. Although he became a citizen of South Africa, he was recalled to England, after serving the missions for twelve years, because he had become too outspoken against the evils of apartheid. In the preface to his book he states that he wrote it whenever he could over a period of a year, that it "has certainly come red hot out of the crucible," and that "it springs from a personal experience which is limited and confessedly partial." In 1960 he was consecrated Bishop of Masasi, in Tanganyika.

Sophiatown! How hard it is to capture and to convey the magic of that name! Once it is a matter of putting pen to paper, all the life and colour seem to leave it; and failing to explain its mysterious fascination is somehow a betrayal of one's love for the place. It is particularly important to me to try to paint the picture that I know and that is yet so elusive, for in a few years Sophiatown will cease to exist. It will be, first of all, a rubble heap, destruction spreading like some contagion through the streets (it has begun already), laying low the houses, good and bad alike, that I have known; emptying them of the life, the laughter, and the tears of the children—till the place is a grey ruin lying in the sun. Then, I suppose, the factories will begin to go up, gaunt impersonal blocks of cement, characterless and chill, however bright the day. And in a few years men will have forgotten that this was a living community and a very unusual one. It will have slipped away into history, and that a fragmentary history of a fraction of time. Perhaps it will awaken faint echoes in the memory of some who recall that it was to Sophiatown that Kumalo came seeking Absalom, his son. But they will never remember what I remember of it; and I cannot put my memories on paper, or, if I do, they will only be like the butterflies pinned, dead and lustreless, on the collector's board. Nevertheless, I must try.

Sophiatown! The name has about it a certain historical and almost theological sound. It recalls Sancta Sophia, Holy Wisdom, and the dreaming city where her temple is built. I have never heard of another Sophiatown in the world, though I suppose there must be one; it is such a euphonious name, for one thing. And, of course, it has a history and a meaning as romantic in its way as anything connected with the Eastern Mediterranean. As romantic but also about as different as it could well be.

Some fifty years ago, when Johannesburg was still a mining dorp, a planned and growing town yet small and restricted in area, a certain Mr. Tobiansky dreamed of a European suburb in the west, on the rocky outcrop which is shadowed by the spur known as Northcliff. It is quite a long way from the centre of town, about four and a half miles in fact, but not an impossible distance. It was a most attractive site in every way, for it had "features": it was not like the flat and uninteresting central area of the city. It could hold its own in natural beauty with Parktown and Houghton, soon to become the most fashionable suburbs, and, like them, it had iron-red rock for a foundation and for a problem in civil engineering.

Mr. Tobiansky bought a large plot of ground and named it in gratitude and admiration after his wife, Sophia. As he pegged out the streets he named many of them after his children: Edith and Gerty and Bertha and Toby and Sol. So from the very beginning Sophiatown had a homely and "family" feel about it. There was nothing "upstage" or snobbish about those names, just as there was nothing pretentious about the kind of houses which began to spring up. In fact, there was nothing very planned about it either. Still the veldt and the rock were more noticeable than the houses: the streets ran up and down the *kopje* and stopped short when the *kopje* became too steep. There was on one side a wide sweep of what you might call meadowland: an empty plot of ground which provided clay for the bricks and a good playing field for the children.

There seemed to be no reason on earth why Sophiatown should not be as popular a suburb as Parktown itself, perhaps even more popular because it was more open, higher up on the six-thousand-foot plateau which is Johannesburg. But Mr. Tobiansky had reckoned without the Town Council; or perhaps already that mischievous and unpredictable voice had whispered something about the future. Whatever it was, the Council decided that a growing town must have sewage-disposal facilities: and it decided further that those facilities must be in the Western Area of the young Johannesburg. The natural and immediate consequence of this decision was the end of Mr. Tobiansky's dream. Sophiatown ceased to be attractive in any way to those Europeans who wished to buy land and to build homes in the suburbs. Mr. Tobiansky could not sell to white Johannesburg and for a while he could not sell to anyone else.

Then once again the Town Council intervened. The First World War brought a wave of industrialisation, and with it the need for African labour. The only existing location, Pimville, had been planned and planted some ten miles from the centre of the town. There was certainly need for another location which would house the African workers and which might be a little more conveniently sited for their work. The Western Area was once more chosen. Sewage disposal and a native location seemed to go together. The Western Native Township, with accommodation for some three thousand families, was built. A tall iron fence was erected all round it. The Africans moved in. So, some forty years ago, began the African occupation of the western suburbs.

As soon as the location was established, Tobiansky found himself in an area where the non-European was in the majority. There was nothing to prevent him selling his land to Africans, coloureds, and Asiatics. Under one of President Kruger's laws he was perfectly safe-guarded for doing so, and as a good businessman he did the obvious thing. The obvious thing but not the most usual in South Africa. For when Tobiansky sold freehold properties to African purchasers, he was in fact establishing a unique situation. He was making possible an African—or at least a non-white—suburb in Johannesburg. He knew, no doubt, what he was doing. He could hardly have known the far-reaching consequences of his action. For as Johannesburg expanded, so did its need for African labour. Apart from the squalid slums of Vrededorp and the distant corrugated-iron location of Pimville, there was nowhere for the people to live except the Western Native Township and the suburbs of Sophiatown, Martindale, and Newclare which surrounded it. Houses sprang up in Edith Street and elsewhere: houses of all types, all sizes, all colours. They crept up towards the rocks on top of the hill; they spread out towards the brickfields. By 1920 or thereabouts it had become quite obvious that here was an area which belonged by right of possession to the non-European half of Johannesburg. It was not so evident at that time that white suburbia was also spreading rapidly westwards and that it was becoming especially the residential area of the European artisan. Sophiatown had come to maturity, had a character and an atmosphere of its own, and in the succeeding thirty-odd years that character and that atmosphere deepened and became only the more permanent. When I arrived to take over as priest-in-charge of the Anglican mission in September 1943, the place had for many years assumed the appearance it has today. It is that which I wish so greatly to put into words. Yet I know I cannot succeed.

They say that Sophiatown is a slum. Strictly in terms of the Slums Act they are absolutely correct, for the density of the population is about twice what it should be—70,000 instead of 30,000. But the word "slum" to describe Sophiatown is grossly misleading and especially to people who know the slums of Europe or the United States. It conjures up immediately a picture of tenement buildings, old and damp, with crumbling stone and dark cellars. The Dickensian descriptions come to mind, and the gloom and dreariness which he could convey so vividly are there in the imagination as soon as the word "slum" is read or recognised. In that sense Sophiatown is not and never has been a slum. There are no tenements; there is nothing really old; there are no dark cellars. Sometimes, looking up at Sophiatown from the Western Native Township across the main road, I have felt I was looking at an Italian village somewhere in Umbria. For you do "look up" at Sophiatown, and in the evening light, across the blue-grey haze of smoke from braziers and chimneys, against a saffron sky, you see close-packed, red-roofed little houses. You see on the farthest sky line the tall and shapely blue-gum trees (which might be cypresses if it were really Italy). You see, moving up and down the hilly streets, people in groups: people with colourful clothes; people who, when you come up to them, are children playing, dancing, and standing round the braziers. And above it all you see the Church of Christ the King, its tower visible north, south, east, and west, riding like a great ship at anchor upon the grey and golden waves of the town beneath. In the evening towards the early South African sunset there is very little of the slum about Sophiatown. It is a human dwelling place. It is as if old Sophia Tobiansky herself were gathering her great family about her, watching over them before they slept. Essentially Sophiatown is a gay place and, for all the occasional moments of violence and excitement, a kindly one too. But like every other place with a character, you have to live in it, to get the feel of its life, before you can really know it. And in the whole of South Africa there are only a handful of white citizens who have had that privilege.

The decision to move the Western Areas, to destroy all the properties built there, and to transplant the whole population to Meadowlands, four miles farther away from the city, was taken by people who had no firsthand knowledge of the place at all. How could they be expected to know it, when in their eyes it represents the very antithesis of a sound "native policy"? Freehold rights and permanence, the building up of a living community—these things are contrary to the whole doctrine of *apartheid*. They assume that the African has a right to live in the city as well as to work in it. Such an assumption is heresy to Dr. Verwoerd. It cannot be allowed. But what is it that makes Sophiatown so precious? Why should we care so much to preserve what, on any showing, is two thirds a slum area? I have asked myself that question a thousand times as I have walked its streets, visited its people in their homes, taken the Blessed Sacrament to the sick and dying. I have asked it when the dust was flying and the wind tossing the refuse about in those sordid and overcrowded back yards, and I have asked it when, looking for someone at night, I have stumbled in the dark across children asleep on the floor, packed tight together beneath a table to make room for others also to sleep. I have asked it when, on a blisteringly hot December day, the sun has beaten down on the iron ceiling of a shack and the heat has mercilessly pressed its substance upon that old, frail creature lying on the bed. I have asked it as I lay awake at night listening to the drunken shouts and the noisy laughter from the yard behind the mission. In other words, I know Sophiatown at its worst: in all weathers, under all conditions, as a slum living up to its reputation. I still love it and believe it has a unique value. But why?

In the first place, because it is not a "location." Part of the meaning of white South Africa's attitude to the African is revealed in that word "location." In America it generally has reference to part of the technique of the cinema industry. A film is made "on location" in order to give it the genuine flavour and atmosphere required by the story. But everywhere else in the world, so far as I know, the word just means a place, a site, a prescribed area. That is why, no doubt, it was chosen by the European when he decided that the African must have somewhere to live when he came to work in the towns and cities of his own country. He could not live in a suburb. He could not live in a village. He could not live in the residential area of the town itself. He could only work in those places. And because he is an abstraction— "a native"—he must have an abstraction for his home. A location in fact, a place to be in for so long as his presence is necessary and desirable to his European boss. A place from which to move on when it ceases to be necessary or desirable that he should stay.

The locations of South Africa for the most part live up to their name. They are abstract, colourless places. Every town has one on its outskirts. Today it is necessary by law that there should be a buffer strip at least five hundred yards wide between any location and the town it serves. There must be the same distance between a location and a main road. Nothing must be erected on the buffer strip—not even a pair of football goal posts. It must mark that tremendous and vital distinction between civilisation and barbarism upon which the doctrine of white supremacy rests. No one of either race may linger on that strip of land, for in that way it might become a meeting place. It is, in exact and literal terms, a no man's land; and it is meant to be just that.

There is a noticeable and depressing similarity about all locations. It is not only that for the most part the houses are built on mass-production lines and at the lowest cost compatible with minimum housing standards. It is that at the same time they are sited in the most monotonous way imaginable, as if to say: "There must be no variety in a location. Variety is a characteristic of the human being. His home is a reflection of that characteristic. But because the African is a native, it is a quality which simply does not exist." Sometimes, with the older locations, tall iron fences were erected and give the impression not only of a kind of imprisonment but of a fortification, as though the location were totally alien to the life around it and had to be defended at all costs from any contact with it. Today the buffer strip serves the

same purpose and is less expensive. So, in a location, you have row
upon row of small boxlike houses of almost identical shape and size.
Such variation as there is marks the end of one housing contract and
the beginning of another or the start, perhaps, of some new experiment
in pre-fab construction. It is never variety for its own sake. It is a
location—not a village, you must remember. As such it is unnecessary
for the streets to be named. You simply number the houses from one to
two or ten thousand and you leave it at that. If, later on, a few streets
receive baptism, it is too late for old habits to be broken. Mrs. Kambula
lives at 6002A Orlando. Mrs. Marite lives "in the four thousands."
It all helps to keep the idea of abstraction alive.

The great advantage of the location is that it can be controlled.
People who come to visit their friends for the weekend must have
permits before they can set foot upon that arid, municipal turf. It is
so much easier, too, to prevent the native feeling himself a permanent
resident in our cities if nonpayment of rent is a criminal offence rather
than a civil one. The presence, in every location, of a European superintendent with his small army of officials, black and white, and his
municipal police, is a sound and healthy reminder that in South Africa
the African needs the white man to guide and direct his daily life.
And in the sphere of broader strategy it is also wiser to have the native
living in one large but easily recognisable camp than scattered around
the town in smaller groupings. If there is trouble in Johannesburg, for
instance, Orlando can be "contained" by a comparatively small force.
It is not a bad target from the air either. And its buffer strip ensures
that no European suburb will be hit by mistake.

In the larger locations there are shops, and they are even allowed
under licence to be owned and run by Africans. All the essential services
are provided, though lighting for your house is not necessarily regarded
as essential. It is not untypical of the location concept that in Johannesburg the largest power station in the Southern Hemisphere stands at
the gate of Orlando. It supplies electricity to the city. Orlando is lit by
candles and paraffin lights. Churches, schools, and clinics exist in
locations through the effort of the various missionary and voluntary
organisations. Municipal social workers go about their business. Men
and women live there and make their family life a reality. But always
I have the feeling (and I am sure I am meant to have it, as are the
inhabitants themselves) that a location cannot *belong* to anyone except
the people who control it, the European officials who live far away
in the city, that other abstraction, "the municipality." Always, even in

considering the better aspects of location life (and there are some, I suppose), I seem to hear the voice of the Manager of Non-European Affairs saying: "We are going to do you good, whether you like it or not, for we alone know what is good for you!"

Sophiatown is not a location. That is my first reason for loving it. It is so utterly free from monotony in its siting, in its buildings, and in its people. By a historical accident it started life as a suburb, changed its colour at an early moment in its career, and then decided to go all out for variety. A £3000 building jostles a row of single rooms: an "American" barber's shop stands next door to an African herbalist's store with its dried roots and dust-laden animal hides hanging in the window. You can go into a store to buy a packet of cigarettes and be served by a Chinaman, an Indian, or a Pakistani. You can have your choice of doctors and clinics even, for they also are not municipally controlled. There are churches of every denomination and of almost every imaginable sect. There is one, for example, known as the "Donkey Church," upon whose squat, square tower there stands, in place of the traditional weathercock, an ass. I would not know its real origin, except that it is, I believe, a schism from the Methodist Church. Nor do I wish to suggest any approval for schism as such: for nothing has done so much damage to African Christianity than its fissiparousness. But somehow or other that little donkey represents the freedom that has existed down the years in Sophiatown, and when I pass it I metaphorically lift my hat. It reminds me, for one thing, of the truth that G. K. Chesterton so simply and so profoundly taught in his poem:

> The tattered outlaw of the earth
> Of ancient crooked will;
> Starve, scourge, deride me: I am dumb,
> I keep my secret still.
>
> Fools! For I also had my hour:
> One far fierce hour and sweet:
> There was a shout about my ears,
> And palms before my feet.

Basically, white South Africa has the same benign or unbenign contempt for the African as man for the donkey. Was it not Smuts himself who said once that "the African has the patience of the ass"? And so Sophiatown is written off as a slum area; its values must be those of the slum; its people must be dirty, undesirable, and, above all, unseen. Like the donkey that stands as a symbol above their streets, they are useful for their labour, for they are strong. But, as Dr. Verwoerd says, there is no place for them above that level in society itself. "I keep my

secret still. . . ." The secret of Sophiatown is not only its variety, it is
its hidden heroisms, or rather its unknown heroes and heroines, its
saints uncanonised and unsung. I know very many.

In the first place, let me say it frankly, any young person who keeps
straight when the dice are loaded so heavily against him needs virtue
of a heroic quality. The overcrowded rooms of Sophiatown, wherein
whole families must sleep and must perform all their human functions
as best they may, do not make morality an easy thing. The lack of
opportunity for fulfilling his personality in any productive way does
not make it easy, either, for a lad to escape the street-corner gang and
the excitement of gambling. The endless, grey vista of an existence
which is based upon poverty is not the kind of outlook which helps to
keep a boy or his girl friend alive to ultimate standards of beauty, truth,
and goodness.

Again and again, hearing confessions, I have asked myself how I
could advise these children, how warn them, how comfort them when
they have fallen. ". . . I have sinned exceedingly in thought, word,
and deed, by my fault, my own fault, my own most grievous fault. . . ."
Have you *really*? No doubt the actual sin is grave enough—fornication
or stealing or fighting—but what would I have done in your place?
And whose fault is it in the sight of God? And what, anyway, can I
advise?

"Don't let yourself get into bad company. . . . Don't be idle. . . . Find
some other interest than gambling. . . . Love? Well, it's not so easy to
describe it . . . it must have the quality of unselfishness."

God forgive me! I find myself giving advice that, in those circumstances, I *know* I could not follow. And yet, again and again, those
gentle men and women, those fresh, gay lads and girls try to follow,
try desperately hard to obey it, and even in their failures do not make
environment or circumstance an excuse. To keep your self-respect
when you are *expected* to have less than your white *baas;* to keep your
home neat and tidy and to dress your children in fresh clothes; to pay
for their school books regularly and to see that they are fed properly.
All this against a background of overcrowding, of the need to be up
and away to work before you have time to eat your own breakfast or
to clean the room that is your home. It needs the kind of virtue which
most European Christians in South Africa have never come within a
mile of. And it is common in Sophiatown. I do not refer just to our
own church people, though naturally they are the ones I know best
and most intimately. There is in that "black spot" (to use the minister's

offensive title) a great well of courage and cheerfulness in face of adversity which has been through the years an inspiration and a challenge to at least one Christian priest. I can shut my eyes for a moment and see old blind Margaret tapping her way along the street in the darkness which has been hers for many long years. Always, half an hour before the early Mass, she will be there in church, prostrate in prayer. Day by day I will find her spending an hour or more before the statue of Our Lady which she has never seen, and if I stop her in the street I will be greeted with that wonderful smile and the lifting of her sightless eyes to my face. . . .

Or, after Mass on Sunday morning, there will be old Tryphena Mtembu. She has spent all her years (at least all those that I have known) mending sacks and inhaling cement dust into her old lungs, so that she is never free from a fierce cough. She lives in a single dark room and "does" for herself, although a few years ago she fell and broke her leg and has to fight her way on to the early-morning bus with a crutch in one gnarled and work-lined hand. Tryphena has a wonderful flow of language, and her epithets are not always what you might expect from a devout and faithful old lady. She is, in fact, very much a product of the Old Kent Road, and were it not for her broken leg I believe she would sing and dance to "Knees up, Mother Brown" with the best of them. I also believe that her place in heaven is assured. For how could it be otherwise with one who fronts adversity with those twinkling and mischievous brown eyes and defies poverty to get her down with that marvellous and undaunted faith?

Or, again, there is Piet, who put all his money into the house in Millar Street, where he now sits, crippled with arthritis, and hoping to die before they come and demolish his home over his head. Old Piet, our churchwarden for so long, who worked for over thirty years in one of the best furniture shops in the city and was rewarded by his employers with a pittance which would not keep him alive. Never have I heard him complain, even when it was obvious that the handling of great bales of material was too much for him in his old age, even when it was a painful and weary journey for him to climb the short hill to the church he loved.

It would be easy but not very interesting, I suppose, to list a score of others of all ages and types who have lived in Sophiatown for the better part of their lives and who by their very living have enriched and beautified it greatly. A priest can see these things. Sometimes he cannot find words in which to express them. But Johannesburg knows nothing of them and can know nothing, for it does not care. To Johannesburg, Sophiatown is a slum: a native slum at that. How could it possibly have any human dignity about it?

But there is one feature of life in Sophiatown which everyone can recognise—everyone who goes there, that is. It is inescapable from the first moment when you step out of your car or stop to ask the way from the tram stop to the mission. It does not matter much what time of day it is either. Nor does it make a great deal of difference who you are or what your business—provided you are not a policeman in uniform. It is the children.

I remember the first day of my arrival there on a September morning twelve years ago. After breakfast at the mission I was told, "There's a school Mass on in the church. They'd like to see you. Will you come across?" The church is a large one by any standards. As I stood at the back and looked towards the High Altar I could see nothing but row upon row of black, curly heads. It seemed impossible to imagine that there could be quite so many children—impossible, anyhow, to imagine myself getting to know even a fraction of them. But I was wrong on both counts. This congregation represented only about half the children in one school. Soon, within a few weeks, I was beginning not only to know them but to compare them mentally with other children I had known in England. I found that I quite easily thought of their names, their features, and their characters in the same terms as of those who were already part of my family, part of my very life. And the reason was not hard to discover.

The Sophiatown child is the friendliest creature on earth and the most trusting. God knows why it should be so, but it is. You will be walking across the playground and suddenly feel a tug at your sleeve or a pressure against your knee; and then there will be a sticky hand in yours. "Hallo, Farther, hallo, Seester, how are you? Hallo, hallo, hallo. . . ." You will come back from Johannesburg, as I have done a thousand times, fed up and sick with weariness from that soulless city, and immediately you are caught in a rush and scurry of feet, in faces pressed against your car window, in arms stretching up to reach yours whether you like it or not. You are *home.* Your children are around you—ten of them, a hundred, a thousand; you belong to them and they will never let you forget it. How, then, can you fail to love the place where such things happen? Its dusty, dirty streets and its slovenly shops, its sprawling and unplanned stretches of corrugated-iron roof: its fetid and insanitary yards? ". . . and the streets of the city shall be

full of boys and girls playing in the streets thereof . . ." is a description
of the heavenly Jerusalem. It is a good one. And anyone who has lived
as I have in that "slum" called Sophiatown will recognise how swiftly,
through the presence of its children and through their unspoilt and
unassailable laughter, heaven can break in upon this old and dreary
world.

I have said that Sophiatown is a gay place. It is more. It has a
vitality and an exuberance about it which belong to no other suburb
in South Africa, certainly to no white suburb. It positively sparkles with
life. Sometimes when I have been depressed by the apparent success
of the present government in selling the idea of "white supremacy,"
I have pulled myself up by thinking just for a moment or two of the
African people as I know them in Sophiatown. There is something so
robust and strong about their way of dealing with each frustration,
which is each day, that it is even laughable to think that such an idea
can endure. And in fact it is by laughter, so often, that the problems
and the sorrows are fronted and overcome. It is by that magnificent
sense of humour and by the fitness with which it is expressed that
victory is won in the daily struggle and will ultimately be won in the
struggle for true nationhood.

A good example of the kind of humour I have known and loved is
to be seen in Sophiatown any weekend, when the "Sophiatown Scottish"
are on the march. In the distance, on a Sunday afternoon, you will
hear the beating of a drum and the sound of a far trumpet. Soon, at the
farthest end of Victoria Road, you will see a small crowd moving towards you and becoming a large crowd as it moves. Then, if you are
wise, you will wait, and witness the unique and heartening sight of an
all-African, all-female band dressed in tartan kilts, white gloves, bands-
man's staff, and accoutrement, swinging down the road with marvellous gusto. Behind them will come the spectators, not marching in
step but dancing with complete abandon and, surrounding them as
always when there's a sight, a crowd of the children, dancing, too, and
singing as they dance. Somehow the "Sophiatown Scottish" stand for
so much more than a happy Sunday afternoon. They stand for the joy
and gaiety which is *there,* deep in the heart of the African and ready
to break out in one form or another whenever and wherever he is at
home.

Another example of the same thing I have seen very often at political
meetings, especially when European police are present to take names
and to record speeches. What could so easily, in other circumstances,

become a dangerously tense situation through the provocative and contemptuous attitude of the authorities becomes a ridiculous and irrelevant matter. "After all," the Africans seem to say, "this is only an incident, and a minor one, in our progress to freedom and to fulfilment. Why not laugh at it, shrug it off with a song?" And so they do.

Sophiatown! It is not your physical beauty which makes you so lovable; not that soft line of colour which sometimes seems to strike across the greyness of your streets; not the splendour of the evening sky which turns your drabness into gold—it is none of these things. It is your people. Yet somehow I do not think it can be the same when you yourself have been destroyed and your houses are just rubble and the factories begin to go up and to smother you with their bulk and size. Even though your people will still be here in Johannesburg, in the wide symmetry of some location such as Meadowlands, there will have been a loss immeasurable. The truth is that Sophiatown is a community, a living organism which has grown up through the years and which has struck its roots deep in this particular place and in this special soil. So have I known it to be. A community with all the ordinary problems of a community and made up of people and families both bad and good. A community, not an abstraction, and therefore *personal* and real in all its aspects. And because it is an African community, living in a city of South Africa, it has to grow together in a unique way. Xosa and Mosotho, Shangaan and Motswana, Indian and Chinese, coloured and white have all contributed something to it. And in my opinion they have all had something of value to contribute. The place is cosmopolitan in a real sense and has about it that atmosphere which belongs to cosmopolitan towns the world over. It is, in that sense, unique. The most unlikely and unexpected things can happen there and not appear at all unlikely or seem incongruous. So you have to be prepared, if you live in the midst of it as a priest, for every conceivable problem at every hour of the day or night. How, then, can you fail to love it?

A great deal is said by sociologists and others of "the breakdown of tribal custom" and "the disastrous impact of Western industrialism upon the urban African." That sentence itself is stiff with the jargon of the race-relations textbook. But when you live in Sophiatown you don't see it that way at all. You see Mrs. X., who has a drunken husband and five children to support—and what must she do? You see Mr. Y., whose wife left him two years ago and the kids are growing up; what is he to plan for them, can the "Father" help him? You see young Joel, who has just left school and got a "tea-boy" job in the city, but he longs to do his Matric, and can't find the time or the money or the quietness for work that he needs. You are called to that room in Tucker Street, where Joseph is fighting for his life against advanced t.b., and in spite of all your efforts you can't get a bed anywhere and you wonder—well, you wonder what it all means within the Providence of God. And you hear that Jane has got into trouble and the boy won't admit his fault; and you run *posthaste* to see her father before he goes out with a sjambok. . . . And then there's George, arrested for carrying *dagga,* and there's Michael, whom you've not seen for weeks, but you hear he's drinking. . . . But behind them all, behind the "problems" which come the way of every priest in every parish in Christendom, there is that great mass of folk who live ordinary lives in extraordinary conditions and who *are* the Christian community in Sophiatown. And a more vital Christian community it would be hard to find anywhere.

I wonder, for instance, how many parishes in England today would have a Mass in the dark of a winter morning at half-past five and get a congregation of twenty or thirty people? And that not just once, but week after week? I wonder how many churches today are full on Sunday morning at six o'clock and again at eleven? Yet this is but the outward form of something far deeper and more profound. It is in fact the answer to the sociologist's question—at least it is part of the answer. The only thing which is meeting the need for a sense of "community," of "belonging," in the broken and shattered tribalism of the town-dwelling African is the Church. It is for that reason that these present years of crisis are of such tremendous significance. If the Church fails in bearing her witness on the colour question *now,* she will never, in my opinion, have a second opportunity. Here in Sophiatown over the past thirty years and more we have been engaged in building a Christian community. It is that community which is now being smashed to pieces in the interests of a racial ideology. And as we watch our people's homes being reduced to heaps of rubble we watch also the destruction of something which cannot be built again so easily or so fair. When Sophiatown is finally obliterated and its people scattered, I believe that South Africa will have lost not only a place but an ideal.

> Day that I have loved, day that I have loved,
> The night is here. . . .

Questions and Suggestions

1. In the first paragraph, Huddleston makes an indirect reference to Alan Paton's celebrated novel *Cry, the Beloved*

Country; if you have read it, you will have a better grasp of this essay.

2. What are the major issues which Huddleston recognizes?
3. Why is Sophiatown being destroyed?
4. What would be some of the local, national, and international reactions to this act of the South African government?
5. What are some of the moral problems that Huddleston raises?
6. How do the churches in your community bear "witness on the colour question *now*"?
7. What are some of the terms with local meanings that Huddleston must define to make the situation clear to those readers who do not know Sophiatown, Johannesburg, or South Africa? Where is Sancta Sophia located? What is the meaning of *dorp*? Could you use the term for an American community? You may need to consult an unabridged dictionary or the glossary in the Paton novel for the meaning of *veldt, kopje, Xosa, sjambok,* and *dagga.* Are there other words which are new to you but which you can understand because of their context? What is the meaning of *fissiparousness?*

Ideas for Writing

1. From what you have learned in your general reading about situations of unrest in most parts of Africa, discuss one of the moral problems that Huddleston's essay raises.
2. If among strangers or in a hostile society, how much moral and political courage would you have?
3. How altruistic should a man be?
4. Discuss the influence of a home or community environment upon a friend, or an example of a friend or acquaintance who was able to escape the "street-corner gang."
5. Discuss the housing difficulties that members of minority groups in your community encounter.
6. Can you describe an example of racial snobbery, even in its inverse form?
7. Explain how some of the streets in your community received their names.

DACHAU REVISITED

TERENCE PRITTIE

A frequent contributor to *The Guardian,* Terence Cornelius
Farmer Prittie (1913–) often writes about conditions in post-war
Germany. British readers know him not only as the author of
Escape to Freedom and *Western Germany on Trial* but also as
a writer about cricket.

Munich, December.

Once Dachau was an obscure railway junction on the main
line from Munich to Ingolstadt and the north, a dozen miles from
the Bavarian capital, with low hills to the north of it and a dreary
swamp to the south-east, bordering the road from Munich. Hitler found
this lonely swamp useful. In this area of rutted car tracks, stagnant
drains, and waterlogged fields he built his first and perhaps most
famous concentration camp.

Iniquity dies hard. In many of the huts that once housed innocent
people marked for death by the Nazis now live equally innocent victims of history—or, rather, of that phase of history that Hitler inaugurated,—German refugees from the East. Raggety children play
along the gutters; households of old women peer through blurred and
broken window-panes; and the grass is growing mercifully over the
dirt-tracks where a captured British Secret Service agent saw typhus-
ridden creatures crawling in April, 1945.

Innocence is not always a virtue. "Down that road and second on the
right," a middle-aged man told me when I asked him the way to the
concentration camp crematorium. He was in no way embarrassed.
"Along that stretch of broken wire and the gate is on the left," said a
youth in answer to my question, and I could swear he winked.

The crematorium stands in its own little park, perfectly preserved,
with a well-kept two-acre garden around it and a single American
sentry at the gate. The garden is not quite what it seems at first sight.

At one end is a mound, surmounted with wreaths and with a head-
stone which bears the inscription "Mass-Grave of Many Thousands."
Just to the north is a long, low ridge of soil, labelled "Execution-Range"
and running the whole length behind it is the "Blood Ditch," which
is covered still with the broken wooden trellis which survived in 1945.
Here S.S. execution squads used to line up their victims, turn them
about, and shoot them in the back of the head. By a natural reflex
they pitched half over the ridge of soil and their blood drained into the
ditch—just one tidy little part of the Master Plan.

Beyond the Blood Ditch is a "Pistol Range" where guards used their
victims for target practice. Beyond again is another mass grave. Just
across the garden is the gallows-stand and at one corner the "Gallows
Tree" which sometimes did supernumerary duty. With its gravel walks,
grass lawns, and flowerbeds, the garden is perfectly kept.

At the western end of the garden are two buildings, the "old" and
the "new" crematoria. The first was simply designed for the burning
of corpses, a small, square building with a single huge oven inside.
Long before the war was half lost the old crematorium became hopelessly inadequate. The new crematorium was run up by slave labourers
who, as likely as not, later died within its red brick, inoffensively
suburban walls.

The new crematorium is labelled "Building 243 A." Its doors are
kept always open, for it is a museum of misery. It contains five main
rooms, the first small and empty. Empty, that is, save for the thousands
of names and messages scribbled on its bare walls. They are accompanied often by a cross, a pierced heart, or the Star of David. There
are little messages—"Les Soissonais à leurs Martyrs," "Stanley Joa-
chimiak was here K.Z. Dauchau 1941–1945."

Beyond this room are the ovens, a big double oven flanked by two
single ones and all three transformed into shrines. On them hang the
flags of many nations, tattered vestments which have presumably been
handed down from the churches that functioned in the camp, pine and
laurel wreaths on nails. Some of them carry messages, "A nos morts,"
"Aux chers disparus." A bronze plaque has been let into one oven,
bearing the names of the Brothers Vaarwel, of Antwerp.

Beyond the cremation-chamber is the "Death Room" with two
gratings in the floor down which blood and excrement were swept.
The Death Room is empty, utterly empty, and not even names live here.
For the walls, for obvious reasons, are lead-lined.

The last two rooms only began to play their part in the life of the crematorium towards the end of the war, when Himmler's advisers evolved the idea of gassing. This does not seem to have been more effective or even cheaper than other Nazi methods of mass murder. But it appealed to their niggling instinct for tidiness.

The fourth room in Dauchau crematorium is the "Undressing Room," with benches along the walls for the victims' clothes. Here, again, the walls are covered with signatures and over the door into the gas chamber is the mocking word "Brausebad"—"Shower-bath"—for no one was to know, officially, that he was going to his death. It probably fooled very few. For, to speed up the process of asphyxiation, the roof is set only 6 ft. 6 in. high. It still contains the eighteen vents through which gas, and not water, was pumped in upon the occupants of the room. Otherwise the room is empty to-day.

The Dachau gas chamber was installed too late to play the same part in mass murder as those of Auschwitz or Treblinka. Only a small proportion of the many thousands who died in Dauchau were gassed. Perhaps that is why a German newspaper published the story that the gas chamber was only installed by the Americans to "pin guilt" on Germany. Himmler explained that

> The proletarianised Jewish masses of the Eastern countries . . . were infected with dreadful epidemics: in particular, spotted typhus raged. I myself lost thousands of my best S.S. men through these epidemics. . . . In order to put a stop to these epidemics we were forced to burn the bodies of incalculable numbers of people who had been destroyed by disease. We were therefore forced to build crematoria. . . .

Some Germans may believe this. Goebbels, they say, was so right about the Bolsheviks, and foolish Western statesmen are just finding that out. Why should Himmler not have been right too? It must have been a coincidence that one and a half hundredweight of bullets was dug out of the soil of the crematorium garden.

I saw Dachau crematorium on a November day when the thermometer registered exactly zero and a biting wind blew across the marshy ground to the east, with its pot-holed roads and mantle of ground mist. But it is on just this kind of day that the Bavarian sky stays strangely clear and a glowing red sun sank quietly behind the single, sinister black chimney of the crematorium. Sinister? Or just picturesque? Either way, there will no longer be an American sentry at the gate in a year's time and the grim little notices in the garden may not be so easy to read. Dachau, after all, is only an obscure railway junction on the main line from Munich to Ingolstadt and the north.

Questions and Suggestions

1. What purpose does Prittie have in mind by beginning this account in the manner of a fairy tale? What effect would this essay have on a person who reads it over a morning cup of coffee?
2. How effective is the word *tidy* in the essay?
3. What does he imply by the final sentence of his report? Does it carry more connotations than at first appears, or is it merely a method of unifying the last with the first sentence of the selection?
4. What is Prittie's impression of post-war Germans?
5. Which monument do you suppose Simone de Beauvoir would find the more impressive—the Dachau crematorium and its garden or the monument to the Unknown Soldier at Arlington?
6. What was the "Master Plan"?
7. What connection do you find between the building numbered "243 A" and the numbers in the Sophiatown district of Johannesburg?
8. Both Prittie and Muir noticed a sunset. What difference do you distinguish in their accounts?

Ideas for Writing

1. Contrast the tone of this essay with A. M. Rosenthal's "There Is No News from Auschwitz," in *The New York Times Magazine,* April 16, 1961, and August 31, 1958. Other accounts worth your attention are Michel del Castillo's *Child of Our Times,* and Giles Playfair and Derrick Sington's "Irma Grese" in *The Offenders.* Certainly you might consult other works in your college library that deal with life and death in the concentration camps.
2. What did our own nation do with the Nisei during World War II?
3. Discuss an example of man's inhumanity to man which has taken place in your own community, not elsewhere.
4. Himmler gave misleading reasons for the deaths of the Jews. Are you familiar with a political act in your state which was deceitfully explained away?
5. Describe the present state of war memorials in your locality.
6. Why do you dislike jokes that derive their supposed humor from the use of such terms of opprobrium as *dagos, kikes, micks, skibbies, darkies,* and *hunkies?*

THE TOWN DUMP

WALLACE STEGNER

As a child Wallace Stegner (1909–), who was born on a farm
near Lake Mills, Iowa, lived in Iowa, North Dakota, Washington,
Saskatchewan, Montana, Utah, Nevada, and California. Because
his family was usually on the move, he was able to establish roots
in only two places—Eastend, Saskatchewan, and Salt Lake City.
A graduate of the Universities of Utah and Iowa, he has been
for a number of years Professor of English and the Director of
the Creative Writing Center at Stanford University. He is the
author of a number of prize-winning volumes, his creative interests centering around the novel and the short story.

The town dump of Whitemud, Saskatchewan, could only
have been a few years old when I knew it, for the village was born
in 1913 and I left there in 1919. But I remember the dump better
than I remember most things in that town, better than I remember
most of the people. I spent more time with it, for one thing; it had more
poetry and excitement in it than people did.

It lay in the southeast corner of town, in a section that was always
full of adventure for me. Just there the Whitemud River left the hills,
bent a little south, and started its long traverse across the prairie and
the international boundary to join the Milk. For all I knew, it might
have been on its way to join the Alph: simply, before my eyes, it
disappeared into strangeness and wonder.

Also, where it passed below the dumpground, it ran through wil-
lowed bottoms that were a favorite campsite for passing teamsters,
gypsies, sometimes Indians. The very straw scattered around those
camps, the ashes of those strangers' campfires, the manure of their
teams and saddle horses, were hot with adventurous possibilities.

It was as an extension, a living suburb, as it were, of the dumpground that we most valued those camps. We scoured them for arti-

From *The Atlantic Monthly*, Oct., 1959. Copyright © 1959 by
Wallace Stegner. Reprinted by permission of The Viking Press, Inc.
This will be a chapter in a forthcoming book by Wallace Stegner.

facts of their migrant tenants as if they had been archaeological sites
full of the secrets of ancient civilizations. I remember toting around
for weeks the broken cheek strap of a bridle. Somehow or other its
buckle looked as if it had been fashioned in a far place, a place where
they were accustomed to flatten the tongues of buckles for reasons that
could only be exciting, and where they made a habit of plating the
metal with some valuable alloy, probably silver. In places where the
silver was worn away the buckle underneath shone dull yellow: probably gold.

It seemed that excitement liked that end of town better than our
end. Once old Mrs. Gustafson, deeply religious and a little raddled in
the head, went over there with a buckboard full of trash, and as she
was driving home along the river she looked and saw a spent catfish,
washed in from Cypress Lake or some other part of the watershed,
floating on the yellow water. He was two feet long, his whiskers hung
down, his fins and tail were limp. He was a kind of fish that no one
had seen in the Whitemud in the three or four years of the town's
life, and a kind that none of us children had ever seen anywhere.
Mrs. Gustafson had never seen one like him either; she perceived at
once that he was the devil, and she whipped up the team and reported
him at Hoffman's elevator.

We could hear her screeching as we legged it for the river to see
for ourselves. Sure enough, there he was. He looked very tired, and he
made no great effort to get away as we pushed out a half-sunken
rowboat from below the flume, submerged it under him, and brought
him ashore. When he died three days later we experimentally fed
him to two half-wild cats, but they seemed to suffer no ill effects.

At that same end of town the irrigation flume crossed the river.
It always seemed to me giddily high when I hung my chin over its
plank edge and looked down, but it probably walked no more than
twenty feet above the water on its spidery legs. Ordinarily in summer
it carried about six or eight inches of smooth water, and under the
glassy hurrying of the little boxed stream the planks were coated with
deep sun-warmed moss as slick as frogs' eggs. A boy could sit in the
flume with the water walling up against his back, and grab a cross
brace above him, and pull, shooting himself sledlike ahead until he
could reach the next brace for another pull and another slide, and so
on across the river in four scoots.

After ten minutes in the flume he would come out wearing a dozen
or more limber black leeches, and could sit in the green shade where

darning needles flashed blue, and dragonflies hummed and darted and stopped, and skaters dimpled slack and eddy with their delicate transitory footprints, and there stretch the leeches out one by one while their sucking ends clung and clung, until at last, stretched far out, they let go with a tiny wet *puk* and snapped together like rubber bands. The smell of the river and the flume and the clay cutbanks and the bars of that part of the river was the smell of wolf willow.

But nothing in that end of town was as good as the dumpground that scattered along a little runoff coulee dipping down toward the river from the south bench. Through a historical process that went back, probably, to the roots of community sanitation and distaste for eyesores, but that in law dated from the Unincorporated Towns Ordinance of the territorial government, passed in 1888, the dump was one of the very first community enterprises, almost our town's first institution.

More than that, it contained relics of every individual who had ever lived there, and of every phase of the town's history.

The bedsprings on which the town's first child was begotten might be there; the skeleton of a boy's pet colt; two or three volumes of Shakespeare bought in haste and error from a peddler, later loaned in carelessness, soaked with water and chemicals in a house fire, and finally thrown out to flap their stained eloquence in the prairie wind.

Broken dishes, rusty tinware, spoons that had been used to mix paint; once a box of percussion caps, sign and symbol of the carelessness that most of those people felt about all matters of personal or public safety. We put them on the railroad tracks and were anonymously denounced in the *Enterprise*. There were also old iron, old brass, for which we hunted assiduously, by night conning junkmen's catalogues and the pages of the *Enterprise* to find how much wartime value there might be in the geared insides of clocks or in a pound of tea lead carefully wrapped in a ball whose weight astonished and delighted us. Sometimes the unimaginable outside world reached in and laid a finger on us. I recall that, aged no more than seven, I wrote a St. Louis junk house asking if they preferred their tea lead and tinfoil wrapped in balls, or whether they would rather have it pressed flat in sheets, and I got back a typewritten letter in a window envelope instructing me that they would be happy to have it in any way that was convenient for me. They added that they valued my business and were mine very truly. Dazed, I carried that windowed grandeur around in my pocket until I wore it out, and for months I saved the letter as a souvenir of the won-

dering time when something strange and distinguished had singled
me out.

We hunted old bottles in the dump, bottles caked with dirt and
filth, half buried, full of cobwebs, and we washed them out at the
horse trough by the elevator, putting in a handful of shot along with the
water to knock the dirt loose; and when we had shaken them until our
arms were tired, we hauled them off in somebody's coaster wagon and
turned them in at Bill Anderson's pool hall, where the smell of lemon
pop was so sweet on the dark pool-hall air that I am sometimes awakened by it in the night, even yet.

Smashed wheels of wagons and buggies, tangles of rusty barbed
wire, the collapsed perambulator that the French wife of one of the
town's doctors had once pushed proudly up the planked sidewalks
and along the ditchbank paths. A welter of foul-smelling feathers and
coyote-scattered carrion which was all that remained of somebody's
dream of a chicken ranch. The chickens had all got some mysterious
pip at the same time, and died as one, and the dream lay out there with
the rest of the town's history to rustle to the empty sky on the border of
the hills.

There was melted glass in curious forms, and the half-melted office
safe left from the burning of Bill Day's Hotel. On very lucky days we
might find a piece of the lead casing that had enclosed the wires of the
town's first telephone system. The casing was just the right size for
rings, and so soft that it could be whittled with a jackknife. It was a
material that might have made artists of us. If we had been Indians of
fifty years before, that bright soft metal would have enlisted our
maximum patience and craft and come out as ring and medal and
amulet inscribed with the symbols of our observed world. Perhaps there
were too many ready-made alternatives in the local drug, hardware, and
general stores; perhaps our feeble artistic response was a measure of
the insufficiency of the challenge we felt. In any case I do not remember that we did any more with the metal than to shape it into crude
seal rings with our initials or pierced hearts carved in them; and these,
though they served a purpose in juvenile courtship, stopped something
short of art.

The dump held very little wood, for in that country anything burn-
able got burned. But it had plenty of old iron, furniture, papers, mattresses that were the delight of field mice, and jugs and demijohns
that were sometimes their bane, for they crawled into the necks and
drowned in the rain water or redeye that was inside.

If the history of our town was not exactly written, it was at least hinted, in the dump. I think I had a pretty sound notion even at eight or nine of how significant was that first institution of our forming Canadian civilization. For rummaging through its foul purlieus I had several times been surprised and shocked to find relics of my own life tossed out there to rot or blow away.

The volumes of Shakespeare belonged to a set that my father had bought before I was born. It had been carried through successive moves from town to town in the Dakotas, and from Dakota to Seattle, and from Seattle to Bellingham, and Bellingham to Redmond, and from Redmond back to Iowa, and from there to Saskatchewan. Then, stained in a stranger's house fire, these volumes had suffered from a house-cleaning impulse and been thrown away for me to stumble upon in the dump. One of the Cratchet girls had borrowed them, a hatchet-faced, thin, eager, transplanted Cockney girl with a frenzy, almost a hysteria, for reading. And yet somehow, through her hands, they found the dump, to become a symbol of how much was lost, how much thrown aside, how much carelessly or of necessity given up, in the making of a new country. We had so few books that I was familiar with them all, had handled them, looked at their pictures, perhaps even read them. They were the lares and penates, part of the skimpy impedimenta of household gods we had brought with us into Latium. Finding those three thrown away was a little like finding my own name on a grave-stone.

And yet not the blow that something else was, something that impressed me even more with the dump's close reflection of the town's intimate life. The colt whose picked skeleton lay out there was mine. He had been incurably crippled when dogs chased our mare, Daisy, the morning after she foaled. I had labored for months to make him well; had fed him by hand, curried him, exercised him, adjusted the iron braces that I had talked my father into having made. And I had not known that he would have to be destroyed. One weekend I turned him over to the foreman of one of the ranches, presumably so that he could be cared for. A few days later I found his skinned body, with the braces still on his crippled front legs, lying on the dump.

Not even that, I think, cured me of going there, though our parents all forbade us on pain of cholera or worse to do so. The place fascinated us, as it should have. For this was the kitchen midden of all the civilization we knew; it gave us the most tantalizing glimpses into our lives as well as into those of the neighbors. It gave us an aesthetic distance from which to know ourselves.

The dump was our poetry and our history. We took it home with us by the wagonload, bringing back into town the things the town had used and thrown away. Some little part of what we gathered, mainly bottles, we managed to bring back to usefulness, but most of our gleanings we left lying around barn or attic or cellar until in some renewed fury of spring cleanup our families carted them off to the dump again, to be rescued and briefly treasured by some other boy with schemes for making them useful. Occasionally something we really valued with a passion was snatched from us in horror and returned at once. That happened to the mounted head of a white mountain goat, somebody's trophy from old times and the far Rocky Mountains, that I brought home one day in transports of delight. My mother took one look and discovered that his beard was full of moths.

I remember that goat; I regret him yet. Poetry is seldom useful, but always memorable. I think I learned more from the town dump than I learned from school: more about people, more about how life is lived, not elsewhere but here, not in other times but now. If I were a sociologist anxious to study in detail the life of any community, I would go very early to its refuse piles. For a community may be as well judged by what it throws away—what it has to throw away and what it chooses to—as by any other evidence. For whole civilizations we have sometimes no more of the poetry and little more of the history than this.

Questions and Suggestions

1. Explain Stegner's statement that Whitemud's town dump "gave us an aesthetic distance from which to know ourselves."
2. What insights into human behavior did Stegner acquire while exploring the town dump?
3. Consider his judgment that the dump possessed more poetry and excitement than did the people.
4. Study the pattern of organization in the essay. Note the use of incident, detail, and diction.
5. Why is it particularly important that Stegner present his childhood experiences vividly?
6. If you are not familiar with the *River Alph,* read Coleridge's "Kubla Khan." See if you can determine the meanings of *lares, penates, Latium,* and *midden* from the context before you consult your dictionary.

Ideas for Writing

1. This essay aptly illustrates the importance of perceptive and imaginative observation. Recall what has impressed you about a community auction, a rummage sale, or a farmers' market. Write an account that recreates the "institution" and its memorable qualities.

2. Describe the chaos of moving or of cleaning the basement, attic, or garage, and consider how such activity calls attention to the way your family lives.

3. Evaluate your community in terms of "what it has to throw away and what it chooses to."

4. Defend your attachment to some object or interest that is generally considered "useless" or impractical.

5. Write a character sketch of a hoarder, a miser, or a scavenger.

6. Study, with the possibility of a paper in mind, the people whom you find buying objects at the local Salvation Army, Good-Will, or St. Vincent de Paul second-hand store.

7. In 1658, Sir Thomas Browne wrote *Hydriotaphia,* a work now better known by its English subtitle, *Urn-Burial; or, A Discourse of the Sepulchral Urns Lately Found in Norfolk.* He, too, was impressed by the finding of relics from the past. What differences in depth of meaning and style do you note in the following paragraphs taken from Chapter V of *Urn-Burial* and in the last two paragraphs of Stegner's essay?

Oblivion is not to be hired. The greater part must be content to be as though they had not been, to be found in the register of God, not in the record of man. Twenty-seven names make up the first story before the flood, and the recorded names ever since contain not one living century. The number of the dead long exceedeth all that shall live. The night of time far surpasseth the day, and who knows when was the equinox? Every hour adds unto that current arithmetick, which scarce stands one moment. And since death must be the *Lucina* of life, and even Pagans could doubt, whether thus to live were to die; since our longest sun sets at right descensions, and makes but winter arches, and therefore it cannot be long before we lie down in darkness, and have our light in ashes;* since the brother of death daily haunts us with dying mementos, and time that grows old in itself, bids us hope no long duration;—diuturnity is a dream and folly of expectation.

* According to the custom of the Jews, who place a lighted wax-candle in a pot of ashes by the corpse.

Darkness and light divide the course of time, and oblivion shares with memory a great part even of our living beings; we slightly remember our felicities, and the smartest strokes of affliction leave but short smart upon us. Sense endureth no extremities, and sorrows destroy us or themselves. To weep into stones are fables. Afflictions induce callosities; miseries are slippery, or fall like snow upon us, which notwithstanding is no unhappy stupidity. To be ignorant of evils to come, and forgetful of evils past, is a merciful provision in nature, whereby we digest the mixture of our few and evil days, and, our delivered senses not relapsing into cutting remembrances, our sorrows are not kept raw by the edge of repetitions. A great part of antiquity contented their hopes of subsistency with a transmigration of their souls,—a good way to continue their memories, while, having the advantage of plural successions, they could not but act something remarkable in such variety of beings, and enjoying the fame of their passed selves, make accumulation of glory unto their last durations. Others, rather than be lost in the uncomfortable night of nothing, were content to recede into the common being, and make one particle of the public soul of all things, which was no more than to return into their unknown and divine original again. Egyptian ingenuity was more unsatisfied, contriving their bodies in sweet consistencies, to attend the return of their souls. But all was vanity, feeding the wind, and folly. The Egyptian mummies, which Cambyses or time hath spared, avarice now consumeth. Mummy is become merchandise, Mizraim cures wounds, and Pharaoh is sold for balsams.

part four ✂ *Books and schoolrooms*

THE PLEASURES OF IGNORANCE

L. A. G. STRONG

Leonard Alfred George Strong (1896–1958) was born near Plymouth, England. Because his parents had strong family connections with Ireland and because he spent the summers of his childhood in Dublin, Strong came to realize that he had inherited two cultural backgrounds. A prolific writer, expressing himself in novels, poems, essays, and plays, he was also passionately interested in teaching others how to use their voices when reciting verse or prose.

The other morning I found myself suddenly awake some minutes before my time. Just as suddenly, and without premeditation, I found myself reviewing the extent of my knowledge and, before it

From *Personal Remarks* by L. A. G. Strong. Published by Peter Nevill, Ltd. Copyright 1953. Reprinted by permission of A. D. Peters.

was time to get up, I had come to the conclusion that I knew practically nothing about anything.

This conclusion was not reached in any spirit of self-abasement, or
even of modesty. The time was not two-thirty a.m., but seven-forty-five.
I woke from no nightmare, but was in calm and contented possession
of my faculties. I experienced a very definite pleasure from the fact
that I might remain for several minutes where I was. The conviction
of my own ignorance was a sane, happy, and (I think) irrefutable
conviction. It did not depress me because there appeared to be good
reasons why I need do nothing about it; good reasons, in fact, for
thinking that I am better as I am.

First of all, what is the positive extent of my knowledge? Apart from
immediate personal experiences, such as the fact that it is unwise to
take hold of the little door in front of a coal range in one's fingers,
(learnt at the age of seven), that a mixture of sherbet and milk chocolate in equal parts produces disconcerting results (discovered at eight),
and that it is socially inexpedient to make jokes about false teeth (impressed on me a little later), the number of things which I can positively say I know is very limited. I know the genitive singular of a
number of Latin words and a much smaller number of Greek ones. I
know, with less certainty, a few things that happened during a certain
limited period of English history; though even these depend upon data
which I am personally unable to verify. I know a few mathematical
formulae, impressed upon me by trial—and error—in relation to my
banking account. I can play, with a dubious proportion of success, the
game of applying to English thoughts and objects the names under
which similar thoughts and objects seem to be known in France. I can
inform a German that the mountain is bedecked with snow, and a
Spaniard that his brother's hat is in the warehouse. I can tell an
Italian railway porter that his tiny hand is frozen. Still, as opportunities
for imparting such information occur but seldom, the knowledge is not
much use to me. I know who wrote a limited number of plays and
poems and pieces of music, and can in certain cases even give a sketchy
account of what they contain. I know, very roughly, the views held by
the various rival practitioners of a science which is as yet so tentative
that no two of them use the same term in the same way. I know the
words and tunes of a few songs. I can repeat several anecdotes.

The acquisition of this inconsiderable store has cost me fifty-six years
and my parents a good deal of money. Compared with all that I do not
know, it seems, to say the least, an inadequate return. I do not under-

stand the major phenomena of the world around me. I do not understand half the contrivances which I use, such as wireless, and the
telephone. I am unable to repair an electric bell. I have a very imperfect
knowledge of my own personal mechanism. What is worse, I am not particularly curious about these things. When I put three pennies into an
automatic machine, and receive a ticket to Tottenham Court Road, I am
not devoured by any desire to know how the miracle is worked. I am simply
grateful to be saved standing in a queue at the booking office. I am so
unobservant that I cannot even draw an accurate picture of the outside
of the house in which I am living. I do not think I could draw a bus,
or the outline of Big Ben, without going first to look at it. In fact, as I
said, outside the range of my own immediate experience, and such deductions of cause and effect as seem to be constant when I come into
contact with them, I know next to nothing—and that at the end of an
elaborate and costly education.

It sounds tragic, and I suppose that as a civilised human being I
ought to be depressed. Yet I was not depressed as I lay comfortably in
bed that morning, and I am not depressed now. After all, when we
put theories aside, and come down to brass tacks, why should I be? My
ignorance does me no harm. Why should I bother how automatic
machines work, so long as they give me my ticket? What does it matter
how my voice is carried to Dorset, provided it reaches the person I
want to talk to? Why should my limited understanding be tossed about
on long and short waves, provided I can switch over from the programme I don't want to the one I do?

What does it matter if I do not know the facts involved in a book
which I have to review? I can look them up in a textbook or in the
encyclopedia, and they will then be accurate, whereas my memory
might deceive me. As long as one is aware of it, ignorance can be the
greatest help to one. Not long ago, I made an appalling howler through
satisfaction at my own knowledge. I had to review a book on a technical
subject. 'Aha', I thought, 'he ought to have included such-and-such':
and so pleased was I with my own erudition that I omitted to do more
than hastily survey the list of contents before expressing my dignified
surprise that the author had neglected, etc. etc. etc. By a quite un-
deserved stroke of good luck, I discovered a couple of days later to my
horror that the author had not neglected, etc. etc. etc. He had dealt
very fully with the matter. A burst of telephoning at the last minute,
and the error was corrected just in time. Phew! Give me ignorance!

The happily ignorant man, the man aware of his own ignorance, and

perfectly content with it, does not misquote. He does not confuse
William with Henry James, mix up the Strausses, or joyfully praise
W. B. Yeats as the author of *Berry & Co.* He invests his money with
caution, and only bets on certainties. He consults his lawyer before he
gives rein to his just indignation. He is not knowledgeable enough to
fall victim to the confidence trickster. In fact, such a premium has our
civilisation put upon ignorance, he gets along very comfortably indeed.

This, of course, is what it has come to. Knowledge is at a discount.
Why need I bother to learn this, that, and the other thing, when a walk
to my bookcase, or, at the worst, to the nearest reference library, will
tell me all I want? Why should I be ashamed of my ignorance, when in
the nature of things I can only know a very little about a very little?
Since that early morning enlightenment, when I realised the true extent
of my ignorance, I have gone my way serene and happy. I need not
bother. It is all done for me. Sometimes I need hardly walk as far as
my bookcase. I can sit in my chair, and listen to a broadcast talk upon
the very subject about which I desire information. The gentleman who
gives the talk is persuasive and kind. He knows infinitely more than I.
It would be downright discourteous to oppose to his discourse the
obstacle of any previous knowledge. We can leave all the knowing to
him. It is his business to—

A horrible thought has struck me. I myself stand on platforms and
give lectures. I myself broadcast. Am I just (I must be, surely) am I
just a surreptitious, disgraceful exception to a rule of enlightenment?
Am I the only one who does not know? . . . I mean, are all the others?
. . . Is it possible that some of them, too. . . ?

I had better stop, before my newly-won content evaporates.

Questions and Suggestions

1. Why does Strong insist that he was sane when he concluded
   that he knew virtually nothing? What advantages does he cite
   for such an awareness of ignorance?

2. Discuss his view that we value ignorance and discount knowledge.

3. Upon what thesis or point does Strong firmly insist?

4. Is the use of the "I" appropriate?

5. Why did he not combine the first two paragraphs?

6. Note the frequent use of questions and interruptions in the
   essay, especially in the last three paragraphs. What is the
   effect of these devices? If Smythe wrote "Avalanche" for

readers, what indication do you find that Strong intended this essay for listeners?

7. In "Calculated Spontaneity," a talk originally given on the B.B.C. and reprinted in *The Oxford Book of English Talk,* John Hilton stated that he always spoke his sentences aloud as he wrote them—if he wished to make his words sound like talk. How applicable is his rule to your own work?

Ideas for Writing

1. What is the "positive extent" of your own knowledge?
2. Discuss, in a light-hearted fashion, the cost in time and money of what you have already learned in college. See Robert Benchley's "What College Did to Me," in *The Early Worm.*
3. Portray an individual unaware of his own ignorance, or describe a social situation involving several serenely ignorant people.
4. See if you can describe, from memory, the house or dormitory in which you live.
5. In "Conversation Piece, 1945," included in *Spring in Fialta,* Vladimir Nabokov brilliantly recreates an evening a Russian exile accidentally spends in an upper-class Boston home with a group of very talkative "murderers or fools." Although a number of the people present were European in origin, their ignorance of what happened in Europe before and during World War II and their completely false versions of other situations, revealing chauvinistic pride and racial hatreds, terrify the unexpected guest. Can you question the validity of some of the conversations you have overheard since coming to college or some of those in which you have inadvertently taken part?

REFLECTIONS ON PEDANTRY AND PEDANTS

JOSEPH ADDISON

Born in his father's rectory near Amesbury, Wiltshire, England, Joseph Addison (1672–1719) studied Classics at Oxford. After making the grand tour, he returned to London where he became a favorite with the Whigs, holding several secretaryships. Friends and enemies alike recognized the power of his mind, the charm of his conversation, his social graces, and his pleasant temper. A contributor to Sir Richard Steele's *Tatler,* Addison wrote 274 of the *Spectator* papers. It was his success with the essay form that did much to establish the pattern and popularity of the familiar essay with future writers.

A man who has been brought up among books, and is able to talk of nothing else, is a very indifferent companion, and what we call a pedant. But, methinks, we should enlarge the title, and give it to everyone that does not know how to think out of his profession and particular way of life.

What is a greater pedant than a mere man of the town? Bar him the play-houses, a catalogue of the reigning beauties, and an account of a few fashionable distempers that have befallen him, and you strike him dumb. How many a pretty gentleman's knowledge lies all within the verge of the court? He will tell you the names of the principal favorites, repeat the shrewd sayings of a man of quality, whisper an intrigue that is not yet blown upon by common fame; or, if the sphere of his observations is a little larger than ordinary, will perhaps enter into all the incidents, turns, and revolutions in a game of ombre. When he has gone thus far he has shown you the whole circle of his accomplishments, his parts are drained, and he is disabled from any farther conversation. What are these but rank pedants? And yet these are the men who value themselves most on their exemption from the pedantry of colleges.

I might here mention the military pedant, who always talks in a camp, and is storming towns, making lodgments, and fighting battles from one end of the year to the other. Everything he speaks smells of gunpowder; if you take away his artillery from him, he has not a word to say for himself. I might likewise mention the law pedant, that is perpetually putting cases, repeating the transactions of Westminster Hall, wrangling with you upon the most indifferent circumstances of life, and not to be convinced of the distance of a place, or of the most trivial point in conversation, but by dint of argument. The state pedant is wrapped up in news and lost in politics. If you mention either of the

From *The Spectator,* No. 105, June 30, 1711. The title of this selection has been added by the editors.

kings of Spain or Poland, he talks very notably; but if you go out of the *Gazette* you drop him. In short, a mere courtier, a mere soldier, a mere scholar, a mere anything, is an insipid pedantic character, and equally ridiculous.

Of all the species of pedants which I have mentioned, the book pedant is much the most supportable; he has at least an exercised understanding and a head which is full though confused, so that a man who converses with him may often receive from him hints of things that are worth knowing, and what he may possibly turn to his own advantage, though they are of little use to the owner. The worse kind of pedants among learned men are such as are naturally endued with a very small share of common sense, and have read a great number of books without taste or distinction.

The truth of it is, learning, like traveling and all other methods of improvement, as it finishes good sense, so it makes a silly man ten thousand times more insufferable by supplying variety of matter to his impertinence, and giving him an opportunity of abounding in absurdities.

Questions and Suggestions

1. How does Addison define a pedant? Do we still need "to enlarge the title," as he suggests? Do you know people in various fields who fit his definition?
2. What is Addison's main point or thesis? How does he develop it?
3. Why does he prefer the book pedant to the other kinds?
4. This selection is from an eighteenth century essay. List the words and phrases that are no longer in common usage.
5. Are his sentences literary or do they have the lilt of spoken prose? Do any of the sentences seem unduly complicated or strange in construction?
6. Does he express his ideas clearly?
7. Compare his views with those of his contemporary, Jonathan Swift, who also satirized the pedant in Part III of *Gulliver's Travels*.

Ideas for Writing

1. In a brief essay define "a person of taste," taking care to be clear and to provide sufficient illustrations.
2. If you share a room with another student, do you find any clashes of temperament developing over differences in your tastes?

3. Why is one of your friends a bore?
4. Analyze your own way of life for signs of pedantry.
5. With Addison's definition in mind, describe a pedant who is representative or typical of a certain profession or occupation.
6. Recreate an evening when you heard adults participate only in "shop talk" or in "small talk," making clear your own reaction to their conversation.

BOOKS

RALPH WALDO EMERSON

The son of a Unitarian minister, Ralph Waldo Emerson (1803–1882) was born in Boston and graduated from Harvard. Three professors had a major influence on his intellectural growth: Ticknor, in modern languages; Everett, in Greek; and Channing, in English composition. For three years Emerson was a Unitarian minister in Boston. Resigning because he could not accept all the dogmas, he developed in his own fashion the philosophy of Transcendentalism. Philosopher he was, but not one without a sense of humor. After a successful trip abroad, he settled in Concord where he had an opportunity to develop his ideas, either in the form of lectures, poems, essays, or entries in his *Journals*. Revered by many during his lifetime for the clarity of his thought and his wisdom, Emerson still has much to say that is of great value, especially in such works as "Self-Reliance," "The American Scholar," *Representative Men, The Conduct of Life,* and *English Traits.*

It is easy to accuse books, and bad ones are easily found; and the best are but records, and not the things recorded; and certainly there is dilettanteism enough, and books that are merely neutral and do nothing for us. In Plato's "Gorgias," Socrates says: "The shipmaster walks in a modest garb near the sea, after bringing his passengers from Ægina or from Pontus, not thinking he has done anything extraordinary, and certainly knowing that his passengers are the same, and in no respect

From *Society and Solitude,* 1870.

better than when he took them on board." So is it with books, for the most part: they work no redemption in us. The bookseller might certainly know that his customers are in no respect better for the purchase and consumption of his wares. The volume is dear at a dollar, and, after reading to weariness the lettered backs, we leave the shop with a sigh, and learn, as I did, without surprise, of a surly bank director, that in bank parlors they estimate all stocks of this kind as rubbish.

But it is not less true that there are books which are of that importance in a man's private experience, as to verify for him the fables of Cornelius Agrippa, of Michael Scott, or of the old Orpheus of Thrace, —books which take rank in our life with parents and lovers and passionate experiences, so medicinal, so stringent, so revolutionary, so authoritative,—books which are the work and the proof of faculties so comprehensive, so nearly equal to the world which they paint, that, though one shuts them with meaner ones, he feels his exclusion from them to accuse his way of living.

Consider what you have in the smallest chosen library. A company of the wisest and wittiest men that could be picked out of all civil countries, in a thousand years, have set in best order the results of their learning and wisdom. The men themselves were hid and inaccessible, solitary, impatient of interruption, fenced by etiquette; but the thought which they did not uncover to their bosom friend is here written out in transparent words to us, the strangers of another age.

We owe to books those general benefits which come from high intellectual action. Thus, I think, we often owe to them the perception of immortality. They impart sympathetic activity to the moral power. Go with mean people, and you think life is mean. Then read Plutarch, and the world is a proud place, peopled with men of positive quality, with heroes and demigods standing around us, who will not let us sleep. Then, they address the imagination: only poetry inspires poetry. They become the organic culture of the time. College education is the reading of certain books which the common-sense of all scholars agrees will represent the science already accumulated. If you know that,—for instance in geometry, if you have read Euclid and Laplace,—your opinion has some value; if you do not know these, you are not entitled to give any opinion on the subject. Whenever any sceptic or bigot claims to be heard on the questions of intellect and morals, we ask if he is familiar with the books of Plato, where all his pert objections have once for all been disposed of. If not, he has no right to our time. Let him go and find himself answered there.

Meantime the colleges, whilst they provide us with libraries, furnish no professor of books; and, I think, no chair is so much wanted. In a libra:y we are surrounded by many hundreds of dear friends, but they are imprisoned by an enchanter in these paper and leathern boxes; and, though they know us, and have been waiting two, ten, or twenty centuries for us,—some of them,—and are eager to give us a sign, and unbosom themselves, it is the law of their limbo that they must not speak until spoken to; and as the enchanter has dressed them, like battalions of infantry, in coat and jacket of one cut, by the thousand and ten thousand, your chance of hitting on the right one is to be computed by the arithmetical rule of Permutation and Combination,—not a choice out of three caskets, but out of half a million caskets all alike. But it happens in our experience, that in this lottery there are at least fifty or a hundred blanks to a prize. It seems, then, as if some charitable soul, after losing a great deal of time among the false books, and alighting upon a few true ones which made him happy and wise, would do a right act in naming those which have been bridges or ships to carry him safely over dark morasses and barren oceans, into the heart of sacred cities, into palaces and temples. This would be best done by those great masters of books who from time to time appear,—the Fabricii, the Seldens, Magliabecchis, Scaligers, Mirandolas, Bayles, Johnsons, whose eyes sweep the whole horizon of learning. But private readers, reading purely for love of the book, would serve us by leaving each the shortest note of what he found.

There are books; and it is practicable to read them, because they are so few. We look over with a sigh the monumental libraries of Paris, of the Vatican, and the British Museum. In 1858, the number of printed books in the Imperial Library at Paris was estimated at eight hundred thousand volumes; with an annual increase of twelve thousand volumes; so that the number of printed books extant to-day may easily exceed a million. It is easy to count the number of pages which a diligent man can read in a day, and the number of years which human life in favorable circumstances allows to reading; and to demonstrate that, though he should read from dawn till dark, for sixty years, he must die in the first alcoves. But nothing can be more deceptive than this arithmetic, where none but a natural method is really pertinent. I visit occasionally the Cambridge Library, and I can seldom go there without renewing the conviction that the best of it all is already within the four walls of my study at home. The inspection of the catalogue brings me continually back to the few standard writers who are on every private shelf;

and to these it can afford only the most slight and casual additions. The crowds and centuries of books are only commentary and elucidation, echoes and weakeners of these few great voices of Time.

The best rule of reading will be a method from nature, and not a mechanical one of hours and pages. It holds each student to a pursuit of his native aim, instead of a desultory miscellany. Let him read what is proper to him, and not waste his memory on a crowd of mediocrities. As whole nations have derived their culture from a single book,—as the Bible has been the literature as well as the religion of large portions of Europe,—as Hafiz was the eminent genius of the Persians, Confucius of the Chinese, Cervantes of the Spaniards; so, perhaps, the human mind would be a gainer, if all the secondary writers were lost,—say, in England, all but Shakspeare, Milton, and Bacon,—through the profounder study so drawn to those wonderful minds. With this pilot of his own genius, let the student read one, or let him read many, he will read advantageously. Dr. Johnson said: "Whilst you stand deliberating which book your son shall read first, another boy has read both: read anything five hours a day, and you will soon be learned."

Nature is much our friend in this matter. Nature is always clarifying her water and her wine. No filtration can be so perfect. She does the same thing by books as by her gases and plants. There is always a selection in writers, and then a selection from the selection. In the first place, all books that get fairly into the vital air of the world were written by the successful class, by the affirming and advancing class, who utter what tens of thousands feel though they cannot say. There has already been a scrutiny and choice from many hundreds of young pens, before the pamphlet or political chapter which you read in a fugitive journal comes to your eye. All these are young adventurers, who produce their performance to the wise ear of Time, who sits and weighs, and, ten years hence, out of a million of pages reprints one. Again it is judged, it is winnowed by all the winds of opinion, and what terrific selection has not passed on it before it can be reprinted after twenty years,—and reprinted after a century!—it is as if Minos and Rhadamanthus had indorsed the writing. 'T is therefore an economy of time to read old and famed books. Nothing can be preserved which is not good; and I know beforehand that Pindar, Martial, Terence, Galen, Kepler, Galileo, Bacon, Erasmus, More, will be superior to the average intellect. In contemporaries, it is not so easy to distinguish betwixt notoriety and fame.

Be sure, then, to read no mean books. Shun the spawn of the press on the gossip of the hour. Do not read what you shall learn, without asking, in the street and the train. Dr. Johnson said, "he always went into stately shops"; and good travellers stop at the best hotels; for, though they cost more, they do not cost much more, and there is the good company and the best information. In like manner, the scholar knows that the famed books contain, first and last, the best thoughts and facts. Now and then, by rarest luck, in some foolish Grub Street is the gem we want. But in the best circles is the best information. If you should transfer the amount of your reading day by day from the newspaper to the standard authors— But who dare speak of such a thing?

Questions and Suggestions

1. What does Emerson say, in this portion of a longer essay, about the books we should select to read, the benefits we can derive from them, and the ways we should read them?
2. Does he develop one point carefully before he proceeds to another? Is there a kind of continuum and overlapping of ideas? Where, for example, does his point about the selection of books appear?
3. Elaborate on his statements: (a) ". . . it is the law of their limbo that they must not speak until spoken to." (b) "College education is the reading of certain books which the common-sense of all scholars agrees will represent the science already accumulated." (c) "Shun the spawn of the press on the gossip of the hour."
4. Find examples in this essay of Emerson's use of contrasts.
5. Cite sentences that you find memorable and account for their appeal.

Ideas for Writing

1. Write an essay developing Emerson's statement, "Go with mean people, and you think life is mean."
2. Describe your library, or the one you are acquiring, and evaluate your selection of books by Emerson's principles.
3. What friend or acquaintance best fits Emerson's title "Professor of Books"?
4. Define the "successful class" that Emerson mentions near the end of the essay.
5. What advice would you give to a semi-mature acquaintance who does not read for pleasure? To arouse his curiosity in such a way that books will become important to him, would

you have him start with the great books or with more
ephemeral matter? E. B. White's "The Future of Reading,"
in *The Second Tree from the Corner,* presents a contemporary
case for the value of reading.

IN MY LIBRARY

E. M. FORSTER

Most readers feel a sense of disappointment that Edward Morgan
Forster (1879–), the distinguished novelist, essayist, short-story
writer, lecturer, biographer, and librettist, has not been an even
more prolific writer. *A Passage to India* is his best known novel.
Famous for being generous to young writers, Forster avoids stuffi-
ness. He has great personal humility. In addition, his was one of
the most effective voices heard in defense of Lady Chatterly at
her trial held in Old Bailey. Since 1946, when he gave up his
home at Abinger, Surrey, England, he has been an honorary
Fellow of King's College, Cambridge, his alma mater. For a non-
collegiate view of Forster in his college rooms, surrounded by his
books, read Mollie Panter-Downes's profile in *The New Yorker*
for September 19, 1959.

You are soon in my library and soon out of it, for most of the
books are contained in a single room. I keep some more of them in a
bedroom and in a little sitting-room and in a bathroom cupboard, but
most of them are in what we will politely term the library. This is a
commodious apartment—twenty-four feet by eighteen—and a very
pleasant one. The ceiling is high, the paint white, the wallpaper rib-
boned-white, and the sun, when it shines, does so through lofty windows
of early Victorian Gothic. Even when it does not shine, the apartment
remains warm and bright, for it faces south. Round the walls are a
dozen wooden bookcases of various heights and shapes, a couple of them
well designed, the others cheap. In the middle of the room stands a

From *Two Cheers for Democracy.* Copyright 1938, 1939, 1947,
1949, 1951 by E. M. Forster. Reprinted by permission of Harcourt,
Brace & World, Inc., and Edward Arnold (Publishers) Ltd.

curious object; a bookcase which once belonged to my grandfather. It
has in its front a little projecting shelf supported on two turned pillars
of wood, and it has a highly polished back. Some say it is a converted
bedstead. It stood in a similar position in the middle of his study over
a hundred years ago—he was a country clergyman. Bedstead or not, it
is agreeable and original and I have tried to fill it with volumes of
gravity, appropriate to its past. Here are the theological works of Isaac
Barrow, thirteen volumes, full morocco, stamped with college arms.
Here are the works of John Milton, five volumes, similarly garbed. Here
is Evelyn's Diary in full calf, and Arnold's *Thucydides* and Tacitus and
Homer. Here are my grandfather's own works bearing titles such as
One Primeval Language, The Apocalypse its own Interpreter and
Mohammedanism Unveiled. Have you read my grandfather's works?
No? Have I read them? No.

My grandfather then is one of the influences that I can trace in my
little collection. I never knew him in the flesh. He must have been
rather alarming. His character was dogmatic and severe and he would
not approve of some of the company which I oblige him to keep to-day.
For close by, in a bookcase between the two windows, lurk works of
another sort—Anatole France, Marcel Proust, Hérédia, André Gide—
the type of Frenchman whose forerunners he denounced in a sermon
preached to his village in 1871 on the occasion of the Fall of Paris. It
is ironical that the book belonging to him which I most cherish should
be a French book. This is a great encyclopaedia in fifty-two volumes—
the *Biographie Universelle* of 1825. Each volume bears his dignified
bookplate with our family arms and also the bookplate of Sir James Mack-
intosh, its previous owner. It is in bad condition—all the backs off—
but it is a useful work of reference of the leisurely type, and makes
excellent reading. There is nothing slick about it. It dates from the days
before the world broke up, and it is a good thing occasionally to go
back to those days. They steady us.

The next influence I have to note is that of his daughter, my aunt.
I inherited her possessions and had to sell or give away most of her
books before I could fit into my present quarters. But I kept what I
liked best, and enough to remind me of her cultivated and attractive
personality. She was a maiden lady of strong character, and a great
reader, particularly of good prose. Trollope, Jane Austen, Charlotte
Yonge, Malory, sound biographies of sound Victorians—these have
come down from her. Books on birds also—Bewick and Morris. The
birds remind me of her bookplate. She had a charming personal one

of a foliated arabesque round a shield, and from the arabesque peep out
birds, dogs and a squirrel—some of the living creatures who surrounded
her country home where she led a quiet, happy and extremely useful
life. She was interested in crafts—she started classes for leather-work
in the village. She was herself a designer and worker, she designed and
executed book-covers which were made up at the binder's, and my
shelves (to which we now return) are enriched by several examples
of her skill. Here are the Letters of Charles Darwin (whom she had
known), and Ruskin's *Praeterita,* and Ruskin's *Giotto*—a fine example
in pigskin, introducing the legendary O of Giotto and her own initials.
The most ambitious of all her bindings—the *Rubaiyat of Omar Khay-
yam*—I gave away after her death to an oriental friend. I still miss that
lovely book and wish I possessed it. I still see the charming design with
which she decorated its cover—polo players adapted from an ancient
Persian miniature—a design for which the contemporary dust jacket
is a poor substitute.

However I am contemporary myself and I must get on to myself and
not linger amongst ancestral influences any longer. What did I bring
to my library? Not much deliberately. I have never been a collector,
and as for the first edition craze, I place it next door to stamp collecting—I can say no less. It is non-adult and exposes the book-lover to
all sorts of nonsense at the hands of the book-dealer. One should never
tempt book-dealers. I am myself a lover of the interiors of books, of the
words in them—an uncut book is about as inspiriting as a corked up
bottle of wine—and much as I enjoy good print and good binding and
old volumes they remain subsidiary to the words: words, the wine of
life. This view of mine is, I am convinced, the correct one. But even
correctness has had its disadvantages and I am bound to admit that my
library, so far as I have created it, is rather a muddle. Here's one sort
of book, there's another, and there is not enough of any sort of book
to strike a dominant note. Books about India and by Indians, modern
poetry, ancient history, American novels, travel books, books on the
state of the world, and on the world-state, books on individual liberty,
art-albums, Dante and books about him—they tend to swamp each
other, not to mention the usual pond of pamphlets which has to be
drained off periodically. The absence of the collector's instinct in me,
the absence of deliberate choice, have combined with a commendable
variety of interests to evolve a library which will not make any definite impression upon visitors.

I have not a bookplate—too diffident or too much bother. I cannot arrange books well either; shall it be by subjects or by heights? Shall a tall old Froissart stand beside *The Times Atlas,* or beside a tiny Philippe de Commines? I do not bang or blow them as much as I should, or oil their leather backs, or align those backs properly. They are unregimented. Only at night, when the curtains are drawn and the fire flickers, and the lights are turned off, do they come into their own, and attain a collective dignity. It is very pleasant to sit with them in the firelight for a couple of minutes, not reading, not even thinking, but aware that they, with their accumulated wisdom and charm, are waiting to be used, and that my library, in its tiny imperfect way, is a successor to the great private libraries of the past. 'Do you ever lend books?' someone may say in a public-spirited tone of voice at this point. Yes, I do, and they are not returned, and still I lend books. Do I ever borrow books? I do, and I can see some of them unreturned around me. I favour reciprocal dishonesty. But the ownership of the things does give me peculiar pleasure, which increases as I get older. It is of the same kind, though not so strong, as the desire to possess land. And, like all possessiveness, it does not go down to the roots of our humanity. Those roots are spiritual. The deepest desire in us is the desire to understand, and that is what I meant just now when I said that the really important thing in books is the words in them—words, the wine of life —not their binding or their print, not their edition value or their bibliomaniac value, or their uncuttability.

One's favourite book is as elusive as one's favourite pudding, but there certainly are three writers whom I would like to have in every room, so that I can stretch out my hand for them at any moment. They are Shakespeare, Gibbon and Jane Austen. There are two Shakespeares in this library of mine, and also two outside it, one Gibbon, and one outside it, one Jane Austen and two outside it. So I am happily furnished. And, of course, I have some Tolstoy, but one scarcely wants Tolstoy in every room. Shakespeare, Gibbon and Jane Austen are my choice, and in a library one thinks of Gibbon most. Gibbon loved books but was not dominated by them. He knew how to use them. His bust might well stand on my grandfather's bookcase, to my grandfather's indignation.

Questions and Suggestions

1. What does Forster mean when he says that his grandfather's encyclopaedia has "nothing slick about it" and that "it dates from the days before the world broke up"? How does the

reference to the contemporary dust jacket illustrate this contrast between the past and present?

2. Why would the grandfather disapprove of many of Forster's choices of books?

3. In what ways does Forster value his library? What is the "really important thing in books"? Are the references to wine apt? How many do you find?

4. Would Forster and Emerson agree about the books that one should read and know; would Forster and Dr. Johnson agree?

5. Study the plan of this essay. Does the contrast between past and present figure prominently in its organization?

6. Consult a rhetoric for examples of inductive and deductive paragraphs. Contrast the organization and development of the first paragraph with that of the next to the last paragraph.

Ideas for Writing

1. Write a personal essay on one of the following: (a) people who influenced your love of books; (b) the risks connected with lending books; (c) arranging books; (d) "Reciprocal dishonesty"; (e) "The desire to understand"; (f) your taste in books as opposed to that of your parents or grandparents.

2. Are you in favor of open or closed stacks in a university library?

3. Contrast two living rooms or two "dens," one with and one without books. Or contrast the two periods in a person's life —his "wild" youth with his "tame" and conservative old age.

4. Did you ever have a teacher who gave the impression that he had no regard for books? If so, evaluate the effect his attitude had upon you.

THE OLD AND THE NEW SCHOOLMASTER

CHARLES LAMB

Charles Lamb (1775–1834), a native of London, was reasonably happy during the seven years he studied at Christ's Hospital, a charitable educational institution. Before leaving Christ's Hospital, Lamb had developed skills in Greek and Latin, but because his

family was poor and because he suffered from a speech impedi-
ment, he was unable to continue his education. During those
formative years, however, he did make a life-long friend with
another student, Samuel Taylor Coleridge. For most of his adult
life, Lamb earned a small but regular income by working as a
clerk in the East India House, thus supporting himself and his
sister Mary. Two essays, in particular, serve as companion pieces
to the one included in this text: "On Christ's Hospital, and the
Character of the Christ's Hospital Boys," and "Christ's Hospital
Five-and-thirty Years Ago."

My reading has been lamentably desultory and immethodical.
Odd, out of the way, old English plays, and treatises, have supplied
me with most of my notions, and ways of feeling. In every thing that
relates to *science*, I am a whole Encyclopædia behind the rest of the
world. I should have scarcely cut a figure among the franklins, or country gentlemen, in king John's days. I know less geography than a schoolboy of six weeks' standing. To me a map of old Ortelius is as authentic
as Arrowsmith. I do not know whereabout Africa merges into Asia;
whether Ethiopia lie in one or other of those great divisions; nor can
form the remotest conjecture of the position of New South Wales, or
Van Diemen's Land. Yet do I hold a correspondence with a very dear
friend in the first-named of these two Terræ Incognitæ. I have no
astronomy. I do not know where to look for the Bear, or Charles's Wain;
the place of any star; or the name of any of them at sight. I guess at
Venus only by her brightness—and if the sun on some portentous morn
were to make his first appearance in the West, I verily believe, that,
while all the world were gasping in apprehension about me, I alone
should stand unterrified, from sheer incuriosity and want of observation.
Of history and chronology I possess some vague points, such as one
cannot help picking up in the course of miscellaneous study; but I
never deliberately sat down to a chronicle, even of my own country.
I have most dim apprehensions of the four great monarchies; and sometimes the Assyrian, sometimes the Persian, floats as *first* in my fancy.
I make the widest conjectures concerning Egypt, and her shepherd
kings. My friend M., with great painstaking, got me to think I understood the first proposition in Euclid, but gave me over in despair at the
second. I am entirely unacquainted with the modern languages; and,

From *Elia, Essays which have Appeared under that Signature in The
London Magazine,* 1823.

like a better man than myself, have "small Latin and less Greek." I am
a stranger to the shapes and texture of the commonest trees, herbs,
flowers—not from the circumstance of my being town-born—for I
should have brought the same inobservant spirit into the world with me,
had I first seen it in "on Devon's leafy shores,"—and am no less at a
loss among purely town-objects, tools, engines, mechanic processes.—
Not that I affect ignorance—but my head has not many mansions, nor
spacious; and I have been obliged to fill it with such cabinet curiosities
as it can hold without aching. I sometimes wonder, how I have passed
my probation with so little discredit in the world, as I have done, upon
so meagre a stock. But the fact is, a man may do very well with a very
little knowledge, and scarce be found out, in mixed company; every
body is so much more ready to produce his own, than to call for a
display of your acquisitions. But in a *tête-à-tête* there is no shuffling.
The truth will out. There is nothing which I dread so much, as the
being left alone for a quarter of an hour with a sensible, well-informed
man, that does not know me. I lately got into a dilemma of this sort.—

In one of my daily jaunts between Bishopsgate and Shacklewell, the
coach stopped to take up a staid-looking gentleman, about the wrong
side of thirty, who was giving his parting directions (while the steps
were adjusting), in a tone of mild authority, to a tall youth, who seemed
to be neither his clerk, his son, nor his servant, but something partaking
of all three. The youth was dismissed, and we drove on. As we were
the sole passengers, he naturally enough addressed his conversation to
me; and we discussed the merits of the fare, the civility and punctuality
of the driver; the circumstance of an opposition coach having been
lately set up, with the probabilities of its success—to all which I was
enabled to return pretty satisfactory answers, having been drilled into
this kind of etiquette by some years' daily practice of riding to and fro
in the stage aforesaid—when he suddenly alarmed me by a startling
question, whether I had seen the show of prize cattle that morning in
Smithfield? Now as I had not seen it, and do not greatly care for such
sort of exhibitions, I was obliged to return a cold negative. He seemed
a little mortified, as well as astonished, at my declaration, as (it appeared) he was just come fresh from the sight, and doubtless had hoped
to compare notes on the subject. However he assured me that I had
lost a fine treat, as it far exceeded the show of last year. We were now
approaching Norton Falgate, when the sight of some shop-goods
ticketed freshened him up into a dissertation upon the cheapness of
cottons this spring. I was now a little in heart, as the nature of my

morning avocations had brought me into some sort of familiarity with the raw material; and I was surprised to find how eloquent I was becoming on the state of the India market—when, presently, he dashed my incipient vanity to the earth at once, by inquiring whether I had ever made any calculation as to the value of the rental of all the retail shops in London. Had he asked of me, what song the Sirens sang, or what name Achilles assumed when he hid himself among women, I might, with Sir Thomas Browne, have hazarded a "wide solution."* My companion saw my embarrassment, and, the almshouses beyond Shoreditch just coming in view, with great good-nature and dexterity shifted his conversation to the subject of public charities; which led to the comparative merits of provision for the poor in past and present times, with observations on the old monastic institutions, and charitable orders;—but, finding me rather dimly impressed with some glimmering notions from old poetic associations, than strongly fortified with any speculations reducible to calculation on the subject, he gave the matter up; and, the country beginning to open more and more upon us, as we approached the turnpike at Kingsland (the destined termination of his journey), he put a home thrust upon me, in the most unfortunate position he could have chosen, by advancing some queries relative to the North Pole Expedition. While I was muttering out something about the Panorama of those strange regions (which I had actually seen), by way of parrying the question, the coach stopping relieved me from any further apprehensions. My companion getting out, left me in the comfortable possession of my ignorance; and I heard him, as he went off, putting questions to an outside passenger, who had alighted with him, regarding an epidemic disorder, that had been rife about Dalston; and which, my friend assured him, had gone through five or six schools in that neighbourhood. The truth now flashed upon me, that my companion was a schoolmaster; and that the youth, whom he had parted from at our first acquaintance, must have been one of the bigger boys, or the usher.—He was evidently a kind-hearted man, who did not seem so much desirous of provoking discussion by the questions which he put, as of obtaining information at any rate. It did not appear that he took any interest, either, in such kind of inquiries, for their own sake; but that he was in some way bound to seek for knowledge. A greenish-coloured coat, which he had on, forbade me to surmise that

*Urn Burial.

he was a clergyman. The adventure gave birth to some reflections on the difference between persons of his profession in past and present times.

Rest to the souls of those fine old Pedagogues; the breed, long since extinct, of the Lilys, and the Linacres: who believing that all learning was contained in the languages which they taught, and despising every other acquirement as superficial and useless, came to their task as to a sport! Passing from infancy to age, they dreamed away all their days as in a grammar-school. Revolving in a perpetual cycle of declensions, conjugations, syntaxes, and prosodies; renewing constantly the occupations which had charmed their studious childhood; rehearsing continually the part of the past; life must have slipped from them at last like one day. They were always in their first garden, reaping harvests of their golden time, among their *Flori* and their *Spici-legia;* in Arcadia still, but kings; the ferule of their sway not much harsher, but of like dignity with that mild sceptre attributed to king Basileus; the Greek and Latin, their stately Pamela and their Philoclea; with the occasional duncery of some untoward Tyro, serving for a refreshing interlude of a Mopsa, or a clown Damætas!

With what a savour doth the Preface to Colet's, or (as it is sometimes called) Paul's Accidence, set forth! "To exhort every man to the learning of grammar, that intendeth to attain the understanding of the tongues, wherein is contained a great treasury of wisdom and knowledge, it would seem but vain and lost labour; for so much as it is known, that nothing can surely be ended, whose beginning is either feeble or faulty; and no building be perfect, whereas the foundation and ground-work is ready to fall, and unable to uphold the burden of the frame." How well doth this stately preamble (comparable to those which Milton commendeth as "having been the usage to prefix to some solemn law, then first promulgated by Solon, or Lycurgus") correspond with and illustrate that pious zeal for conformity, expressed in a succeeding clause, which would fence about grammar-rules with the severity of faith-articles!—"as for the diversity of grammars, it is well profitably taken away by the king majesties wisdom, who foreseeing the inconvenience, and favourably providing the remedie, caused one kind of grammar by sundry learned men to be diligently drawn, and so to be set out, only everywhere to be taught for the use of learners, and for the hurt in changing of schoolmaisters." What a *gusto* in that which follows: "wherein it is profitable that he can orderly decline his noun, and his verb." *His* noun!

The fine dream is fading away fast; and the least concern of a teacher in the present day is to inculcate grammar-rules.

The modern schoolmaster is expected to know a little of every thing, because his pupil is required not to be entirely ignorant of any thing. He must be superficially, if I may so say, omniscient. He is to know something of pneumatics; of chemistry; of whatever is curious, or proper to excite the attention of the youthful mind; an insight into mechanics is desirable, with a touch of statistics; the quality of soils, &c. botany, the constitution of his country, *cum multis aliis.* You may get a notion of some part of his expected duties by consulting the famous Tractate on Education addressed to Mr. Hartlib.

All these things—these, or the desire of them—he is expected to instil, not by set lessons from professors, which he may charge in the bill, but at school-intervals, as he walks the streets, or saunters through green fields (those natural instructors), with his pupils. The least part of what is expected from him, is to be done in school-hours. He must insinuate knowledge at the *mollia tempora fandi.* He must seize every occasion—the season of the year—the time of the day—a passing cloud—a rainbow—a waggon of hay—a regiment of soldiers going by —to inculcate something useful. He can receive no pleasure from a casual glimpse of Nature, but must catch at it as an object of instruction. He must interpret beauty into the picturesque. He cannot relish a beggar-man, or a gipsy, for thinking of the suitable improvement. Nothing comes to him, not spoiled by the sophisticating medium of moral uses. The Universe—that Great Book, as it has been called— is to him indeed, to all intents and purposes, a book, out of which he is doomed to read tedious homilies to distasting schoolboys.—Vacations themselves are none to him, he is only rather worse off than before; for commonly he has some intrusive upper-boy fastened upon him at such times; some cadet of a great family; some neglected lump of nobility, or gentry; that he must drag after him to the play, to the Panorama, to Mr. Bartley's Orrery, to the Panopticon, or into the country, to a friend's house, or to his favourite watering-place. Wherever he goes, this uneasy shadow attends him. A boy is at his board, and in his path, and in all his movements. He is boy-rid, sick of perpetual boy.

Boys are capital fellows in their own way, among their mates; but they are unwholesome companions for grown people. The restraint is felt no less on the one side, than on the other.—Even a child, that "plaything of an hour," tires *always.* The noises of children, playing

their own fancies—as I now harken to them by fits, sporting on the
green before my window, while I am engaged in these grave speculations at my neat suburban retreat at Shacklewell—by distance made
more sweet—inexpressibly take from the labour of my task. It is like
writing to music. They seem to modulate my periods. They ought at
least to do so—for in the voice of that tender age there is a kind of
poetry, far unlike the harsh prose accents of man's conversation.—I
should but spoil their sport, and diminish my own sympathy for them,
by mingling in their pastime.

I would not be domesticated all my days with a person of very
superior capacity to my own—not, if I know myself at all, from any
considerations of jealousy or self-comparison, for the occasional communion with such minds has constituted the fortune and felicity of
my life—but the habit of too constant intercourse with spirits above
you, instead of raising you, keeps you down. Too frequent doses of
original thinking from others, restrain what lesser portion of that faculty
you may possess of your own. You get entangled in another man's mind,
even as you lose yourself in another man's grounds. You are walking
with a tall varlet, whose strides out-pace yours to lassitude. The constant
operation of such potent agency would reduce me, I am convinced, to
imbecility. You may derive thoughts from others; your way of thinking,
the mould in which your thoughts are cast, must be your own. Intellect
may be imparted, but not each man's intellectual frame.—

As little as I should wish to be always thus dragged upwards, as
little (or rather still less) is it desirable to be stunted downwards by
your associates. The trumpet does not more stun you by its loudness,
than a whisper teases you by its provoking inaudibility.

Why are we never quite at our ease in the presence of a schoolmaster?—because we are conscious that he is not quite at his ease in
ours. He is awkward, and out of place, in the society of his equals. He
comes like Gulliver from among his little people, and he cannot fit the
stature of his understanding to yours. He cannot meet you on the
square. He wants a point given him, like an indifferent whist-player.
He is so used to teaching, that he wants to be teaching *you*. One of
these professors, upon my complaining that these little sketches of mine
were any thing but methodical, and that I was unable to make them
otherwise, kindly offered to instruct me in the method by which young
gentlemen in *his* seminary were taught to compose English themes.—
The jests of a schoolmaster are coarse, or thin. They do not *tell* out of
school. He is under the restraint of a formal and didactive hypocrisy

in company, as a clergyman is under a moral one. He can no more let his intellect loose in society, than the other can his inclinations.—He is forlorn among his co-evals; his juniors cannot be his friends.

"I take blame to myself," said a sensible man of this profession, writing to a friend respecting a youth who had quitted his school abruptly, "that your nephew was not more attached to me. But persons in my situation are more to be pitied, than can well be imagined. We are surrounded by young, and, consequently, ardently affectionate hearts, but *we* can never hope to share an atom of their affections. The relation of master and scholar forbids this. *How pleasing this must be to you, how I envy your feelings,* my friends will sometimes say to me, when they see young men, whom I have educated, return after some years absence from school, their eyes shining with pleasure, while they shake hands with their old master, bringing a present of game to me, or a toy to my wife, and thanking me in the warmest terms for my care of their education. A holiday is begged for the boys; the house is a scene of happiness; I, only, am sad at heart—This fine-spirited and warm-hearted youth, who fancies he repays his master with gratitude for the care of his boyish years—this young man—in the eight long years I watched over him with a parent's anxiety, never could repay me with one look of genuine feeling. He was proud, when I praised; he was submissive, when I reproved him; but he did never *love* me—and what he now mistakes for gratitude and kindness for me, is but the pleasant sensation, which all persons feel at revisiting the scene of their boyish hopes and fears; and the seeing on equal terms the man they were accustomed to look up to with reverence. My wife too," this interesting correspondent goes on to say, "my once darling Anna, is the wife of a schoolmaster.—When I married her—knowing that the wife of a schoolmaster ought to be a busy notable creature, and fearing that my gentle Anna would ill supply the loss of my dear bustling mother, just then dead, who never sat still, was in every part of the house in a moment, and whom I was obliged sometimes to threaten to fasten down in a chair, to save her from fatiguing herself to death—I expressed my fears, that I was bringing her into a way of life unsuitable to her; and she, who loved me tenderly, promised for my sake to exert herself to perform the duties of her new situation. She promised, and she has kept her word. What wonders will not woman's love perform?—My house is managed with a propriety and decorum, unknown in other schools; my boys are well fed, look healthy, and have every proper accommodation; and all this performed with a careful economy, that

never descends to meanness. But I have lost my gentle, *helpless* Anna!
—When we sit down to enjoy an hour of repose after the fatigue of
the day, I am compelled to listen to what have been her useful (and
they are really useful) employments through the day, and what she
proposes for her to-morrow's task. Her heart and her features are
changed by the duties of her situation. To the boys, she never appears
other than the *master's wife,* and she looks up to me as the *boys' master;*
to whom all show of love and affection would be highly improper, and
unbecoming the dignity of her situation and mine. Yet *this* my gratitude forbids me to hint to her. For my sake she submitted to be this
altered creature, and can I reproach her for it?"—For the communication of this letter, I am indebted to my cousin Bridget.

Questions and Suggestions

1. Contrast Lamb's reading with the kind Emerson advocated.
   Is Lamb a "book pedant" according to Addison's definition?
   Are Lamb and L. A. G. Strong at all alike?

2. Elaborate upon Lamb's reference to the modern schoolmaster
   as being "sick of perpetual boy" and as having to be "superficially . . . omniscient."

3. Explain why Lamb believes a teacher can exert too constant
   an influence for a student's good. Would that danger be
   more likely to develop and flourish in a public or a preparatory school?

4. Do you agree with Lamb that the "fine old Pedagogues . . .
   who . . . came to their task as to a sport" are now extinct?

5. Jot down the main subjects discussed in this essay and consider their relationship.

6. What purpose does the quoted letter serve? Does Lamb write
   a unified, logically developed essay? Does the form of the
   essay correspond to the approach to knowledge that he describes in the first paragraph?

7. What point does the second paragraph develop? Where is
   the thesis stated?

8. Are the few short paragraphs inconsistent and out of place
   among the long ones that dominate the essay?

9. How does Lamb's vocabulary reveal the contribution that
   Latin made to English? Do you find him using any words
   that are no longer in current usage?

10. Consult the *Dictionary of National Biography* (DNB) for
    brief lives of William Lyly, Thomas Linacre, and John Colet,
    each of whom was connected with famous English schools.

Ideas for Writing

1. Develop a well-organized essay on Lamb's point about the danger of being "stunted downwards by your associates."
2. Write informally of your own experience in getting along with very little knowledge of a subject.
3. Describe an evening you spent with a person who was too anxious to display his own knowledge.
4. Contrast two teachers who you feel currently represent the old and new schoolmasters.
5. Utilizing your own observation and knowledge, present your view on Lamb's point that a teacher's "juniors cannot be his friends."

THESE NICE KIDS

STRINGFELLOW BARR

The son of an Episcopal clergyman, Stringfellow Barr (1897–) was born in Suffolk, Virginia. A graduate of the University of Virginia, he served in the army during World War I, afterwards attending Oxford as a Rhodes Scholar. From 1937 to 1946, Dr. Barr was president of St. John's College, Annapolis. Since then he has taught courses in political science and has been president of the Foundation for World Government, being most active in international organizations that support peace and the alleviation of hunger.

Schneider glanced with a practiced eye at his class and judged there might be thirty students ranged in front of him waiting for him to begin his lecture on the last decades of the nineteenth century. Theoretically, there should have been fifty-three; but May had come around again; his students were beginning to cram for finals; the evenings were getting pleasantly warm; the fancy of the young men was lightly turning to thoughts of girl students, even to some girl students who had left them quite unmoved during the long and bitter winter. So they sat up late now; and lay abed till noon. In short, spring fever had combined with the pressures of memorization to disintegrate Schneider's class.

He supposed he should call the roll and report the absentees. But he had always hated rolls. They had seemed to him so eloquent of the fact that most students found most lectures truly not worth attending and would have been better off in their rooms or at the library, reading. Now and then a form card from the Dean's office reminded him that he was expected to report absences promptly; and he usually did so for several weeks immediately after receiving such a reminder. But he always stopped it again as soon as he dared.

He sat waiting for the bell to ring before beginning his lecture. One or two more students might straggle in. He glanced at his notes. But why repeat these so-called facts about the nineteenth century? Their textbook gave them. The Britannica gave them. Dozens of other books in the library gave them. Why should he make sure their lecture notes gave them too? Why on earth, as a matter of fact, should there be lecture notes? And why should these nice kids be asked to listen to fifteen so-called lectures a week on five different and apparently unrelated subjects?

Had they learned anything whatever from him since September? He wondered. They could scarcely be expected to learn much. He had ample evidence that they had never previously learned to read except in a very loose sense of the word; and, when they took quizzes, their writing was nothing short of terrifying. He already looked forward with horror to the examinations he must grade next month. They would be illegibly written, grossly ungrammatical, whimsically punctuated, and misspelled. As a professional historian who had worked in manuscript collections in several languages, he believed he could decipher nearly any handwriting, on condition that the writer was literate, could spell, could punctuate, and had some notions of grammar. He was confident also that he could read a manuscript with no punctuation whatever, if the words were recognizably spelled and the grammatical structure reasonably intact. But you had to have leverage somewhere.

These nice kids, here in front of him now, had never learned their own mother tongue. Brought up on comic strips, they had listened in infancy to soap operas, and in adolescence they had sat for hours before the television screen. These things had been their books. And,

in terms of what he wanted to say in his lecture this morning, it would
be interesting to know precisely why. How and why do civilizations
collapse and crumble like Nineveh into dust, with or without benefit
of guided missiles? He intended to talk this morning about the period
of European history between 1870 and 1914, a period that slightly
overlapped his own lifetime. He ached to take these students back in
time, into that extraordinary nineteenth-century world, so confident
of continuous progress, so sure of the imminent triumph of man, so
innocent of the horrors just ahead, the massacres, the tortures, the
exiles. But these kids could probably not even remember Hiroshima,
much less Hitler's rape of Poland. The Second World War was now
jumbled in with the other blurred memories of their early childhood.

Some of them just conceivably may have had an elder brother who
fought, or even died, in Korea. But mostly, thought Schneider, they
have lived their lives in a country steadily more and more stupefied by
comfort, more and more hypnotized by the television screen, a country
of "viewers." For viewers they are; spectators; waiting to be amused, and
to be sold. They have lived their lives in a country where it pays not to
say things that other people are not saying. They hope for jobs in business, and they expect their careers to be scrutinized by some monstrous
I.B.M. machine in some automated, chrome-plated office. They do not
propose to join anything or say anything that may cause an I.B.M.
machine to retch, or snort, or even gasp. Although they are terribly
bored from the eyebrows up, they have never known any other state.
And since they are excited and amused from the eyebrows down, it
is not accurate to say that they are depressed.

They live in a mild euphoria, enhanced now by the spring. Schneider
noted that, as spring progressed, they tended to pair off heterosexually
in their choice of seats in his lecture room. At times, he noted, they
even held hands. Not ecstatically, not in the delicious agony of the
romantic, but bucolically. It was clear that, although they were drawn
to each other sexually, it was less as the great lovers of legend than as
puppies who lick food off each other's mouths. They merely took
pleasure in each other. If one of them found a third pup with a stickier
mouth, he or she wandered off and formed a new symbiosis; and,
although Schneider supposed that the deserted pup must feel some
pang or other of rejection and pain, yet some fourth accommodating
pup was likely to turn up all too soon. And so they all went their
dreamlike, pleasant, unstrenuous, unexhilarated way through the merry
month of May, promiscuous and tolerant, viewers and spectators, dy-

namic conservatives, their young hearts bursting with singing commercials.

But aren't these kids ultimately Europeans? he asked himself. It is true that the student body contained a small sprinkle of Negro Americans, of Chinese Americans, of Mexican Americans; but it happened that none of them was in his class. He glanced from the faces before him to his class roll. European names. Almost all of them North European. British, German, Scandinavian, Dutch, one or two Irish. Their grandparents in many cases, their parents perhaps in one or two cases, had been born in Europe. But they had swarmed across the sea to this new Europe of ours, shaking the dust of old Europe unregretfully from their shoes. They had swarmed across the Appalachians, and even across the broad Mississippi. Perhaps they were merely displaced persons, modern history's first vast consignment of D.P.s. Perhaps, thought Schneider, we are viewers primarily because we are the first wave of D.P.s, not yet recovered from the trauma of displacement, missing we know not what, half remembering the things we want to forget, resenting the efforts of Woodrow Wilson and Franklin Roosevelt to pull us back into Europe's orbit, drawn by our manifest destiny toward the Pacific and beyond, haunted by the old dream of Cathay and the newer dream of the Open Door in China, remembering with anger the white crosses of our soldiers killed in Europe's stupid wars, yet eager to shoot Japanese in the Pacific, to seize Pacific islands and to hold them, to follow the setting sun as we have followed it for generations. Would these D.P.s in front of him, dwelling now in their well-fed, hygienic euphoria, their amoral and unstrenuous promiscuity, want to hear about their Homeland of a hundred years ago? Should they want to? He noted their names on the roll, and for the first time his historian's eye was caught by the dullness of their names. Westward the course of dullness takes its way, bringing with it a faceless flotsam with names that remind one of nothing—names, he added to himself, like Schneider.

The class bell jangled shrilly, like a factory bell calling all men to the assembly line. Well, he thought, flotsam and jetsam that we are, here we go together. Let us now remember. He kept his seat at the little table and began to speak. He had thrust his notes from him.

"In the second half of the nineteenth century," he said, "we enter the Age of Progress. It is the age I was myself born into, although in 1914, when it came crashing to the ground, I was too young to know that my world had tottered. It is a world which, of course, you never lived in; but your grandfathers lived in it, and I should like to suggest this morning what sort of world they lived in and what gods they believed in. For clearly I do not mean that modern science and technology stopped progressing in 1914. Even if I told you it had, you wouldn't believe me. You know better.

"But when you and I started this course together, you may remember I pictured to you a Europe filled with petty wars, it is true, but united also by common memories of the crusades, worshiping in cathedrals dedicated to the same saints, tilling the fields for their daily bread, and living—at least, most Europeans—in similar huts and cottages. I tried to suggest that the El Dorado Columbus sought when he sailed west, a land of gold and gems, took the place in many men's imaginations of the Christian Paradise; and that the very painters of Europe in the Renaissance turned from the religious insights of Italian primitives to the brilliant, joyous portrayal of this world. I said that Luther and Calvin tried to call Europe back to her love of the invisible and unworldly, but that Shakespeare and Racine were calling European man to go forward to his tragic destiny. Galileo was calling him to the truth of his universe, in defiance of the Church's edicts. I told you about the great capitalists like Fugger of Augsburg; of the slave traders that ransacked the coasts of Africa for human labor to develop El Dorado and enrich their owners. I told you of the conquest of India, and eventually of much of Asia. Of the little children working under the lash in England's factories at the new machines; of the armies of Napoleon smashing the feudal structure of Western Europe.

"Now I want to speak of the middle-class paradise that the new machines built in Europe, with the help of millions of sweating, starving, dying coolies in Asia, and Negroes in the two Americas. Actually, we have been trying for eight months to understand a series of religions that Christendom has tried to substitute for the Christian doctrines of the Middle Ages. This morning I want to talk about the religion of progress, of the theology of science, of man's worship of the machine, and of his firm belief that by his own efforts he could bring Heaven to earth for you and me, his descendants.

"So-called pure science was as remote from the average man as God the Father had been, and maybe remoter. But it rapidly became applied science and entered the familiar daily world of Western man. Abstract scientific laws became incarnate in the machine, took on flesh, became modern man's mediator and redeemer. The machine mediated by becoming like man and dwelling among men: by pump-

ing out mines as he had pumped out mines, by drawing his water,
hewing his wood, spinning his thread and weaving his garments, by
bearing his burdens faster than he could bear them, paddling his boats,
plowing his fields, reaping his grain, and making his daily bread. The
machine redeemed man from toil—or promised to. It entered into the
hospital to heal him of sickness, or to protect him from pain. It trans-
figured itself into a telegraph and carried his messages by code; or into
a telephone and put him in communion with all those who truly turn
to the telephone; or into a radio and brought him knowledge and entertainment in his loneliness. It became a telescope and let him gaze at
stars no man had seen. It became a submarine and took him to the
depths that only the fish had known. It took on wings and lifted him
toward the heavens themselves."

Schneider had started speaking quietly; but as he spoke, such an
overpowering vision of Western man's dream of material progress seized
him that the words poured uncontrollably from his mouth. However,
when he looked around, he saw that a good half of his class was not
with him. Some were studying for a quiz that loomed ahead of them
later in the day. One was covertly reading the comics. A couple of co-eds
were busy with their make-up, studying their faces in the mirrors of
their compacts. A singularly pretty girl, with a shapely body and
empty, regular face, who never wore jeans but always dressed in charming skirts, had as usual managed to arrange her skirt and her legs so
that Schneider and only Schneider could catch just a glimpse of one
white thigh. She had often paid Schneider this personal compliment
in the past: whether from sheer exhibitionism or to see whether she
could put him out of countenance, or to soften him up when he came
to grade her wretched examination paper, he could never guess. He
had always in the past found her stimulating, but today he barely saw
her in his excitement over a period into which he, though not she,
had been born.

As a matter of fact, something else had caught his eye. A lad halfway
back on the other side of the room had started to lean forward as
Schneider spoke. He had a pale, oval face, quite unlike the acres of
uncharted flesh that most of his students used for faces. His hair was
slightly disordered. His eyes were fixed on Schneider and were burning
with interest as Schneider evoked these lost and confident decades.
Schneider forgot the others and hurried on, as if he were talking to
him and to him alone. But as his own excitement grew, he rose from
his chair and paced slowly in front of the blackboard while he spoke.

"The machine," he said, "would mediate between abstract science and the daily, concrete needs of man only if man imitated his new redeemer by achieving increased mechanical efficiency. And so man learned to imitate the machine, by living intimately with it, by serving it faithfully and promptly. It was a severe discipline, but it promised him redemption from all the evils of this life. It promised him his lost 'dominion over creation.' It promised him power and proud citizenship in a new city, the City of Nature, whose name is Industrialism, whose inexorable rulers are Matter and Force, and whose missionaries are commanded to spread ceaselessly the use of the machine. Like Augustine's City of God, this city too would be a pilgrim city, moving through the desert of agrarian peasant society with its primitive techniques, its poverty, its ignorance, and its military impotence."

He talked on, engrossed by the vision before him, and the young student with the burning eyes never glanced from his face. They were both unconscious of the co-eds who now manicured, of the students who jotted down for no genuine reason fragments of Schneider's tumultuous lecture, of one student who had fallen asleep. And Schneider spoke of the doubts that John Ruskin and William Morris had expressed; of the artists, like Van Gogh, who had gone insane, or, like Gauguin, to the South Seas; of the impressionists, the cubists. Of that new animal, the social scientist, who reported the facts of the social order and who more often than not failed to ask what a good life was. Of naturalism in literature. And of Baudelaire's bitter eloquence about the horrible burden of boredom.

He spoke, too, of the immigrants who crowded from Europe to America.

"What this river of immigrants," he said, "contributed to America besides their muscle, their energy, and their skill depends in part on what was in their hearts when they left Europe. There are no statistics on that, and there can of course be none. But all the evidence suggests that they sought primarily economic opportunity, the nineteenth-century form of personal salvation. They sought, too, freedom from the burden of military conscription, that burden which the democratic era had brought Europe's system of sovereign nation-states. And in America, where even second-rate skills fetched rewards that first-rate skills in Europe could not guarantee, they learned better even than Europe the optimism of the Age of Progress. They learned that land can be not only a peasant's family heritage but real estate, capable of bringing enormous unearned increment. They learned the joys of an anarchical economic system in an environment of apparently unlimited resources. They learned to reverse exactly the medieval hierarchy of economic pursuits; to respect, first the financier, whose backing would open a golden West; next, the businessman, the industrialist, who supplied clothes and shelter; and last, the farmer, who produced only the food without which all would perish, but who was thrust aside in American esteem by the growing power of urban business."

But America was Cardwell's field, and Schneider guiltily skipped back to Europe, to Auguste Comte, to *Lockesley Hall*, to Victor Hugo, to Darwin, and to Herbert Spencer's vision of necessary progress.

"By the opening years of this century you were born in," he said, while the boy's eyes burned brightly in the sea of bored or neutral faces, "the citizens of Christendom proudly stood on a pinnacle of material power that exceeded every previous dream of man. Moreover, the pinnacle had been built by man's own efforts and hence invited an understandable pride. It had been built by human reason, by 'the scientific method,' by a rapidly growing technology. The rules were already known by which this mighty skyscraper city could be built even higher. To the critic who scoffed that it was a purely material achievement, modern man could reply that not only were he and his fellow citizens more comfortable physically than their fathers had been but that liberalism was everywhere triumphant or about to triumph, that political privilege had been sharply curtailed, that economic privilege was under attack, that, in short, social justice was a goal universally professed. If religion and art seemed often to be lagging, might not that be that they still lacked an adequate material base? Seek ye first a high standard of living, and all these things shall be added unto you. It was good to be alive in the years of man's unbelievable power and of man's increasing hope for the future. It was good to be alive in the opening years of the twentieth century, this century, your century and mine, for they were in all truth wonderful, glittering years."

He paused and looked about him as if in sudden pain. Some of his students stared curiously. Breathing harder, he began again.

"From this bourgeois, Baconian Eden modern man was ejected with a sudden violence unique in his experience. In a few days, millions of men were mobilized to kill and be killed. It was as if some terrible madness had seized on the citizens of the city that Matter and Force had so benignly ruled. Across the tranquil, smiling, midsummer countryside of Europe swept vast armies, bearing more deadly weapons than man had ever known. The earth rocked and the sky reeled. The great gray ships of the British Royal Navy hurried silently to their appointed posts. It was the summer of 1914."

Suddenly, such violent emotions arose in Schneider that he knew he could not go on. He glanced at his watch. There was lots of time left— but it was time he could not use. His throat became dry; his voice came to his own ears as if from a great distance. He felt slightly dizzy.

"I cannot discuss the First World War today. I am sorry."

He bowed slightly, rose clumsily to his feet, and left his classroom. What had he said, he wondered. Had any of it made sense? It seemed to him to have a certain rhythm. Had it had any genuine, logical structure? Whether it had or not, they were not interested, except for that one boy. They would remember nothing.

Questions and Suggestions

1. Do you agree with Professor Schneider about college students? Is he unduly bitter?

2. Have his students met the standards for reading set by Emerson?

3. How do "these nice kids" differ from L. A. G. Strong's "happily ignorant" men?

4. What tendency in education is revealed by Schneider's sudden recollection: (a) that Cardwell taught American history; and (b) his realization that most students rely on last minute memorization?

5. What does Schneider mean when he suggests that progress in science and technology stopped in 1914?

6. Analyze the paragraphing and sentence structure of his lecture. Do you find many examples of parallelism? Does he illustrate his points and expand them sufficiently?

7. Schneider thinks and speaks as one inspired. Analyze his use of such familiar phrases as "manifest destiny," "westward the course," "dwelling among men," and "Seek ye first." What does he mean by *Baconian Eden, bucolically, symbiosis, trauma,* and *euphoria*?

Ideas for Writing

1. Write a paper, preferably taking a stand, on today's "substitutes for books," "notes and lectures," or "the Age of Progress."

2. Recreate one of your own history classes, comparing your teacher with Schneider and your classmates with the students in his class.

3. By consulting files of newspapers and by talking with people who experienced the effects of the depression of the 1930's, write an essay that conveys your impression of the uncertainty and hardship of those years. Or choose some other " 'world . . . you never lived in' " and do the same for it. You could try to recreate such war-time experiences as those suffered by the people of Hiroshima, soldiers in combat, and civilians in an occupied city. Books such as John Hersey's *Hiroshima,* Stephen Crane's *The Red Badge of Courage,* and Anne Frank's *The Diary of a Young Girl* offer vivid presentations of such ordeals.

A BITTER FARCE

DELMORE SCHWARTZ

A native of Brooklyn, Delmore Schwartz (1913–) studied at Columbia, Wisconsin, Harvard, and New York University. He has been a teacher and lecturer at various colleges and universities. Mr. Schwartz is best known as a poet, translator, editor, critic, and the author of a number of short stories and experimental plays. *Genesis,* told in prose and poetry, is the story of the making of an American, Hershey Green, a child of New York whose parents came from Europe at the turn of the century.

The summer was a very difficult summer for Mr. Fish, youthful teacher of composition and author of promise. He had never before taught in the wet heat of summer, and now he was teaching Navy students, some of whom had been in action in the Pacific. He also taught a class of girls which differed in no way from his former classes in composition.

It was soon clear to Mr. Fish that the students of the Navy must be taught elementary things carefully and clearly. Yet such was the heat and the difficulty of teaching during the summer that he was quickly drawn from discussions of spelling and grammar to other matters, matters which are sometimes referred to as topics of the day.

Soon the two Navy classes regarded Mr. Fish as an authority. The

From *The World is a Wedding.* Copyright 1948 by Delmore Schwartz. Reprinted by permission of New Directions, Publishers.

reason or reasons for this view were obscure both to Mr. Fish and his students. It was a view vague, strong and general; and Mr. Fish thought that perhaps his worn indifference had entered into his tone when he expressed opinions, and thus impressed the boys as authoritative.

This was the second summer of America's part in the war. The feeling of mid-war was everywhere because no one was able to see how the war might end very soon. Hence it was that Mr. Fish was asked by his students to express his opinions as to the establishment of a second front, the existence of a secret weapon, and Hitler's generalship.

Had he been cooler and more energetic, he would often have refused the seductions of such discussion or his replies would have been of a different character. As it was, he was worn and warm enough to state both sides of every question so that they both appeared to be very true. The boys were charmed by the somersaults of dialectic and did not mind in the least. They begged Mr. Fish to begin a discussion at the least pretext.

Thus he was asked about when the second front would be launched and if it would be successful.

"The question of opening a second front will be fully understood in a hundred years, very little will be understood until the end of the war," he observed, before beginning a new discussion of grammar and spelling. "The war, however, will be over long before some members of the Navy learn how to spell. But let us make an effort."

These judicious evasions and quick transitions delighted the Navy students.

And when the Detroit race riots occurred during this second summer of the war, the Navy's students wished to know what Mr. Fish thought of the Negro problem.

"It can't be stated in black and white," he said, and the students groaned as he had known they would, although on the other hand he had little idea that he was about to fall into a pun when he began the sentence.

"What do you think ought to be done?" asked one of the students, inspired in part by interest and in part by a desire to avoid the serious drill in grammar.

"What I think can be done or ought to be done," said the withdrawn Mr. Fish, touched somewhat by the interest of the boys in his opinion, "cannot conceivably have much effect on anyone. Yet, for the little that it is worth, which is probably nothing, I will say this: that nothing at all can be done in the South, except for the Negroes to

depart from the South. Any other course would result in a resumption
of the Civil War. On the other hand, this is a very big country, and it
is as yet largely unsettled. There is no reason why some region cannot
be chosen where a strict equality would be enforced. Yet equality
cannot be dictated merely by signing a bill. The process would take a
hundred years. By that time all of us will be dead and you will have no
way of knowing if this is a good idea—"

At least half of the students in the Navy were from the South, as
Mr. Fish knew very well. One of them raised his hand and waved it
like a baseball bat, being excited.

"Where will this region be?" he asked in a hurry.

"Don't be disturbed," said Mr. Fish. "This is merely the idle idea of
a teacher of composition who plays no part in the fabulous destiny of
the aging republic—"

He knew that this student feared that the imaginary region might
be near his own home, which was Missouri, one of the border states.

Another boy raised his hand. This boy's name was Murphy, and he
had often been disturbed by Mr. Fish. Tall, strong, broad-shouldered,
and black-haired, his face often wore an expression of anger.

"It's just like a dog show, sir," he said, speaking of the race riots.
"The thoroughbred dogs will always fight with the mongrels."

"Mr. Long," said Mr. Fish, speaking to a student who came from
Texas, "Mr. Murphy has just called all Southerners dogs: are you going
to let him get away with that?"

The class laughed and Mr. Murphy looked disgusted. He felt that
he had made a serious point and the instructor had dismissed it with
a play on words.

"Now," said Mr. Fish, "we had better return to the difference between the use of the semicolon and the comma. It is possible, as I said
the other day, that the absence of a comma may result in the death of
a man—"

"Sir," said one of the boys in the back of the classroom, a Mr. Kent,
who had not awaited the recognition of his raised hand, "I want to ask
just one more question about your idea about the blacks: would you
marry a Negro woman?"

Mr. Fish had anticipated the possibility of this question the moment
that the question of the Negroes had arisen. And from previous conversations in very different circumstances, he had derived an answer,
which was to be uttered in the mock-grand style. He was going to say
that he would marry any woman to whom he made love because other-

wise his children might be illegitimate. He felt that this might touch both the sense of honor and the memory of experience in some of them.

(Mr. Fish felt that in this way he turned the tables on his questioners and put them on the defensive. In the same way, when the war began, he was prepared to be asked why he was not in uniform and he was going to reply, "That is a very good question. Why don't you write to my draft board? I will give you the address." But the question was never asked, a significant silence.)

So, as these thoughts passed quickly through the teacher's head, he decided that it would be ill-advised to make such an answer, for any reference to sexual intercourse brought about an unfortunate period in the classroom, a period in which the giggle and the smirk entered like English horn and flute.

"Your question is an old one," said Mr. Fish, to gain time, "and an interesting one."

Mr. Fish knew very well that if he confessed a willingness to marry a Negro woman, he would lose face with his students. They would not forgive him the admission. On the other hand, if he said that he would not marry a black woman, his students would regard him as having admitted that he believed in social inequality, just as they did. And this would be a betrayal of the principles he supposed himself to believe with his whole mind and heart.

"The fact is," continued Mr. Fish, speaking to the waiting and troubled boys, "I don't know any Negroes. I don't know why I don't, certainly I have not been avoiding them: it just happens that I have not been introduced to any of them. Hence the question is one which in a sense has no meaning for me—"

The students groaned in a species of triumph, for they regarded this as an obvious evasion and confession.

Prompted by the groan, Mr. Fish felt that he must go further. Self-contained and constricted was his appearance; but his inner being was suddenly full of fear and trembling.

"I would not marry a Negro woman," he said having decided quickly, "but there are many white women whom I would not marry for the same reasons that I would not marry a Negro woman. Thus it is not a question of discrimination against the Negro race. Enough now of this discussion of my private life and marriage—"

The class relaxed. The boys from the South were relieved to hear that Mr. Fish would not marry a black woman. Some of the students did not really understand what Mr Fish had answered. Mr. Fish at the moment was wondering just what he meant, although he had no doubt about the success of his answer. Most of the students felt then that Mr. Fish would not marry many white women as well as Negro women because he was a Jew. And this pleased them very much; they were pleased to the depths of their being. However, they had misunderstood him.

After teaching the students of the Navy at the University, Mr. Fish went to get his lunch. He ate in a state of abstraction, thinking of all the remarks he might have made and had not made about the problem of race prejudice. He said to himself that he was only a teacher of the ways to use the powerful English language. But language was involved in all things, and he felt now a sense of insufficiency and withdrawal. He had turned aside, as often before; he had side-stepped a matter about which he felt that he ought to be direct, blunt and frank as to his conviction and belief. Soon, in less than an hour, he was going to meet some of the students in his class of girls. For two years now he had taught a class of boys and then walked across the campus to teach a class of girls, and at times it seemed to him that it was as if he went to teach in another country when he taught the girls, or at least as if he taught another subject. For the girls were unlike the boys as students in many ways. They did not like to argue, but the boys argued at the drop of a hat. They were passive, polite and docile, the antithesis of the boys in each of these things. And this made it necessary that the teacher be more active. It was often useful to use the method of asking questions and discussing the answers, so that instead of the oppression of passive listening, the students participated in the hour as if they played a game.

To some extent it was possible to make more progress with female students when they came to what was termed conference, a period of half an hour during which the teacher conversed privately with the student, either reviewing themes which had already been corrected, or trying to help the student in thinking about the subject of a new theme. The girls were often selfconscious and constrained then, for they were still adolescent and to be alone with a young man summoned up such feelings in them. But on the whole, this part of teaching, which was very like tutoring, was interesting and useful so far as Mr. Fish was concerned. It was for him a way of coming to know human beings with whom otherwise he would never have had much acquaintance.

The girls had of late been asked to keep a journal in which each night they made observations of the interesting things they had seen or heard during the day. The purpose of this journal was to create the

habit of articulating one's perceptions, of moving in mind habitually
from thing to word; and then also the improvised and informal character of the journal was intended to free the student from the inhibitions overpowering them when they had to write a formal theme. This
task of the journal had proved to be a very successful one when introduced during the previous year.

When Mr. Fish came to his office, Miss Lucy Eberhart awaited him.
She was a tall blonde and blue-eyed girl, who looked as if she might
become pretty at some later date. Now, at eighteen, she looked somewhat gawky, and she was both nervous and self-conscious, a fact which
expressed itself in unwieldy movements of her limbs. As she sat down
in the chair which faced the teacher's desk, she pulled down the skirt
over her bare legs with an unnecessary emphasis; she pulled it down
as if it had been up too high and as if the instructor had been glancing
at her legs. But he had not; he had begun to read the first entry of her
journal, which was entitled, for that day:

Just Some Thoughts

At lunch today, two of my friends and I had a most interesting
discussion. One of the girls suddenly asked: "If you had to marry
one of them, which of these three would you choose, a Chinaman, a Jew, or a Negro?" We all immediately agreed that we
wouldn't marry at all! But for the sake of argument we agreed
that we had to marry one, and that all of them were intelligent,
well-educated, and also good-looking for their respective races.
Each of the three was a native of his particular home country,
although all could speak English and were refined gentlemen.
I, for one, positively could not make up my mind. My two pals,
after pondering the situation for several minutes, guessed that
they would choose the Chinaman, certainly not the Negro. "And
why would you marry the Chinaman? Why not the Jew?" I asked.
"Even if he were from Syria, I think he would be more like us
physically than the Chinaman." My friends were not very definite.
They pointed out that there is something about Jews that other
races can't stand. It always comes out sooner or later. Some Jews
are charming people, but even the best simply are not liked, because, well, they are demanding, grasping, almost unscrupulous
about the way they get what they want. On the other hand according to my friends, the Chinese are very friendly, and the educated
ones seem unusually intelligent.

But I wonder if there is not another reason for their choice.
Although perhaps there is less prejudice here against the races
than in some other countries, America has its share of intolerance.

Because the Negroes were once our slaves, it is easy to see that even now we consider them distinctly inferior. There is certainly prejudice against the Jews as well. Possibly some of it is jealousy because the Jews have managed to wangle themselves into good positions and make money. But it seems that everywhere they go, they make enemies by their attitude, and barbarous methods of reaching their goals. Ah! but the Chinamen! For years we have been trying to help the Chinese—today they are our allies in war! We have no bone to pick with them, and we are sorry for them.

If the choice of my two friends was influenced by these factors, in my mind their selection was not quite just. Therefore, I think if I were placed in that horrible position, and must marry one of the three men, I would choose the one who was the fairest and most honest, the kindest, and he whose ideas most nearly coincided with mine.

"This is very interesting, Miss Eberhart," said Mr. Fish, amazed to such an extent that for the moment his only emotion was amazement. He asked the student if the other two girls were also in the same English class, and he was told that one of them was, and the one who was had told her not to make the conversation about marriage the subject of her journal entry, but she had decided to do so anyway.

"O no, Miss Eberhart," said Mr. Fish, "to say what you think and to be sincere, to use what is in your own mind is the purpose of this kind of assignment. Your writing improves if you draw directly upon your feelings. However, there are faults in expression here. As I have pointed out before, you ought not to use such a colloquialism as 'wangled' in a piece of writing. And then, to speak of 'refined gentlemen' is a redundancy, since the idea of gentleman includes the idea of refinement. You make an error in idiomatic usage also when you write 'in my mind,' and not 'to my mind.' Be careful with prepositions especially, for most errors in idiom occur in the use of prepositions. As for the content of your entry, I don't think that it is necessary for me to make any comment upon it."

"I didn't mean to take a crack at anybody," said Miss Eberhart to Mr. Fish's surprise, for nothing in his tone seemed to him to express resentment or distaste.

Mr. Fish was silent for a moment. He was seeking to consult his feelings, and he felt only that certain feelings were absent which perhaps should be present.

Miss Eberhart gazed at him and waited for a final word before she departed from the conference.

"Apart from the errors I have mentioned, Miss Eberhart," said Mr. Fish at last, "this is a satisfactory piece of work, and a fulfillment of the assignment. I believe there are some Chinese at the university at present—"

He paused. I don't want to say that, he said to himself, for Miss Eberhart's nostrils had flared as he spoke.

"But," he continued, compelled, "I am told that on the Pacific Coast, the Chinese are disliked very much too, or were for a time, until the Exclusion Act was passed.

"However, I can speak with authority only on matters of the choice of words, sentence structure, and clear thought. If you have no questions, that will be all for today." He had become more and more formal as he continued, formality being his only recourse when worn out.

"No crack was intended," said Miss Eberhart, perplexed and nervous.

"Miss Eberhart, to use words like crack or words like wangle is to succumb to slang usages. You can be simple, natural, and direct without using slang."

"Thank you very much, Mr. Fish," said Miss Eberhart, departing because Mr. Fish had given her her notebook in a way that meant that the conference was concluded.

It would be hard to say why Mr. Fish did not think more of this incident after it was concluded. Perhaps the concerns of his private life were such that his mind had no time to be occupied with it. Certainly he did not like the occurrence. Yet it provoked in him few strong feelings.

Two days after, when he went to teach his students of the Navy, the classroom work was supposed to be based upon a reading assignment in the textbook especially prepared for the Navy boys. The assignment on this day was an essay on the immigrant in America by Louis Adamic. The essay was fitly entitled "Plymouth Rock and Ellis Island," and its gist, made with many careful qualifications, was that America's power and glory had been made possible by immigrant labor, by the acceptance of differences among human beings, by the diversity of many racial strains. The hope of the world, said Adamic, was here just because of this diversity of peoples; and this made the possibility of a universal culture, a pan-human culture, such as had never before existed on the globe. And this was the American Dream and the American Tradition. Adamic made his argument specific by speaking of the Germans, the Jews, and the Negroes especially as peoples who might be subjected to race-prejudice, to the hatred of those who are different from oneself.

And he observed that if the German people had produced Hitler, they had also produced Thomas Mann.

Mr. Fish revolved the essay in his mind as he walked to the classroom. It was natural that he should be reminded of his conference with Miss Eberhart, and his classroom discussion of the Negroes. He resolved to review the essay quickly and not permit the hour to be wasted in a general discussion which would accomplish nothing at all but the expression of dark opinions.

And yet, since Mr. Fish had as a matter of habitual method often expressed grave doubts as to the assigned reading, he found himself criticizing Adamic too. It was a matter of method with him because he had often told his students never to accept anything printed without rigorous examination. And as he drew forth by means of questions a summary of Adamic's argument, he said:

"What Adamic has to say is true, in part; but we ought also to remember that if America has always been the land of liberty, it has also been the land of the witch-hunt and the lynching party, the land of persecution and the land where everyone feared that he was a stranger or was conscious of a fear of the stranger. That this is true does not in the least deny or contradict the truth of what Adamic says. This has been the land of liberty and of persecution from the days when witches were burned in Salem until the day four weeks ago when the race riot occurred in Detroit, or the riot in May in Los Angeles when the sailors beat up the zoot suit boys. These riots, riots of just this kind, would not occur if this were not also the land of liberty."

The instructor's criticism of Adamic emboldened the black-haired Mr. Murphy who also disagreed with the text.

"Take the Jews, sir," said Mr. Murphy, "Adamic says that there is [and now he read from his book] 'a tendency among the Jews in many parts of the country to suppress their talents, and to draw apart.' That's not true. And not only that, there is something wrong with a lot of Jews. Some of them are all right. But a lot of them are not. I know from personal experience because I worked for a couple of them—"

There were three Jewish students in this Navy class, and Mr. Fish's glance took in their responses. One of them made believe that he was intent upon his textbook, and one of them turned white. The third looked stolidly ahead at the blackboard, and Mr. Fish was unable in a quick glance to make out what his feelings were. But the dead white face of one of the Jewish boys made Mr. Fish feel that something must be said; or perhaps he spoke for a deeper reason of which he was unaware; or perhaps he was merely feeling fluent and argumentative on that day; or perhaps he had in mind Miss Eberhart's journal.

"You say," he said to the black-haired Murphy, "that you know from personal experience that some Jews, indeed many Jews, are no good. Are you Irish?" He knew very well that Murphy was Irish.

Murphy affirmed that both his mother and his father were Irish.

"Do you know what is said of the Irish very often in this city? It is said that the Irish are drunken and truculent. Now I know from personal experience that the man who lives next door to me, who is Irish, gets drunk on Saturday nights and beats up his wife. Does that mean that I have justification for hating most of the Irish or condemning them as drunken and truculent?"

"I know the Irish," said Murphy, "and I know that that's not true of most of them."

"I know the Jews, I might say to you," said Mr. Fish, "and I know that what you say of them can be shown to be untrue in many instances. On the other hand, there are instances which prove the truth of what is said of both the Jews and the Irish. It is true that the Jews, since they have engaged for centuries in financial dealings, practice some of the methods which make the commercial world infamous. You're a Catholic: do you know why the Jews have been more a commercial people than anything else?"

"I don't know," said Murphy with the tone of one who is judicious enough to admit his own ignorance when it is true that he is ignorant.

"They have been a commercial people," said Mr. Fish, "because that is all they were permitted to be by the decree of the Catholic Church. Do you know why the Pope decreed that the Jews might be usurers? Because usury was a sin against nature; and one which led to the damnation of the soul. It was all right for Jews to be usurers because they were damned in any case, in view of the Holy Father. Thus by civil and theological decree, the Jews were prevented from doing that which is right and condemned to do that which is a mortal sin. Do you think that that is a good, noble or religious way to treat a people?"

"Well, why did they do it?" asked Murphy.

"They had no choice: and I might ask you why the Holy Apostolic Church behaved in this way? To get others to do your usurious banking for you is no less a sin than to get another man to do your murdering for you, or is it?" said Mr. Fish, carried away by his own rapid association of ideas, for he had never thought of the matter in this way before this particular occasion, and knew nothing of usury.

"The Jews seem to have taken it pretty well," said Murphy. "They were suited for it."

"How did they get to be suited for it?" said Mr. Fish, feeling in himself the rise of a flood of rhetoric.

"I don't know," said Murphy pensively. His face wore the look of one who was involved in much more than he had intended or expected. He hesitated. "They are traitors by inheritance, I guess."

"How can you be a traitor by inheritance?" asked Mr. Fish, rising to a pitch of intensity in tone. "Can a moral act be inherited? Can anyone be condemned to death as a murderer because his father is a murderer?"

To this surprising question there was no answer.

By now the classroom was silent and electrified.

"No," said Mr. Fish, "among the civilized nations, no man is by law responsible for the crimes of another man. Hence, even if the worst that is said of the Jews were true, it is illegal (and it is also immoral) to blame any Jew in advance—"

(By this time Mr. Fish was anticipating in his own mind objections and questions which would never have occurred to his students.)

"For even if we grant that there are inherited patterns of behavior, like inherited diseases and inherited features, no one can be sure in advance that any person, starting from the moment of his birth, is bound to have a certain kind of character. How many great men have had great sons? Very few. Nonetheless, even if we grant a certain tendency to behave as one's parents, it is an abomination to condemn any man before he has committed a crime. And this is exactly what race prejudice does: it is a denial of the freedom of the will and of moral responsibility. How many in this class are Irish?"

Half the class raised hands, including a boy named Cohan, who looked very Jewish or Irish. Mr. Fish thought that he was joking, but this was untrue.

"Let me state at this point," said Mr. Fish, pleased by what he took to be Cohan's wit and the class's good humor, "that some of my best friends are Irish—"

He awaited laughter, but the boys did not understand.

"—and some of my best friends are anti-Semitic: what can I do?"

Again the boys were perplexed, though interested.

"Two of the modern authors I admire most of all are Irish, and it might be maintained that if they had not been Irish but English, they might not have been great authors—"

This meant nothing to the boys. Mr. Fish decided to use a new argument.

"Let us consider," said Mr. Fish, "the proposition Mr. Murphy stated just before, that the Jews were traitors by inheritance."

Quickly Mr. Fish drew a crude map of Ireland upon the blackboard. He was inspired at the moment by James Joyce.

"If we wish to indulge in prejudice, then this map shows how the Irish are traitors visibly upon the map. That author I spoke of a moment ago once wrote that all Ireland was battling against the rest of Ireland. He referred to the division between Ireland and Ulster."

Mr. Fish pointed to the map. "The Irish to one who does not like them may be said to be traitors by tradition. Their efforts at liberation have often been weakened or betrayed by renegade Irishmen."

"I myself," said Mr. Fish, after a rhetorical silence, "am of Russian-Jewish distinction. I mean detraction. I feel very proud of my ancestors, who wrote the Bible and other great works of aspiration, morality and fiction which have been the basis of Western culture for the past two thousand years at least. My ancestors, in whom I take pride, but not personal pride, were scholars, poets, prophets and students of God when most of Europe worshipped sticks and stones: not that I hold that against any of you, for it is not your fault if your forbears were barbarians grovelling and groping about for peat or something.

"Nonetheless I must confess a great shame to you, an ancestor of mine who was also a barbarian."

Mr. Fish told the class to observe his high cheek bones and wide-set eyes.

"My face bears the mark of some Mongolian rapist. Some Mongolian barbarian raped one of my greatgrandmothers. In the Jewish community a man was honor bound to accept such a child of rape as his own; thus I am, alas, as the mirror repeats to me often, a mongrel Mongol.

"But here a very important question presents itself: it appears to be likely that the Mongolians are the ancestors of the American Indians, who are the only true natives of this country of ours, America. Thus I may say that from the point of view of race I am of Indian distraction or destruction. I am a hundred and fifty per cent American. Hence I may say to you, Mr. Murphy, why don't you go back where you came from, if you don't like the class of people here?"

It was difficult to say whether the teacher and the class were more pleased or appalled by this formulation.

The bell rang, concluding the hour. Four excited students of the
Navy stood at Mr. Fish's desk to discuss the whole matter with him.
Everyone was in good spirits. Mr. Murphy also waited to speak to
Mr. Fish.

"It is better in the Southwest," said a boy from Texas, "there Jews
and white people intermarry and no one thinks anything about it—"

"I am olive-skinned myself," said Mr. Fish, "but I know just what
you mean" (for the Texan had intended to be amiable and condemn
the wicked decadent East).

"Another wasted hour," said Mr. Fish as he took up books and papers,
and prepared to depart from the classroom in the company of the four
students.

"Do you know," he said to one of them, "a good many of the things
I have just said to the class were merely verbalism—ratiocination—"
(he searched for the word which would be clear to them, gazing at
their perplexed looks)—"I was just playing a game with facts and with
words, after a time."

Then Mr. Fish saw that Murphy still waited apart to speak to him.

He bade the other boys goodbye and Murphy made his approach.

"Sir," said Murphy, "they shouldn't have put such essays in the
textbook. They're troublemakers."

Now they walked upon the campus, crowded with the students of
changing classes.

"Mr. Murphy," said Mr. Fish, "I don't really care what you say. But
you ought not to say such things. It is foolish of you. Even if it is true, it
is a foolish thing to say and if you said it in another class, you might
get into trouble. I don't know what the rules about such expressions of
race feeling are, but I suspect that it is forbidden to bring such feelings
into the open air of the classroom."

"I have nothing against you," said Murphy, "you always give me a
square deal."

"I am glad that you think so," said Mr. Fish, "an interesting thought
just entered my mind: if I reported you to your commanding officer,
then you might get into trouble, for as an officer-to-be you have shown
an extraordinary lack of tact and discretion. Perhaps it is my duty to
report this incident to your commanding officer, although I certainly
will not report you."

"Thanks a lot," said Murphy, his brows contracted with concern,
"they certainly ought to be more careful about what they put in these
textbooks."

"There is nothing wrong with the textbook," said Mr. Fish. "I must go now, but I want to ask you one more question, which is, since I am a Jew and since you have publicly insulted my own people, why don't I report you?"

"I told you I knew that some Jews are all right," said Murphy.

"Answer my question," said Mr. Fish, "why don't I report you, since perhaps I ought to report you?"

"I don't know why," said Mr. Murphy.

"Neither do I," said Mr. Fish as he returned to his home to await the arrival of innumerable anxiety feelings which had their source in events which had occurred for the past five thousand years.

Questions and Suggestions

1. Compare Mr. Fish's navy students and Mr. Schneider's postwar class.

2. Do you agree with Murphy that collections of essays should not contain "troublemakers"? How might Murphy feel about this story?

3. Discuss Fish's reaction to the student's journal.

4. Why were many of the students pleased by Fish's answer to the question about marriage? Why does he virtually repudiate his impassioned argument against racial intolerance? What does the last sentence in the story mean?

5. What does the story reveal about human behavior?

6. Does Schwartz tell this story from a single point of view? Is it in any sense like a play? Recall the conclusion you reached about Laurie Lee's "The Kitchen."

7. Discuss Fish's use of *distraction* and *detraction*. What is the etymological meaning of *pun*?

8. Explain "somersaults of dialectic," "a rhetorical silence," and "a state of abstraction." What is the meaning of *verbalism* and *ratiocination*?

9. How effective is the title?

Ideas for Writing

1. Write a journal entry similar to Lucy Eberhart's in which you record your reaction to a situation involving irrational behavior.

2. Analyze a generalization about another race or nationality group that you have accepted as being true.

3. Poignant situations serve as the focal point in the following stories: "A Gift of Light," in Elizabeth Enright's *The Riddle*

of the Fly; "A Bad Streak," in Brian Glanville's *A Bad Streak;*
"A Home for Highland Cattle," in Doris Lessing's *Five;* and
"The Dignity of Night" in Klaus Roehler's *The Dignity of
Night.* Compare or contrast one of these episodes with a
personal experience.

4. Consider this story against the background of recent events
and then give your reaction to one of the following statements: (a) "Yet equality cannot be dictated merely by signing
a bill." (b) ". . . they certainly ought to be more careful about
what they put in these textbooks." (c) ". . . race prejudice
. . . is a denial of the freedom of the will and of moral
responsibility."

WHAT WE DON'T KNOW
WILL HURT US

A. WHITNEY GRISWOLD

In 1950, Dr. A. Whitney Griswold (1906–) became the sixteenth
president of Yale University. Born in Morristown, New Jersey, he
received his degrees from Yale. In 1933 he became an instructor
in the history department, rising to a full professorship by 1947.
His first book, *The Far Eastern Policy of the United States,* appeared in 1938. It was through the study of history that Dr.
Griswold came to his conviction that many young Americans must
have a chance at a liberal education, an education "that contributes directly to knowledge, freedom and civilization." Further,
he agrees with Jefferson: " 'If a nation expects to be ignorant and
free, in a state of civilization, it expects what never was and
never will be.' "

The conflict which rages around our schools is not a conflict
between public and private institutions. It is a conflict between two

From *Liberal Education and the Democratic Ideal and Other Essays.*
Copyright © 1959. Published by Yale University Press, Inc. Reprinted
by the generous permission of the author.

different types of learning. Until we understand it as such, we are not likely to solve the many problems it involves—the acute shortage of teachers and schoolrooms, the financial exigencies, and the curricular confusion that fill the headlines.

Whatever the origin of this conflict, its tactics, polemics, and political pros and cons, its chief casualty has been the liberal arts. Yet of all learning, and to all learning, the wisest men of every generation—from the age of Pericles to the age of Eisenhower—have deemed these studies the most essential.

The liberal arts have constituted the basic studies from which all phases of the educational process—general, vocational, professional; elementary, secondary, and higher—draw nourishment and without which they languish and fail. Three hundred and fifty years ago, in the fifth century of Oxford and a quarter century before the founding of the first American university, Francis Bacon perceived this relationship and stated it as follows:

> First therefore, amongst so many great foundations of colleges in Europe I find it strange that they are all dedicated to professions, and none left free to arts and sciences at large. For if men judge that learning should be referred to action, they judge well, but in this they fall into the error described in the ancient fable, in which the other parts of the body did suppose the stomach had been idle, because it neither performed the office of motion, as the limbs do, nor of sense, as the head doth, but yet notwithstanding it is the stomach that digesteth and distributeth to all the rest. So if any man think philosophy and universality to be idle studies, he doth not consider that all professions are from thence served and supplied. And this I take to be a great cause that hath hindered the progression of learning, because these fundamental knowledges have been studied but in passage. For if you will have a tree bear more fruit than it hath used to do, it is not any thing you can do to the boughs, but it is the stirring of the earth and putting new mould about the roots that must work it.

No one since Bacon has improved upon his statement of the case.

Why has it been so difficult for us to perceive the role of the liberal arts? One reason is the nature of the controversy in which American education is now involved. A second Battle of the Books is in progress —and, as in the first, the "quarrel is so inflamed by the warm heads of either faction, and the pretensions somewhere or other so exorbitant, as not to admit the least overtures of accommodation." At times the quarrel seems as pointless as Englishmen criticizing Germans for not speaking English, or golfers ridiculing tennis players for playing tennis with rackets instead of golf sticks. There is an exchange of invective but no exchange of meaning.

This quarrel has confused the issue. The adversaries in Swift's satire were ancient versus modern learning, as Swift knew them at the end of the seventeenth century. At first glance, today's adversaries would seem to be their lineal descendants: the same Ancients (who by now have recruited most of Swift's Moderns including Swift himself) versus the Moderns of 1954. A closer look reveals that this is not precisely the case. It would appear from the polemics that the Ancients were now opposed by a wholly different adversary known as instrumentalism, which sprang full-flowered from the brow of John Dewey and entered the lists against classical learning barely half a century ago. It would seem that most of the troubles or triumphs of American education (depending upon how one looks at them) had resulted from the application of this brand-new American invention to the educational process.

Such an oversimplification of history distorts the educational problem and hinders its solution. Granting the considerable (and demonstrable) influence of Mr. Dewey and his followers on our educational system, particularly upon our schools of education, teachers' colleges, and public schools, it has been but one of many historical forces that have contributed to the present situation.

Let us look more closely at today's Battle of the Books. If its adversaries are not logical counterparts of Swift's, what are they? They are proponents of two different types of learning which have existed and competed with one another since ancient times—not as old versus new, but as two distinct sets of purposes and methods. The purposes and methods of the liberal arts were first defined by the Greeks. They are expounded in the writings of Plato and Aristotle; and though they have passed through ancient, medieval, and modern phases, they still retain their original meaning. They are not a body of revealed truths or logical absolutes or a quantum of knowledge. They are studies designed to develop to capacity the intellectual and spiritual powers of the individual. Their aim is to make the most of a man in order that he may make the most of his calling, his cultural opportunities, and his responsibilities as a citizen. Such was the meaning of the liberal arts in Plato's time and such is it today.

Instrumentalism is just as old as the liberal arts and fundamentally just as consistent in meaning. In current usage, instrumentalism has become a synonym for pragmatism, especially as applied to education. Essentially it means the identification of truth with utility. That is true or good which works, which accomplishes results, or which gives emotional satisfaction to the believer.

"The true, to put it very briefly," William James once wrote in a summary of pragmatism, "is only the expedient in the way of thinking, just as the 'right' is only the expedient in the way of our behaving. Expedient in almost any fashion; and expedient in the long run and on the whole, of course."

These words should not be read out of moral context. Both James and Dewey believed that immorality, even according to traditional standards, would be found inexpedient. But the words forge a link with the Sophists of the fifth century B.C., whose slogan was "Man is the measure of all things" and whose intensely practical instruction in law, rhetoric, or—in the case of the versatile Hippias—almost any trade, emphasized the subjective desires of their pupils and their satisfaction in utilitarian skills and occupations.

I leave for the moment the relative merits of these two educational philosophies. Liberal education has periodically dried up in formalism and is never proof against illiberal teaching. Bacon himself takes certain contemporary Cambridge professors to task for teaching "words and not matter." Form without substance, polish without purpose, have always been a "distemper of learning" to the liberal arts. It we think of utilitarian education in the sense of occupational training, we will find that it has always had a respectable place in society; it had such a place in the medieval guild system; it has it in our secondary schools today.

If, on the other hand, we think of it in the sense of instrumentalism, this too has made useful contributions to the educational process, especially at the level of elementary education. My point, however, is not the respective merits of liberal and utilitarian education but their common antiquity. Once this is appreciated, the present dispute assumes its true character. It is not a dispute between Ancients and Moderns, or tradition and invention. It is a dispute between two Ancients which has been going on a long time.

Another thing the Sophists and instrumentalists have in common is that each arose in answer, as it were, to a specific set of practical demands. All philosophy reflects its times, in language and metaphor if not in theory. Even Plato, with his insistence upon the independent reality of ideas, was sensitive to the conditions in which he lived. But while Plato towered over his times, the Sophists fitted into them as hand into glove. The Sophists were a group of professional teachers who responded to the demands of young men for practical education that would help them get ahead in the world. Some of these young men were members of a rising plutocracy and anxious for instruction in the ways of democracy. Others were just looking for careers, uninterested in philosophy and the arts but eager to learn a trade. To all of these demands the Sophists responded with a body of teachings and a point of view so congenial to modern pragmatism that Schiller, the English pragmatist, called himself their disciple. For all the latter-day strictures upon them, their teachings flourished in the same society that sustained Plato and Aristotle.

Pragmatism made its modern appearance in the United States toward the close of the nineteenth century and in the early years of the twentieth in the writings of C. S. Peirce, William James, and John Dewey. These were the years in which the United States was passing through a highly self-conscious phase of nationalism that expressed itself in our war with Spain and a short-lived flurry of imperialism. Business was booming, and obsessing our thoughts and energies to a degree unparalleled in history. These trends were accompanied by an exuberant nativism that strove for expression in our cultural life. Ties with the past, and with older civilizations, were being cut. Optimism, improvisation, and Americanism were the order of the day. It is hard to conceive of a doctrine more perfectly suited to these conditions and attitudes than pragmatism.

Much the same can be said of pragmatism in the form of instrumentalism as Dewey and his followers applied it to our schools. The first half of the present century saw changes in the character and composition of our schools, particularly our secondary schools; this doctrine was ideally suited to accommodate them. Because of the decisive part secondary education plays in liberal education—which must begin in high school if it is to begin at all—it will repay us to consider some of these changes in detail. To sum them up, they produced, as though from dragon's teeth, an enormous new secondary school population, most of which was entirely innocent of the liberal arts and their purposes. The demand placed upon our schools for the kind of utilitarian education that the young Athenians demanded of the Sophists was overwhelming. The schools rose to meet the demand with the ancient doctrine of instrumentalism.

The brunt of this new educational burden was borne by our public secondary schools. Compulsory school-attendance laws and child-labor laws gradually accumulated throughout the states, with the effect of keeping in school boys and girls who used to quit after the eighth grade. As automatic machinery developed and the labor market became more crowded, labor union policies had the same effect. The appeal of secondary education—whether for some vocation, for life, or, via higher education, for a profession—became more positive and more popular. As college degrees became standard requirements for entrance into the professions and all but standard for many types of business, high school diplomas acquired a similar if lesser material value. Meanwhile, as a force in itself and a prime mover behind all these laws and polices, the population of the United States rose from 76,000,000 to 150,000,000.

The results of these trends reveal themselves in three dramatic sets of figures. From 1910 to 1940 the percentage of the 14- to 15-year age group in the nation's labor force declined from 30 per cent to 5 per cent. The percentage of the 17-year age group enrolled in high school rose from 30 per cent to 60 per cent; and the total high school population increased from 1,111,000 to 7,113,000. The comparable increase of enrollment in elementary education in these three decades was from 18,450,000 to 21,050,000. In other words, while elementary school enrollment increased by less than one-sixth, high school increased by more than six times. From 1900 to 1950 it rose from around 10 per cent to 75 per cent of its age group. What this amounted to was the creation, almost overnight, of a huge new educational population.

In curricular preference this population was overwhelmingly vocational. A disproportionately large part of it consisted of the children of immigrants. These immigrants poured into the country in such numbers in the first quarter of the century (over a million a year for six of the years between 1900 and 1920) that their total number together with their children reached a peak of 38,000,000. At no time between 1900 and 1950 was it below 25,000,000. In 1920, for example, it stood at 35,000,000, exactly a third of our total population of 105,000,000.

The overwhelming majority of this group of immigrant and recent immigrant origin lacked even a smattering of liberal education or comprehension of its purposes. Allowing for exceptions—more numerous among certain national and cultural groups than among others—the typical immigrant of these years was a person of humble origin and circumstances who had been denied access to liberal education by the highly selective educational systems prevailing abroad. How therefore could he be expected to understand it and transmit its motivations to his children? If he had ever thought of the liberal arts at all, the chances are it was as one of the aristocratic class privileges which he had come to America to escape. I know that with some it worked the other way, and that among these men and women are some of the staunchest supporters of liberal education the country has ever had. But the rank and file were innocents.

It was precisely this group, moreover, that the child-labor and school-attendance laws forced into our high schools in greatest numbers, since it was from them that so much of our unskilled and semi-skilled factory labor was recruited. Schools take their character not only from their pupils but from parents, whether the parental influence (or lack of it) stems from home, parent-teachers' association, ballot-box, or school board. The schools cannot set and maintain standards unless parents understand and support them. My point is not that our foreign population opposed liberal education. It is that through lack of previous opportunity they failed to comprehend it and therefore failed to support it. We may weigh the effect of this failure upon the liberal arts by asking ourselves what the effect on curriculum might have been if they all had been graduates of European universities; or American colleges; or, for that matter, of American public high schools of an earlier generation.

Our immigrant population was not the only such weight in these scales. Among our native population fifteen million Negro citizens, heretofore lacking any but the most primitive educational opportunities, became rightful claimants to the benefits of secondary education. For want of previous opportunity they too lacked comprehension of the liberal arts. In 1920 their number was 10,400,000. If we add this to the number of foreign-born and their children in that year, it gives us a total of 45,000,000 out of 105,000,000 Americans, beyond the pale, so to speak, of the liberal arts.

Nor does this complete the total. Liberal education characteristically begins where elementary education leaves off and carries through to the end of college. A recent study places the most critical phase of liberal education in the last two years of secondary school and the first two years of college. Certain it is that a heavy share of responsibility for it devolves upon secondary education, not only in its curriculum but in disseminating a general awareness of its purposes and benefits through society. In 1900 barely 10 per cent of its age group finished high school. Millions of native white citizens sent their children to high school in the years that followed with no idea of what liberal education was and no encouragement from home to find out. The frontiersman's hostility toward book learning was still strong. Materialism was rampant. Plunkitt of Tammany Hall spoke with scorn of "college professors and philosophers who go up in a balloon to think"; and the voice of Plunkitt was the voice of the nation.

Is it any wonder that in this suddenly expanded realm of secondary education, where from time immemorial the liberal arts have had to prove themselves in competition with utilitarian education of all kinds —where they have always had to make a case for themselves or give ground—they gave ground? They did not give it in an objective test of merit or by decision of policy. They gave it by default.

No matter how or why the ground was given, it was a serious setback to education in general. Its seriousness can be measured not merely in hypothetical conjectures about human happiness but in concrete losses of manpower. These show up vividly in studies of the number and type of high school graduates entering college today. From such studies two telling facts appear. The first is that of the 25 per cent of our high school graduates best qualified for higher education, 40 per cent do not continue with it for lack of motivation. The second fact is that most of these intellectually competent yet unmotivated young men and women come from homes representing the cultural groups and attitudes we have been discussing. How great a loss we have sustained by this wastage of human talent we can only surmise.

Could the schools have provided a better understanding of the liberal arts, through their own teachers and curricula, in spite of all the cultural odds against them? To have done so they would have needed, first, much more specific and powerful assistance from parents; but the parental tendency was to default responsibilities to the schools and then criticize the schools for not discharging them. The result was to force into both liberal and vocational curricula subjects previously treated in the home or (at times) behind the woodshed. The increasing secularization of American life contributed to the same result, causing both home and church to look to the schools for moral discipline. And to these new burdens, government added its demand for training in citizenship. The whole imposed upon the schools a crude lay morality of "life adjustment" which their hard-pressed teachers made shift to

impart in the classroom—to the common loss of the liberal arts and
of really useful occupational training.

To have resisted or modified these trends, the schools would have
needed, secondly, much greater financial support than was forthcoming,
particularly for teachers' salaries. I know this is an old story and that it
is sometimes exaggerated—that it has perhaps even been used as an
excuse for not undertaking educational reforms which could at least
have been started without money. But as I write these very words, my
morning paper carries the headline, "Teacher Scarcity at Critical Stage,"
and a report from the President of the American Association of School
Administrators that our average annual teacher salary is $3,600, "with
large numbers getting $2,000 or less." There is a direct cause-and-
effect relationship between the salary and the headline. The report
goes on to recommend the spending of $26,600,000,000 for school
buildings during the next six years. I do not mean to labor this all-too-
familiar argument. Yet no explanation of our educational predicament
can possibly ignore it. We have the resources to solve this financial
problem. A stronger representation of the liberal arts among teachers
and students as well as among parents, school boards, and taxpayers
would expedite its solution.

To have put forth a greater effort in the interest of liberal education,
the schools would have needed, finally, much more specific—and
sympathetic—assistance from the liberal arts colleges and universities
than they received—particularly from the universities. In the nineteenth century there was institutional as well as intellectual continuity
between the secondary and higher phases of liberal education. To preserve this continuity, two things are required above all others. These
are, first, the closest possible cooperation between school and college in
such matters as the planning of curriculum and the testing and guidance of students; and, second, both secondary school and college
teachers aware of and prepared for these responsibilities. In the nineteenth century such continuity was ensured, partly by the liberal arts
curricula prevailing generally throughout our secondary schools and
partly by the fact that these schools recruited their teachers almost
entirely from the liberal arts colleges.

Toward the turn of the century this continuity began to be disrupted.
It is difficult to say exactly how the disruption started, but the colleges
and universities were at least partly to blame. As the elective system
gained headway in the colleges, liberal education lost character and in
extreme cases became so dissipated as to be hardly recognizable. In part

the elective system was the result of European (particularly German) influence that emphasized specialization culminating in graduate work. In even larger part it resulted from the deficiencies of the liberal arts themselves, from their failure to keep fresh and vital and reveal their meaning to their own disciples. It began in the 1870s, a good thirty years before Dewey published his *School and Society.*

By disrupting the unity of the liberal arts on a horizontal plane the elective system greatly abetted the disruption of their continuity on a vertical plane. The result in curricular terms was a tide rip of vocational and liberal currents. The liberal arts colleges—partly out of conviction and partly in deference to the professional schools and the professions—continued to offer liberal education, however diluted by vocational and other electives, and to require preparation in the liberal arts on the part of entering freshmen. The schools met this requirement with a curricular mixture of liberal, vocational, and life-adjustment courses in which the liberal element became steadily more diluted.

The results are epitomized in a letter which I have before me. It contains the transcript of a high school senior applying for admission to the liberal arts curriculum of Yale University. The transcript shows that of twelve junior and senior courses offered as the first half of the liberal arts continuum, two were in English, one in American history, and the other nine were as follows: typing, speech, (2) chorus, (2) physical education, journalism, personality problems, and marriage and family. The subjects required, in varying combination, for admission to Yale are English language and literature, two foreign languages, mathematics, history, and the natural sciences. An answer frequently given me to the question raised by this obvious conflict is that the student should not have been allowed to apply for Yale. A more satisfactory answer would be that his innate aptitude and competence should have been discovered in time for his high school to assign him to those studies which would have made his admission to Yale possible.

The gap in the continuity of liberal education between school and college grew wider when the liberal arts faculties in the universities relinquished responsibility for the training of secondary school teachers to special schools and departments of education in the universities and to the newly founded teachers' colleges. This is not to suggest that the liberal arts were willfully suppressed or utterly forsaken. On the contrary they struck new roots in the teachers' colleges, in some of which they flourished—and continue to flourish—more than in some so-called liberal arts institutions. It is to say, rather, that what might have been a united effort became a divided one, which had lost the support of its strongest potential ally, the liberal arts faculties of the universities.

This process, which in its early stages appears to have been largely involuntary, was abetted by the demand for teachers that was caused by the soaring high school enrollment. It was further abetted by the comparably increasing need for university and college teachers, and the growing concern of the liberal arts faculties with that need. The relatively unfavorable working conditions, compensation, and intellectual opportunities of high school teaching also played a part.

Here again liberal education lost ground by default. The sad part of it is that what began as an involuntary and almost imperceptible schism culminated in an acrimony and a second Battle of the Books. It is not necessary to become embroiled in the battle to recognize the harmful effect of this dissidence on liberal education. To prepare for instruction in one set of values and purposes formerly represented by one faculty, there were now two faculties—one passive, the other active, with conflicting purposes. What should have been a colloquium turned into a conflict in which no one gained and liberal education was the heavy loser.

The liberal arts faculties of the universities did not want this conflict and did not start it. It is simply a rather more acute manifestation than usual of the ancient competition between two kinds of learning. If, in this conflict, the liberal arts faculties have been more sinned against than sinning, they too did some sinning.

My conclusion from all these facts is that the schools did not receive the support in liberal education they needed from the colleges and universities to uphold their end of the bargain.

The entire country has been the loser and the entire country is responsible for its own loss. The educational process is indivisible. Each part of it depends upon every other part. If we single out the universities as standard-bearers we must not forget that these standards, too, require the support of parents—a cultural base of comprehension and sympathy—or they cannot be maintained. If the truth be told, there was little comprehension of the power of the liberal arts in American society because American society was incurious and inarticulate concerning its own political and social philosophy. Not since the great days of the Federal Convention, the Federalist Papers, the writings and teachings of Adams and Jefferson, and the seminal decisions of John Marshall had we bothered to inquire much into the meaning of our democracy and the vital part of it represented by liberal education. The glow of that early enlightenment soon faded in the American sky, and while we remained furiously awake in business and politics, in philosophy we went to sleep. We were not roused from this sleep and impelled to re-examine first principles until economic collapse, followed by the threat of fascist and then of communist totalitarianism, forced us to look into the meaning of many things we had taken for granted. Then and only then (and I speak of the last two decades) did we begin to discover the meaning that liberal education held for Plato and Aristotle and Adams and Jefferson.

No one was more sympathetic to education in all its phases than Jefferson. He spoke constantly of "a general diffusion of knowledge" as the corollary to self-government; and he made comprehensive plans which included vocational as well as liberal education. He believed that all Americans should be taught "reading, writing, and common arithmetic"; that all should learn some useful trade or calling; and that all who had the ability should go just as far in higher education as their ability permitted them; and he saw no incompatibility between these three principles. At the same time, as his personal correspondence and the whole record of his life reveal, it was liberal education that enriched his own mind and spirit and through them conveyed transcendent benefits to all American education.

The same can be said of Lincoln, who had almost no formal education and whose discovery and use of liberal education for this very reason offers a truly pragmatic demonstration of its powers. "It was a wild region," he wrote in 1859 of Spencer County, Indiana, whither his uneducated father moved the family from Kentucky in Lincoln's eighth year, "with many bears and other wild animals, still in the woods."

> There I grew up. There were some schools, so called; but no qualification was ever required of a teacher beyond "readin, writin, and cipherin" to the Rule of Three. If a straggler supposed to understand latin happened to sojourn in the neighborhood, he was looked upon as a wizzard (sic). There was absolutely nothing to excite ambition for education. Of course when I came of age I did not know much. . . . I could read, write and cipher to the Rule of Three; but that was all. I have not been to school since. The little advance I now have upon this store of education, *I have picked up from time to time under the pressure of necessity.*

Whither did this practical motive lead him? It led him to English grammar at the age of twenty-three; to Euclid when he was a member of Congress; to the Bible; to Bunyan, Shakespeare, Defoe, Burns, and

Byron; to Blackstone's *Commentaries;* to American history; to Voltaire, Gibbon, and Paine. It led him, in short, to liberal education, and this in turn led on to greater things.

Was it Lincoln's genius or his education that took him the rest of the way? It was both. He was no towering intellectual. The nature of his genius was that he so perfectly represented the ideals and aspirations of his country and his fellow men. Without this education he might have continued to represent those ideals and aspirations in the back woods of Illinois. With the help of a liberal education he represented them, and not only represented but advanced and strengthened them, for the world. What liberal education offered Lincoln in his time, a proper diffusion of its power through our educational system offers us all today.

We neglect this knowledge at our peril.

Questions and Suggestions

1. In one sentence state the thesis or central idea and then explain the title.

2. How does this essay show that a knowledge of the past illumines the present? What light does a part of this essay throw on Whitman's hopes for the future? Does it explain any of Baldwin's father's reaction to foreigners?

3. Why does Griswold think that the present "battle of books" differs from the "battle" that Swift described?

4. Does the quotation from Bacon explain, at least in part, Prof. Schneider's phrase "Baconian Eden"?

5. How successful are Bacon's analogies?

6. In order to grasp more of the meaning from Griswold's survey of the changes that took place in America around the turn of the century, reread Highet's essay.

7. What are the principles or ideas of pragmatism? How have they been applied to education? Why does Griswold say this philosophy is well-suited to "optimism, improvisation, and Americanism"?

8. When this essay first appeared, Roman numerals indicated four divisions in its thought. Identify these parts and sum up each in a single sentence. Be sure that your statements include nothing incompatible with the general thesis.

9. Consider the meaning of Griswold's statement, "All philosophy reflects its times, in language and metaphor if not in theory." See if this principle also applies to the manner in which an essayist expresses his views. Contrast, for example, Lamb's

style with Griswold's, noticing differences in diction, allusions, sentence structure, and paragraphing.

10. Explain Griswold's allusions to "the age of Pericles," "dragon's teeth," and "from the brow of John Dewey." Define *exigencies, polemics, secularization, transcendent, instrumentalism,* and *formalism.*

Ideas for Writing

1. What knowledge did you acquire during the first twelve years of your schooling that should have been taught to you at home by interested parents or friends?

2. Analyze your reasons for coming to college and write at length upon the reason you consider most important.

3. Did your parents provide you with the proper incentive for your coming to college?

4. Define "getting ahead in the world." Contrast its popular meaning with your present views on the subject.

5. Consider the following passages as bases for papers: (a) "The schools cannot set and maintain standards unless parents understand and support them." (b) "The educational process is indivisible." (c) ". . . while we remained furiously awake in business and politics, in philosophy we went to sleep."

6. From what you knew of your classmates in the twelfth grade, how wise do you think states are in establishing laws for the legal age when a student can stop attending school? If you were establishing a college, where would you draw a line between the courses that produce a form of mental culture and those that give more practical results? Between the fine arts and recreation?

part five 〰 *The mind of the scientist*

THE STARS

C. P. SNOW

Born in Leicester, England, Charles Percy Snow (1905–) came from a poor family. With the help of scholarships he studied at University College, Leicester, and later at Christ's College, Cambridge, receiving his Ph.D. in 1930. During World War II he was chief of the scientific personnel for the British Ministry of Labour. *The Search,* first published in 1935 but revised and reprinted in 1958, was his first serious work of fiction. However, it lies outside the monumental series of eleven novels that are centered around Lewis Eliot. Snow, who was knighted in 1957, is married to the novelist Pamela Hansford Johnson. In recent years he has been a frequent lecturer in American universities.

When I was a child of about eleven, a new excitement suddenly flared up in my life.

It must have been a Sunday night, for my father and I were walking after church. I had not been to the service myself; my father would
never have thought of taking me. But occasionally on Sunday evenings
he would look embarrassed and tell me: "I shall be in Wentworth
Street at eight o'clock, if you'd like to come along." Wentworth Street
was round the corner from our parish church, but we were not supposed to know where he was going. He would set off, as though he and
the church-bell had nothing in common.

This particular Sunday night was warm and twilit, and I fancy
summer was nearly over. As we came to the end of the town, the sun
had just gone down behind the river, and—I remember it as though it
were yesterday—in the yellow sunset sky there was a sickle of new
moon, and high over our heads a sprinkling of stars just coming dimly
out. We stopped and looked.

My father said:

"I wonder if they're what we think they are? Stars! Stars like this!"
He waved vaguely. "People think we know about them. I wonder if
we do."

I gazed up at him.

"I wonder if we *can*," he added.

I didn't know what he was thinking. All of a sudden I felt that all
the things around me were toys to handle and control, that I had the
power in a tiny, easy world.

"I wonder if they are what we think they are," my father was saying again.

"Let's find out," I said. And then:

"I'm going to find out."

My father looked puzzled. "Well," he said.

The night had taken hold of me. I wanted to do something with
those stars. I did not quite know what, but I was elated. Their beauty
stirred me, but it was not only that. If I had been older, I should have
said I wanted to know, to understand, to alter. I wanted to rush out
and have them for my own. I laughed:

"I'm going to find out all about them."

I remember my father's face as he stared at me. His eyes were kindly
and bewildered, he was chewing one end of his moustache, there was
a sort of baffled amusement round his mouth.

"Perhaps you will," he reflected. We began to walk home.

"A lot of people have tried, you know," he said doubtfully. "Sir Isaac Newton—and Sir Robert Ball—and Sir William Herschel—and Sir Oliver Lodge——" My father's reading was odd, I discovered later, and he always found it an effort to shorten a title. He must have called his friends "Mr.——" when he was alone with them. "Sir Oliver Lodge," he repeated. "Very great men. They've all tried."

"I don't care," I said defiantly.

My father had lost himself in some more speculations. "They may be wrong after all," he was saying to himself. "All these stars. Bigger than the world. Bigger than the sun. It seems strange if they're put there just for nothing. It doesn't seem right."

But I was full of schemes by now. As soon as we got home I rushed to the book-case and took out all the eight volumes of the *Children's Encyclopædia* and began to turn the new shiny-smelling pages in search of pictures I hazily remembered. I didn't know anything of indexes then; and, despite my father's gentle wishes, I had scarcely glanced through the Encyclopædia, which he had bought for me a year or so before. While I dashed over the pages, my mother kept calling me in to supper. At last I found what I was looking for. My mother was placated as soon as I began to eat some of the trifle or fruit or blanc-mange—it must have been one of the three which we had for supper that night. Soon I broke out:

"Father!" I only used the word very rarely, when I wanted all his attention.

"Father! I want you to help me make a telescope."

"Why?" he said.

"To look at the stars." We smiled at each other.

"I used to think I'd like a telescope," my father said. "But somehow I never got one——"

"It's ever so easy to make one," I hurried on. "It'll only take us an hour or two. The Encyclopædia tells you all about it. You only want a cardboard tube and two magnifying glasses and some sticking stuff—and you can see mountains on the moon! And moons round some of the stars! We must make one!"

"We'll see after supper," he said.

I leant out of my bedroom window that night, and the stars seemed like friends.

The next evening, when he came home, my father laid a parcel on the table. Usually he started tea as soon as he came in, but now he watched while I untied the string and found a cardboard tube, some extra cardboard, two lenses and oddments in the way of wax and seccotine and string.

"Oh fine!" I shouted. "Let's make it now."

"My tea," he murmured, but I said:

"Come on, it won't take long," and we began. We fixed one lens into the tube and it looked so much like the Encyclopædia picture that we laughed with delight. But then the difficulties began. For the other lens we had to make a thinner tube out of cardboard; it sounded simple, and I cut out and my father glued, and everything seemed straight-forward. In a minute or two, though, my father was chewing his moustache a little puzzledly.

"It's not a very straight tube," he said.

"It's not far off," I said.

It was, in fact, a queer-looking sort of cone.

"We'll have to try again," he said dubiously.

We cut and glued time and time again, but the best we could do was a poor irregular thing beside our fine bought tube.

"Perhaps it'll do." My father held it in his hand and closed one eye and stared along it. "After all, we're just starting, aren't we?"

I was worried and anxious, but I tried to smile.

"I'm sure it will do," I said.

Then, very gingerly, he began to put the small lens into the tube we had made. I remember seeing him stand there, his fingers a little tentative and uncertain, his forehead puckered, his bluish friendly eyes undecided: his hand slipped, and the lens got lodged in at an angle.

"Oh confound it!" he said. "I never could do anything with my hands."

I felt like crying, but he looked so wretched that I knew I mustn't.

"Let's try it like that. It may be all right."

"Shall we?" He held the thing in his hands. "It may not—it may not be so bad after all."

"We'll go and look at the moon." I turned my face away from him. I was afraid everything had gone wrong: I was hoping that we should manage to see something. Anxiously we went upstairs and rested our contraption on the window-sill; the moon had just risen, a crescent over the bank of clouds on the sky-line. With a catch at my heart, I looked at it through our lenses. I saw a faint distorted shape.

"I can see it," I said. "Much better than I can without the telescope. Ever so much better."

My father gazed down the tube himself.

"I can see something," he said, after a pause. "I wonder if it *is* better."

"Of course it is," I replied. He mustn't be disappointed, I knew in some half-conscious way. "Wait till it's a full moon. We'll see the mountains." Privately, I vowed I would make the telescope myself by that time.

My father still looked worried. "It would be better if I'd got the lens in straight," he said, and went disconsolately off to tea.

For a day or two I was busy with tubes and lenses, petulant at times, but going on with a rush of hope. In a way, my father's failure had made me more certain that it was left for me to know about the stars: he couldn't do it, no one could do it—but I knew I could myself, and I read the Encyclopædia and an old handbook of astronomy my father had picked up somewhere, and made tubes more or less cylindrical, while my mother grumbled that I was leaving meals half-finished, going to bed late, and littering rooms with scraps of paper. Proudly I told her: "I'm doing astronomy."

When I had the telescope about half ready, and was mastering the gumming of tubes and fixing of lenses, my father came in one evening and watched me begin on the eye-piece. I noticed he was smiling.

"Don't bother about that," he said.

"It'll soon be finished," I replied.

"No, it won't. Look here." His hand came from behind his back with a new telescope a foot long, all shining in gold and bronze, so bright that I could see my face in the barrel as he handed it to me. "This is for you."

I felt a choke in my throat. I knew that the gift was far too expensive for him, but his eyes were bright with enjoyment.

"It's better to buy things than make them," he was saying, "if they've got to be exact. These things must be exact. Exactness is important, you know. Exact scientific instruments . . ." he trailed off, smiling.

Perhaps I had a twinge that my own telescope, made by my own hands, was dishonoured for ever. The cardboard looked shabby, hopelessly—hopelessly futile, by the side of the metallic perfection of this newcomer. But the resentment flickered and passed; here was a better thing ready to use, a real way to find out about the stars.

"Oh thanks," I shouted, and, looking back, I think my father must have felt repaid.

That night I saw two of the moons of Jupiter. There were no clouds those nights, I remember, and there comes back to me the sight of silvery circles floating on the glowing luminous black-purple of the sky. The black-purple into which, beyond which, I longed to go: often I would lie awake thinking of how I could see into the dark space which lay beyond the stars.

I kept a record of my watchings. There were drawings of Saturn's rings, sometimes like a thin straight line, sometimes like a tilted saucer: of Mars, and I was sure there were rivers and canals and tracks: of all the stars invisible to my eyes that the telescope enabled me to see. Evening after evening at sunset, I would watch for a sight of Mercury flashing across the west; and many dawns I got up, unknown to my mother, until I had assured myself that the morning star was really Venus reappearing. Once, I followed a comet that would not come again for forty years.

All the time my mind was investing what I saw. Before long I was peopling the planets and devising expeditions to the stars.

Questions and Suggestions

1. These pages have been taken from the opening chapter of the novel. Are there any suggestions or hints in them that the boy, Arthur Miles, will become a "pure idealist in science"?
2. Why did the father never think of taking his son to the evening services? How does Mr. Miles differ from the father in Lagerkvist's "Father and I"?
3. Does Mr. Miles have the intellectual qualities necessary to be an alert and stimulating parent? Explain your answer in light of what you learned from Addison, Griswold, and Highet.
4. Do the child and father agree that it is better to " 'buy things than make them . . . if they've got to be exact' "?
5. Learn why *Newton, Ball, Herschel,* and *Lodge* are famous. Consult your dictionary for the meaning and origin of *trifle, blancmange, petulant,* and *nebulous.* You should read Snow's novel, *The New Men,* that deals with some of the ethical problems nuclear scientists face, and also his essays *Two Cultures and the Scientific Revolution* and *Science and Government.* For generous excerpts from his address, "The Moral Un-Neutrality of Science," see *The New York Times* for December 28, 1960.

Ideas for Writing

1. Explain in detail how you failed with a do-it-yourself project. For a delightful and pertinent attack on the great mass of "literature" that tells one how to do anything, read Dwight

Macdonald's "Onward and Upward with the Arts: How-toism," in the May 22, 1954, issue of *The New Yorker.*

2. Recall the night when you first became consciously aware of the moon and stars, or the time when you made your first sightings through a telescope.

3. Describe the incident when you received a gift that was obviously too expensive for your parents to have given to you.

4. Does your father want you to have advantages that he lacked?

5. Contrast your father's reactions to science, literature, or religion with the views held by Mr. Miles.

6. Discuss the pros and cons of a parent being a "pal."

7. Explain the process you used in making or repairing an object.

THE AUTUMN STARS

EDWIN WAY TEALE

Edwin Way Teale (1899–) was born in Joliet, Illinois, and spent his youth in the dune country of northern Indiana. It was some years after he graduated from Earlham College and Columbia before he became a full-time writer. Even now he writes slowly, often rewriting. One way he achieves his desired accuracy is by keeping a notebook in which he records on-the-spot descriptions of places and his thoughts. His favorite authors are Thoreau, W. H. Hudson, Hardy, and Conrad. He considers the opening verses of the twelfth chapter of Ecclesiastes to be the finest 225 words in literature.

Down the long, gradual decline of the Appalachian Plateau, far into Ohio, we rode next day. America is the Land of the Turning Wheel—a myriad of wheels turning in factories, millions of wheels turning on the highways. Here in the Middle West, with its Akrons and Detroits, we were riding through one of the strongholds of the

wheel. But here also we noted another side of America. That under-
current of poetic feeling that runs through the great mass of men was
revealing itself everywhere on place-signs and on rural mailboxes.
Here, as all across the land, it was finding expression in the names
bestowed by farmers on their homesteads. The Seven Pines, Hidden
Acres, Long Furrow Farm, Willow Bend, Green Pastures, Killdee
Farm, Far Hills, Hickory Stick Farm, The Windy Oaks, Meadow
Lane Farm.

That morning we had started early. We met—as we were to meet
in so many other dawns—the same sequence: the milkman, the
bakeryman, the cats sitting beside doors; then the workmen waiting
for busses, schoolchildren with books and lunches, and finally busi-
nessmen and salesmen on the road. The signs of autumn were all
around us in this land of buckeyes and shagbark hickories. Teasels
stood dry in the sunshine. Every larger pond held a coot or two, birds
we could visualize among the great spatter-dock leaves of lower Florida
where many spend their winter months. Everywhere across the open
fields, browning the weed tops, ran the rust of autumn. Cutting down
the length of Ohio from east to west, we were crossing the path of
monarch butterflies moving south. Once again the coming of fall was
ushering in one of the great insect migrations of the world.

This was September. This was the first of the "ber" months of fall.
Name aloud the twelve months of the year and you will find that the
four that comprise autumn, the only months that end in "ber," have
the most round and melodious sounds of all—September, October,
November, December. And three of the four, appropriately for a time
when the fires of the year are dying down, end in "ember."

On this day we noticed many things. We saw a robin shoot up and
over a speeding automobile and speculated on how many birds are
saved from death by the streamlining of the modern car. We observed
how television antennas provide a new kind of signpost—pointing
ahead as we approached big cities, pointing back after we had passed
them by. About noon we stopped at a filling station for gasoline. On
the grass near by lay a spotted dog sound asleep. The dog wore sun-
glasses.

"That," the attendant told us, "is the laziest dog in the world. He
sleeps all day long. Two hours ago I put those glasses on him as a
joke, and he doesn't even know they are there yet!"

Not long after we passed Broken Sword Creek, near Oceola, we
noticed a kind of toning to the woodlot trees. The creeping hues

of autumn had run along the edges while the inner trees were green. This perhaps was due to the stronger winds at the woodland's edge— for one scientist found that in the interior of an Ohio woods the wind had been slowed down to one tenth its velocity at the border— or it may have been the consequence of some local condition, some thermal belt or topographical effect such as we were to encounter all across the autumn. There are always these little seasons within the seasons, little retreats and advances within the great retreats and advances.

In the twilight that evening, just before we settled down for the night, we passed a vaguely seen bird in a dead treetop.

"A sparrow hawk," I said. "Or was it a flicker? It could have been a crow."

And we both laughed, recalling that favorite passage in the *Journal* of Henry Thoreau:

"November 1, 1853. Saw three of those birds . . . They must be either sandpipers, telltales . . . or plovers (?) Or may they be the turnstone?"

The next morning we rode the Lincoln Highway into Delphos. Less than thirty miles from the Indiana line, this Ohio town with its population of 6,000 lies on the old Miami and Erie Canal. At one time it was surrounded by extensive fields of clover and was known as The Honey Center of the World. Today its fame rests less on honey than on comets. For Delphos is the home of the noted comet collector Leslie C. Peltier. Searching the night sky from his cornfield and backyard observatories, he has discovered eleven comets, a record unequaled by any other amateur astronomer in America.

I found Peltier, near the western edge of Delphos, cutting his grass with a power mower. A slender man with graying hair and a quiet and engaging sincerity of manner, he was in his early fifties. He has been fascinated by the night sky since he was sixteen. That year he bought his first telescope, a thirty-power glass advertised in *The American Boy*. It cost eighteen dollars. We found ourselves on a common ground of experience when he recalled how he had earned those dollars. Long ago, as a small boy in the sandhill country of northern Indiana, I picked something like 20,000 strawberries, at two cents a quart, to earn my first camera. Peltier, too, had picked strawberries, at the same rate of pay, to earn his first telescope.

He brought it from the house, a spyglass with sliding tubes made by the A. S. Aloe Company, of St. Louis. It had arrived in July, right after the strawberry picking season had ended. I squinted into the eyepiece, looking at distant trees and a far-away passing plane. With the brass tubes fully extended, it gave a magnification of thirty diameters; with an auxiliary lens in place, the magnification was boosted to eighty diameters. This is the only telescope Peltier has ever owned. The two instruments he has used subsequently in his comet hunting were loaned him by Eastern universities. The first of these, a four-inch glass, was forwarded by Harvard University. The second, which he has used since 1923, is a six-inch telescope sent on loan by Princeton.

During the months that followed the arrival of the original spyglass, the sixteen-year-old farm boy contented himself with looking at the Milky Way and the rings of Saturn and the craters of the moon. No one else in all that region had any special interest in astronomy. Two years later one of his presents at Christmas was William Tyler Olcott's *Field Book of the Stars*. It was a footnote in this book that turned him to a serious study of the sky. It asked all readers interested in undertaking definite projects in star-watching to write to the author. Peltier did. As a result, at the age of eighteen, he began studying those pinpoints of brilliance that wax and wane in brightness—the variable or "flare" stars. He sent in his first variable star report in March 1918 and he has not missed a month in all the years that have followed. This record of more than 400 months without a break is another distinction of his that is unapproached by any other amateur.

In 1925, two years after the Princeton telescope arrived, Peltier discovered his first comet. In the middle of the strawberry patch, which by then had become a cornfield, he had constructed, with his father's help, a nine-foot observatory with a revolving dome of galvanized sheet metal. We drove four miles east of Delphos that afternoon to see the discarded dome, which still lay like an immense white mushroom behind a red barn on the farm where Peltier spent his boyhood. He pointed out an old black-walnut tree that stood at the edge of the cornfield. Long ago, from the top of that tree, he had snapped a bird's-eye view of his observatory with a folding Kodak. It was from this observatory, on the night of November 13, 1925, that he saw the first of his eleven comets.

He had swung his telescope toward the constellation Hercules. Each pinpoint of brightness in that part of the sky was as familiar to him as the lights of the neighboring farmhouses. Instantly he noticed a spot of brilliance where no light had been on the night before.

He studied it minute after minute for nearly an hour until there was no possibility of doubt. The far-away light was that great prize, dreamed of by every amateur astronomer, a new comet.

Peltier leaped on his bicycle and began pedaling four miles through the dark to Delphos. The official discoverer of a comet in America is the first to get word to the Harvard Observatory at Cambridge, Massachusetts. The telegraph office, when he reached it, was dark and deserted. He raced toward the signal tower of the Pennsylvania Railroad. There emergency telegrams could be dispatched at night. It was a little after midnight when breathlessly he reached the top of the stairs. A few minutes later his message was on the way. A Russian astronomer independently discovered the same comet. But that was four days later. Peltier's cornfield telescope was the first in the world to be trained on this speeding visitor in outer space.

"That was on Friday the thirteenth," he told me. "I'm not superstitious but I notice that on every Friday the thirteenth in November I look over the sky with special care."

For no reason that he can suggest, he has made more discoveries in February than in any other month of the year. So far he has never discovered a comet in December.

"Someday," he said, "I hope to get one in December as a special kind of Christmas present."

The reason he has found more new comets than any other amateur is, he believes, simple. No one else has spent so many hours hunting in the night skies. He has averaged more than an hour at his telescope for every clear night in the past thirty-six years. Even on nights of intermittent clouds he studies the heavens in the open spaces. On bright moonlit nights, when observation is impossible, he often gets up at two or three o'clock in the morning, after the moon has set, to spend an hour or two in comet hunting and variable-star watching, before going back to bed. We calculated the total time he has spent at the eyepiece of his telescope and found it came to more than 225 continuous days and nights of concentrated observation.

Because comets are brightest when nearest the sun, a favorite hunting ground for these heavenly bodies is the eastern sky just before dawn and the western sky just after sunset. Most comets are reported from these portions of the firmament. Peltier, however, spends little time searching there. All around the world observers have their telescopes trained on these spots. So he hunts elsewhere. As a consequence his finds are less likely to be anticipated by others. It was while thus

engaged, searching the northern heavens near the Pole Star on the
night of May 15, 1936, that he made his greatest discovery, a comet
so brilliant that by July of that year it could be seen with the naked
eye. In honor of the farm-boy astronomer it was named the Comet
Peltier.

   After he left the farm and moved to Delphos, where he is designer
for a furniture factory, Peltier built his second observatory in his back
yard. It is even smaller and more economical than the first. We walked
out to it, a simple white box about six feet square, resting on a concrete foundation at the edge of a dahlia garden next to a patch of late
sweet corn. The sheet metal of its flat roof was below the level of
my eyes. This observatory, in which Peltier has discovered five of his
comets, was made mainly from odds and ends. Its total cost was fifteen
dollars—less than the amount paid for the original spyglass telescope.

   He swung open the door. On hot summer nights it is held ajar by
the pressure of a down-bent portion of the edge of the metal roof; in
winter weather it is kept shut by means of a simple hook and eye. Everything about the observatory is unpretentious, often improvised. The "dew
shield" at the end of the telescope is merely a sheet of corrugated cardboard held loosely around the barrel by a strand of wire. It can be
slipped forward to protect the lens or pushed back along the barrel
out of the way when the telescope is lowered into the box observatory
and the opening in the roof is closed to make the interior watertight.

   I peered inside. Just within the door one half of the front seat of
a junkyard automobile had been mounted behind the eyepiece of the
telescope. I eased myself into this seat and looked around the crowded
interior. The counterweights on the telescope were pieces of lead from
a discarded battery. Just in front of my knees there rose a steering
wheel salvaged from another junked automobile. I turned it and the
whole box of the observatory began rotating on small flanged wheels
that followed the circle of a single rail mounted on the concrete foundation. Above my right hand a disk of wood carried a knob at its edge.
Winding this disk elevated or depressed the end of the telescope.
Elbow-high on my right, a shelf held a loose-leaf book of star maps
and jottings on the backs of envelopes beneath a ten-watt photographic
safelight in a crook-necked lamp. This faint illumination is all that is
needed for making notes, and it does not affect Peltier's eyes sufficiently
to upset his judgment of the comparative brilliance of distant stars.
Thrust forward under the telescope, my feet rested on the bars of a
shallow cage. It contained an old electric hot plate—a foot warmer

for winter nights. Peltier, not infrequently, maintains his lonely vigil in zero weather and on at least one occasion he followed his hunting across the skies on a night when the thermometers stood at twenty degrees below zero.

I slid out of the seat and we walked back toward the house. That evening, as soon as it became dark, we planned to return to this telescope that had brought first intelligence to the world of the existence of nearly a dozen comets. Through it we would watch the autumn stars.

Amid the Everglades of Florida, at the start of our trip north with the spring, Nellie and I had seen the arc of the sun steadily mounting the sky. Now, in these latter months of the year, the movement was reversed. Day by day the course of the sun was descending, sinking steadily, if almost imperceptibly, into the south. Shadows at noon were growing longer. The astronomy of fall was ushering in the fall.

This third season, according to Greek mythology, was born of the Silver Age. First came the Golden Age when all the year was spring. Then, a step downward, followed the Silver Age. Spring shrank to a single season, and summer, autumn and winter came into being. Thus the ancients accounted for the four seasons of the year. Now we know that their source is rather the position of the tilted earth on its journey around the sun. At night, we see our shifting relationship to the center of our universe reflected in the course of the stars. Our fate, so far as it is affected by the seasons, is written in the sky. During these initial days of our travels westward, the movement of heavenly bodies—without haste, without pause—was bringing to the Northern Hemisphere the earliest of all the multiform changes of autumn.

The night before, we had watched the constellations stretching across a clear and brilliant firmament above the level darkness of an Ohio countryside. We had seen the "evening star" of this autumn sky, the planet Venus, hanging low in the west, just above the ebbing colors of the sunset, when twilight came. The nearest of all the planets, almost a twin of the earth in size, Venus is surrounded by a heavy blanket of silvery vapor. It is this vapor, reflecting the rays of the sun, that makes it the brightest planet in our sky—the "Splendor of Heaven" as the Arabs called it. Although the maximum light it reflects to earth is only about $\frac{1}{4,000}$ that of the full moon, it is concentrated into one small spot in the heavens. Venus as the "evening star" is a feature of the autumn sky of only certain years. But the rising of Orion, the brightest of the constellations, ascending higher and higher in the eastern sky each night, is a feature of every fall. The annual bluish swarm of meteors, the November Leonids, is another. But the greatest, the most far-reaching, event in the firmament during this season of the year is the apparent southward journey of the sun.

This illusion is owing to the fact that the axis of the earth, on which the globe spins, is tilted 23½ degrees away from vertical to the plane of the earth's orbit around the sun and always points in the same direction. In consequence, the Northern Hemisphere is inclined toward the sun in summer and away from it in winter. This fact, in combination with the curvature of the earth's surface, results in uneven heating at the same moment at various latitudes. The more vertical the rays, the more heat they bring to the surface of the planet. This is both because they travel through less heat absorbing atmosphere and because they are spread over less area than are slanting rays striking the curved surface of the globe.

During autumn, the Northern Hemisphere progressively tilts more and more away from the sun. In spring, of course, the reverse takes place. Only twice a year—at the time of the spring and the autumnal equinox—do the rays of the sun fall vertically on the equator. The word equinox, coming from the Latin, means "equal night." On these two occasions only are day and night of approximately equal length all over the earth except near the poles. Autumn, incidentally, is warmer than spring. In fall, the hemisphere is slowly cooling off; in spring, it is slowly warming up. And there is a lag in both of these seasonal changes.

As we waited for evening to come to Delphos, that afternoon, the astronomy of the season was working toward an event 9,000 miles away above far-off Molucca Strait, near the island of Celebes, in the Dutch East Indies. There, 123 degrees, 21 minutes, 54 seconds longitude east of Greenwich, England, at 9:24 P.M., Eastern Standard Time, on a day not far distant now, the sun would reach the Celestial Equator. It would shine straight down on the lonely sea that forms this portion of the earth's equator. And for all the Northern Hemi-sphere, at that precise moment, autumn officially would begin.

At Delphos the evening came at last. And while the twilight deepened into darkness we lingered over the chicken, the hot biscuits, the muskmelons, the peach cobbler, the long train of dishes of a midwestern feast Mrs. Peltier had prepared. We listened to recollections of a time when Peltier, just married, made a living collecting rocks in the Southwest for the Ward's Natural History Establishment, of Rochester, N. Y.

It was after eight o'clock when we finally started for the observatory. At that moment the great disappointment of the trip enveloped us. Ever since the storm at Cape May the skies had been clear. For half a month afterwards the nights were cloudless and brilliant with stars. On this one evening of all those many evenings, dense overcast had swiftly spread across the sky, sheeting it from horizon to horizon, making invisible every planet, blanketing every star.

It was a long time before I could accept the reality of this fact. Endlessly I turned the steering wheel that revolved the observatory. Endlessly I wound the wooden disk that raised and lowered the telescope. I was like a pilot caught above fog, seeking a hole through which to escape. Everything was one uniform blankness. Only once the telescope recorded light—a sudden glow of brilliant red like some rare heavenly body. It was the ruby warning lamp at the top of a radio tower.

At length I gave up. The looked-forward-to experience was not for us. We had, however, met a man of lasting interest and that was worth traveling far to find; we had made friends in Delphos. But the stars and planets still moved invisible behind their veil of overcast when we bade the Peltiers good-by that night. Yet, seen or unseen, by night and by day, we knew, the movement of these heavenly bodies across the firmament was foreshadowing all the impending changes of fall. The flow of the seasons already had altered its direction; we would feel its current quicken during the weeks ahead. For autumn advances like the rising tide. It has its warmer days and its days of increasing chill. Its waves move forward, then retreat. But all the while its average progress—like that of ocean water rising to the flood —is set in one direction.

Questions and Suggestions

1. Locate some of the details that Teale uses in showing that autumn has arrived. Where do you find them in the essay and why?

2. What evidence do you have that Teale is an accurate observer, a careful writer? Do you find any hint that some of the material for this essay might first have gone into a notebook?

3. How does the author view the relationship between the costs of materials and the creative results? How could a careless reader be misled by the figure given for the cost of Peltier's observatory?

4. What importance does Teale seem to consider environment has on a man's mental development?
5. How does Teale get you to make your own evaluation of Peltier?
6. Does the essay have any controlling themes? What are the major divisions?
7. Does the opening image of the "Turning Wheel" have more than one meaning for the essay?
8. Teale's transitions are worth careful study.
9. Notice how he uses both time and place, or a combination of the two, to get some of his desired effects.
10. Consult your dictionary for the origins of the names of the autumn months, *Orion,* and the *November Leonids.* What is the meaning of *celestial equator, variable stars, Pole Star,* and the prefix *hemi?*

Ideas for Writing

1. Describe a man whose outward appearance belies his mental agility, or the reverse.
2. Peltier's life was changed by a footnote. Perhaps one book has already produced changes in your life. If it has, you might organize a good paper around a cause and effect scheme.
3. Recount your difficulties in maintaining an interest in a hobby or idea when you could find no one with whom you could share your enthusiasms.
4. In what ways might you seem odd to someone else?
5. Using a map, if necessary, develop a paper around the place names in your locale, explaining what the names reveal. Before writing your paper, read Stephen Vincent Benet's short poem "American Names," or portions of George R. Stewart's *Names on the Land.*
6. Through the use of details gathered from direct observation, show how you are aware that the seasons are in the process of change.
7. Comment on a meeting you had with an individual who was most enthusiastic about his avocation. Consider its effect on his life.
8. After doing some research in the library, write about the origins and the appropriateness of the names we use for the months, or how some of the constellations came to get their names.
9. How successful was your visit to the planetarium?

HUMBUG IN SCIENCE

MAGNUS PYKE

Dr. Magnus Pyke (1908–) was born in London, studied at McGill, served during World War II in the Scientific Adviser's Division of the British Ministry of Food, and is now director of a research laboratory in Scotland. Each of the fourteen essays in *Nothing Like Science* shows "that science is something more than a process for inventing useful things—that it is, indeed, one way of finding out the truth."

Science, with all its great material successes to its credit, has become today an important way of thought. It is indeed probably the most important intellectual influence in our modern philosophy. There is a danger, therefore, that it may tend to be taken too solemnly, too uncritically. Science, as we have said, is the precise assessment and collation of facts. Any conclusions drawn from these facts must be verifiable by experiment. But one thing which has been unduly neglected by scientists is the old question as to whether a tree that falls in the desert makes any noise when nobody is there to hear it. And this is odd because it was Einstein, the greatest of them all, who pointed out that any particular scientist was mistaken in assuming that two things happened simultaneously in two different places when he could never be in two places at once to see both things happening. Einstein, in fact, suggested in his polite mathematics, which were mercifully incomprehensible not only to lay people but to most scientists as well, that confident scientific assumptions such as these might be humbug. Quite recently, however, there is some evidence that the tide of scientific solemnity is turning. One or two papers have appeared in the literature in which humbug is seriously discussed. And it may not be long before it is recognized that humbug plays an important role in certain branches of science.

When a research worker sets out systematically to discover whether vitamin tablets—let us say—prevent your catching cold, it is no good his giving them to a group of people throughout the winter and asking them at the end whether they have had fewer colds than during the year before. Neither is it enough to give vitamins to half the people in a large group and compare them with the other half who are given nothing. The power of the mind over the body is such that some of the people receiving the pills will be affected one way or the other by the very fact that *something* is being done to them. This being so, the competent experimenter is now trained to give vitamin tablets, or whatever it is he may be testing, to one group of people and dummy tablets to another exactly comparable group. The dummy pills are commonly termed, in the technical vernacular, 'placebos'.

Until lately little attention has been paid to the nature of the placebo itself. Provided that it was inert, that was all that mattered. This is now changed. Although describing it as a 'humble humbug', a writer in a recent number of the *Transactions of the College of Physicians of Philadelphia* pointed out the necessity of close scientific study being made of the placebo, now dignified with the title of a 'research tool'. Another writer in the *American Journal of Medicine* goes into some detail on the matter. He considers that when humbug is required for scientific purposes it should be efficient. A placebo medicine should, it now appears, be red, yellow or brown, *not* blue or green, which are colours associated with liniments or poisons. The taste should be bitter but not unpleasant. Capsules or tablets should be coloured and either very small—implying that they are excessively potent—or impressively large; and they should not look like everyday things such as aspirin.

Just as Einstein's events which happen in two places at once may be influenced by the person who observes them, so, it is now argued, a particular drug cannot, in a scientific sense, be said to have a particular effect on any organ of the body without taking into account the personality of the man or woman to whom the body belongs. The *Journal of Pharmacology* published a learned article not long ago pointing out that when a drug is being tested for its effect, let us say, on the pain from wounds, as is only right and proper, half of the group of patients are injected with an inert placebo—usually salt and water. It is nearly always found that some of these patients report that the placebo has relieved their pain. A scientific study of these 'placebo reactors', as they are called, shows that, like people who are 'accident prone', they possess certain characteristics. These people who are particularly susceptible to humbug, we must assume, are more grateful to the doctors who are experimenting on them, more co-operative with the nurses, and more talkative than 'normal' individuals.

As soon as one starts to investigate humbug in science, it is surprising how many scientists one discovers whose whole lives are devoted to the subject. The 'meat cutlet' of the vegetarian restaurant, complete with its paper frill round its artificial 'bone' of uncooked macaroni, is achieved without the aid of science, but the whole army of chemists busy fabricating artificial cream, or artificial colours simulating egg in cake or oak smoke in kippers, or artificial egg albumen for baking are all engaged in harnessing scientific knowledge to the humbug business.

When we discuss the shortage of scientific manpower which is hampering the full development of this country in a competitive world, it is salutary to recall that highly qualified colloid chemists are devoting their talents and the fruits of prolonged training and education to such problems as the best method to prevent the orange pulp in orange squash settling to the bottom of the bottle. In the field of brewing, a great research foundation has been established one of whose major preoccupations is to prevent beer from becoming cloudy. Not long ago, when beer was consumed from pewter vessels, science would have been relieved of the pursuit of this piece of amiable humbug.

The scientific problems which arise in the study of the humbug demanded by modern fancy are very real ones. No one has ever been known to contract a disease from a loaf of bread which is handled with reasonable care. But today, just as our Victorian grandmothers used to avoid the improper sight of uncovered legs—*any* kind of legs —by affixing little skirts to the legs of dining-room tables, so do we eschew the sight of uncovered food by insisting that bread be wrapped. This innocent desire sets the research chemists several difficult conundrums. Microbiologists must be employed to study the types of mould which tend to develop inside the wrapping paper. Organic chemists are required to investigate possible antimycotic agents which could prevent the moulds from growing. Cereal chemists must be engaged to research into the nature of crumb toughness.

To the scientist, the nature of the problem is everything. The purpose for which the work is done is very little. He will work with as much devotion to perfect a colour or a varnish so that a new model of a motor-car can claim to be the 'most beautiful object on four wheels' as he will to invent a new anaesthetic. And this is right and

proper, for who knows what may be the ultimate outcome of a
scientific investigation?

Humbug, however, can come into science in a different and less
attractive form. For example, a few years ago two young men who
were engaged in an investigation into the composition of wool discovered a new method of analysis. Such a discovery is of fundamental
importance in science since progress is often brought to a halt by the
inability of classical analytical methods to separate chemical substances of distinct but similar nature. The technique invented by
these two young men, Drs. Martin and Synge, for which, very appropriately, they were awarded a Nobel Prize, was sublimely simple as
so many strokes of genius often are. Its principle was as follows. If
you drop red ink on to blotting-paper the mixed pigments in the ink
separate into their different colours as the blot expands. In the same
way, if a mixture of, say, the different sugars that occur naturally
in honey are allowed to spread slowly down a strip of blotting-paper
they also will separate out and the quantities of the individual sugar-
types can be measured. The original form of the process consisted of hanging a long wet strip of paper overnight in a container which kept the
atmosphere moist. In the learned paper announcing the discovery to
a meeting of the Biochemical Society, the inventors described how
they used lengths of earthenware drainpipe for the purpose. Nowadays,
although lots of chemists still use equally simple apparatus for this
work, there are on the market elaborate and expensive vessels fitted
with all kinds of gadgets for carrying out 'paper-partition chromatography'. In fact these elegant pieces of apparatus, although sometimes
more convenient than the old-fashioned drainpipes, do the same job.
And there are research workers who try them. The scientist, after all,
is only a man. He needs constantly to be kept awake to reality if he
is not to forget that this type of thing, together with the chromium-
plated taps you turn on with your feet, may in fact be nothing but
humbug.

Another bit of humbug in science is found with the use of a special
language. There is no harm in this of itself; indeed, much of science
is so complicated that the employment of a specialised jargon, the
words of which possess a precise technical meaning, is of convenience
as a species of shorthand. But there are occasions when technical
language is used to make something that is, in fact, simple and commonplace sound as if it were important and learned. For example, to
an ordinary person 'literature' is a written record of something worth

saying, well said. To a scientist, however, 'the literature' is anything at all, important or unimportant, that has appeared in a technical journal about the subject under discussion. And in this 'literature' the scientist may wrap himself up and hide himself away from reality in the liturgy of a ritual passive voice. Oddly enough, he is compelled to use this grammatical form by the insistence of scientific editors. But if he were allowed to write straight down what he had done, without humbug, he might not publish any report until he really *had* made a discovery. As it is, we get this sort of thing:

> The test was made immediately after *the subjects* had consumed meals, the solid portions of which varied from 6 to 18 oz. From the results *it was found that* the effect of size of meal on number of words typed was *highly significant,* the typist working best after meals, the portions of which weighed 9 to 12 oz. However, in *further tests it was found* that the effect of size of meal was rendered insignificant if *motivation* to do well were sufficiently great.

In other words, the scientific nutrition of one's typist helps her with her work—unless it doesn't.

Throughout the whole period of his academic training the scientist is gradually conditioned by the language of his textbooks as well as by the kind of prose favoured by the editorial boards of learned journals to use long, pompous, Latin words when he could use short Anglo-Saxon ones. The phrases to be found in his illiterate 'literature' are usually long and involved rather than short and pithy. Dr. Johnson illustrated the effect of this way of writing. In English, the sentence is: 'It has not wit to keep it sweet.' With the assistance of Latinised words this becomes: 'It has not vitality to preserve it from putrefaction.'

Not long ago, R. Whitehead writing in the *Lancet* pointed out that scientists when they meant 'say' would try to make their statements seem more impressive by using 'affirm', 'allege', 'assert', 'aver', 'claim', 'contend', 'declare', 'intimate', 'maintain', or 'state' instead. Surely, this is humbug. Instead of 'much', they write 'a considerable amount of', 'a great deal of', 'a large proportion of', or 'quite a large quantity of' and their prose is peppered with such phrases as 'circular in outline', 'complex in character', 'large in size', 'next in order', and most popular of all, 'red in colour'.

This brings me to a difficult and important aspect of humbug in science. The question whether a modern scientist is an educated man.

For a long time it has been thought that only a liberal knowledge of the classics justified a man considering himself to be an educated person in the full sense. Such an education gave him an understanding of men and affairs, of literature and philosophy, and of the languages and customs of countries other than his own. In recent years, Cabinet Ministers, senior Civil Servants and other Powerful People have begun to realise that science could achieve material results unattainable otherwise. The detonation of the first atomic bomb really brought home the fact that scientists were, at least on this striking material plane, to be reckoned with. Consequently, those in positions of authority were not entirely unwilling to be convinced by the argument put forward by scientists with increasing assurance that a 'scientific training' was, in fact, a liberal education.

It is difficult to assert, in the face of the great and increasing mass of technical publications printed each year, that a scientific education, as at present administered, conduces to much elegance in literary style. Once upon a time it was the custom for scientific workers to move about and study in other countries. Most of the older generation of scientists used to work for a period in a German laboratory. A vestigial remnant of this internationalism remains in the British practice of setting chemists an examination in German translation. But this is now recognised to be of no cultural significance and few English-speaking chemists can do better than scramble through a German technical paper with a dictionary as a crutch.

We must face the fact that in the practical world of affairs science is not accepted as a philosophy but as a way of doing things. A scientific education is designed to teach the student the factual knowledge to enable him to handle chemicals or electrical apparatus or machinery in its various sorts. The illiterate scientists, it must be admitted, are many, the scientific philosophers are few. Sometimes, in the hope that the assertion is true and not humbug, that scientific education fits a man for the affairs of the world, the research worker is brought from his back room and taken into the boardroom. There he sits in barely concealed boredom while general matters are being discussed. Only when his own items are reached in the agenda does he hold forth, *ex cathedra*—and then stops.

The study of Latin verbs or Greek syntax cannot of itself be claimed to furnish the mind with much else than a set of more or less arbitrary rules. But the *Odyssey* (as has been shown by the enormous sales of the Penguin translation) by reporting the behaviour and feelings of

men three thousand years ago gives us ideas to guide our own behaviour today. The modern teaching of chemistry and physics and
mechanics produces a competent technologist. Sometimes it produces
a scientist. But if it produces a philosopher this is quite accidental.
The contribution of science has been the thesis that logical study, ex-
perimentation and the acceptance of conclusions based on fact no
matter how unexpected or unpalatable are the way to truth. Scientific
education teaches its pupils to apply these principles only to material
things. Until the philosophy with all its implications is taught as
applying also to government, social affairs, even religion itself perhaps,
there surely is an element of humbug in claiming that the study of
'science' as we understand the word produces educated men.

One more piece of humbug might be included here: the belief
that the scientist, the dedicated research worker, does his job to benefit
humanity. This extraordinary delusion is held to apply most directly
to scientific persons involved in medical matters. There are in hos-
pitals whole laboratories full of scientifically trained men and women,
all busily engaged in matching blood samples, analysing what are
euphemistically called 'specimens', looking at slices of flesh under
microscopes and carrying out the whole complex programme of the
tests that prudent doctors demand, not necessarily to help the patients,
but to protect their attendants from subsequent legal action if, as is
bound to occur eventually in this mortal scene, the patient does not
recover. These scientists do their jobs as well as anybody else, but the
measure of service to humanity in their work is no greater than that
of motor mechanics.

Dr. L. W. Batten in the course of a lecture to the final-year medical
students at St. Bartholomew's Hospital, London, pointed out that,
although modern medicine depends on science and the continuing
work of scientists, the practice of medicine is an art. He also pointed
out that all artists work partly for money. Shakespeare wrote his plays,
Bach composed his Brandenburg concerto, Michelangelo got his David
out of that lump of marble—partly for money; although none of them
got very rich. The popular impression of a doctor selflessly serving
suffering humanity is exaggerated. Good doctors, says Dr. Batten, are
seldom dedicated to the service of humanity. Partly, like the rest of
us, they work for money and partly they work for the praise of their
peers. But though they do not say so, the best of them are dedicated
to the practice of medicine. That is to say, they are interested in their
work.

It is as unreasonable to single out the doctors and nurses for special gratitude for scientific activity on behalf of suffering mankind, merely because we see them actually dealing with sufferers, as it is to tip the waiter but not the cook or the kitchen maid when we go to a restaurant. Louis Pasteur was applying his chemical acumen to preventing wine going sour when he developed the discovery that solved the problem of infectious disease. Service to suffering humanity did not come into it. The scientist who did more to earn the gratitude of suffering humanity than a complete Royal-College-full of medical consultants was the engineer who thought out the process for making iron pipes and thus enabled us to keep the sewage separate from the drinking water. It was this scientific advance that rendered possible the great populous cities that we find necessary for our happiness today.

The popular imagination is strange and unpredictable. It is traditional folk-lore of our time to think of a civil servant as a dried-up sort of fellow with a rolled umbrella and a well developed contempt for the ordinary citizen, who arrives at his office late in the morning, continuously drinks cups of tea while he is there and enjoys six weeks' holidays plus six weeks' sick leave every year. Yet a civil servant is far more directly concerned with benefiting humanity than a scientist. He often has to think about humanity—or at least about that section of it with which he is employed to deal. A scientist engaged, let us say, by a great chemical company may be far removed from any thoughts of humanity, suffering or otherwise. Yet, just as it was said of McCormick that his invention of the mechanical reaper straightened the bent backs of the peasants of the world, so equally could it be held that the anonymous inventors of nylon allowed the weary housewives of at least a substantial proportion of the world to put down their darning needles. But it is clearly humbug to believe that the research team that made the discovery, and the chemical engineers and administrators who made the nylon, and the investors and boards of directors and shareholders who made it possible for the manufacture to take place at all were impelled by altruistic notions about the sufferings of mankind.

Thus we see that although science is a potent means of making material things, of creating power and of controlling Nature and, most important of all, is the dominant philosophy by which our Western technology is directed, nevertheless humbug enters into its operation in a number of ways. Humbug is a necessary and useful feature in the 'controls' used to measure the effectiveness of new drugs and new vitamins, the very existence of which it would sometimes be impossible to establish without it. But humbug in science has only a limited function for good. Usually it is bad because it is by its very nature false, and the core of science is truth. Elaborate and unnecessarily complex apparatus designed to impress rather than to enlighten is a hindrance to discovery. There is the sad story from the United States of a first-rate scientist who was studying the nature of the proteins in blood plasma. For part of his research he needed to use a machine called an 'ultra-centrifuge'. This is a large, complicated and very expensive piece of equipment which separates substances suspended in liquid by spinning a test tube full of the mixture at extremely high speed. His studies yielded interesting results which were published. But instead of being able to proceed with the next logical step in his intricate research he found himself bombarded with samples of blood plasma from other doctors all over the place who had half-understood the significance of his published report. They had the idea that his kind of studies *might* be useful for some of their patients. But above all, they were impressed by his expensive and unusual apparatus. When last heard of he was set up in a big office in an institute with *four* ultra-centrifuges, so bombarded with miscellaneous blood samples as to have no time left to think or to carry out new research.

The adaptability of the modern citizen to the stresses of the crowded world in which he is subjected to all sorts of scientific marvels is remarkable. He quickly tends to develop, to a greater or lesser degree, a protective armour against a good deal of the humbug by which he is assailed. The scientist also must in his professional life defend himself against the same influences. Sometimes he needs to use humbug as part of his science. Usually, however, he needs to be on the defensive against the special dangers of pompous and obscure language, of woolly, grandiose thoughts about the cultural significance of his activities, of windy beliefs in his mission in the world, or, most dangerous of all, of coming to believe his own humbug.

Questions and Suggestions

1. List in your own words some of the sources that Pyke gives for the presence of humbug in science.
2. Does he consider some forms of scientific humbug to be more valuable and some more dangerous than others?
3. What implications do you find in the essay that the shortage of scientists working on major projects could be reduced?

4. On what point is he clearly in agreement with Teale?

5. Is the tone of the essay consistent?

6. Does Pyke hold some non-conformist views concerning scientists and their education?

7. One of his major concerns is with the language and "literature" of scientists, whether they be British or American. What faults does he find? What does he mean by the "ritual passive voice"? Why does he prefer *placebo* to *research tool* or *placebo reactors*? Consult your dictionary for the meaning of *pleonasm, tautology,* and *redundancy.* Does Pyke quote any examples of such errors?

8. For further improvement in your writing, study the structure of his paragraphs.

9. Because a number of words in this essay may not be in your active vocabulary, be sure you know the meaning that Pyke has in mind for *vernacular, inert, colloid, eschew, antimycotic, chromatography, vestigial, altruistic, ex cathedra,* and *acumen.*

Ideas for Writing

1. Discuss the validity of a psychological test in which you served as one of the guinea pigs. Be as objective as possible in stating your conclusion.

2. Using specific details to develop one or more dramatic situations or related incidents, reveal your reaction to a hypochondriac. In another paper you might show how a person's imagination, either through the power of association or outside influence, allows him to believe he is either well or sick, or that the medicine has or has not been of much help.

3. Study a page in one of your science texts and show why the prose is or is not "illiterate 'literature,' " and explain why the author is or is not guilty of humbug.

4. Analyze a portion of a text for its jargon.

5. Consider situations in which an authority in a certain field may give the impression of being uneducated. Base your paper on an expert or specialist whom you know well.

6. Define "the educated man."

DR. HEIDEGGER'S EXPERIMENT

NATHANIEL HAWTHORNE

Nathaniel Hawthorne (1804–1864), a native of Salem, Massachusetts, was widely read before he entered Bowdoin College, where he graduated in 1825. Although he invested some money in the Brook Farm experiment, at West Roxbury, he found the group uncongenial. Nor could he, as was Muir, be a hero-worshiper of Emerson; but he was pleasantly acquainted with Thoreau. With the publication of his stories, novels, and journals, Hawthorne gradually came to be recognized as one of America's most important writers.

That very singular man, old Dr. Heidegger, once invited four venerable friends to meet him in his study. There three white-bearded gentlemen—Mr. Medbourne, Colonel Killigrew and Mr. Gascoigne—and a withered gentlewoman whose name was the Widow Wycherly. They were all melancholy old creatures who had been unfortunate in life, and whose greatest misfortune it was that they were not long ago in their graves. Mr. Medbourne, in the vigor of his age, had been a prosperous merchant, but had lost his all by a frantic speculation, and was now little better than a mendicant. Colonel Killigrew had wasted his best years and his health and substance in the pursuit of sinful pleasures which had given birth to a brood of pains, such as the gout and diverse other torments of soul and body. Mr. Gascoigne was a ruined politician, a man of evil fame—or, at least, had been so till time had buried him from the knowledge of the present generation and made him obscure instead of infamous. As for the Widow Wycherly, tradition tells us that she was a great beauty in her day, but for a long while past she had lived in deep seclusion on account of certain scandalous stories which had prejudiced the gentry of the town against her. It is a circumstance worth mentioning that each of these three old gentlemen—Mr. Medbourne, Colonel Killigrew and Mr. Gascoigne—

From *Twice-Told Tales.* This story first appeared in the January, 1837 issue of *Knickerbocker Magazine,* under the title, "The Fountain of Youth".

were early lovers of the Widow Wycherly, and had once been on the point of cutting each other's throats for her sake. And before proceeding farther I will merely hint that Dr. Heidegger and all his four guests were sometimes thought to be a little beside themselves, as is not infrequently the case with old people when worried either by present troubles or woeful recollections.

"My dear old friends," said Dr. Heidegger, motioning them to be seated, "I am desirous of your assistance in one of those little experiments with which I amuse myself here in my study."

If all stories were true, Dr. Heidegger's study must have been a very curious place. It was a dim, old-fashioned chamber festooned with cobwebs and besprinkled with antique dust. Around the walls stood several oaken bookcases, the lower shelves of which were filled with rows of gigantic folios and black-letter quartos, and the upper with little parchment-covered duodecimos. Over the central bookcase was a bronze bust of Hippocrates, with which, according to some authorities, Dr. Heidegger was accustomed to hold consultations in all difficult cases of his practice. In the obscurest corner of the room stood a tall and narrow oaken closet with its door ajar, within which doubtfully appeared a skeleton. Between two of the bookcases hung a looking-glass, presenting its high and dusty plate within a tarnished gilt frame. Among many wonderful stories related of this mirror, it was fabled that the spirits of all the doctor's deceased patients dwelt within its verge and would stare him in the face whenever he looked thitherward. The opposite side of the chamber was ornamented with the full-length portrait of a young lady arrayed in the faded magnificence of silk, satin and brocade, and with a visage as faded as her dress. Above half a century ago Dr. Heidegger had been on the point of marriage with this young lady, but, being affected with some slight disorder, she had swallowed one of her lover's prescriptions and died on the bridal-evening. The greatest curiosity of the study remains to be mentioned: it was a ponderous folio volume bound in black leather, with massive silver clasps. There were no letters on the back, and nobody could tell the title of the book. But it was well known to be a book of magic, and once, when a chambermaid had lifted it merely to brush away the dust, the skeleton had rattled in its closet, the picture of the young lady had stepped one foot upon the floor, and several ghastly faces had peeped forth from the mirror, while the brazen head of Hippocrates frowned and said, "Forbear!"

Such was Dr. Heidegger's study. On the summer afternoon of our tale a small round table as black as ebony stood in the center of the room, sustaining a cut-glass vase of beautiful form and elaborate workmanship. The sunshine came through the window between the heavy festoons of two faded damask curtains and fell directly across this vase; so that a mild splendor was reflected from it on the ashen visages of the five old people who sat around. Four champagne glasses were also on the table.

"My dear old friends," repeated Dr. Heidegger, "may I reckon on your aid in performing an exceedingly curious experiment?"

Now, Dr. Heidegger was a very strange old gentleman whose eccentricity had become the nucleus for a thousand fantastic stories. Some of these fables—to my shame be it spoken—might possibly be traced back to mine own veracious self; and if any passages of the present tale should startle the reader's faith, I must be content to bear the stigma of a fiction-monger.

When the doctor's four guests heard him talk of his proposed experiment, they anticipated nothing more wonderful than the murder of a mouse in an air-pump, or the examination of a cobweb by the microscope, or some similar nonsense with which he was constantly in the habit of pestering his intimates. But without waiting for a reply Dr. Heidegger hobbled across the chamber and returned with the same ponderous folio bound in black leather which common report affirmed to be a book of magic. Undoing the silver clasps, he opened the volume and took from among its black-letter pages a rose, or what was once a rose, though now the green leaves and crimson petals had assumed one brownish hue and the ancient flower seemed ready to crumble to dust in the doctor's hands.

"This rose," said Dr. Heidegger, with a sigh—"this same withered and crumbling flower—blossomed five and fifty years ago. It was given me by Sylvia Ward, whose portrait hangs yonder, and I meant to wear it in my bosom at our wedding. Five and fifty years it has been treasured between the leaves of this old volume. Now, would you deem it possible that this rose of half a century could ever bloom again?"

"Nonsense!" said the Widow Wycherly, with a peevish toss of her head. "You might as well ask whether an old woman's wrinkled face could ever bloom again."

"See!" answered Dr. Heidegger. He uncovered the vase and threw the faded rose into the water which it contained. At first it lay lightly on the surface of the fluid, appearing to imbibe none of its moisture. Soon, however, a singular change began to be visible. The crushed and dried petals stirred and assumed a deepening tinge of crimson, as if the flower were reviving from a deathlike slumber, the slender stalk and twigs of foliage became green, and there was the rose of half a century, looking as fresh as when Sylvia Ward had first given it to her lover. It was scarcely full-blown, for some of its delicate red leaves curled modestly around its moist bosom, within which two or three dewdrops were sparkling.

"That is certainly a very pretty deception," said the doctor's friends—carelessly, however, for they had witnessed greater miracles at a conjurer's show. "Pray, how was it effected?"

"Did you never hear of the fountain of youth?" asked Dr. Heidegger, "which Ponce de Leon, the Spanish adventurer, went in search of two or three centuries ago?"

"But did Ponce de Leon ever find it?" said the Widow Wycherly.

"No," answered Dr. Heidegger, "for he never sought it in the right place. The famous fountain of youth, if I am rightly informed, is situated in the southern part of the Floridian peninsula, not far from Lake Macaco. Its source is overshadowed by several gigantic magnolias which, though numberless centuries old, have been kept as fresh as violets by the virtues of this wonderful water. An acquaintance of mine, knowing my curiosity in such matters, has sent me what you see in the vase."

"Ahem!" said Colonel Killigrew, who believed not a word of the doctor's story; "and what may be the effect of this fluid on the human frame?"

"You shall judge for yourself, my dear colonel," replied Dr. Heidegger. "And all of you, my respected friends, are welcome to so much of this admirable fluid as may restore to you the bloom of youth. For my own part, having had much trouble in growing old, I am in no hurry to grow young again. With your permission, therefore, I will merely watch the progress of the experiment."

While he spoke Dr. Heidegger had been filling the four champagne glasses with the water of the fountain of youth. It was apparently impregnated with an effervescent gas, for little bubbles were continually ascending from the depths of the glasses and bursting in silvery spray at the surface. As the liquor diffused a pleasant perfume, the old people doubted not that it possessed cordial and comfortable properties, and, though utter skeptics as to its rejuvenescent power, they were inclined to swallow it at once. But Dr. Heidegger besought them to stay a moment.

"Before you drink, my respectable old friends," said he, "it would be well that, with the experience of a lifetime to direct you, you should draw up a few general rules for your guidance in passing a second time through the perils of youth. Think what a sin and shame it would be if, with your peculiar advantages, you should not become patterns of virtue and wisdom to all the young people of the age!"

The doctor's four venerable friends made him no answer except by a feeble and tremulous laugh, so very ridiculous was the idea that, knowing how closely repentance treads behind the steps of error, they should every go astray again.

"Drink, then," said the doctor, bowing; "I rejoice that I have so well selected the subjects of my experiment."

With palsied hands they raised the glasses to their lips. The liquor, if it really possessed such virtues as Dr. Heidegger imputed to it, could not have been bestowed on four human beings who needed it more woefully. They looked as if they had never known what youth or pleasure was, but had been the offspring of Nature's dotage, and always the gray, decrepit, sapless, miserable creatures who now sat stooping round the doctor's table without life enough in their souls or bodies to be animated even by the prospect of growing young again. They drank off the water and replaced their glasses on the table.

Assuredly, there was an almost immediate improvement in the aspect of the party—not unlike what might have been produced by a glass of generous wine—together with a sudden glow of cheerful sunshine, brightening over all their visages at once. There was a healthful suffusion on their cheeks instead of the ashen hue that had made them look so corpse-like. They gazed at one another, and fancied that some magic power had really begun to smooth away the deep and sad inscriptions which Father Time had been so long engraving on their brows. The Widow Wycherly adjusted her cap, for she felt almost like a woman again.

"Give us more of this wondrous water," cried they, eagerly. "We are younger, but we are still too old. Quick! give us more!"

"Patience, patience!" quoth Dr. Heidegger, who sat watching the experiment with philosophic coolness. "You have been a long time growing old; surely you might be content to grow young in half an hour. But the water is at your service." Again he filled their glasses with the liquor of youth, enough of which still remained in the vase to turn half the old people in the city to the age of their own grandchildren.

While the bubbles were yet sparkling on the brim, the doctor's four

guests snatched their glasses from the table and swallowed the contents
at a single gulp. Was it delusion? Even while the draught was passing
down their throats it seemed to have wrought a change on their whole
systems. Their eyes grew clear and bright; a dark shade deepened among
their silvery locks: they sat around the table, three gentlemen of middle
age and a woman hardly beyond her buxom prime.

"My dear Widow, you are charming!" cried Colonel Killigrew, whose
eyes had been fixed upon her face while the shadows of age were flitting
from it like darkness from the crimson daybreak.

The fair widow knew of old that Colonel Killigrew's compliments
were not always measured by sober truth; so she started up and ran to
the mirror, still dreading that the ugly visage of an old woman would
meet her gaze.

Meanwhile, the three gentlemen behaved in such a manner as
proved that the water of the fountain of youth possessed some intoxicat-
ing qualities—unless, indeed, their exhilaration of spirits were merely
a lightsome dizziness caused by the sudden removal of the weight of
years. Mr. Gascoigne's mind seemed to run on political topics, but
whether relating to the past, present or future could not easily be
determined, since the same ideas and phrases have been in vogue these
fifty years. Now he rattled forth full-throated sentences about patriotism,
national glory and the people's right; now he muttered some perilous
stuff or other in a sly and doubtful whisper, so cautiously that even his
own conscience could scarcely catch the secret; and now, again, he
spoke in measured accents and a deeply-deferential tone as if a royal
ear were listening to his well-turned periods. Colonel Killigrew all this
time had been trolling forth a jolly bottle-song and ringing his glass
in symphony with the chorus, while his eyes wandered toward the
buxom figure of the Widow Wycherly. On the other side of the table,
Mr. Medbourne was involved in a calculation of dollars and cents with
which was strangely intermingled a project of supplying the East Indies
with ice by harnessing a team of whales to the polar icebergs. As for
the Widow Wycherly, she stood before the mirror courtesying and
simpering to her own image and greeting it as the friend whom she
loved better than all the world besides. She thrust her face close to
the glass to see whether some long-remembered wrinkle or crow's-foot
had indeed vanished; she examined whether the snow had so entirely
melted from her hair that the venerable cap could be safely thrown

aside. At last, turning briskly away, she came with a sort of dancing step to the table.

"My dear old doctor," cried she, "pray favor me with another glass."

"Certainly, my dear madam, certainly," replied the complaisant doctor. "See! I have already filled the glasses."

There, in fact, stood the four glasses brimful of this wonderful water, the delicate spray of which, as it effervesced from the surface, resembled the tremulous glitter of diamonds.

It was now so nearly sunset that the chamber had grown duskier than ever, but a mild and moonlike splendor gleamed from within the vase and rested alike on the four guests and on the doctor's venerable figure. He sat in a high-backed, elaborately-carved oaken armchair with a gray dignity of aspect that might have well befitted that very Father Time whose power had never been disputed save by this fortunate company. Even while quaffing the third draught of the fountain of youth, they were almost awed by the expression of his mysterious visage. But the next moment the exhilarating gush of young life shot through their veins. They were now in the happy prime of youth. Age, with its miserable train of cares and sorrows and diseases, was remembered only as the trouble of a dream from which they had joyously awoke. The fresh gloss of the soul, so early lost and without which the world's successive scenes had been but a gallery of faded pictures, again threw its enchantment over all their prospects. They felt like new-created beings in a new-created universe.

"We are young! We are young!" they cried, exultingly.

Youth, like the extremity of age, had effaced the strongly-marked characteristics of middle life and mutually assimilated them all. They were a group of merry youngsters almost maddened with the exuberant frolicsomeness of their years. The most singular effect of their gayety was an impulse to mock the infirmity and decrepitude of which they had so lately been the victims. They laughed loudly at their old-fashioned attire—the wide-skirted coats and flapped waistcoats of the young men and the ancient cap and gown of the blooming girl. One limped across the floor like a gouty grandfather; one set a pair of spectacles astride of his nose and pretended to pore over the black-letter pages of the book of magic; a third seated himself in an armchair and strove to imitate the venerable dignity of Dr. Heidegger. Then all shouted mirthfully and leaped about the room.

The Widow Wycherly—if so fresh a damsel could be called a widow

—tripped up to the doctor's chair with a mischievous merriment in her rosy face.

"Doctor, you dear old soul," cried she, "get up and dance with me;" and then the four young people laughed louder than ever to think what a queer figure the poor old doctor would cut.

"Pray excuse me," answered the doctor, quietly. "I am old and rheumatic, and my dancing-days were over long ago. But either of these gay young gentlemen will be glad of so pretty a partner."

"Dance with me, Clara," cried Colonel Killigrew.

"No, no! I will be her partner," shouted Mr. Gascoigne.

"She promised me her hand fifty years ago," exclaimed Mr. Medbourne.

They all gathered round her. One caught both her hands in his passionate grasp, another threw his arm about her waist, the third buried his hand among the glossy curls that clustered beneath the widow's cap. Blushing, panting, struggling, chiding, laughing, her warm breath fanning each of their faces by turns, she strove to disengage herself, yet still remained in their triple embrace. Never was there a livelier picture of youthful rivalship, with bewitching beauty for the prize. Yet, by a strange deception, owing to the duskiness of the chamber and the antique dresses which they still wore, the tall mirror is said to have reflected the figures of the three old, gray, withered grandsires ridiculously contending for the skinny ugliness of a shriveled grandam. But they were young: their burning passions proved them so.

Inflamed to madness by the coquetry of the girl-widow, who neither granted nor quite withheld her favors, the three rivals began to interchange threatening glances. Still keeping hold of the fair prize, they grappled fiercely at one another's throats. As they struggled to and fro the table was overturned and the vase dashed into a thousand fragments. The precious water of youth flowed in a bright stream across the floor, moistening the wings of a butterfly which, grown old in the decline of summer, had alighted there to die. The insect fluttered lightly through the chamber and settled on the snowy head of Dr. Heidegger.

"Come, come, gentlemen! Come, Madam Wycherly!" exclaimed the doctor. "I really must protest against this riot."

They stood still and shivered, for it seemed as if gray Time were calling them back from their sunny youth far down into the chill and darksome vale of years. They looked at old Dr. Heidegger, who sat in his carved armchair holding the rose of half a century, which he had rescued from among the fragments of the shattered vase. At the motion of his hand the four rioters resumed their seats—the more readily because their violent exertions had wearied them, youthful though they were.

"My poor Sylvia's rose!" ejaculated Dr. Heidegger, holding it in the light of the sunset clouds. "It appears to be fading again."

And so it was. Even while the party were looking at it the flower continued to shrivel up, till it became as dry and fragile as when the doctor had first thrown it into the vase. He shook off the few drops of moisture which clung to its petals.

"I love it as well thus as in its dewy freshness," observed he, pressing the withered rose to his withered lips.

While he spoke the butterfly fluttered down from the doctor's snowy head and fell upon the floor. His guests shivered again. A strange chillness—whether of the body or spirit they could not tell—was creeping gradually over them all. They gazed at one another, and fancied that each fleeting moment snatched away a charm and left a deepening furrow where none had been before. Was it an illusion? Had the changes of a lifetime been crowded into so brief a space, and were they now four aged people sitting with their old friend Dr. Heidegger?

"Are we grown old again so soon?" cried they, dolefully.

In truth, they had. The water of youth possessed merely a virtue more transient than that of wine; the delirium which it created had effervesced away. Yes, they were old again. With a shuddering impulse that showed her a woman still, the Widow clasped her skinny hands before her face and wished that the coffin-lid were over it, since it could be no longer beautiful.

"Yes, friends, ye are old again," said Dr. Heidegger, "and, lo! the water of youth is all lavished on the ground. Well, I bemoan it not; for if the fountain gushed at my very doorstep, I would not stoop to bathe my lips in it—no, though its delirium were for years instead of moments. Such is the lesson ye have taught me."

But the doctor's four friends had taught no such lesson to themselves. They resolved forthwith to make a pilgrimage to Florida and quaff at morning, noon and night from the fountain of youth.

Questions and Suggestions

1. In what ways might Dr. Heidegger resemble modern scientists? In what ways does this tale foreshadow some medical and psychological methods currently in use?
2. What attitude does the narrator hold concerning scientific experiments?

3. Who tells the tale? Is Hawthorne as interested in his characters as he is in the general idea or theme? What is the theme?
4. Is the story primarily realistic or symbolic? What is the meaning of Dr. Heidegger's final speech?
5. Why does the doctor not name the acquaintance who sent him the elixir?
6. What association does Hawthorne intend for you to make when you read the description of the study? Are the details appropriate to his purpose?
7. Recent tests indicate that human subjects have hallucinations or bad side effects from a medicine or experiment, if they know they are expected to; but, under clinically similar conditions, they do not experience the same results when given placebos. Was it through unconscious persuasion that Dr. Heidegger got his results? The effect of such persuasion upon communities is graphically recorded by Aldous Huxley in *The Devils of Loudun* and by Arthur Miller in *The Crucible*.

Ideas for Writing

1. Describe specific individuals who regularly attend health clubs, spas, rejuvenation centers, or who consult quacks.
2. Explain why a friend or acquaintance underwent plastic surgery.
3. Can you describe the quality of false youthfulness in an older person, or a friend who does not like to act his age?
4. Recreate a visit you paid to an astrologer, palmist, or faith healer. Were you affected by the surroundings and the abracadabra, or did you remain a skeptic?
5. Recall the time when you or a friend was persuaded to believe, even if only momentarily, something which you knew could not be true.
6. Study the cosmetic advertisements in one of the glossy magazines. What conclusions do you reach, either from the pictures or the copy? Do the advertising agencies agree with Dr. Heidegger's belief about life?
7. Write your own story about a daydreamer. If you have ever wanted to be a player in the major leagues, read George Plimpton's *Out of My League*, a fine account of a wish that came true.

LIVING THINGS IN THE FRAME OF NATURE

CHARLES RAVEN

Since 1955, Charles Earle Raven, D.D. (1885--) has been
Chaplain to Queen Elizabeth, having been chaplain to her father
and grandfather. Educated at Cambridge, he was Regius Professor
of Divinity at Cambridge for eighteen years. The recipient of many
honorary degrees, Dr. Raven has held numerous academic posts
as well as high positions in the Church of England. He has also
served as president of the Botanical Society of the British Isles.
His two books that have the greatest connection with this essay
are *John Ray, Naturalist,* and *English Naturalists from Neckam
to Ray,* a prize-winning volume.

It is typical of the customary outlook upon the history of science to append a section on the study of living organisms to a record
concerned almost entirely with mathematics, astronomy, physics and
chemistry. This is all a part of the tendency, still so prevalent, to
identify science with weight and measurement and to treat biology
and psychology under mechanical categories and by laboratory methods.
Here we cannot be concerned with the failings of this procedure or the
recent revolts against it. But upon the story of the making of the modern
world it has had a seriously distorting effect.

For, in fact, the scientific movement—in its origin among the general changes which we call the Renaissance—owed far more to medicine, to the study of plants and animals, the development of new
foodstuffs and flowers and the exploration of new lands and seas, than
to Copernicus and his successors. Not until the eighteenth century
could it be said of science: 'There is now no room for natural philosophy: mathematics hath engrossed all'. Of the remarkable achievements
which had created an orderly and scientific botany and zoology before

From *The Listener,* August 13, 1959. Reprinted by permission of
the author. This was the last talk in a series entitled "The Making of
Modern Science," produced on the Third Programme.

the Copernican cosmology had become generally accepted we have in fact a much fuller knowledge than we have of the early alchemists or even the astronomers, let alone the engineers and the mechanics.

It is indeed arguable that gastronomy, not astronomy, is the oldest science and that the first application of the method of observation and experiment was made in the primitive kitchens of the cave-men, and was soon expanded into the fields of medicine, hunting, and agriculture. And although it was speedily obscured by superstitions and traditions, fables and fancies, it was never wholly abandoned even in the darkest ages. European culture and education owe a great debt to the Hippocratic oath and the Hippocratic colleges which set apart the medical profession as a dedicated and educated caste long before any other calling had been similarly and adequately equipped. Salerno and its medical school exerted an influence on the universities not only of Italy, like Padua, but also in other countries, as at Leyden. This has not been adequately acknowledged.

Moreover, thanks to Dioscorides and Galen, who had provided the standard text-books for pharmacology and for medicine, the tradition of Greek science had been kept alive more effectively than in any other of its departments. When the Renaissance re-created a demand for classical manuscripts, and the printing presses gave them unprecedented circulation, the commentaries upon Dioscorides's herbs and the disputes about Galen's anatomy originated the scientific research which was to spread all over western Europe by the middle of the sixteenth century. By then five commentators in various parts of Europe had expounded Dioscorides; and Vesalius of Belgium and John Caius of England had inaugurated the criticism and defence of Galen. Moreover, scholars of the early Renaissance in northern Italy had initiated inquiries into the plants mentioned by Pliny; and as Latin and Greek source-books were edited, substantial additions not only to botany but to zoology were made; and the process so familiar in the field of religion which compared the medieval fables of the herbals and bestiaries with the sober records and observation of classical authors added a great mass of material for the beginnings of biological studies.

The great pioneer who brought together all the evidence from the classics, from the traditions, and from a lifetime of study and inquiry— the man who has perhaps the best claim to be regarded as the founder of modern science—was Conrad Gesner, the Swiss. His four great folios on the *History of Animals, Reptiles, Birds and Fishes,* his collections of material for projected volumes on insects and plants, his vast number of other books, his hundreds of letters to doctors and students of nature all over Europe, and perhaps above all his excellent pictures illustrating the *History* so well that nearly all the creatures mentioned can still be easily identified—all this meant that he had not only produced the necessary material for zoological and botanical studies, but had given to students everywhere a sense of partnership and a standard of excellence which constituted a real scientific movement. We in Britain can see from our two first biologists, William Turner and John Caius, how much Gesner meant to them; and his many pupils in the next generation were scientists in the modern sense of the word.

The rapidity with which the new study of nature kindled the imagination and excited the interest of Western man was due in large part to the discoveries which the great voyagers and explorers brought home with them. The potato and the turkey, tobacco and quinine, tea, coffee, and chocolate, these were tangible proofs of the value of 'natural philosophy': for their human interest they were far more important than Copernican astronomy and more immediately rewarding than developments in mining and machinery.

The actual course of biological studies began inevitably with the naming of the plants and animals which medicine, literature, and observation made familiar. A chief incentive for identifying plants came from the traditional 'compound' drugs and antidotes to poison which had a sacrosanct reputation but no certainty as to their ingredients. The stylized pictures in the herbals derived remotely from Greek originals had long lost any resemblance to living flowers; and in any case they represented species from the Aegean or Asia Minor. We know how laboriously every classical reference was extracted and categorized and compared: but with useless illustrations and almost worse descriptions the results were at best speculative. Popular names and legends were based on the strange doctrine of signatures: this assumed that every plant testified by colour or shape or structure to its uses and value to man; this had controlled pharmacy for centuries. But the precise herbs which were actually used were hard to identify.

One essential and yet accidental cause of the speed and success of this first phase of biological study was the excellence of the artists who devoted themselves to depicting the flora and fauna of their world. It is I think true that no one has ever drawn plants or animals better than Dürer; and that the teams of experts who produced the woodcuts for the first herbals fully deserve to be classed with the Master. They worked from newly gathered specimens and though some of them, the borages for example, faded too fast for them, no plant that they dealt with could ever be mistaken for anything else. The pictures of animals and birds reproduced by Gesner are not so good: the attitudes are often stilted and the shapes occasionally distorted: but in the birds most of those taken from life are plainly recognizable; and the animals, those for example drawn by John Caius from specimens in the London Docks and the Lion Gate of the Tower, are usually easy to name. With such guides it was possible not only to identify large numbers of particular species but to observe their affinities and arrange them in an appropriate system. And this was in fact being done before the dawn of the seventeenth century.

Fortunately, also, the great publishing house of Plantin of Antwerp acquired large collections of woodcuts which, starting with those of Fuchs's herbal, were constantly increased and were used by our British herbalists. To Plantin and his successors botanical studies owe an incalculable debt: it is largely due to their diligence in producing, translating, and distributing the voluminous works of the sixteenth-century pioneers that the study of plants reached its scientific status before this had been attained in any other subject, and that gardening and agriculture were so soon to encourage serious study of soils and culture, of variations and hybridization. There were dozens of named forms of pinks and carnations before the start of the seventeenth century. And the tulip-mania of Holland had begun within fifty years of the introduction of the first scarlet tulip into Europe; William Turner had urged the growing of flax and had brought lucerne (alfalfa) into England as a fodder-plant, and de l'Ecluse developed potato-culture in Germany, Austria, France, and the Low Countries, and was the first serious student of mycology. By the end of the century the famous brothers Gaspard and Jean Bauhin had brought botany to a point of excellence at which it had to stick until fuller knowledge of plant physiology and of the chemistry of soils was available.

Some progress of a scientific as well as a speculative kind had already been made in this direction. Paracelsus by his experiments with metallic and chemical remedies and Van Helmont with his study of what he was the first to call gas, his interest in fermentation and his research on the growth of a willow, had opened up problems which went far beyond matters of identification and nomenclature. Van Helmont especially, by sharing the philosophical and mystical ideas of the Renaissance Platonists of Italy, did much to prevent science from becoming absorbed in practical and mechanistic inquiries. His influence was not without effect upon the medicine of the seventeenth century and its great pioneer William Harvey, whose massive collection of material was destroyed in the Civil War but who published his *De Generatione* in 1651. Writing a generation before Leeuwenhoek's discovery of spermatozoa, Harvey's knowledge of the physiology of impregnation was necessarily incomplete, but his observations on pregnancy and still more on courtship are full of interest: he was a pioneer in the study of the living animal—an element in biology which has only in recent years become pre-eminent.

It was in the latter half of the seventeenth century, when the work of Bacon and Comenius and the foundation of scientific societies gave an inspiration and unity to all branches of study, that the next forward move in biology began. This was twofold. In the first place a closer attention was paid to the structure and habits of living organisms; concepts of specific distinctness, of relationships and of a natural system of classification, became established; and problems of form and function and of the evidence for design suggested themselves. In the second the development of observation and experiment challenged and destroyed fabulous traditional beliefs like spontaneous generation or the degradation of one species into another, and purged zoology of its legendary and emblematic elements—the phoenix, the gryphon, the were-wolf, and the unicorn. As a consequence, the period of exploration and identification naturally led on to the expansion of natural philosophy into the ordered system of the sciences; and biological studies were enlarged to include the whole organic field and deepened by attention to anatomy and physiology and the first concern with palaeontology. It is from this period that we can best date the coming of the modern age.

Typical of this great advance, and to some degree responsible for it, was the development in Britain. The writings of John Ray, greatest of naturalists, and his friend Francis Willughby produced not only the first system of classification of plants and the most complete history of them, but also similar histories of birds and fishes, animals, reptiles, and insects—a *systema naturae* half a century before that of Linnaeus —and the first inquiry into the problems of the relationship of the organism to its environment and of its form and function—an inquiry which led by way of Paley's *Natural Theology* to the work of Charles Darwin. Contemporary workers in many fields brought biological studies to a level beyond which they could hardly advance until physics had been emancipated from the ancient belief in the four elements and chemistry purged of astrology and alchemy and applied to a serious study of the structure of the earth and of its organic inhabitants. We have only to compare Ray's inquiries into problems of adaptation and behaviour with his attempts to explain respiration to realize the difficulty of the situation. It was inevitable that biology should mark time until the work of Haller and Lavoisier and their contemporaries made possible a scientific interpretation of the relation between the living creature and its environment. The studies in botany and zoology which had explored new worlds in the sixteenth and seventeenth centuries could only confine themselves to nomenclature and a rather superficial taxonomy until a deeper analysis of the whole order of nature made it possible to attain a sense of the interdependence and mutual relationships of its parts. Even then mechanistic categories and analogies dominated the world of science and tended to degrade the status and even to deny the characteristics of the world of life.

Thus it is plain that when interest in organic development was revived the attention that had to be paid to physiology and bio-chemistry reduced biology to little more than the study of dead organisms in a laboratory or their display in a museum. The living creature was almost lost to view: it was studied, if at all, in strict confinement, in cages and mazes: and theories as to its way of life were deduced from its structure and coloration rather than from observation in the field and in its normal surroundings. Until recently the range covered by naturalists like Ray lay outside the limits accepted as proper to the professional scientists, and the questions which he had asked were left unanswered by nearly two centuries. The recent study of animal psychology and of ecology is beginning to restore the wider and more coherent outlook of earlier days.

Now that we are at last escaping from this period of analysis and mensuration it is easy to see how the concentration upon physics and chemistry and their application to industrial development has led to an interpretation of the history of the New Philosophy which has tended to ignore the primacy of medical and biological studies, to identify science with mathematics and astronomy, and to trace back its pedigree to a succession of investigators, Copernicus, Kepler, Galileo, and Newton. Immensely important as they have been in establishing a reign of law and an urban and materialistic society, they neither initiated the emergence nor gave rise to the transformation of modern man. The heliocentric cosmology was less disturbing than the rejection of spontaneous generation, of creation as an act rather than a continuing process and of witchcraft, astrology, and magic. Charles Kingsley's welcome to Darwinism was: 'Men now find that they have got rid of an interfering God: they have to choose between the absolute empire of accident, and a living, immanent, ever-working God'. This gives its proper emphasis to the revolution—though it is sad that so many zoologists . . . still accept the former alternative and talk profanely of randomness. Enough said: it may be permissible to summarize the chief changes that we have been considering so far as they concern biology.

Instead of regarding the origin and development of life on our planet as caused by a single creative act (such as Milton described in *Paradise Lost*) and continued by a series of dramatic interventions, we see the whole as a process continuous, orderly, and coherent. In this process real novelties emerge. Death and the extinction of creatures ill-adjusted to their environment have been the accompaniments and to some extent the causes of progress. Life moves, and new levels of achievement both in structure and in behaviour are attained. Physically and mentally, individually and collectively, there is advance—though this is neither automatic nor mechanical. From the beginning of life there is a measure of free response, leading up to conscious intention and so to increasing control and co-operation. So the way has been prepared for man.

Though the new interpretation has challenged the traditions and transformed the outlook of former times, it is giving us a deeper and clearer insight into the nature of the universe, of life and its manifold development, and, for ourselves, of its values and of our goal.

Questions and Suggestions

1. Why does Raven believe that Conrad Van Gesner, rather than Copernicus, should be considered the father of modern science? Do you find Raven's case convincing?
2. Why does he disapprove of identifying scientific thought and methods with "weight and measurement" as well as with "mechanistic categories and analogies"? Restate what he says concerning the increased use of observation and experiment.
3. Why did biology lose its initial place of importance?
4. Scientists for several centuries have been indebted to Christophe Plantin and his successors. Why?
5. Explain in your own words why the rejection of the theory of "spontaneous generation" proved to be revolutionary and disturbing.
6. What common flowers are found in the *borage* family? What

is the meaning of *gastronomy, palaeontology, taxonomy, mensuration, heliocentric, cosmology,* and the *Hippocratic oath?*

Ideas for Writing

1. Taking examples from what you have read in works of science fiction or from any of the science fiction films you may have seen, show how some of us still believe in fabulous concepts that equal or surpass some medieval beliefs. If you wish to know more about fabulous beasts, consult T. H. White's translation of a twelfth century manuscript, *The Book of Beasts.*

2. Describe an afternoon you spent in a laboratory, pointing out what you learned or failed to grasp from an experiment. For another paper you could evaluate a field trip.

3. Discuss the value that specific illustrations in one of your scientific texts have for you.

4. After studying this essay, attempt a general account of some phase of the growth of scientific knowledge. If you find that you need to know more than the essay itself reveals concerning Dioscorides, Galen, Pliny, Paracelsus, Linnaeus, Comenius, Paley, Lavoisier, Kepler, Vesalius, and Newton, consult any standard reference work.

5. Write a brief biography of one of the celebrated persons whom Raven mentions. Be sure to use the best sources available in your library.

ROLE OF THE INTELLECTUAL AND THE SCIENTIST

NORBERT WIENER

Norbert Wiener (1894–), who was born in Columbia, Missouri, received his A.B. degree from Tufts and subsequent degrees from Harvard, and has done advanced study at Cornell, Columbia, Cambridge, Göttingen, and Copenhagen. Since 1919 he has been closely associated with the department of mathematics at the Massachusetts Institute of Technology. It was the publication of

Cybernetics, in 1948, that first brought Dr. Wiener to the attention of the general reading public. To see for yourself what a verbal craftsman he is, study the first edition of this essay in conjunction with the revised edition in your text.

This book argues that the integrity of the channels of internal communication is essential to the welfare of society. This internal communication is subject at the present time not only to the threats which it has faced at all times, but to certain new and especially serious problems which belong peculiarly to our age. One among these is the growing complexity and cost of communication.

A hundred and fifty years ago or even fifty years ago—it does not matter which—the world and America in particular were full of small journals and presses through which almost any man could obtain a hearing. The country editor was not as he is now limited to boiler plate and local gossip, but could and often did express his individual opinion, not only of local affairs but of world matters. At present this license to express oneself has become so expensive with the increasing cost of presses, paper, and syndicated services, that the newspaper business has come to be the art of saying less and less to more and more.

The movies may be quite inexpensive as far as concerns the cost of showing each show to each spectator, but they are so horribly expensive in the mass that few shows are worth the risk, unless their success is certain in advance. It is not the question whether a show may excite a great interest in a considerable number of people that interests the entrepreneur, but rather the question of whether it will be unacceptable to so few that he can count on selling it indiscriminately to movie theaters from coast to coast.

What I have said about the newspapers and the movies applies equally to the radio, to television, and even to bookselling. Thus we are in an age where the enormous per capita bulk of communication is met by an ever-thinning stream of total bulk of communication. More and more we must accept a standardized inoffensive and insignificant product which, like the white bread of the bakeries, is made rather for its keeping and selling properties than for its food value.

This is fundamentally an external handicap of modern communication, but it is paralleled by another which gnaws from within. This is the cancer of creative narrowness and feebleness.

In the old days, the young man who wished to enter the creative arts might either have plunged in directly or prepared himself by a general schooling, perhaps irrelevant to the specific tasks he finally undertook, but which was at least a searching discipline of his abilities and taste. Now the channels of apprenticeship are largely silted up. Our elementary and secondary schools are more interested in formal classroom discipline than in the intellectual discipline of learning something thoroughly, and a great deal of the serious preparation for a scientific or a literary course is relegated to some sort of graduate school or other.

Hollywood meanwhile has found that the very standardization of its product has interfered with the natural flow of acting talent from the legitimate stage. The repertory theaters had almost ceased to exist when some of them were reopened as Hollywood talent farms, and even these are dying on the vine. To a considerable extent our young would-be actors have learned their trade, not on the stage, but in university courses on acting. Our writers cannot get very far as young men in competition with syndicate material, and if they do not make a success the first try, they have no place to go but college courses which are supposed to teach them how to write. Thus the higher degrees, and above all the Ph.D., which have had a long existence as the legitimate preparation of the scientific specialist, are more and more serving as a model for intellectual training in all fields.

Properly speaking the artist, the writer, and the scientist should be moved by such an irresistible impulse to create that, even if they were not being paid for their work, they would be willing to pay to get the chance to do it. However, we are in a period in which forms have largely superseded educational content and one which is moving toward an ever-increasing thinness of educational content. It is now considered perhaps more a matter of social prestige to obtain a higher degree and follow what may be regarded as a cultural career, than a matter of any deep impulse.

In view of this great bulk of semi-mature apprentices who are being put on the market, the problem of giving them some colorable material to work on has assumed an overwhelming importance. Theoretically they should find their own material, but the big business of modern advanced education cannot be operated under this relatively low pressure. Thus the earlier stages of creative work, whether in the arts or in the sciences, which should properly be governed by a great desire on the part of the students to create something and to communicate it to the world at large, are now subject instead to the formal requirements of finding Ph.D. theses or similar apprentice media.

Some of my friends have even asserted that a Ph.D. thesis should be the greatest scientific work a man has ever done and perhaps ever will do, and should wait until he is thoroughly able to state his life work. I do not go along with this. I mean merely that if the thesis is not in fact such an overwhelming task, it should at least be in intention the gateway to vigorous creative work. Lord only knows that there are enough problems yet to be solved, books to be written, and music to be composed! Yet for all but a very few, the path to these lies through the performance of perfunctory tasks which in nine cases out of ten have no compelling reason to be performed. Heaven save us from the first novels which are written because a young man desires the prestige of being a novelist rather than because he has something to say! Heaven save us likewise from the mathematical papers which are correct and elegant but without body or spirit. Heaven save us above all from the snobbery which not only admits the possibility of this thin and perfunctory work, but which cries out in a spirit of shrinking arrogance against the competition of vigor and ideas, wherever these may be found!

In other words, when there is communication without need for communication, merely so that someone may earn the social and intellectual prestige of becoming a priest of communication, the quality and communicative value of the message drop like a plummet. It is as if a machine should be made from the Rube Goldberg point of view, to show just what recondite ends may be served by an apparatus apparently quite unsuitable for them, rather than to do something. In the arts, the desire to find new things to say and new ways of saying them is the source of all life and interest. Yet every day we meet with examples of painting where, for instance, the artist has bound himself from the new canons of the abstract, and has displayed no intention to use these canons to display an interesting and novel form of beauty, to pursue the uphill fight against the prevailing tendency toward the commonplace and the banal. Not all the artistic pedants are academicians. There are pedantic *avantgardistes*. No school has a monopoly on beauty. Beauty, like order, occurs in many places in this world, but only as a local and temporary fight against the Niagara of increasing entropy.

I speak here with feeling which is more intense as far as concerns the scientific artist than the conventional artist, because it is in science that I have first chosen to say something. What sometimes enrages me and always disappoints and grieves me is the preference of great schools of learning for the derivative as opposed to the original, for the conventional and thin which can be duplicated in many copies rather than the new and powerful, and for arid correctness and limitation of scope and method rather than for universal newness and beauty, wherever it may be seen. Moreover, I protest, not only as I have already done against the cutting off of intellectual originality by the difficulties of the means of communication in the modern world, but even more against the ax which has been put to the root of originality because the people who have elected communication as a career so often have nothing more to communicate.

Questions and Suggestions

1. What is the thesis statement? What are some of the changes in communication that have had adverse effects upon our society?
2. Why does Wiener attack contemporary education? Are his reasons and examples valid? Wherein do he and Pyke agree about the education our scientists receive? Do they agree about the way some scientists use language? What do they say about the value of many scientific reports?
3. Do Emerson and Wiener agree about the ways in which universities should educate youth?
4. Explain why Wiener does not believe that one school of art has all the best answers? What relationship does he point out between "scientific artists" and "conventional artists"?
5. Would Wiener and Raven agree as to the founder of modern science?
6. What does the author mean by his reference to Rube Goldberg?
7. What connotative effect does Wiener achieve when he speaks of "colorable material" being given to semi-mature apprentices?

Ideas for Writing

1. Discuss the value of studying a hundred great books rather than sundry textbooks. Check the *Reader's Guide to Periodical Literature* as far back as 1935 for titles of articles about St. John's College.
2. Explain why a specific film was "a standardized, inoffensive and insignificant product."
3. Describe the processes and pleasures of baking bread at home, barbecuing a round of beef, or of preparing a mousse. Or

comment upon specific examples of flavorless foods that come from scientific "kitchens" and are enticingly packaged.

4. Use a pseudonym for one of your friends in explaining how you know that he wants a degree for "social prestige" rather than because of "any deep impulse."

5. Study one issue of your local paper and evaluate the syndicated material; or comment on how much national and international news it contains in proportion to its size. If possible, contrast two of your local papers for their effective coverage of the news.

6. If a copy of the 1950 edition of *The Human Use of Human Beings* is in your library, study it to see what types of revisions Dr. Wiener made.

SCIENTIST AND HUMANIST: CAN THE MINDS MEET?

I. I. RABI

Isidor Isaac Rabi (1898–) born in Rymanow, Austria-Hungary, was brought to America in 1899. He received his undergraduate degree from Cornell and his Ph.D. from Columbia. The recipient of many honorary degrees and awards, Dr. Rabi won the Nobel Prize in 1944 for his work in nuclear physics; his other fields of interest being quantum mechanics, molecular beams, and magnetism. Active in the development of atomic theories, he has served as chairman of a number of national and international committees dealing with atomic energy, especially in its development for peaceful uses. Since 1950 Dr. Rabi has been Higgins Professor, in the department of physics, at Columbia.

For more than half a century, from the period of the Darwinian controversy till the end of the 1930s, science remained almost unchallenged as the source of enlightenment, understanding, and hope for a better, healthier, and safer world. The benefits brought by science

From *The Atlantic Monthly*, January 1956. Copyright © by I. I. Rabi. Reprinted by permission of I. I. Rabi, and *The Atlantic Monthly*.

were and are still visible everywhere one looks. Human ills are being overcome; food supplies are becoming more abundant; travel and communication are quick and easy; and the comforts of life, especially for the common man, are vastly increased. In the person of Albert Einstein science enjoyed a world-wide respect almost akin to reverence and hardly equaled since the time of Isaac Newton.

In the last decade or so we have begun to detect signs of significant change. The knowledge and techniques developed through science for the illumination of the mind and the elevation of the spirit, for the prolongation and the amelioration of life, have been used for the destruction of life and the degradation of the human spirit. Technological warfare, biological warfare, psychological warfare, brainwashing, all make use of science with frightening results.

I do not suggest that warfare and its attendant horror is a result of modern science. Ancient Greece, at the zenith of that remarkable civilization, in a land united by a common culture and a common religion, destroyed itself in a bitter and useless war more thoroughly than Europe has done in the present century even with the aid of electronics, aviation, and high explosives. What I mean is that our epoch in history, which has produced one of the greatest achievements of the human race, may be passing into a twilight that does not precede the dawn.

Science, the triumph of the intellect and the rational faculties, has resulted in the hydrogen bomb. The glib conclusion is that science and the intellect are therefore false guides. We must seek elsewhere, some people say, for hope and salvation; but, say the same people, while doing so we must keep ahead of the Russians in technology and in the armaments race. Keep the fearsome fruits but reject the spirit of science. Such is the growing mood of some people at the present time. It is a mood of anti-intellectualism which can only hasten the destruction which these people fear. Anti-intellectualism has always been endemic in every society, perhaps in the heart of every human being. In times of stress this attitude is stimulated and people tend to become impatient and yield to prejudice and emotion just when coolness, subtlety, and reason are most needed.

We are told, and most of us believe, that we are living in a period of crisis unequaled in history. To be cheerful and proud of our accomplishment and optimistic of the future is almost akin to subversion. To be considered objective and realistic, one must view with alarm. Yet we are not living in a period of hard times and unemployment! We have, I cannot say enjoyed but, rather, bemoaned, a period of prosperity and world-wide influence for good unequaled in history. Nevertheless, despite all, we seem to be acquiring a complacency of despair. In this mood, unable to adjust to new values, we hark back to a past which now looks so bright in retrospect, and we raise the banner of "Back to the Humanities."

What is meant by the slogan "Back to the Humanities"? What are people really looking for? What knowledge, what guidance, what hope for salvation, what inspiration, or what relief from anxiety does a practical-minded people like ours expect from a knowledge of the humanities? They do not wish to re-establish the study of the Greek and Roman classics in their original tongues, or to re-create the Greek city-state in Metropolitan Boston.

I venture to suggest that what they mean is something quite different from what is meant by the humanities. The progress of civilization in the modern age, especially in our own century, has brought with it an immense increase of knowledge of every kind, from archaeology to zoology. More is known of the history of antiquity than was known to Herodotus. We have penetrated farther into the heavens and into the innermost secrets of the structure of matter than anyone could have dreamt of in previous generations. We have run through the satisfactions of representational art to the puzzling outlines of abstract art. The increase in physical comfort and in communication has brought with it a whole set of new problems. The great increase in population necessarily means further crowding and additional social and cultural adjustment. Under these circumstances, it is natural for people to look for guidance toward a balanced adjustment.

What people are really looking for is wisdom. To our great store of knowledge we need the added quality of wisdom.

Wisdom is inseparable from knowledge; it is knowledge plus a quality which is within the human being. Without it knowledge is dry, almost unfit for human consumption, and dangerous in application. The absence of wisdom is clearly noticeable; the learned fool and the educated bore have been with us since the beginnings of recorded history. Wisdom adds flavor, order, and measure to knowledge. Wisdom makes itself most manifest in the application of knowledge to human needs.

Every generation of mankind has to remake its culture, its values, and its goals. Changing circumstances make older habits and customs valueless or obsolete. New knowledge exposes the limitations and the contingent nature of older philosophies and of previously accepted guides to action. Wisdom does not come in formulas, proverbs, or wise saws, but out of the living actuality. The past is important for understanding the present, but it is not the present. It is in a real sense created in the present, and changes from the point of view of every generation.

When change is slow, the new is gradually assimilated, and only after a number of generations is it noticeable that the world is really different. In our century enormous changes in the circumstances of our lives and in our knowledge have occurred rapidly—in every decade. It is therefore not at all surprising that our intellectual, our social, and our political processes have failed to keep abreast of contemporary problems. It is not surprising that we become confused in the choice of our goals and the paths which we must take to reach them.

Clearly a study of the Greek and Roman classics in their original tongues or even in a good translation is a most rewarding venture in itself. This literature has never been surpassed in any age. And in reading this literature one is struck by how applicable the situations are to the present day. The fact that we can still be moved strongly by this literature is an illustration not merely of the constancy of structure of the human nervous system but also of the fact that great art and profound insights have a character which is independent of any age.

The humanities preserve and create values; even more they express the symbolic, poetic, and prophetic qualities of the human spirit. Without the humanities we would not be conscious of our history; we would lose many of our aspirations and the graces of expression that move men's hearts. Withal the humanities discern but a part of the life of man—true, a vital part but only a part.

It has often been claimed that the chief justification for the study of the humanities is that it teaches us values. In fact some people go even further and claim that the humanities, in which literature, parts of philosophy, and the history and appreciation of the fine arts are included, are the *only* sources of values other than the more spiritual values of religion.

This claim cannot pass without challenge. It cannot be said that it is absurd, but rather that it is a symptom of our failure in the present age to achieve a unity and balance of knowledge which is imbued with wisdom. It is a symptom of both ignorance and a certain anti-rational attitude which has been the curse of our century. It betrays a lack of self-confidence and faith in the greatness of the human spirit in contemporary man. It is the expression of a form of self-hatred which is rationally unjustifiable although deeply rooted.

Man is made of dust and to dust returneth; he lives in a universe of which he is also a part. He is free only in a symbolic sense; his nature is conditioned by the dust out of which he is made. To learn to understand himself he must learn to understand the universe in which he lives. There is more than enough in this enterprise to engage the boldest, the most imaginative, and the keenest minds and spirits of every generation. The universe is not given to us in the form of a map or guide. It is made by human minds and imaginations out of slight hints which come from acute observation and from the profound stratagems of experiments.

How can we hope to obtain wisdom, the wisdom which is meaningful in our own time? We certainly cannot attain it as long as the two great branches of human knowledge, the sciences and the humanities, remain separate and even warring disciplines.

Why is science, even more than the humanities, as a living component of our society so misunderstood? A glance at a current dictionary definition may give us a clue.

Science: "A branch of knowledge dealing with facts or truths systematically arranged and showing the operation of general law."

This definition brings to my mind a solitaire player or head bookkeeper for a mail-order concern. It is a partial truth which is also a caricature. It is out of harmony with the picture of Archimedes jumping out of his bath crying Eureka! or Galileo in misery and degradation during his trial and recantation, or Einstein creating the universe out of one or two deductions from observation and a profound aesthetic feeling for symmetry. Nor does this definition account for the violence of the opposition to scientific discovery which still exists in the same quarters in our own age.

It is often argued that physical science is inherently simple, whereas the study of man is inherently complicated. Yet a great deal is known of man's nature. Wise laws for government and personal conduct were known in remotest antiquity. The literature of antiquity shows a profound understanding of human natures and emotions. Not man but the external world was bewildering. The world of nature instead of seeming simple was infinitely complex and possessed of spirits and demons. Nature had to be worshiped and propitiated by offerings, ceremonies, and prayers. Fundamentally nature was unpredictable, antagonistic to human aspiration, full of significance and purpose, and generally evil.

Knowledge of nature was suspect because of the power which it brought, a power which was somehow allied with evil. There were of course always men who had insights far beyond these seemingly naïve notions, but they did not prevail over what seemed to be the evidence of the senses and of practical experience.

It was therefore not until late in the history of mankind, not until a few seconds ago so to speak, that it was recognized that nature is understandable and that a knowledge of nature is good and can be used with benefit; that it does not involve witchcraft or a compact with the devil. What is more, any person of intelligence can understand the ideas involved and with sufficient skill learn the necessary techniques, intellectual and manual.

This idea which is now so commonplace represents an almost complete break with the past. To revere and trust the rational faculty of the mind—to allow no taboo to interfere in its operation, to have nothing immune from its examination—is a new value which has been introduced into the world. The progress of science has been the chief agent in demonstrating its importance and riveting it into the consciousness of mankind. This value does not yet have universal acceptance in this country or in any other country. But in spite of all obstacles it will become one of the most treasured possessions of all mankind because we can no longer live without it. We have gone too far along the direction which it implies ever to turn back without unimaginable disaster.

The last world war was started in an attempt to turn back to dark reaction against the rational faculty and to introduce a new demonology into the world. It failed as will every other such attempt. Once the mind is free it will be destroyed rather than be put back in chains.

To my mind the value content of science or literary scholarship lies not in the subject matter alone; it lies chiefly in the spirit and living tradition in which these disciplines are pursued. The spirit is almost always conditioned by the subject. Science and the humanities are not the same thing; the subject matter is different and the spirit and tradition are different. Our problem in our search for wisdom is to blend these two traditions in the minds of individual men and women.

Many colleges and universities are trying to do just this, but there is one serious defect in the method. We pour a little of this and a little of that into the student's mind in proportions which result from mediation between the departments and from the particular predilections of the deans and the president. We then hope that these ingredients will combine through some mysterious alchemy and the result will be a man educated, well-rounded, and wise. Most often, however, these ingredients remain well separated in the compartmentalized mind, or they may form an indigestible precipitate which is not only useless but positively harmful, until time the healer washes it all away.

Wisdom is by its nature an interdisciplinary quality and not the product of a collection of specialists. Although the colleges do indeed try to mold the student toward a certain ideal of the educated man of the twentieth century, it is too often a broad education administered by specialists. The approximate counterpart to this ideal of the educated man, embodied in a real living person, is a rare being on any college faculty. Indeed, in most colleges and universities the student is the only really active connecting link between the different departments. In a certain paradoxical sense the students are the only broadly educated body in the university community, at least in principle.

The affairs of this country—indeed of almost every country— whether in government, education, industry, or business, are controlled by people of broad experience. However, this broad experience rarely includes the field of science. How can our leaders make wise decisions now in the middle of the twentieth century without a deep understanding of scientific thought and feeling for scientific traditions? The answer is clear in the sad course that events have taken.

This anguished thought has impelled many scientists, often to their own personal peril, to concern themselves with matters which in the past were the exclusive domain of statesmen and military leaders. They have tried to advise, importune, and even cajole our leaders to include the scientific factor in our fateful policy decisions. They have been successful, but only in special instances.

I am not making a plea for the scientist statesman comparable to the philosopher king. The scientist rarely has this kind of ambition. The study of nature in its profundity, beauty, and subtlety is too attractive for him to wish to forsake his own creative and rewarding activity. The scientist away from his science is like an exile who longs for the sights and sounds of his native land. What the scientist really desires is for his science to be understood, to become an integral part of our general culture, to be given proper weight in the cultural and practical affairs of the world.

The greatest difficulty which stands in the way of a meeting of the

minds of the scientist and the non-scientist is the difficulty of communication, a difficulty which stems from some of the defects of education to which I have alluded. The mature scientist, if he has any taste
in these directions, can listen with pleasure to the philosopher, the
historian, the literary man, or even to the art critic. There is little
difficulty from that side because the scientist has been educated in our
general culture and lives in it on a day-to-day basis. He reads newspapers,
magazines, books, listens to music, debates politics, and participates in
the general activities of an educated citizen.

Unfortunately this channel of communication is often a one-way
street. The non-scientist cannot listen to the scientist with pleasure and
understanding. Despite its universal outlook and its unifying principle,
its splendid tradition, science seems to be no longer communicable to
the great majority of educated laymen. They simply do not possess the
background of the science of today and the intellectual tool necessary
for them to understand what effects science will have on them and on
the world. Instead of understanding, they have only a naïve awe mixed
with fear and scorn. To his colleagues in the university the scientist
tends to seem more and more like a man from another planet, a creature scattering antibiotics with one hand and atomic bombs with the
other.

The problems to which I have addressed myself are not particularly
American. The same condition exists in England, France, and indeed
in all other countries. From my observation we are perhaps better off
than most. Our American colleges and universities, since they are fairly
recent and are rapidly expanding, have not settled into complacency.
They are quite ready to experiment to achieve desired ends. Our experimental methods have taught us how to impart the most diverse forms
of knowledge. Although wisdom is more elusive, once the objective is
clear that the ultimate end of education is knowledge imbedded in
wisdom we shall find ways to move toward that ideal. The ideal of the
well-rounded man is a meaningless ideal unless this sphericity means
a fusion of knowledge to achieve balanced judgment and understanding,
which are qualities of wisdom.

The problems are, of course, depressingly difficult. In the secondary
schools—with their overcrowding, their teachers overworked and inadequately trained, the school boards, and, not least, the powerful clique
of professional educators who form a society within our society—all that
is unique and characteristic of science and mathematics is being crowded
out of the curriculum and replaced by a fairy tale known as general

science. The colleges and universities are in much better shape, although the great population increase is about to hit them with masses of inadequately prepared students. Most people would be quite content with a holding operation in which we could maintain the quality that is already possessed.

However, it seems to me that something could be done even now with the faculty members of the colleges and the universities. Wisdom can achieve a hybrid vigor by crossing the scientist and the humanist through a more extensive and intensive interaction within the faculty. Why should not the professor of physics be expected to refresh himself periodically by taking a course in aesthetics or comparative literature or in the Greek drama? Why shouldn't the professor of medieval philosophy or the professor of ancient history take a course in modern physics and become acquainted with the profound thoughts underlying relativity and quantum mechanics? It would let in some fresh air, or at least different air, to blow away some of the cobwebs which grow in the unventilated ivory towers.

Somewhere a beginning has to be made to achieve a more architectural quality in our culture, a quality of proportion and of organic unity, and it is reasonable to start with the members of the faculties of our institutions of higher learning. Here are all the strands of the tapestry which is to represent our culture, living in close proximity but separate, adding up to nothing more than the sum of the parts. The scientists must learn to teach science in the spirit of wisdom and in the light of the history of human thought and human effort, rather than as the geography of a universe uninhabited by mankind. Our colleagues in the non-scientific faculties must understand that if their teachings ignore the great scientific tradition and its accomplishments, their words, however eloquent and elegant, will lose meaning for this generation and be barren of fruit.

Only with a united effort of science and the humanities can we hope to succeed in discovering a community of thought which can lead us out of the darkness and the confusion which oppress all mankind.

Questions and Suggestions

1. Compare the failures and successes that Rabi notes in our university and college systems with what Wiener has observed. Do the two scientists hold any other views in common, such as the conclusions about the lack of communication of ideas and the growth of anti-intellectualism?

2. Reread that section of Pyke's essay that deals with education. Wherein do Rabi and Pyke agree, differ?

3. In the last decades what has brought about a change in the public's attitude toward science? Can you give examples from your own experience or reading that would sustain this point?

4. What distinction does Rabi make between wisdom and knowledge?

5. Where does he state most succinctly his major thesis?

6. What hope does he hold for the future?

7. Do Rabi and Pyke reach any similar conclusions concerning the classics?

8. What reasons does Rabi cite for the difficulty of communication between scientists and non-scientists? Reread "These Nice Kids." Do Schneider's ideas about the fifteen lectures a week on "apparently unrelated subjects" bear out any of Dr. Rabi's fears?

9. Rabi believes that the acceptance of one value has changed modern man's whole concept of the world. Do you think that he and Raven would agree?

Ideas for Writing

1. Explain why comic-book versions of the classics and the *Bible* fail to embody and impart the wisdom of the past.

2. After reading *The Book of Ruth, Job,* or the account of Ulysses's return home after his years of wandering, show how the experiences of these individuals are still applicable to ourselves—how we can learn from them.

3. Perhaps you have already come to believe that there is little give and take between the scientists and non-scientists in your college. Explain how you came to recognize this situation. Describe a teacher who is both scientist and humanist or one who is chiefly a scientist.

4. By using a number of intimate details, show how the lack of stimulating talk in your own home has limited your development, or how the opposite situation has prevailed and influenced you.

RELIGION AND SCIENCE

ALFRED NORTH WHITEHEAD

Alfred North Whitehead (1861–1947), the son of a Canon in the Anglican church, was born in Ramsgate, England. He studied at Trinity College, Cambridge, remaining after he graduated to become a most influential lecturer in mathematics. Before leaving Cambridge to become lecturer at the Imperial College of Science, in London, he and his former student Bertrand Russell collaborated on a most important work, *Principia Mathematica.* In 1924, rather than retiring, Whitehead moved to Harvard where he became Professor of Philosophy and was a senior member of Harvard's Society of Fellows. Deeply and emotionally religious, Whitehead was always something of a mystic.

The difficulty in approaching the question of the relations between Religion and Science is, that its elucidation requires that we have in our minds some clear idea of what we mean by either of the terms, 'religion' and 'science.' Also I wish to speak in the most general way possible, and to keep in the background any comparison of particular creeds, scientific or religious. We have got to understand the type of connection which exists between the two spheres, and then to draw some definite conclusions respecting the existing situation which at present confronts the world.

The *conflict* between religion and science is what naturally occurs to our minds when we think of this subject. It seems as though, during the last half-century, the results of science and the beliefs of religion had come into a position of frank disagreement, from which there can be no escape, except by abandoning either the clear teaching of science, or the clear teaching of religion. This conclusion has been urged by controversialists on either side. Not by all controversialists, of course, but by those trenchant intellects which every controversy calls out into the open.

The distress of sensitive minds, and the zeal for truth, and the sense of the importance of the issues, must command our sincerest sympathy. When we consider what religion is for mankind, and what science is, it is no exaggeration to say that the future course of history depends upon the decision of this generation as to the relations between them. We have here the two strongest general forces (apart from the mere impulse of the various senses) which influence men, and they seem to be set one against the other—the force of our religious intuitions, and the force of our impulse to accurate observation and logical deduction.

A great English statesman once advised his countrymen to use large-scale maps, as a preservative against alarms, panics, and general misunderstanding of the true relations between nations. In the same way in dealing with the clash between permanent elements of human nature, it is well to map our history on a large scale, and to disengage ourselves from our immediate absorption in the present conflicts. When we do this, we immediately discover two great facts. In the first place, there has always been a conflict between religion and science; and in the second place, both religion and science have always been in a state of continual development. In the early days of Christianity, there was a general belief among Christians that the world was coming to an end in the lifetime of people then living. We can make only indirect inferences as to how far this belief was authoritatively proclaimed; but it is certain that it was widely held, and that it formed an impressive part of the popular religious doctrine. The belief proved itself to be mistaken, and Christian doctrine adjusted itself to the change. Again in the early Church individual theologians very confidently deduced from the Bible opinions concerning the nature of the physical universe. In the year A. D. 535, a monk named Cosmas* wrote a book which he entitled, *Christian Topography*. He was a travelled man who had visited India and Ethiopia; and finally he lived in a monastery at Alexandria, which was then a great centre of culture. In this book, basing himself upon the direct meaning of Biblical texts as construed by him in a literal fashion, he denied the existence of the antipodes, and asserted that the world is a flat parallelogram whose length is double its breadth.

In the seventeenth century the doctrine of the motion of the earth was condemned by a Catholic tribunal. A hundred years ago the extension of time demanded by geological science distressed religious people, Protestant and Catholic. And to-day the doctrine of evolution is an equal stumbling-block. These are only a few instances illustrating a general fact.

*Cf. Lecky's *The Rise and Influence of Rationalism in Europe*, Ch. III.

But all our ideas will be in a wrong perspective if we think that this recurring perplexity was confined to contradictions between religion and science; and that in these controversies religion was always wrong, and that science was always right. The true facts of the case are very much more complex, and refuse to be summarised in these simple terms.

Theology itself exhibits exactly the same character of gradual development, arising from an aspect of conflict between its own proper ideas. This fact is a commonplace to theologians, but is often obscured in the stress of controversy. I do not wish to overstate my case; so I will confine myself to Roman Catholic writers. In the seventeenth century a learned Jesuit, Father Petavius, showed that the theologians of the first three centuries of Christianity made use of phrases and statements which since the fifth century would be condemned as heretical. Also Cardinal Newman devoted a treatise to the discussion of the development of doctrine. He wrote it before he became a great Roman Catholic ecclesiastic; but throughout his life, it was never retracted and continually reissued.

Science is even more changeable than theology. No man of science could subscribe without qualification to Galileo's beliefs, or to Newton's beliefs, or to all his own scientific beliefs of ten years ago.

In both regions of thought, additions, distinctions, and modifications have been introduced. So that now, even when the same assertion is made to-day as was made a thousand, or fifteen hundred years ago, it is made subject to limitations or expansions of meaning, which were not contemplated at the earlier epoch. We are told by logicians that a proposition must be either true or false, and that there is no middle term. But in practice, we may know that a proposition expresses an important truth, but that it is subject to limitations and qualifications which at present remain undiscovered. It is a general feature of our knowledge, that we are insistently aware of important truth; and yet that the only formulations of these truths which we are able to make presuppose a general standpoint of conceptions which may have to be modified. I will give you two illustrations, both from science: Galileo said that the earth moves and that the sun is fixed; the Inquisition said that the earth is fixed and the sun moves; and Newtonian astronomers, adopting an absolute theory of space, said that both the sun and the earth move. But now we say that any one of these three statements is equally true, provided that you have fixed your sense of 'rest' and 'motion' in the way required by the statement adopted. At the date of Galileo's controversy with the Inquisition, Galileo's way of stating the facts was, beyond question, the fruitful procedure for the sake of scientific research. But in itself it was not more true than the formulation of the Inquisition. But at that time the modern concepts of relative motion were in nobody's mind; so that the statements were made in ignorance of the qualifications required for their more perfect truth. Yet this question of the motions of the earth and the sun expresses a real fact in the universe; and all sides had got hold of important truths concerning it. But with the knowledge of those times, the truths appeared to be inconsistent.

Again I will give you another example taken from the state of modern physical science. Since the time of Newton and Huyghens in the seventeenth century there have been two theories as to the physical nature of light. Newton's theory was that a beam of light consists of a stream of very minute particles, or corpuscles, and that we have the sensation of light when these corpuscles strike the retinas of our eyes. Huyghens' theory was that light consists of very minute waves of trembling in an all-pervading ether, and that these waves are travelling along a beam of light. The two theories are contradictory. In the eighteenth century Newton's theory was believed, in the nineteenth century Huyghens' theory was believed. To-day there is one large group of phenomena which can be explained only on the wave theory, and another large group which can be explained only on the corpuscular theory. Scientists have to leave it at that, and wait for the future, in the hope of attaining some wider vision which reconciles both.

We should apply these same principles to the questions in which there is a variance between science and religion. We would believe nothing in either sphere of thought which does not appear to us to be certified by solid reasons based upon the critical research either of ourselves or of competent authorities. But granting that we have honestly taken this precaution, a clash between the two on points of detail where they overlap should not lead us hastily to abandon doctrines for which we have solid evidence. It may be that we are more interested in one set of doctrines than in the other. But, if we have any sense of perspective and of the history of thought, we shall wait and refrain from mutual anathemas.

We should wait: but we should not wait passively, or in despair. The clash is a sign that there are wider truths and finer perspectives within which a reconciliation of a deeper religion and a more subtle science will be found.

In one sense, therefore, the conflict between science and religion is a slight matter which has been unduly emphasised. A mere logical contradiction cannot in itself point to more than the necessity of some readjustments, possibly of a very minor character on both sides. Remember the widely different aspects of events which are dealt with in science and in religion respectively. Science is concerned with the general conditions which are observed to regulate physical phenomena; whereas religion is wholly wrapped up in the contemplation of moral and aesthetic values. On the one side there is the law of gravitation, and on the other the contemplation of the beauty of holiness. What one side sees, the other misses; and vice versa.

Consider, for example, the lives of John Wesley and of Saint Francis of Assisi. For physical science you have in these lives merely ordinary examples of the operation of the principles of physiological chemistry, and of the dynamics of nervous reactions: for religion you have lives of the most profound significance in the history of the world. Can you be surprised that, in the absence of a perfect and complete phrasing of the principles of science and of the principles of religion which apply to these specific cases, the accounts of these lives from these divergent standpoints should involve discrepancies? It would be a miracle if it were not so.

It would, however, be missing the point to think that we need not trouble ourselves about the conflict between science and religion. In an intellectual age there can be no active interest which puts aside all hope of a vision of the harmony of truth. To acquiesce in discrepancy is destructive of candour, and of moral cleanliness. It belongs to the self-respect of intellect to pursue every tangle of thought to its final unravelment. If you check that impulse, you will get no religion and no science from an awakened thoughtfulness. The important question is, In what spirit are we going to face the issue? There we come to something absolutely vital.

A clash of doctrines is not a disaster—it is an opportunity. I will explain my meaning by some illustrations from science. The weight of an atom of nitrogen was well known. Also it was an established scientific doctrine that the average weight of such atoms in any considerable mass will be always the same. Two experimenters, the late Lord Rayleigh and the late Sir William Ramsay, found that if they obtained nitrogen by two different methods, each equally effective for that purpose, they always observed a persistent slight difference between the average weights of the atoms in the two cases. Now I ask you, would it have been rational of these men to have despaired because of this conflict between chemical theory and scientific observation? Suppose that for some reason the chemical doctrine had been highly prized throughout some district as the foundation of its social order: —would it have been wise, would it have been candid, would it have been moral, to forbid the disclosure of the fact that the experiments produced discordant results? Or, on the other hand, should Sir William Ramsay and Lord Rayleigh have proclaimed that chemical theory was now a detected delusion? We see at once that either of these ways would have been a method of facing the issue in an entirely wrong spirit. What Rayleigh and Ramsay did was this: They at once perceived that they had hit upon a line of investigation which would disclose some subtlety of chemical theory that had hitherto eluded observation. The discrepancy was not a disaster: it was an opportunity to increase the sweep of chemical knowledge. You all know the end of the story: finally argon was discovered, a new chemical element which had lurked undetected, mixed with the nitrogen. But the story has a sequel which forms my second illustration. This discovery drew attention to the importance of observing accurately minute differences in chemical substances as obtained by different methods. Further researches of the most careful accuracy were undertaken. Finally another physicist, F. W. Aston, working in the Cavendish Laboratory at Cambridge in England, discovered that even the same element might assume two or more distinct forms, termed *isotopes,* and that the law of the constancy of average atomic weight holds for each of these forms, but as between the different isotopes differs slightly. The research has effected a great stride in the power of chemical theory, far transcending in importance the discovery of argon from which it originated. The moral of these stories lies on the surface, and I will leave to you their application to the case of religion and science.

In formal logic, a contradiction is the signal of a defeat: but in the evolution of real knowledge it marks the first step in progress towards a victory. This is one great reason for the utmost toleration of variety of opinion. Once and forever, this duty of toleration has been summed up in the words, 'Let both grow together until the harvest.' The failure of Christians to act up to this precept, of the highest authority, is one of the curiosities of religious history. But we have not yet exhausted the discussion of the moral temper required for the pursuit of truth. There are short cuts leading merely to an illusory success. It is easy enough to find a theory, logically harmonious and with important applications in the region of fact, provided that you are content to disregard half your evidence. Every age produces people with clear logical intellects, and with the most praiseworthy grasp of the importance of some sphere of human experience, who have elaborated, or inherited, a scheme of thought which exactly fits those experiences which claim their interest. Such people are apt resolutely to ignore, or to explain away, all evidence which confuses their scheme with contradictory instances, what they cannot fit in is for them nonsense. An unflinching determination to take the whole evidence into account is the only method of preservation against the fluctuating extremes of fashionable opinion. This advice seems so easy, and is in fact so difficult to follow.

One reason for this difficulty is that we cannot think first and act afterwards. From the moment of birth we are immersed in action, and can only fitfully guide it by taking thought. We have, therefore, in various spheres of experience to adopt those ideas which seem to work within those spheres. It is absolutely necessary to trust to ideas which are generally adequate, even though we know that there are subtleties and distinctions beyond our ken. Also apart from the necessities of action, we cannot even keep before our minds the whole evidence except under the guise of doctrines which are incompletely harmonised. We cannot think in terms of an indefinite multiplicity of detail; our evidence can acquire its proper importance only if it comes before us marshalled by general ideas. These ideas we inherit—they form the tradition of our civilisation. Such traditional ideas are never static. They are either fading into meaningless formulae, or are gaining power by the new lights thrown by a more delicate apprehension. They are transformed by the urge of critical reason, by the vivid evidence of emotional experience, and by the cold certainties of scientific perception. One fact is certain, you cannot keep them still. No generation can merely reproduce its ancestors. You may preserve the life in a flux of form, or preserve the form amid an ebb of life. But you cannot permanently enclose the same life in the same mould.

The present state of religion among the European races illustrates the statements which I have been making. The phenomena are mixed. There have been reactions and revivals. But on the whole, during many generations, there has been a gradual decay of religious influence in European civilisation. Each revival touches a lower peak than its predecessor, and each period of slackness a lower depth. The average curve marks a steady fall in religious tone. In some countries the interest in religion is higher than in others. But in those countries where the interest is relatively high, it still falls as the generations pass. Religion is tending to degenerate into a decent formula wherewith to embellish a comfortable life. A great historical movement on this scale results from the convergence of many causes. I wish to suggest two of them which lie within the scope of this chapter for consideration.

In the first place for over two centuries religion has been on the defensive, and on a weak defensive. The period has been one of unprecedented intellectual progress. In this way a series of novel situations have been produced for thought. Each such occasion has found the religious thinkers unprepared. Something, which has been proclaimed to be vital, has finally, after struggle, distress, and anathema, been modified and otherwise interpreted. The next generation of religious apologists then congratulates the religious world on the deeper insight which has been gained. The result of the continued repetition of this undignified retreat, during many generations, has at last almost entirely destroyed the intellectual authority of religious thinkers. Consider this contrast: when Darwin or Einstein proclaim theories which modify our ideas, it is a triumph for science. We do not go about saying that there is another defeat for science, because its old ideas have been abandoned. We know that another step of scientific insight has been gained.

Religion will not regain its old power until it can face change in the same spirit as does science. Its principles may be eternal, but the expression of those principles requires continual development. This evolution of religion is in the main a disengagement of its own proper ideas from the adventitious notions which have crept into it by reason of the expression of its own ideas in terms of the imaginative picture of the world entertained in previous ages. Such a release of religion from the bonds of imperfect science is all to the good. It stresses its own genuine message. The great point to be kept in mind is that normally an advance in science will show that statements of various religious beliefs require some sort of modification. It may be that they have to be expanded or explained, or indeed entirely restated. If the religion is a sound expression of truth, this modification will only exhibit more adequately the exact point which is of importance. This process is a gain. In so far, therefore, as any religion has any contact with physical facts, it is to be expected that the point of view of those facts must be continually modified as scientific knowledge advances. In this way, the exact relevance of these facts for religious thought will grow more and more clear. The progress of science must result in the unceasing codification of religious thought, to the great advantage of religion.

The religious controversies of the sixteenth and seventeenth centuries put theologians into a most unfortunate state of mind. They were always attacking and defending. They pictured themselves as the garrison of a fort surrounded by hostile forces. All such pictures express half-truths. That is why they are so popular. But they are dangerous. This particular picture fostered a pugnacious party spirit which really expresses an ultimate lack of faith. They dared not modify, because they shirked the task of disengaging their spiritual message from the associations of a particular imagery.

Let me explain myself by an example. In the early medieval times, Heaven was in the sky, and Hell was underground; volcanoes were the jaws of Hell. I do not assert that these beliefs entered into the official formulations: but they did enter into the popular understanding of the general doctrines of Heaven and Hell. These notions were what everyone thought to be implied by the doctrine of the future state. They entered into the explanations of the influential exponents of Christian belief. For example, they occur in the *Dialogues* of Pope Gregory,* the Great, a man whose high official position is surpassed only by the magnitude of his services to humanity. I am not saying what we ought to believe about the future state. But whatever be the right doctrine, in this instance the clash between religion and science, which has relegated the earth to the position of a second-rate planet attached to a second-rate sun, has been greatly to the benefit of the spirituality of religion by dispersing these medieval fancies.

Another way of looking at this question of the evolution of religious thought is to note that any verbal form of statement which has been before the world for some time discloses ambiguities; and that often such ambiguities strike at the very heart of the meaning. The effective sense in which a doctrine has been held in the past cannot be determined by the mere logical analysis of verbal statements, made in ignorance of the logical trap. You have to take into account the whole reaction of human nature to the scheme of thought. This reaction is of a mixed character, including elements of emotion derived from our lower natures. It is here that the impersonal criticism of science and of philosophy comes to the aid of religious evolution. Example after example can be given of this motive force in development. For example, the logical difficulties inherent in the doctrine of the moral cleansing of human nature

*Cf. Gregorovius' *History of Rome in the Middle Ages,* Book III, Ch. III, Vol. II, English Trans.

by the power of religion rent Christianity in the days of Pelagius and Augustine—that is to say, at the beginning of the fifth century. Echoes of that controversy still linger in theology.

So far, my point has been this: that religion is the expression of one type of fundamental experiences of mankind: that religious thought develops into an increasing accuracy of expression, disengaged from adventitious imagery: that the interaction between religion and science is one great factor in promoting this development.

I now come to my second reason for the modern fading of interest in religion. This involves the ultimate question which I stated in my opening sentences. We have to know what we mean by religion. The churches, in their presentation of their answers to this query, have put forward aspects of religion which are expressed in terms either suited to the emotional reactions of bygone times or directed to excite modern emotional interests of nonreligious character. What I mean under the first heading is that religious appeal is directed partly to excite that instinctive fear of the wrath of a tyrant which was inbred in the unhappy populations of the arbitrary empires of the ancient world, and in particular to excite that fear of an all-powerful arbitrary tyrant behind the unknown forces of nature. This appeal to the ready instinct of brute fear is losing its force. It lacks any directness of response, because modern science and modern conditions of life have taught us to meet occasions of apprehension by a critical analysis of their causes and conditions. Religion is the reaction of human nature to its search for God. The presentation of God under the aspect of power awakens every modern instinct of critical reaction. This is fatal; for religion collapses unless its main positions command immediacy of assent. In this respect the old phraseology is at variance with the psychology of modern civilisations. This change in psychology is largely due to science, and is one of the chief ways in which the advance of science has weakened the hold of the old religious forms of expression. The nonreligious motive which has entered into modern religious thought is the desire for a comfortable organisation of modern society. Religion has been presented as valuable for the ordering of life. Its claims have been rested upon its function as a sanction to right conduct. Also the purpose of right conduct quickly degenerates into the formation of pleasing social relations. We have here a subtle degradation of religious ideas, following upon their gradual purification under the influence of keener ethical intuitions. Conduct is a by-product of religion—an inevitable by-product, but not the main point. Every great religious teacher has revolted against the presentation of religion as a mere sanction of rules of conduct. Saint Paul denounced the Law, and Puritan divines spoke of the filthy rags of righteousness. The insistence upon rules of conduct marks the ebb of religious fervour. Above and beyond all things, the religious life is not a research after comfort. I must now state, in all diffidence, what I conceive to be the essential character of the religious spirit.

Religion is the vision of something which stands beyond, behind, and within, the passing flux of immediate things; something which is real, and yet waiting to be realised; something which is a remote possibility, and yet the greatest of present facts; something that gives meaning to all that passes, and yet eludes apprehension; something whose possession is the final good, and yet is beyond all reach; something which is the ultimate ideal, and the hopeless quest.

The immediate reaction of human nature to the religious vision is worship. Religion has emerged into human experience mixed with the crudest fancies of barbaric imagination. Gradually, slowly, steadily the vision recurs in history under nobler form and with clearer expression. It is the one element in human experience which persistently shows an upward trend. It fades and then recurs. But when it renews its force, it recurs with an added richness and purity of content. The fact of the religious vision, and its history of persistent expansion, is our one ground for optimism. Apart from it, human life is a flash of occasional enjoyments lighting up a mass of pain and misery, a bagatelle of transient experience.

The vision claims nothing but worship; and worship is a surrender to the claim for assimilation, urged with the motive force of mutual love. The vision never overrules. It is always there, and it has the power of love presenting the one purpose whose fulfilment is eternal harmony. Such order as we find in nature is never force—it presents itself as the one harmonious adjustment of complex detail. Evil is the brute motive force of fragmentary purpose, disregarding the eternal vision. Evil is overruling, retarding, hurting. The power of God is the worship He inspires. That religion is strong which in its ritual and its modes of thought evokes an apprehension of the commanding vision. The worship of God is not a rule of safety—it is an adventure of the spirit, a flight after the unattainable. The death of religion comes with the repression of the high hope of adventure.

Questions and Suggestions

1. In this famous essay Whitehead discusses the conflict that continues to exist between religion and science. Summarize his views.
2. What does he say about the age of this conflict?
3. What changes in theological and scientific doctrines does he mention?
4. What solution to the conflict does he propose?
5. How does Whitehead's definition of science agree with or differ from the definitions which you have already noted in Pyke and Rabi? Is one definition more nearly correct than the others?
6. Why do you accept or deny Whitehead's definition of religion? On what major premise does he base his discussion of religion? To help you reach a clear answer to this question, read Bertrand Russell's "Portraits from Memory: Alfred North Whitehead," in *Harper's Magazine*, December, 1952. Russell and Whitehead, once famous collaborators, failed to agree on philosophical issues.
7. Why does Whitehead believe our interest in religion has declined? Is Rabi's statement that each generation must "remake its culture, its values, and its goals" applicable to this problem?
8. Why does Whitehead recognize the need for tolerance? For additional thought on this subject, informally expressed, see Lucien Price's *The Dialogues of Alfred North Whitehead*.
9. Your grasp of Whitehead's argument will be clearer when you know more concerning *Pelagius, Augustine, Wesley, St. Francis* and *Cardinal Newman*. Consult the *Encyclopedia of Religion and Ethics* for introductory accounts.

Ideas for Writing

1. Show how in your own family there has been a conflict between religion and science, or an intolerance of others' views. Do your values and goals appear to differ from those of your parents?
2. Describe an acquaintance who ignores evidence that might contradict his beliefs—whether they be opinions he holds concerning religious groups, other races, other nations, or the people outside his immediate environment.
3. Use examples which will make it clear that religion for some people in your community has declined "into a decent formula" which they use "to embellish a comfortable life."
4. Analyze a situation which shows that human problems cannot be solved very satisfactorily by imposing rules or "absolute theories." Why can few ethical problems be "summarized in simple terms"?
5. Have your science courses made you question any of your beliefs?

part six ✂ *The significance of art*

ON THE FASCINATION OF STYLE

F. L. LUCAS

During the fighting on the Western front in 1917, Frank Laurence Lucas (1894–) was gassed, having been wounded even earlier. The author of novels, poems, plays, translations, and essays, Mr. Lucas, a native of Yorkshire, has been a most prolific and at the same time a most perceptive writer. For a number of years he has been Fellow and Lecturer of King's College, Cambridge, as well as the University Reader in English. If, after studying this essay, you wish to know more about the development of English prose, read *The Search for Good Sense,* one collection of Lucas's essays that deals brilliantly with four eighteenth century prose stylists.

When it was suggested to Walt Whitman that one of his works should be bound in vellum, he was outraged—"Pshaw!" he snorted, "—hangings, curtains, finger bowls, chinaware, Matthew Arnold!" And he might have been equally irritated by talk of style; for he boasted of "my barbaric yawp"—he would *not* be literary; his readers should touch not a book but a man. Yet Whitman took the pains to rewrite *Leaves of Grass* four times, and his style is unmistakable. Samuel Butler maintained that writers who bothered about their style became unreadable but he bothered about his own. "Style" has got a bad name by growing associated with precious and superior persons who, like Oscar Wilde, spend a morning putting in a comma, and the afternoon (so he said) taking it out again. But such abuse of "style" is misuse of English. For the word means merely "a way of expressing oneself, in language, manner, or appearance"; or, secondly, "a *good* way of so expressing oneself"—as when one says, "Her behavior never lacked style."

Now there is no crime in expressing oneself (though to try to *im-press* oneself on others easily grows revolting or ridiculous). Indeed one cannot help expressing oneself, unless one passes one's life in a cupboard. Even the most rigid Communist, or Organization-man, is compelled by Nature to have a unique voice, unique fingerprints, unique handwriting. Even the signatures of the letters on your breakfast table may reveal more than their writers guess. There are blustering signatures that swish across the page like cornstalks bowed before a tempest. There are cryptic signatures, like a scrabble of lightning across a cloud, suggesting that behind is a lofty divinity whom all must know, or an aloof divinity whom none is worthy to know (though, as this might be highly inconvenient, a docile typist sometimes interprets the mystery in a bracket underneath). There are impetuous squiggles implying that the author is a sort of strenuous Sputnik streaking round the globe every eighty minutes. There are florid signatures, all curlicues and dangle-ments and flamboyance, like the youthful Disraeli (though these seem rather out of fashion). There are humble, humdrum signatures. And there are also, sometimes, signatures that are courteously clear, yet mindful of a certain simple grace and artistic economy—in short, of style.

Since, then, not one of us can put pen to paper, or even open his mouth, without giving something of himself away to shrewd observers, it seems mere common sense to give the matter a little thought. Yet it does not seem very common. Ladies may take infinite pains about having style in their clothes, but many of us remain curiously indifferent about having it in our words. How many women would dream of polishing not only their nails but also their tongues? They may play freely on that perilous little organ, but they cannot often be bothered to tune it. And how many men think of improving their talk as well as their golf handicap?

No doubt strong silent men, speaking only in gruff monosyllables, may despise "mere words." No doubt the world does suffer from an endemic plague of verbal dysentery. But that, precisely, is bad style. And consider the amazing power of mere words. Adolf Hitler was a bad artist, bad statesman, bad general, and bad man. But largely because he could tune his rant, with psychological nicety, to the exact wave length of his audiences and make millions quarrelsome-drunk all at the same time by his command of windy nonsense, skilled statesmen, soldiers, scientists were blown away like chaff, and he came near to rule the world. If Sir Winston Churchill had been a mere speechifier, we might have lost the war; yet his speeches did quite a lot to win it.

No man was less of a literary aesthete than Benjamin Franklin; yet this tallow-chandler's son, who changed world history, regarded as "a principal means of my advancement" that pungent style which he acquired partly by working in youth over old *Spectators;* but mainly by being Benjamin Franklin. The squinting demagogue, John Wilkes, as ugly as his many sins, had yet a tongue so winning that he asked only half an hour's start (to counteract his face) against any rival for a woman's favor. "Vote for you!" growled a surly elector in his constituency. "I'd sooner vote for the devil!" "But in case your friend should not stand . . .?" Cleopatra, that ensnarer of world conquerors, owed less to the shape of her nose than to the charm of her tongue. Shakespeare himself has often poor plots and thin ideas; even his mastery of character has been questioned; what does remain unchallenged is his verbal magic. Men are often taken, like rabbits, by the ears. And though the tongue has no bones, it can sometimes break millions of them.

"But," the reader may grumble, "I am neither Hitler, Cleopatra, nor Shakespeare. What is all this to me?" Yet we all talk—often too much; we all have to write letters—often too many. We live not by bread alone but also by words. And not always with remarkable efficiency. Strikes, lawsuits, divorces, all sorts of public nuisance and private misery, often come just from the gaggling incompetence with which we express ourselves. Americans and British get at cross-purposes because they use the same words with different meanings. Men have been hanged on a comma in a statute. And in the valley of Balaclava a mere verbal ambiguity, about *which* guns were to be captured, sent the whole Light Brigade to futile annihilation.

Words can be more powerful, and more treacherous, than we sometimes suspect; communication more difficult than we may think. We are all serving life sentences of solitary confinement within our own bodies; like prisoners, we have, as it were, to tap in awkward code to our fellow men in their neighboring cells. Further, when A and B converse, there take part in their dialogue not two characters, as they suppose, but six. For there is A's real self—call it A_1; there is also A's picture of himself—A_2; there is also B's picture of A—A_3. And there are three corresponding personalities of B. With six characters involved even in a simple tête-à-tête, no wonder we fall into muddles and misunderstandings.

Perhaps, then, there are five main reasons for trying to gain some mastery of language:

We have no other way of understanding, informing, misinforming, or persuading one another.

Even alone, we think mainly in words; if our language is muddy, so will our thinking be.

By our handling of words we are often revealed and judged. "Has he written anything?" said Napoleon of a candidate for an appointment. "Let me see his *style*."

Without a feeling for language one remains half-blind and deaf to literature.

Our mother tongue is bettered or worsened by the way each generation uses it. Languages evolve like species. They can degenerate; just as oysters and barnacles have lost their heads. Compare ancient Greek with modern. A heavy responsibility, though often forgotten.

Why and how did I become interested in style? The main answer, I suppose, is that I was born that way. Then I was, till ten, an only child running loose in a house packed with books, and in a world (thank goodness) still undistracted by radio and television. So at three I groaned to my mother, "Oh, I *wish* I could read," and at four I read. Now travel among books is the best travel of all, and the easiest, and the cheapest. (Not that I belittle ordinary travel—which I regard as one of the three main pleasures in life.) One learns to write by reading good books, as one learns to talk by hearing good talkers. And if I have learned anything of writing, it is largely from writers like Montaigne, Dorothy Osborne, Horace Walpole, Johnson, Goldsmith, Montesquieu, Voltaire, Flaubert and Anatole France. Again, I was reared on Greek and Latin, and one can learn much from translating Homer or the Greek Anthology, Horace or Tacitus, if one is thrilled by the originals and tries, however vainly, to recapture some of that thrill in English.

But at Rugby I could *not* write English essays. I believe it stupid to torment boys to write on topics that they know and care nothing about. I used to rush to the school library and cram the subject, like a python swallowing rabbits; then, still replete as a postprandial python, I would tie myself in clumsy knots to embrace those accursed themes.

Bacon was wise in saying that reading makes a full man; talking, a ready one; writing, an exact one. But writing from an empty head is futile anguish.

At Cambridge, my head having grown a little fuller, I suddenly found I *could* write—not with enjoyment (it is always tearing oneself in pieces)—but fairly fluently. Then came the War of 1914-18; and though soldiers have other things than pens to handle, they learn painfully to be clear and brief. Then the late Sir Desmond MacCarthy invited me to review for the *New Statesman;* it was a useful apprenticeship, and he was delightful to work for. But I think it was well after a few years to stop; reviewers remain essential, but there are too many books one *cannot* praise, and only the pugnacious enjoy amassing enemies. By then I was an ink-addict—not because writing is much pleasure, but because not to write is pain; just as some smokers do not so much enjoy tobacco as suffer without it. The positive happiness of writing comes, I think, from work when done—decently, one hopes, and not without use—and from the letters of readers which help to reassure, or delude, one that so it is.

But one of my most vivid lessons came, I think, from service in a war department during the Second War. Then, if the matter one sent out was too wordy, the communication channels might choke; yet if it was not absolutely clear, the results might be serious. So I emerged, after six years of it, with more passion than ever for clarity and brevity, more loathing than ever for the obscure and the verbose.

For forty years at Cambridge I have tried to teach young men to write well, and have come to think it impossible. To write really well is a gift inborn; those who have it teach themselves; one can only try to help and hasten the process. After all, the uneducated sometimes express themselves far better than their "betters." In language, as in life, it is possible to be perfectly correct—and yet perfectly tedious, or odious. The illiterate last letter of the doomed Vanzetti was more moving than most professional orators; 18th Century ladies, who should have been spanked for their spelling, could yet write far better letters than most professors of English; and the talk of Synge's Irish peasants seems to me vastly more vivid than the later style of Henry James. Yet Synge averred that his characters owed far less of their eloquence to what he invented for them than to what he had overheard in the cottages of Wicklow and Kerry:

"*Christy.* 'It's little you'll think if my love's a poacher's, or an earl's itself, when you'll feel my two hands stretched around you, and I

squeezing kisses on your puckered lips, till I'd feel a kind of pity for
the Lord God is all ages sitting lonesome in His golden chair.'

"*Pegeen.* 'That'll be right fun, Christy Mahon, and any girl would
walk her heart out before she'd meet a young man was your like for
eloquence, or talk at all.' "

Well she might! It's not like that they talk in universities—more's
the pity.

But though one cannot teach people to write well, one can sometimes
teach them to write rather better. One can give a certain number of
hints, which often seem boringly obvious—only experience shows they
are not.

One can say: Beware of pronouns—they are devils. Look at even
Addison, describing the type of pedant who chatters of style without
having any: "Upon enquiry I found my learned friend had dined that
day with Mr. Swan, the famous punster; and desiring *him* to give me
some account of Mr. Swan's conversation, *he* told me that *he* generally
talked in the Paronomasia, that *he* sometimes gave in to the Ploce,
but that in *his* humble opinion *he* shone most in the Antanaclasis."
What a sluttish muddle of *he* and *him* and *his!* It all needs rewording.
Far better repeat a noun, or a name, than puzzle the reader, even for
a moment, with ambiguous pronouns. Thou shalt not puzzle thy reader.

Or one can say: Avoid jingles. The B.B.C. news bulletins seem
compiled by earless persons, capable of crying round the globe: "The
enemy is re*port*ed to have seized this im*port*ant *port,* and reinforce-
ments are hurrying up in sup*port.*" Any fool, once told, can hear such
things to be insupportable.

Or one can say: Be sparing with relative clauses. Don't string them
together like sausages, or jam them inside one another like Chinese
boxes or the receptacles of Buddha's tooth. Or one can say: Don't flaunt
jargon, like Addison's Mr. Swan, or the type of modern critic who gur-
gles more technical terms in a page than Johnson used in all his *Lives*
or Sainte-Beuve in thirty volumes. But dozens of such snippety precepts,
though they may sometimes save people from writing badly, will help
them little toward writing well. Are there no general rules of a more
positive kind, and of more positive use?

Perhaps. There *are* certain basic principles which seem to me observed by many authors I admire, which I think have served me and
which may serve others. I am not talking of geniuses, who are a law to
themselves (and do not always write a very good style, either); nor of
poetry, which has different laws from prose; nor of poetic prose, like

Sir Thomas Browne's or De Quincey's, which is often more akin to poetry; but of the plain prose of ordinary books and documents, letters and talk.

The writer should respect truth and himself; therefore honesty. He should respect his readers; therefore courtesy. These are two of the cornerstones of style. Confucius saw it, twenty-five centuries ago: "The Master said, The gentleman is courteous, but not pliable: common men are pliable, but not courteous."

First, honesty. In literature, as in life, one of the fundamentals is to find, and be, one's true self. One's true self may indeed be unpleasant (though one can try to better it); but a false self, sooner or later, becomes disgusting—just as a nice plain woman, painted to the eyebrows, can become horrid. In writing, in the long run, pretense does not work. As the police put it, anything you say may be used as evidence against you. If handwriting reveals character, writing reveals it still more. You cannot fool *all* your judges *all* the time.

Most style is not honest enough. Easy to say, but hard to practice. A writer may take to long words, as young men to beards—to impress. But long words, like long beards, are often the badge of charlatans. Or a writer may cultivate the obscure, to seem profound. But even carefully muddied puddles are soon fathomed. Or he may cultivate eccentricity, to seem original. But really original people do not have to think about being original—they can no more help it than they can help breathing. They do not need to dye their hair green. The fame of Meredith, Wilde or Bernard Shaw might now shine brighter, had they struggled less to be brilliant; whereas Johnson remains great, not merely because his gifts were formidable but also because, with all his prejudice and passion, he fought no less passionately to "clear his mind of cant."

Secondly, courtesy—respect for the reader. From this follow several other basic principles of style. Clarity is one. For it is boorish to make your reader rack his brains to understand. One should aim at being impossible to misunderstand—though men's capacity for misunderstanding approaches infinity. Hence Molière and Po Chu-i tried their work on their cooks; and Swift his on his menservants—"which, if they did not comprehend, he would alter and amend, until they understood it perfectly." Our bureaucrats and pundits, unfortunately, are less considerate.

Brevity is another basic principle. For it is boorish, also, to waste your reader's time. People who would not dream of stealing a penny

of one's money turn not a hair at stealing hours of one's life. But that
does not make them less exasperating. Therefore there is no excuse
for the sort of writer who takes as long as a marching army corps to
pass a given point. Besides, brevity is often more effective; the half
can say more than the whole, and to imply things may strike far deeper
than to state them at length. And because one is particularly apt to
waste words on preambles before coming to the substance, there was
sense in the Scots professor who always asked his pupils—"Did ye
remember to tear up that fir-r-st page?"

Here are some instances that would only lose by lengthening:

> It is useless to go to bed to save the light, if the result is twins.
> (Chinese proverb.)
> My barn is burnt down—
> Nothing hides the moon. (Complete Japanese poem.)
> Je me regrette. (Dying words of the gay Vicomtesse d'Houde-
> tot.)
> I have seen their backs before. (Wellington, when French
> marshals turned their backs on him at a reception.)
> Continue until the tanks stop, then get out and walk. (Patton
> to the Twelfth Corps, halted for fuel supplies at St. Dizier,
> 8/30/44.)

Or there is the most laconic diplomatic note on record: when Philip
of Macedon wrote to the Spartans that, if he came within their borders,
he would leave not one stone of their city, they wrote back the one
word—"If."

Clarity comes before even brevity. But it is a fallacy that wordiness
is necessarily clearer. Metternich when he thought something he had
written was obscure would simply go through it crossing out everything
irrelevant. What remained, he found, often became clear. Wellington,
asked to recommend three names for the post of Commander-in-Chief,
India, took a piece of paper and wrote three times—"Napier." Pages
could not have been clearer—or as forcible. On the other hand the
lectures, and the sentences, of Coleridge became at times bewildering
because his mind was often "wiggle-waggle"; just as he could not even
walk straight on a path.

But clarity and brevity, though a good beginning, are only a beginning. By themselves, they may remain bare and bleak. When Calvin
Coolidge, asked by his wife what the preacher had preached on, replied "Sin," and, asked what the preacher had said, replied, "He was
against it," he was brief enough. But one hardly envies Mrs. Coolidge.

An attractive style requires, of course, all kinds of further gifts—

such as variety, good humor, good sense, vitality, imagination. Variety means avoiding monotony of rhythm, of language, of mood. One needs to vary one's sentence length (this present article has too many short sentences; but so vast a subject grows here as cramped as a djin in a bottle); to amplify one's vocabulary; to diversify one's tone. There are books that petrify one throughout, with the rigidly pompous solemnity of an owl perched on a leafless tree. But ceaseless facetiousness can be as bad; or perpetual irony. Even the smile of Voltaire can seem at times a fixed grin, a disagreeable wrinkle. Constant peevishness is far worse, as often in Swift; even on the stage too much irritable dialogue may irritate an audience, without its knowing why.

Still more are vitality, energy, imagination gifts that must be inborn before they can be cultivated. But under the head of imagination two common devices may be mentioned that have been the making of many a style—metaphor and simile. Why such magic power should reside in simply saying, or implying, that A is like B remains a little mysterious. But even our unconscious seems to love symbols; again, language often tends to lose itself in clouds of vaporous abstraction, and simile or metaphor can bring it back to concrete solidity; and, again, such imagery can gild the gray flats of prose with sudden sun-glints of poetry.

If a foreigner may for a moment be impertinent, I admire the native gift of Americans for imagery as much as I wince at their fondness for slang. (Slang seems to me a kind of linguistic fungus; as poisonous, and as short-lived, as toadstools.) When Matthew Arnold lectured in the United States, he was likened by one newspaper to "an elderly macaw pecking at a trellis of grapes"; he observed, very justly, "How lively journalistic fancy is among the Americans!" General Grant, again, unable to hear him, remarked: "Well, wife, we've paid to see the British lion, but as we can't hear him roar, we'd better go home." By simile and metaphor, these two quotations bring before us the slightly pompous, fastidious, inaudible Arnold as no direct description could have done.

Or consider how language comes alive in the Chinese saying that lending to the feckless is "like pelting a stray dog with dumplings," or in the Arab proverb: "They came to shoe the pasha's horse, and the beetle stretched forth his leg"; in the Greek phrase for a perilous cape— "stepmother of ships"; or the Hebrew adage that "as the climbing up a sandy way is to the feet of the aged, so is a wife full of words to a quiet man"; in Shakespeare's phrase for a little England lost in the world's vastness—"in a great Poole, a Swan's-nest"; or Fuller's libel on tall men—"Ofttimes such who are built four stories high are observed to have little in their cockloft"; in Chateaubriand's "I go yawning my life"; or in Jules Renard's portrait of a cat, "well buttoned in her fur." Or, to take a modern instance, there is Churchill on dealings with Russia: "Trying to maintain good relations with a Communist is like wooing a crocodile. You do not know whether to tickle it under the chin or beat it over the head. When it opens its mouth, you cannot tell whether it is trying to smile or preparing to eat you up." What a miracle human speech can be, and how dull is most that one hears! Would one hold one's hearers, it is far less help, I suspect, to read manuals on style than to cultivate one's own imagination and imagery.

I will end with two remarks by two wise old women of the civilized 18th Century.

The first is from the blind Mme. du Deffand (the friend of Horace Walpole) to that Mlle. de Lespinasse with whom, alas, she was to quarrel so unwisely: "You must make up your mind, my queen, to live with me in the greatest truth and sincerity. You will be charming so long as you let yourself be natural, and remain without pretension and without artifice." The second is from Mme. de Charrière, the Zélide whom Boswell had once loved at Utrecht in vain, to a Swiss girl friend: "Lucinde, my clever Lucinde, while you wait for the Romeos to arrive, you have nothing better to do than become perfect. Have ideas that are clear, and expressions that are simple." ("*Ayez des idées nettes et des expressions simples.*") More than half the bad writing in the world, I believe, comes from neglecting those two very simple pieces of advice.

In many ways, no doubt, our world grows more and more complex; sputniks cannot be simple; yet how many of our complexities remain futile, how many of our artificialities false. Simplicity too can be subtle—as the straight lines of a Greek temple, like the Parthenon at Athens, are delicately curved, in order to look straighter still.

Questions and Suggestions

1. Lucas's prose has wit, exuberance, vitality, subtle rhythms, and variety; he offers much admirable advice in a short space. Elaborate upon each of his five reasons for improving one's use of language.

2. What relationship does he recognize between reading and writing, between the mastery of language and an appreciation of literature?

3. What is your reply to the college student who tells you, "I hate being around books"?
4. State Lucas's basic principles or "cornerstones" of style. Are they similar to those advocated by your rhetoric or handbook?
5. Is his interest in style evident in his manner of presenting these principles? Contrast his style with that of your rhetoric.
6. Lucas, as a teacher himself, gives what advice about clarity, pronouns, relative clauses, and jargon?
7. Assay his use of similes, metaphors, allusions, and quotations. Do they give any "concrete solidarity" to his prose? How unusual and striking are his comparisons?

Ideas for Writing

1. Read Arthur Daley's column in the sports section of *The New York Times* and write a paper, analyzing his figures of speech. After listening carefully to everyday speech, write an essay that deals with "the native gift of Americans for imagery" or with "their fondness for slang."
2. Describe the misery you experienced when you had to write in class on an unfamiliar subject.
3. What respect do you show the reader of your themes, your letters? Why do you sometimes fail to read all of a sales letter?
4. What reply would you give to a first grade teacher who tells you, a parent, "We don't want Johnny to be able to read when he comes to school"?
5. What impression of "education" courses do you have from the comments you have heard upperclassmen make?
6. Write on the role or importance of style in one's behavior or appearance, elaborating on some basic principles such as Lucas does in his discussion of writing.
7. Analyze some of the faults in your earlier papers, paying particular attention to the verbs and pronouns.

LOOKING BACK AT WRITING

SEÁN O'FAOLÁIN

A Dubliner by birth, Seán O'Faoláin (1900–) graduated from the National University of Ireland and also from Harvard. After taking an active part in the Irish Revolution, he became a teacher.

It was with the publication of *A Nest of Simple Folk* that he began to receive acclaim in America. Since the publication of that novel he has continued to write fiction, biographies, essays, and to do translations from the Gaelic. Disapproving of censorship, as practiced in Eire, and the insularity of the Irish people (see "Love Among the Irish," *Life,* March 16, 1953), O'Faoláin as an interpreter of Ireland is praised abroad, but his works often produce controversy among his co-nationals.

When I was in my twenties I did not know from Adam what I wanted to say. I had no grasp at all of the real world, of real people. I had met and mingled with them, argued with them, lived with them, shared danger with them. They were mysteries to me. I could only try to convey my astonishment and delight at the strangeness of this bewildering thing called life.

Besides, when I wrote "Fugue," my first successful story, in 1927, I had come out of an experience which had left me dazed—the revolutionary period in Ireland. Not that it was really an experience as I now understand that word. It was too filled with dreams and ideals and a sense of dedication to be an experience in the sense of things perceived, understood, and remembered. I perceived all right, I remembered all right, but it had all been far too much to understand; especially the disillusion at the end of it all, for, as few people who are not Irish now remember, that revolutionary period ended in a civil war, and civil war is of all wars the most difficult thing for its participants to understand. Besides, as I found myself yesterday making a character in a story I am writing say: "It's a terrible and lovely thing to look at the face of Death when you are young, but it unfits a man for the long humiliation of life."

I suppose that is why those early stories were full of romantic boss-words like *dawn*. At that time if you said *dawn* to me, my mouth would begin to dribble. *Dawn* is not a prose writer's word. I doubt if it is any longer a decent word for even a poet to use. It is a sounding word, a rhetorical word. Words like that are all right for Frenchmen. They are able to use rhetoric as if it were not rhetoric; we are not. (The other day a producer said to me: "I'm doing a French play. Every time one of the characters makes a speech I want to make him stand with his

back to the audience. Otherwise he seems as if he were about to take
off in an aeroplane.")

But those first stories I wrote were all the time trying to take off
in an aeroplane. They are, I now see, very romantic, as their weighted
style shows. I have sometimes thought of rewriting them, but I realize
that I should have to change their nature if I were to change their style,
which is full of romantic words, such as *dawn, dew, onwards, youth,
world, adamant, or dusk;* of metaphors and abstractions; of personaliza-
tions and sensations which belong to the author rather than to the
characters. The stories also contain many of those most romantic of
all words, *and* and *but,* which are words that are part of the attempt
to carry on and expand the effect after the sense has been given.
Writers who put down the essential thing, without any cocoon about
it, do not need these *ands* and *buts.* The thing is given and there it lies;
whereas the writer who luxuriates goes on with the echoes of his first
image or idea. His emotions and his thoughts dilate, the style dilates
with them, and in the end he is trying to write a kind of verbal music
to convey feelings that the mere sense of the words cannot give. He
is chasing the inexpressible.

If I were to rewrite those stories, it would be a lie. A story is like a
picture, caught in the flick of a camera's trigger, that comes nearer and
nearer to clarity in the bath of hypo which is the writer's blend of skill
and imagination; he trembles over it as the bleach trembles and wavers
over the sensitive halides of the film, waiting for the final perfection of
his certainty, of his desire. Then the experience, complete or incomplete, is fixed forever. You can rewrite while you are the same man.
To rewrite years after is a form of forgery.

My second volume of stories, *A Purse of Coppers,* appeared after I
had more or less come out of the daze. I came out of it by writing
myself out of it in a novel, *A Nest of Simple Folk,* and a biographical
study of a beautiful Irishwoman, a romantic guerrilla, Constance
Gore-Booth, later Countess Markievicz. The biography was slight and
groping, but it helped me to get all those romantic figures into some sort
of perspective, and myself along with them. I could grin a bit at my
solemn self and at my solemn countrymen. I hope a certain adjustment
and detachment shows itself in the stories that follow "A Broken
World."

Naturally, of course, I still did not know what was happening to
me or what I was doing. Writers never do. For instance, a friend suggested to me that "A Broken World" was my unconscious reply to

Joyce's wonderful story, "The Dead." I certainly did not consciously mean any such thing; but I can agree that what with the snow over Dublin, and the suggestion that Ireland is not dead but sleeping, as against Joyce's feeling that Ireland is paralyzed by its past, one could, I suppose, say that the stories contrast the attitudes of two different generations. After all, Joyce grew up with a strong distaste for Ireland.

But I do not think I had adjusted myself properly until my next volume of stories, *The Man Who Invented Sin*—if even then. Anyway, by the time I had more or less adjusted myself to the life about me, it suddenly broke in on me that Ireland had not adjusted herself to the life about her in the least little bit. Irishmen in general were still thinking about themselves, or rather in their usual way double-thinking or squint-thinking about themselves, in terms of *dawns,* and *ands,* and *buts,* and *onwards,* and *dew,* and *dusk,* while at the same time making a lot of good, hard cash to the evocative vocabulary of *tariff, tax, protection, quota, levy, duties,* or *subsidies,* meanwhile carefully compiling a third and wholly different literary style (*pious, holy, prudent, sterling, gossoons, lassies, maidens, sacred, traditional, forefathers, olden, venerable, mothers, grandmothers, ancestors, deep-rooted, traditions, Gaelic, timeworn,* and *immemorial*) to dodge more awkward social, moral, and political problems than any country might, with considerable courage, hope to solve in a century of ruthless thinking. This ambivalence, if not triplivalence, demanded a totally new approach. I have been trying to define it ever since. For, as long as we were all in a splendidly romantic-idealistic fervor about Ireland, we could all write romantically, or idealistically, about Ireland, as Sean O'Casey did. (He is sometimes called and probably thinks himself a realist, but he is actually the biggest old romantic we ever produced.) Or if we were all being realistic we could write in the realist tradition.

But for any kind of realist to write about people with romantic souls is a most tricky and difficult business, even when he is a Stendhal gifted with a lovely irony, a Chekhov holding on firmly to the stern morality of the doctor, a Turgenev informed by an intelligent humanism, or an E. M. Forster blessed with a talent for quiet raillery. If one has not some such gift the subject is an almost certain pitfall. But when it comes to writing about people who, like the Irish of our day, combine beautiful, palpitating, tea-rose souls with hard, coolly calculating heads, there does not seem to be any way at all of writing about them except satirically or angrily. Once a writer's eye gets chilly about their beautiful souls he becomes like the only sober man at a drunken party, and the only decent thing for him to do then is either to get blind drunk with the rest of the boys (all singing in chorus "I'll take you home again, Kathl-ee-een") or else to go home and scrub himself clean in a raging satire on the whole boiling lot of them.

I have made a few mildly tentative efforts in this direction in some of my later stories. They started out to be satirical; they mostly failed dismally to be satirical; largely, I presume—I observe it to my dismay and I confess it to my shame—because I still have much too soft a corner in my heart for the old land. For all I know I may be still a besotted romantic! Some day I may manage to dislike my countrymen sufficiently to satirize them; but I gravely doubt it—curse them! However, as D. H. Lawrence said, one's passion is always searching for some form that will express or hold it better, letting none of it leak away. And one is always searching for different forms, since otherwise one's passion would have the same form from birth to death, which would merely mean that one had got stuck, or given up, or agreed to compromise on some easy formula somewhere along the line; and that would be premature death, since not to change is to die though still apparently alive.

One thing I find very chastening as I look back at my writing: the thought that although I began writing in 1927—that is really writing, writing well—and have since written lots of other books (far too many of them), all I have to show for all those years by way of short stories —or, at least, all I am content to show—is some thirty titles. One thinks of writers like George Sand pouring out volume after volume while—as Colette observed, enviously, wondering how on earth she managed it—never once neglecting a love affair, never missing one puff of her hookah, never denying herself any experience that came her way.

I think of the time when I wanted to be another Balzac. I saw myself scribbling away madly while the printer's devil stood by my desk picking up the pages of genius and running off with them to the printing press while the ink was still wet. I must have been *very* young then. When I got down to the business of writing, I found that half the art of writing is rewriting, and I would be happy if I achieved two hundred words of lapidary prose in a day.

I have learned in my thirty-odd years of serious writing only one sure lesson: stories, like whiskey, must be allowed to mature in the cask. And that takes so much time! Oh, dear! Why do they tell us in our youth that there are twenty-four hours in a day, seven days in a week, and fifty-two weeks in a year? Balzac, indeed! I shall be content if a half dozen, if even three or four, of my stories that have taken thirty years to write are remembered fifty years hence.

Questions and Suggestions

1. Is O'Faoláin right in saying that writers "never" know what they are doing?
2. Why does he find it difficult to write realistically about the Irish? Has he ever satirized them? For examples of genial satire, consult Sir Richard Steele's portrait of Sir Roger de Coverley, Alva Johnston's *The Legendary Mizners,* and some of the writings of James Thurber.
3. How does O'Faoláin's statement that a young man's sight of "the face of Death" makes him unfit "for the long humiliation of life" bear out his claim that he himself has changed from a romantic to a realist?
4. Discuss O'Faoláin's use of figures of speech. What is the "cocoon" he mentions in the fourth paragraph? What was wrong with the metaphors he used in his early stories? What does he mean by a "weighted style"? Why does he call such words as *dawn, dew,* and *onwards* "romantic boss-words"?

Ideas for Writing

1. Recreate a time when you were especially aware of the mysteriousness of life.
2. Can you explain some personal situation which was, at least at the time, "too much [for you] to understand"?
3. See if you can put into words the essential traits of a person who is imaginative, poetic, or romantic.
4. Look back at some of your earliest creative efforts. Did you try to handle any subjects beyond your youthful ability?
5. Analyze a poem by a friend for evidence of romantic influences upon the subject, diction, and form. Study some of e.e. cummings's early poems.
6. Read "The Teacher" in Sherwood Anderson's *Winesburg, Ohio.* Would Kate Swift's advice to George Willard, a young man interested in becoming a writer, have helped the young O'Faoláin?
7. What is meant by the term "poetic language"?

A POET'S CHILDHOOD

HAROLD NICOLSON

Harold George Nicolson (1886–), who is married to the novelist
Victoria Sackville-West, was born in Tehran, Persia, when his
father was British chargé d'affaires there. After graduating from
Oxford, he entered the diplomatic corps, resigning in 1929. Since
then he has served in the House of Commons and has also been
a frequent contributor to English journals and papers. Nicolson's
work as a biographer and historian has received wide praise.

Second-rate works of art, especially when they are technically
competent, leave us with a sense of depression. First-rate works of art,
in that they enlarge experience and enhance life, in that they reveal
for us new shafts of beauty or fresh aspects of human character,
provide lasting exhilaration. Mr. Laurie Lee's CIDER WITH ROSIE is
a first-rate work of art. Its vigour and delicacy animate the loveliness
of existence.

Mr. Lee describes his childhood in a small Cotswold village, so
isolated from the world that it still retained "the blood and beliefs of
generations who had been in this valley since the Stone Age." He does
not sentimentalise this pastoral simplicity. The valley was a funnel
through which the winds howled bringing with them flood and snow.
The villagers were harsh in their habits, possessing a "frank and un-
fearful attitude to death" and taking violence as a matter of course.

As a baby Laurie Lee would be told stories of "hapless suicides, of
fighting men loose in the snow, of witch-doomed widows disembowelled
by bulls, of child-eating sows." There were legends around him of
ghosts and murders, of hangman's cottage and Jones's goat, of the man
who returned from New Zealand only to be murdered on his first night
home, since he had angered them by his vaunting, of Miss Fluck who
floated, like Ophelia, drowned in the pond.

In contrast to these spectres was his own cottage home, with its "womanly warmth" and the glow of the kitchen fire, "the evening lamp, the vast and easy time": —

> The fire burned clear with a bottle-green light. Their voices grew low and furry. A farm-dog barked far across the valley, fixing the time and distance exactly. Warned by the dog and some hooting owls, I could sense the night valley emptying, stretching in mists of stars and water, growing slowly more secret and late.

There were nine of them in the cottage, their mother and eight children. They were often hungry and to this day Mr. Lee will wake at night clamouring for whole rice puddings and big pots of stew. Their eldest sister, Marjorie, who seems to have been a competent child, helped her mother to clean the house and nurse the invalids and the babies. Their father does not come well out of the story, since he deserted his family, lived in London as a minor Civil Servant, and only very occasionally came to visit them or consented to spare a few shillings to eke out the rent. Mr. Lee refers to his "devout gentility" and concludes that he must have been "a rather priggish young man."

Readers of that excellent periodical, John Murray's *Cornhill,* will already have met Mr. Lee's astonishing and admirable mother. She was descended directly from one of the executioners of Edward II, whose final operation in Berkeley Castle must have demanded strong nerves. She inherited these nerves and resolved that, in spite of her husband's desertion, she would herself face the upbringing of two separate litters. She was not a woman to flinch or to repine. She had a native genius, playing music wildly, learning poetry by heart and drawing "delicate snowflake" sketches of the fields and trees outside. She had a passion for collecting old china and would attend sales and return triumphant with a broken Wedgwood cup or a half-piece of Spode. She was "mischievous, muddle-headed, full of brilliant fancies, half witless, half touched with wonder": —

> She was, after all, a country girl; disordered, hysterical, loving. She was muddled and mischievous as a chimney-jackdaw, she made her nest of rags and jewels, was happy in the sunlight, squawked loudly at danger, pried and was insatiably curious, forgot when to eat or ate all day, and sang when sunsets were red.

In spite of the fact that during her long struggle to bring up two families she was "deserted, debt-ridden, flurried, bewildered, doomed by ambitions that never came off," she retained her "indestructible gaiety which welled up like a thermal spring." In the end, when the daughters had married and the sons were embarked upon the ladder of life, she abandoned all struggle and "reverted gently to a rustic simplicity as a moss-rose reverts to a wild one." It is a beautiful tribute that her famous son pays to her memory: —

> Nothing now that I ever see that has the edge of gold around it—the change of a season, a jewelled bird in a bush, the eyes of orchids, water in the evening, a thistle, a picture, a poem—but my pleasure pays some brief duty to her. She tried me at times to the top of my bent. But I absorbed from birth, as now I know, the whole earth through her jaunty spirit.

Outside the glow of the kitchen fire there spread the village characters and the village events. There was Granny Wallon, who made cowslip wine. There was her enemy, Granny Trill, whose bible was Old Moore's Almanack, and who died at the age of ninety-five. There were the worried school-teacher and the vicar and the aged squire who wept continuously and whom they all revered. There were choir outings and church teas. The little boys at a very early age told each other smutty stories and indulged in sexual experiments. "Manslaughter, arson, robbery, rape cropped up regularly throughout the years. Quiet incest flourished where the roads were bad." It was in this manner that Laurie, drunk with cider and the scent of hay, first learnt the facts of life: —

> But he covered his face and hid his joy
> in a wild-goose web of false directions,
> and hunted the woods for eggs and glow-worms,
> for rabbits tasteless as moss.
>   It was then that I began to sit on my bed and stare out at the nibbling squirrels, and to make up poems from intense abstraction, hour after unmarked hour, imagination scarcely faltering once, rhythm hardly skipping a beat, while sisters called me, suns rose and fell, and the poems I made, which I never remembered, were the first and the last of that time. . . .

I have quoted enough from this *Wahrheit und Dichtung* to indicate the rapturous beauty of his book. The atmosphere of thistle and thistle-down is excellently reflected in Mr. John Ward's illustrations. Grasping his fiddle, and with his sense of wonder still undimmed, Laurie Lee leaves the Cotswolds for the wide, angry and vivacious world.

Questions and Suggestions

1. How does Nicolson distinguish between first-rate and second-rate works of art? What can they have in common?

2. If you consider "The Kitchen" in Part I of your text as being a representative selection from Lee's autobiography, how does the book meet O'Faoláin's standards of realism?

3. Why does Nicolson refer to Lee's account of life as *Wahrheit und Dichtung,* truth and fiction?

4. Why do you agree with Nicolson that Lee does not become sentimental?

5. Consult F. O. Matthiessen's "The Winter Critic" in the October, 1952, issue of *The Atlantic* for advice about book reviewing. Test Nicolson's review against Matthiessen's principles.

6. What methods of book reviewing are exemplified here that are also apparent in the Bowen review? How do the two reviews differ?

Ideas for Writing

1. Imagine that you, as a reviewer, want to suggest what the Lees and their home are like. Include one or two apt quotations in your account.

2. Review Gwen Raverat's *Period Piece,* Mary Ellen Chase's *The White Gate,* Leonard Woolf's *Sowing,* C. Day-Lewis's *The Buried Day,* Frank O'Connor's *An Only Child,* Diana Holman-Hunt's *My Grandmothers and I,* or a similar book about childhood and youth, indicating as Nicolson does who the characters are, what their lives and surroundings are like, and how well the book recreates the life it depicts.

3. Using Matthiessen's standards, evaluate a review given at a meeting of a literary club.

4. What is wrong with digests of books?

5. What opinion do you now hold of high school book reports? Do you have suggestions for improving them?

6. Why is it easy to satirize literary clubs?

THE INVARIABLE BADNESS
OF AMATEUR ACTING

MAX BEERBOHM

Even before he left Oxford, Max Beerbohm (1872–1956), a native of London, was known for his gifts as an essayist and cartoonist. *Zuleika Dobson* remains one of the best novels about English university life. As a young man about town in the nineties, Beerbohm knew everyone whom he needed to know, and at the same time felt free to do brilliant caricatures of their foibles. Because of his many gifts, he was considered the natural choice for dramatic critic of the *Saturday Review* when George Bernard Shaw resigned. Beerbohm, long a resident of Rapallo, Italy, was knighted in 1939. During the war years he did a number of broadcasts for the B.B.C. For an extended portrait of the novelist, artist, critic, essayist, and fabler, read S. N. Behrman's *Portrait of Max.*

January 24 and 31, 1903

There is much to be said for the amateur in other arts. There is nothing to prevent us from taking him quite seriously. His work, at its best, or even at its second best, yields us a quality of pleasure which we could not win elsewhere.

As "amateur" is a rather dubious word, let me explain that I mean by it one who practises an art by the way, as a recreation from some other kind of work, or as a recreation from leisure, and not with any need of emolument from it, nor devoting to it his whole life. Work done with this motive, done under these conditions, may often be trivial, but it never can be vulgar. Professionalism is a very dangerous thing. It tempts a man to accept a popular standard, and to ignore his own standard of what is right and wrong in his art—to aim at what passes muster, not at what himself thinks worthy. Necessitating, moreover, not merely constant labour but also constant output, professionalism tends to foster a fatal fluency, enabling a man to say anything anyhow, robbing him, at length, of the power to express anything from himself. From such dangers the amateur is safe. Working solely for his own pleasure, he is not seduced into doing less than his best for sake of a public which does not exact, or positively will have none of, his best. Under no contract to stand and deliver at stated hours, he can linger over his work as long as ever he care to. He need take no short cuts to sufficiency. He may treat, with deliberate footsteps, the high-road to perfection. He never acquires a cheap ready-made knowledge of "how to do things." Thus he must always be finding out for himself how a thing—how on earth even the easiest, most obvious thing—can be done. And thus the way, when he finds it, is his own way; so that even the easiest, most obvious thing achieved by him has some distinction, some personal flavour and significance. Some beauty, belike, too; for his is "the hand of little employment" that "hath the daintier sense"—the lingering hand, delicately refining. The most exquisite work, in other arts than the art of acting, is always the work of an amateur.

Take an example. No one, I suppose, will dispute that in the art of writing prose the most exquisite work done in our time was the work of an amateur. Essentially an amateur was Walter Pater. There was no worldly need for him to write. Writing was his recreation, his way of enjoying himself. To the last, he was an amateur. And the peculiar value and beauty of his work came from the very fact that he was so amateurish. He never mastered, because there was no need for him to master, the rudiments of writing as a business. He never could express anything off-hand. He had always to fumble and grope in the recesses of his consciousness before he could set down on paper the simplest thought. He had infinite leisure for fumbling and groping there before he need express thoughts more complicated. And thus it is that we have in his writing so exact and vivid a presentment of himself, and a beauty so distinct from any other kind of beauty that is known to us (except, of course, in the work of his disciples). Suppose that Pater had failed to win a Fellowship, and had come "down" to London, there to make worldly use of the specific instinct that was in him. Suppose that he had become a professional writer. And then try to imagine yourself reading with any pleasure such books as he might have left behind him. Pater not exquisite! A poor sort of Pater that would be.

I have taken in Pater, of course, a pre-eminent example—the kind of man bound to do pre-eminent work as an amateur. The average amateur has but little true impulse for the art which he pursues—nothing that is worth expressing, nor much of the gift for achieving a beautiful expression of it. His work does not matter much; but it has, at least, a kind of fragile charm and distinction. The faint reflection of a faint thing is better than the harsh reflection of nothing in particular. And the difference between those two reflections is the difference between the work of the average amateur and the average professional.

Not that I would altogether decry professionalism. Its power for evil is not unlimited; and it is to some extent a power for good. It kills only the exquisite talent. To that rarer phenomenon, genius, it is

of real service. Pater was a great man in a small way, and professionalism would have been fatal to him; but, had he been great in a great
way, he would have been all the better for having to earn his bread by
writing. Take the case of any absolutely great writer who has been
beset by that necessity. Take, for example, Balzac. Had he had enough
money to keep him in ease and comfort, had he not laden himself with
that appalling load of debts, he would not have written more carefully
than he did write. Merely, he would have written less. Professionalism
is a kind of pump. It soon pumps out of a small artist what might have
been valuable had it been expressed by the small artist, slowly, of his
own accord. It does not, on the other hand, exhaust the great artist.
It does but keep him in a constant state of effusion. How much leisure
the great artist has for his work is a question which does not at all
affect the quality of his work. He is so strongly himself that his
hastiest work bears always his own authentic stamp. The great artist
is always at his best. If ever he tried (and he never does try) to be
exquisite, he would not succeed in being so. Exquisiteness is within
the reach only of certain smaller artists. And it is within their reach
only when they are working as amateurs.

As in literature, so is it in painting and in music. For example—
but oh, bother examples! Or rather, I beg you to take them on trust.
I am a simple dramatic critic: I refuse to do more than make general
assertions about music and painting. A priori, of course, one would
expect that a rule deducible from the arts generally would hold good
in the art of acting also. It is among amateur mimes that one would
look to find the most delicate and various interpretation of finer shades
of character. One would not look to find great tragic acting, or even
great comedic acting. But one would expect, at least, a certain exquisite subtlety in the portrayal of "character parts." The average
professional mime offends us with his roughness and readiness. His
experience is such that he never has to think anything out freshly for
himself. He repeats mechanically the tricks which he has played before, and which, maybe, he had picked up, in the first instance, from
other mimes. If he is one who confines himself to a single "line of business," he does the same thing, over and over again, in the same way.
If he is "versatile," he does different things, over and over again, in
the same way. Never is he the character as drawn by the author.
Never is he even himself. He is but a tissue of tedious conventions.
Now, the average amateur has little or no experience. Therefore he
must think for himself. A part is put into his hands, and he must

excogitate what will be the best means of conveying his idea of it to the audience. And it is likely (on the analogy of the other arts) that he, if he have a true bent towards acting, will give a very original and delicate performance. Well, let us test these likelihoods by our experience of amateur acting. We have all, in our time, seen a good deal of amateur acting. For it is acting which has been in our time the most popular of the art-forms, and therefore the most ardently practised by the greatest number of amateurs. In the early part of this century, poetry bore away the palm. So pervasive was the force of Byron that thousands of ladies and gentlemen, who else would never have thought of rhyming love to dove, began to scribble innumerable verses in innumerable albums. Then came Queen Victoria, who was no poet, but was fond of sketching in water-colour. Forthwith, the albums were laid aside, and easels were set up in their stead, and the faltering fingers that had been stained with violet ink were now stained with moist paints. Later came Jenny Lind, and the genteel world sketched no more in water-colour, but warbled. Last of all came Mr. Henry Irving; and the genteel world ceased to warble, and began to act, and has been acting ever since. Acting, indeed, has had, and still has, a greater vogue than came to any of the other art-forms. For, in a sense, it is the easiest of them all. Not every one can write a metrical line, or draw a straight line, or sing a note in tune. But any one who is not dumb and paralysed can come and speak a few lines across a row of footlights, and can imagine that he is speaking them rather nicely. The greater the number of amateurs, of course, the greater the number of duffers. But there is no reason to suppose that among even the greatest number there will not be some persons of real skill and talent. And yet, and yet, did any one of us ever behold an amateur mime whom he could praise without insincerity, or whose performance seemed comparable with even the worst professional performance? None of us ever beheld that amateur mime. Why?

That the vast majority of amateur mimes should merely flounder does not, of course, surprise me. What else should they do? They go in for private theatricals, not with any inward impulse for the art of acting, but just for the fun of the thing, as a variation from the common round of amusements in country-houses. As on the professional stage, so on the amateur stage, the conditions foster a certain freedom between the sexes, and many amateur mimes regard their art less as an end in itself than as a means to flirtation. In such diversions as sport or gambling there can be no sexual element. A woman who rides to hounds, or goes out with the guns, is doing a mannish thing, and ceasing, for the time, to be a woman. She does not distract attention from the fox or the birds, and presumably does not seek to distract it: she, too, is exclusively a minister of death. Similarly, when men and women play cards, their aim is to win one another's money; and this stern enterprise precludes any kind of dalliance. But in rehearsing a play there is nothing to prevent, and much to encourage, a tender familiarity. There is nothing to make either the man forget his manhood or the woman her womanhood. And the fact that the man is impersonating by the way another man, and the woman another woman, creates for them a vague sense of greater freedom and less responsibility. Innumerable other motives there are by which amateur mimes are made. A middle-aged man told me, the other day, that he had taken to amateur acting because of an accident which had slightly injured his eyesight. He had no longer been able to shoot straight, and consequently there had been a heavy fall in the quantity and quality of his invitations. As he was a bachelor, and not very rich, and fond of the country, and gregarious, this had been for him a serious matter. And so he had taken counsel with himself, had thrown himself enthusiastically into the art of acting, and had now won his way back to the favour he had forfeited. "I know I can't act for nuts," he said. "But then, *they* can't act for nuts, either. So what does it matter?" Perhaps a real efficiency in acting would be as disastrous for him as had been his crooked shooting.

Not many amateur mimes are, like this gentleman, conscious of their own defects. And this brings me to one of the solutions for their mysterious badness. They are never told—never told personally— how bad they are, or even that they are not very good indeed. I know that the professional mimes get very little in the way of frank criticism. The average critic finds far greater difficulty in understanding the rudiments of acting than in understanding even the intricacies of dramaturgy. So he takes the safe course of peppering every cast with such epithets as "manly," "sincere," "polished," "sympathetic." In his opinion, what the leading man does is always "perhaps the best thing he has yet done"; and "nothing could" ever "be better than the performance of" the leading lady; and even the small fry always give "valuable assistance" and (as though one might expect them to be treacherous) "loyal help." Nevertheless, there are a few critics who really can (and dare) discriminate bad from good acting. And for these critics the performers have a wholesome respect, and from them learn many wholesome lessons in their art. The amateurs, on the other hand, move in an atmosphere of untainted adulation. Their friends, and their servants, and their villagers, vie with one another in loudness of applause. And even the expert dramatic critic never dreams of being anything but dulcet. Of course, he is not often there at all. Books by amateurs are published, and paintings by amateurs are exhibited, and so are criticised by the experts. But (thank Heaven!) private theatricals are nearly always given in private or remote places, and the expert escapes them. Now and again, however, Fate drops him into one of these private or remote places. And he, basely, does not attempt to improve the occasion by telling the truth. Last year, a well-known expert went to stay at a house in ——shire. His hostess was a lady of much lustre and importance in the county. The expert, when he arrived, found her rehearsing a play. It appeared that the rector of the village church had set his heart on an east-window, and that his appeal for subscriptions had not had a very hearty response. So the expert's hostess had organised a theatrical entertainment, to be given in aid of the fund. Two playlets, of an old-fashioned and unpretentious kind, were to be enacted in the village schoolroom. In each of them the expert's hostess had assigned to herself the leading part. This she had done, not because she had ever acted before, nor because she had any great wish to act now, but rather because she owed it to her position not to appear in a subordinate capacity even on the stage. Her husband disapproved strongly of the whole scheme. It was only under strong protest that he attended the performance. The expert happened to be sitting next to him; and the notion that the husband was with difficulty repressing his contempt and mortification made it the more difficult for the expert to repress his own hysterical mirth at what was passing on the stage. The helpless awkwardness of the untried amateur is not in itself amusing; but when it is brought into an even conflict with the dignity and easy grace of a great lady moving in her own sphere of influence, the result (according to the expert) is something quite irresistibly droll and delightful. Throughout the evening, the husband sat silent. When the curtain fell, he turned to the expert and said, in perfect seriousness and good faith, "Well, I never could have believed it. Of course, she can't do anything really great in such parts as those. Nobody could. But I should like to see her as—well, say as 'La Dame aux Camélias.'" Later, the expert found himself saying to his hostess, for want of anything better to say, "I should like very much to see you as 'La Dame aux Camélias.' It is a part that would suit you." The other day, he heard that the rector was agitating for a new font, and that "La Dame aux Camélias" was in rehearsal.

Certainly, the absence of criticism is one of the blights on amateur acting. But the real mischief lies deeper. It is inherent in the art of acting. Acting is essentially a public art. A man might paint or write, with some pleasure, on a desert island. But he could not act there. Not less than the orator, the actor must have an audience to work on. Now, it were no great gratification to an orator to address none but small and select audiences, even if these audiences were composed of finely critical persons. The fact that his work does not endure beyond the moment of its performance makes it essential for him to be heard at large. Similarly, the man who has any real impulse for acting will not be satisfied with private or semi-private triumphs—would not be satisfied by them even if the private or semi-private audiences were composed of finely critical persons, and not of persons who applaud with equal enthusiasm whatever he may happen to do. Such triumphs may be gratifying enough to the vanity of the duffer but the man who feels that he has it in him to act will crave for a wider field. To that wider field he cannot attain if he continue to be an amateur actor. Consequently, he becomes a professional actor as soon as ever he can. And thus the amateur stage is always automatically deprived of such persons as might, if they tarried on it, become its ornaments. Only the duffers tarry on it.

Questions and Suggestions

1. In spite of his protest against the use of examples, does Beerbohm observe the principle that a writer should be specific?

2. After you and a classmate have outlined this essay, compare and discuss the results. Why do the outlines differ?

3. Distinguish between "exquisite talent" and "genius," the "amateur" and the "professional," and "recreation from . . . work" and "recreation from leisure."

4. Beerbohm makes a distinction between Pater and Balzac; the following examples should help you to grasp Beerbohm's point. The first paragraph is from Pater's "Sebastian Van Storck" in *Imaginary Portraits:*

In complete contrast to all that is abstract or cold in art, the home of Sebastian, the family mansion of the Storcks—a house, the front of which still survives in one of those patient architectural pieces by Jan van der Heyde—was, in its minute and busy wellbeing, like an epitome of Holland itself with all the good-fortune of its "thriving genius" reflected, quite spontaneously, in the national taste. The nation had learned to content itself with a religion which told little, or not at all, on the outsides of things. But we may fancy that something of the religious spirit had gone, according to the law of the transmutation of forces, into the scrupulous care for cleanliness, into the grave, old-world, conservative beauty of Dutch houses, which meant that the life people maintained in them was normally affectionate and pure.

This second paragraph is from Balzac's *The Quest of the Absolute,* translated by Ellen Marriage:

It so happens that human life in all its aspects, wide or narrow, is so intimately connected with architecture, that with a certain amount of observation we can usually reconstruct a bygone society from the remains of its public monuments. From relics of household stuff, we can imagine its owners "in their habit as they lived." Archæology, in fact, is to the body social somewhat as comparative anatomy is to animal organizations. A complete social system is made clear to us by a bit of mosaic, just as a whole past order of things is implied by the skeleton of an ichthyosaurus. Beholding the cause, we guess the effect, even as we proceed from the effect to the cause, one deduction following another until a chain of evidence is complete, until the man of science raises up a whole bygone world from the dead, and discovers for us not only the features of the past, but even the warts upon those features.

Coment on the differences in the sentence constructions in the two passages.

5. Is the "absence of criticism" a blight on writing as well as on acting?

Ideas for Writing

1. Consider the applicability of Beerbohm's distinction between the amateur and the professional to some sport or activity in which you participate.

2. Describe a recent fad that has grown out of public interest in a person and his activities.

3. Review a college theatrical performance, using Beerbohm's views about amateur acting as your standards for judgment.

4. Are you conscious of any "tender familiarity" developing among the students who haunt the local greenroom?

5. After referring to Lucas's comments about the "positive happiness of writing," state as exactly as you can in your journal how you felt as you enjoyed playing a game, acting a part, writing a story, performing a sonata, or painting a picture.

THE TWO FACES OF MÜLLER-ROSÉ

THOMAS MANN

Thomas Mann (1875–1955), Nobel Prize winner for his novels, was born in Lübeck, then a free city. After studying at the University of Munich, he traveled in Italy. It was while he was in Rome, in 1898, that his first collection of stories was published; but his first great success came with *Buddenbrooks,* one of the books burned and banned by Hitler. From 1938 until 1952 Mann lived in America. In the summer that he died, Mann was ready to begin work on the second part of Felix Krull's *Confessions,* the first volume taking Felix only as far as Portugal on his around-the-world "confidence" jaunt.

As I search my mind for further impressions of my youth, I am at once reminded of the day when I first attended the theatre, in Wiesbaden, with my parents. I should mention here that in my description of my youth I am not adhering to strict chronological order, but am treating my younger days as a whole and moving freely from incident to incident. When I posed for my godfather as a Greek god I was between sixteen and eighteen years of age and thus no longer a child, though very backward at school. But my first visit to the theatre fell in my fourteenth year—though even so my physical and mental development, as will presently be seen, was well advanced and my receptivity to impressions of certain kinds much greater than ordinary. What I saw that evening made the strongest impression on me and gave me endless food for thought.

We first visited a Viennese café, where I drank a cup of punch and my father imbibed absinthe through a straw—this in itself was calculated to stir me to the depths. But how can one describe the fever that possessed me when we drove in a cab to the theatre and entered the lighted auditorium with its tiers of boxes? The women fanning their bosoms in the balconies, the men leaning over their chairs to chat; the

hum and buzz of conversation in the orchestra, where we presently took
our seats; the odours which streamed from hair and clothing to mingle
with that of the illuminating-gas; the confusion of sounds as the
orchestra tuned up; the voluptuous frescoes that depicted whole cascades
of rosy, foreshortened nymphs—certainly all this could not but rouse
my youthful senses and prepare my mind for all the extraordinary
scenes to come. Never before except in church had I seen so many
people gathered together in a large and stately auditorium; and this
theatre with its impressive seating-arrangements and its elevated stage
where privileged personages, brilliantly costumed and accompanied by
music, went through their dialogues and dances, their songs and
routines—certainly all this was in my eyes a temple of pleasure, where
men in need of edification gathered in darkness and gazed upward
open-mouthed into a realm of brightness and perfection where they
beheld their hearts' desire.

The play that was being given was unpretentious, a work of the loose-
zoned muse, as people say. It was an operetta whose name I have, to
my sorrow, forgotten. Its scene was Paris, which delighted my poor
father's heart, and its central figure was an idle attaché, a fascinating
rogue and lady-killer, played by that star of the theatre, the well-loved
singer Müller-Rosé. I heard his real name from my father, who enjoyed
his personal acquaintance, and the picture of this man will remain forever in my memory. He is probably old and worn-out by now, like me,
but at that time his power dazzled all the world, myself included; it
made so strong an impression upon me that it belongs to the decisive
experiences of my life. I say dazzled, and it will be seen hereafter how
much meaning I wish to convey by that word. But first I must try to
set down my still vivid recollections of Müller-Rosé's effect on me.

On his first entrance he was dressed in black, and yet he radiated
sheer brilliance. In the play he was supposed to be coming from some
meeting-place of the gay world and to be slightly intoxicated, a state
he was able to counterfeit in agreeable and sublimated fashion. He wore
a black cloak with a satin lining, patent-leather shoes, evening dress,
white kid gloves, and a top hat; his hair was parted all the way to the
back of his head in accordance with the military fashion of the day.
Every article of his attire was so well pressed, and fitted with such
flawless perfection, that it could not have lasted more than a quarter-
hour in real life. He seemed, indeed, not to belong to this world. In
particular his top hat, which he wore nonchalantly tipped forward
over his brow, was the ideal and model of what a top hat should be,

without a particle of dust or roughness and with the most beautiful reflections, just as in a picture. And this higher being had a face to match,
rosy, fine as wax, with almond-shaped, black-rimmed eyes, a small,
short, straight nose, a perfectly clear-cut, coral-red mouth, and a little
black moustache as even as if it had been drawn with a paintbrush,
following the outline of his arched upper lip. Staggering with a fluid
grace such as drunken men do not possess in everyday life, he handed
his hat and stick to an attendant, slipped out of his cloak, and stood
there in full evening dress, with diamond studs in his thickly pleated
shirt front. As he drew off his gloves, laughing and chatting in a silvery
voice, you could see that the back of his hands were white as milk
and adorned with diamond rings, but that the palms were as pink as
his face. He stood before the footlights on one side of the stage and
sang the first stanza of a song about what a wonderful life it was to be
an attaché and a ladies' man. Then he spread out his arms, snapped
his fingers, and drifted delightedly to the other side of the stage, where
he sang the second stanza and made his exit, only to be recalled by
loud applause. The third stanza he sang in midstage in front of the
prompter's box. Then with careless grace he plunged into the action
of the play. He was supposed to be very rich, which in itself lent his
figure a magical charm. He appeared in a succession of costumes:
snow-white sports clothes with a red belt; a full-dress, fancy uniform
—yes, at one ticklish and sidesplitting moment in sky-blue silk drawers.
The complications of the plot were audacious, adventurous, and risqué
by turns. One saw him at the feet of a countess, at a champagne supper
with two ambitious daughters of joy, and standing with raised pistol
confronting a dull-witted rival in a duel. And not one of these elegant
but strenuous exercises was able to disarrange a single fold of his shirt
front, extinguish any of the reflections in his top hat, or overheat his
rosy countenance. He moved so easily within the frame of the musical
and dramatic conventions that they seemed, far from restricting him,
to release him from the limitations of everyday life. His body seemed
informed to the fingertips with a magic for which we have only the
vague and inadequate word "talent," and which obviously gave him as
much pleasure as it did us. To watch him take hold of the silver head
of his cane or plunge both hands in his trouser pockets was a spontaneous delight; the way he rose from a chair, bowed, made his exits
and entrances, possessed such delightful self-assurance that it filled
one's heart with the joy of life. Yes, that was it: Müller-Rosé dispensed
the joy of life—if that phrase can be used to describe the precious

and painful feeling, compounded of envy, yearning, hope, and love, that the sight of beauty and lighthearted perfection kindles in the souls of men.

The audience in the orchestra was made up of middle-class citizens and their wives, clerks, one-year servicemen, and girls in blouses; and despite the rapture of my own sensations I had presence of mind and curiosity enough to look about me and interpret their feelings. The expression on their faces was both silly and blissful. They were wrapped in self-forgetful absorption, a smile played about their lips, sweeter and more lively in the little shopgirls, more brooding and thoughtful in the grown-up women, while the faces of the men expressed that benevolent admiration which plain fathers feel in the presence of sons who have exceeded them and realized the dreams of their youth. As for the clerks and the young soldiers, everything stood wide open in their upturned faces—eyes, mouths, nostrils, everything. And at the same time they were smiling. Suppose we were up there in our underdrawers, how should we be making out? And look how boldly he behaves with those ambitious tarts, as though he had been dealing with them all his life! When Müller-Rosé left the stage, shoulders slumped and virtue seemed to go out of the audience. When he strode triumphantly from backstage to footlights, on a sustained note, his arms outspread, bosoms rose as though to meet him, and satin bodices strained at the seams. Yes, this whole shadowy assembly was like an enormous swarm of nocturnal insects, silently, blindly, and blissfully rushing into a blazing fire.

My father enjoyed himself royally. He had followed the French custom and brought his hat and stick into the theatre with him. When the curtain fell he put on the one and with the other pounded long and loud on the floor. "C'est épatant," he repeated several times, quite weak from enthusiasm. But when it was all over and we were outside in the lobby among a crowd of exalted clerks, who were quite obviously trying to imitate their hero in the way they walked, talked, held their canes, and regarded their reddened hands, my father said to me: "Come along, let's shake hands with him. By God, weren't we on intimate terms, Müller and I! He will be *enchanté* to see me again." And after instructing the ladies to wait for us in the vestibule, we actually went off to hunt up Müller-Rosé.

Our way lay through the darkened director's box beside the stage and then through a narrow iron door into the wings. The half-darkened stage was animated by the eerie activity of scene-shifting. A girl in red livery, who had played the role of a liftboy, was leaning against the wall sunk in thought. My poor father pinched her playfully where her figure was at its broadest and asked her the way to the dressing-rooms, which she irritably pointed out. We went through a white-washed corridor, where naked gas-jets flared in the confined air. From behind several doors came loud laughter and angry voices, and my father gestured with his thumb to call my attention to these mani-festations. At the end of the narrow passage he knocked on the last door, pressing his ear to it as he did so. From within came a gruff shout: "Who's there?" or "What the devil?" I no longer remember the words spoken in that clear, rude voice. "May I come in?" asked my father, whereupon he was instructed to do something quite different, which I must not mention in these pages. My father smiled his dep-recatory smile and called through the door: "Müller, it's Krull, Engel-bert Krull. I suppose I may shake your hand after all these years?" There was a laugh from inside and the voice said: "Oh, so it's you, you old rooster! Always out for a good time, eh?" And as he opened the door he went on: "I don't imagine my nakedness will do you any harm!" We went in. I shall never forget the disgusting sight that met my boyish eyes.

Müller-Rosé was seated at a grubby dressing-table in front of a dusty, speckled mirror. He had nothing on but a pair of gray cotton drawers, and a man in shirt sleeves was massaging his back, the sweat running down his own face. Meanwhile the actor was busy wiping face and neck with a towel already stiff with rouge and greasepaint. Half of his countenance still had the rosy coating that had made him radiant on the stage but now looked merely pink and silly in contrast to the cheese-like pallor of his natural complexion. He had taken off the chestnut wig and I saw that his own hair was red. One of his eyes still had deep black shadows beneath it and metallic dust clung to the lashes; the other was inflamed and watery and squinted at us im-pudently. All this I might have borne. But not the pustules with which Müller-Rosé's back, chest, shoulders, and upper arms were thickly covered. They were horrible pustules, red-rimmed, suppurating, some of them even bleeding; even today I cannot repress a shudder at the thought of them. Our capacity for disgust, let me observe, is in pro-portion to our desires; that is, in proportion to the intensity of our attachment to the things of this world. A cool indifferent nature would never have been shaken by disgust to the extent that I was then. As a final touch, the air in the room, which was overheated by an iron stove, was compounded of the smell of sweat and the exhalations from the pots and jars and sticks of greasepaint that littered the table, so that at first I thought I could not stand it for more than a minute without being sick.

However, I did stand it and looked about—but I can add nothing to this description of Müller-Rosé's dressing-room. Indeed, I should perhaps be ashamed at reporting so little and at such length about my first visit to a theatre, if I were not writing primarily for my own amusement and only secondarily for the public. It is not my intention to maintain dramatic suspense; I leave such effects to the writers of imaginative fictions, who are intent on giving their stories the beautiful and symmetrical proportions of works of art—whereas my material comes from my own experience alone and I feel I may make what use of it I think best.

Questions and Suggestions

1. With Nicolson's distinction between first-rate and second-rate art in mind, evaluate the role played by Müller-Rosé in the operetta.
2. What does this episode reveal about man's inclination to be romantic?
3. Explain: "Our capacity for disgust . . . is in proportion to our desires."
4. How does Mann's narrator, Felix Krull, exemplify Elizabeth Bowen's point about the way we recall past experiences?
5. Contrast Mann's description of the audience with the one he gives of the dressing room.
6. Study the details he uses to develop the contrast between appearance and reality. Notice particularly his selection of images in the account of Müller-Rosé during and after the performance.
7. Although Krull claims in the last paragraph that he is not an artist, has he, in reality, given artistic symmetry to his recollection?

Ideas for Writing

1. Contrast the appearance created by irresponsible advertising or propaganda with the reality that exists behind the carefully contrived façades.
2. Contrast the exterior of a resort hotel, a library, or a college building with its interior; the description in the catalogue

with the college course itself; the creed of an organization
with the group's actual practice.

3. What does Mary look like before she applies her make-up in
the morning?
4. In one well-developed paragraph, rich in imagery, reveal the
most intense disgust you have ever known.
5. How did one theatrical performance in particular cause you
to forget yourself?
6. Has any episode, like Felix Krull's, aroused your own "youthful senses"? Have you ever experienced any conflict between
mental immaturity and physical maturity?
7. What are the advantages or disadvantages of long courtships
and youthful marriages? Should college students marry?

AT MRS. FARRELLY'S

JOSEPH CARROLL

Formerly a newspaperman, script writer for NBC, newscaster,
and Associate Editor of *Collier's,* Joseph Carroll (1911–), who
was born in Chicago, graduated from Loyola. When he first came
to New York, in 1939, he roomed in a house where the landlady
spoke much as does Mrs. Farrelly; in the story, however, for the
sake of propriety, he was forced to make considerable modifications.

Brennan always stayed at Mrs. Farrelly's rooming house when
he was between voyages and when he was on the beach altogether,
waiting for a berth. The house was one of a grimy red-brick row
fronting the North River docks on a downtown street; it was within
easy walking distance of the union hall on Seventeenth Street and close
to Greenwich Village with its opportunities for companionship and
carousal. Brennan had no family except a married sister in Ohio, with
whom he exchanged perfunctorily dutiful letters once a year; and
insofar as he had a home at all, it was Mrs. Farrelly's.

The first time he stayed there, Mrs. Farrelly took an immediate liking to him and he to her. He had been shipping out for more than a year, and he was sick of blowing his pay on hotels; there were better things to blow it on. Brennan never saved any money but he liked to get value for what he spent, even if it was only a howling hangover and the memory of brief luxuries to take back to sea with him. A shipmate steered him to Mrs. Farrelly's when they shipped in from South America, and when she opened the door to him, Brennan could tell he was making an impression.

He was used to being liked by women and wasn't conceited about it: he figured they liked him not for his looks, which were average pleasant, but because he was a nice guy. He knew he was a nice guy and couldn't imagine being anything else. Brennan was only twenty-two, but he'd been kicking around more or less on his own since he was a kid, and he had decided a long time ago that you had an easier time of it if you were a nice guy though it didn't necessarily put money in your pocket. He liked women, too, most of them, so long as they didn't embarrass him with importunities. Brennan liked to do the importuning himself—it was half the fun.

He liked Mrs. Farrelly right away, and not for her looks. She was in her late forties and wouldn't have been a beauty even in her prime. The attempt to dye her hair had clearly been a mistake, for the natural mousy brown showed through under strands of the most startling magenta. Her figure was nothing much, and she had the chalky pallor of so many women who live their lives within the curious limits that a great city, no less than a prairie village, can impose; Mrs. Farrelly was a New Yorker born and bred, but she rarely traveled above Fourteenth Street or below Houston.

But her pale face was kind, and Brennan liked her smile. It was still early forenoon when he arrived with his gear, and Mrs. Farrelly was wearing a frayed robe of faded pink. "Excuse my being in my penorr," she said, "but honest to God if I'm ever awake till noon. I just can't seem to get *started* in the morning." Every vowel came out flat and long, as if someone had been at it with a rolling pin.

She led Brennan up a flight of stairs and into his room. It was a narrow room, with a bed and small table, a chest of drawers, two chairs, and very little else; but it was clean and prettified with various five-and-dime touches, such as the blue ribbons that looped back the gray-white window curtains. On the wall over the chest was a picture in an ornate frame, whose gilt was peeling; the picture, in blurry blues and greens and yellows, showed a child crossing a narrow bridge over an angry stream, and behind him a girlish angel with wings outspread protectively.

Mrs. Farrelly said: "The you-know is down the hall—second door. Two other roomers on this floor and they use it too, but it's all right if everybody just coöperates. If someone's in there too long, keep hammering loud. Nesbitt—he's in the room across the hall—he goes in there with the *Daily News* sometimes. And he'll stay until he's got his horoscope worked out unless you make a racket. Honest, some people don't have the least consideration."

Brennan nodded, but Mrs. Farrelly showed no disposition to go; she wanted to talk. "It'd be a real nice view," she said, pointing to the window, "except the pier fronts are in the way and you can't see the river. I always say what's the use of having a river that you can't see it. Blocks and blocks and you can't see it, unless you go up to the market by Little West Twelfth Street, where they fish off the pier. Honest, isn't that some name? Little West Twelfth, how I love thee! You can see the river from the roof, but it's too cold to go up there now. Summertimes, we go up—Farrelly and me. Farrelly's my husband. It's real pretty at night, all the lights over to Jersey and like on the boats. Some people they just never notice things like that, but Farrelly's different. He's a poet. He *writes* poetry."

Brennan was interested. "You mean for a living?" he asked.

She looked doubtful. "Well, he writes it all the time, but I wouldn't say he made a living out of it. There's not much money in poetry. Farrelly says things are slow for poets these times. People just don't have the money."

Brennan started to laugh, and changed his mind: Mrs. Farrelly wasn't being funny.

"You like poetry?" Mrs. Farrelly said.

"Yeah," Brennan said. "I like it. I'd like to see Far—your husband's."

She shook her head. "He's so *funny*. He won't show it to anybody—except me. He's afraid somebody'll steal it off him. He says poets are clickish—a little bunch of them have it all their own way and without you're in the click you can't have your poems printed up in books. Honest, I guess it's the same in every line. Like the longshoremen—that's what Nesbitt is, a longshoreman—unless they know the **boss** and slip him a little something once and a while they just don't get through the shape-up. Nesbitt hasn't had a day's work in three weeks."

Brennan had an odd vision of poets going through a shape-up and started to laugh again; again he changed his mind. "Yeah," he said, "it's the same in everything. It's not what you know, it's who you know."

Mrs. Farrelly clasped her hands together appreciatively. "I'll have to remember that to tell Farrelly. He likes things that are said neat. It's not what you know, it's who you know," she repeated. She went to the door but then turned; Brennan had started to sit down on the bed. "Sit right down," she said, "I'll be going in a minute. You must be tired. Where was your ship? South America? My! I never been but to Hoboken. You sound educated."

Brennan sat down, shaking his head. "Uh-uh. Grammar school. My old man died and I went to work soon as it was legal. I tried a lot of things, but I like shipping best. You get time to read."

Mrs. Farrelly sighed. "You don't know how lucky you are," she said. "I never get time to read, running this place like I do. Honest, if it isn't this it's that, in a rooming house. Keeping the place clean and going to the stores. I hardly even get to read the papers. Farrelly is a great reader—always was. And of course, he has his poetry to keep up on. He can't do no writing here. Too noisy—trucks going by all the time, and sirens on the river, and the kids yelling out in the street. He goes over to the library up near Eighth Avenue every morning and stays there all day and writes. Honest, he has just pages and pages covered with it, and he won't let me do a thing with it."

She looked at Brennan pensively. "You seem like a real nice boy. I'd like for you to meet Farrelly. When do you ship out?"

"Next week," Brennan said. "I'd like the room until Sunday night."

She looked pleased. "You could eat with us Sunday. We take our big meal in the afternoon and have just cold stuff for supper."

Brennan was touched, and embarrassed. "Wouldn't want to put you to any trouble," he said.

She laughed. "Trouble? Why, all the trouble is putting out another plate. Farrelly and me never had a kid, isn't that funny? We been married long enough to have them older than you. I used to kid him about it. It must be you just simply don't have it, I told him once. And honest, it made him so mad I was scared. He hardly ever gets mad. But he hates anything *vulgar*."

Brennan was blushing a little. "I guess you do, too," she said. "But I don't mean anything by it. It's just my way. I grew up around here— this house was my father's, rest his soul. I had a brother was killed in

an accident on the docks. He was older than me, and he talked real
rough. This is a rough neighborhood. But Farrelly's different."

Brennan couldn't think of anything to say, but she didn't expect
an answer. "You eat with us Sunday," she said, and started out the
door. Then she turned again. "Another thing," she said diffidently.
"I hope you'll excuse me mentioning it. If you want to bring—uh—
anybody up here nights—"

Brennan was now blushing all over, the rough redness at his cheek-
bones spreading throughout his olive face.

"—it's all right if you aren't too noisy about it. It's just we don't
want the police on us. Lots of seamen stay here, and I know how it is.
A person has their passions."

Brennan was looking at the floor.

She coughed, artificially. "I hope you won't take what I'm saying
wrong. You're so kind of young. Watch out for them hustling girls in
the bar and grills. They're no good—and you never know what you
can pick up off them."

She closed the door after her, and Brennan lay back on the bed,
wondering why he liked the damn woman so much.

He met Farrelly at the Sunday meal. It was a good meal: baked ham
and mashed potatoes and green vegetables and a bakery pie for dessert;
but Brennan, who had spent too much time in Bleecker Street bars
the night before, was in no condition to enjoy it.

"You need a drink," Farrelly said, watching him nibble at the food;
and he brought out a bottle of whisky. Mrs. Farrelly poured a hooker
for each of them, but didn't take any herself. She whisked back and
forth between the kitchen and the dining room, which was brightly
papered in a pattern of some yellow flower that made it look as though
someone had been throwing eggs at the wall.

After the drink, Brennan felt better and could eat. He didn't think
Farrelly looked much like a poet, though you never could tell about
poets. Farrelly's hair was all white, which made his face look young.
It was a coarse face in its surfaces: configurations of veins threaded
his cheeks with an unhealthy blue over glittering crimson. Guiltily,
Brennan reflected that his face might come to look like that if he spent
the next five years as strenuously as he had spent it in Bleecker Street
and environs the night before. Farrelly's dissipations had not marred
the odd juvenility of his features; his eyes were large and pale, and
—white hair and all—he looked like an altar boy who had been on
one hell of a toot.

If Mrs. Farrelly was disturbed by these evidences of intemperance, or even aware of them, she didn't show it. She left the bottle close to Farrelly's hand and looked at him dotingly whenever he spoke.

Farrelly was most courteous in his manner toward Brennan. "So you follow the sea?" he said bookishly.

"Yeah," Brennan said. "It gives me something to do."

"Do you admire Conrad?" asked Farrelly.

Brennan thought that was quite a leap, but he answered politely: "Some of him."

"Do you find him true to life?"

Yes and no, Brennan said; he didn't think seamen talked like that, even when Conrad was writing, but he guessed that if anyone ever wrote the way seamen really talked he wouldn't be able to get it printed.

"I like Melville better," Farrelly said. "I read him all the time." Brennan thought to himself that he couldn't have read Melville very carefully because he kept talking about Moby Dick as though it were a man; he said he had once seen John Barrymore in the title role.

All of Farrelly's literary knowledge seemed fragmentary, and some of it was mistaken, Brennan knew. He tried to change the conversation, so as to work Mrs. Farrelly into it. She looked from one to another of them admiringly, and Brennan felt like a phony. He read books when he felt like it, the same way he drank or chased girls, when he felt like that. Unhappily, he told Farrelly that, no, he didn't plan to write a book: he went to sea because it was a living, better than some other ways of making money, at least for him. If he ever got married, he thought he would want a shoreside job.

Farrelly didn't listen to his answers; every question was a topic sentence for himself; and after the meal was over, when he had a lot more drinks, he didn't even bother asking questions: he just talked. At Mrs. Farrelly's urging, he recited a lot of poetry in a declamatory voice.

Brennan didn't think he recited very well, though it might have been the liquor; he stopped at the end of every line, and, unless you knew the poem he was reciting, you wouldn't have been able to make any sense out of it at all. Mrs. Farrelly did not seem to mind this: her rapt face showed that she was having a very good time.

In one of the pauses, she asked Farrelly to bring out his own poetry or recite it to Brennan. Farrelly, whose eyes were pretty glassy by this time, turned to her coldly. "The time hasn't come," he said. "You know that. This is a fine young man"—he pointed to Brennan—"but what do we *know* about him?"

And then he went upstairs, walking rigidly and holding to the banister as he walked.

Mrs. Farrelly hoped Brennan's feelings weren't hurt. "He has to be so careful," she said enigmatically. Brennan said not at all and it was time for him to be going anyway.

The next few times he hit port, Brennan saw a lot of Mrs. Farrelly but very little of her husband. Brennan stayed out till all hours, and it was always late when he got up. Mrs. Farrelly took to asking him down to the kitchen for coffee and talked to him confidentially about Farrelly, who still spent his days at the library.

"He's failing," Mrs. Farrelly said one morning. "All you have to do is look at him to see he's failing. And it isn't as if he was old: he's only fifty-three. He's sick, that's what he is, and is it any wonder with the way he's treated when all he wants is to put in a fair day's work at his poetry? My sisters won't even talk to him—and the way they talk about him would make you sick to your stomach. Nell's the worst. She never married and she's never *been* with anyone. You know the way women like that are?"

Brennan drank his coffee unquiveringly; he had got over blushing at Mrs. Farrelly's occasional physiological allusions, and this one was only mildly blunt. He told her he knew what she meant.

"Nell's got scabs on her knees from going to church every day of her life but all she ever thinks about is the one thing. She's always going on about the Porto Ricans and the colored in the neighborhood, and she like to of died when I had a colored for a roomer. I didn't see there was anything wrong about it, being he was a lot cleaner than most that stay here. But you bust Nell's head open and you'd find only the one thing. Every time she looks at Farrelly I know she's thinking dirty. I know he takes his drop, but I never heard him say a dirty word.

"The other sister—Hattie—has her own man and four kids, but she's never got over it that Pa left this place to me. Farrelly moved in here right after we were married—he was working over to the market then, but he never liked it because he got no time to work on his poetry at all. So after Pa died, he quit, and ever since it's been the poetry."

Flickeringly, her eyes looked wistful, Brennan thought.

"So the two of them are all the time chewing about Farrelly," she went on. "They're the only family I got now but I sent the pair of them flying out of this kitchen only last week for having their foul mouths on Farrelly. It was 'why don't he work?' and 'why do you give him money for drink?' until I told the both of them to kiss the left cheek of my behind and threw them out."

She poured more coffee for Brennan and herself. "He's failing, though. I can see it every day goes by. He don't read out what he's wrote during the day to me any more, like he always used to—and he bites my head off if I ask him about it. He just sits and don't say anything, only to himself, stuff I can't even understand, over and over and over. And you know something? He *cries*. All by himself in the bedroom, he cries. I found him like that last night and I told him, 'What's the matter, lovey?' And he just said to go away, and kept on crying."

Brennan stood up quickly. "I have to meet a fellow," he said.

She followed him to the front door. "You think—you think maybe I shouldn't let him have money for the drink, like Hattie says? It's the only thing he takes any pleasure in, except the poetry."

Brennan said awkwardly, "I don't know, Mrs. Farrelly. Maybe you better call a doctor to look at him."

"He hates doctors," Mrs. Farrelly said. "I might call one, if he gets worse."

Brennan went out.

Brennan shipped out on the longest trip he had ever made, and what with layovers for repairs and weather delays, it was more than three months before he saw Mrs. Farrelly again. His ship docked late on a summer afternoon, but after he was paid off he stopped in a saloon on South Street where he met the union delegate from his ship and got in an argument about the handling of a beef on the trip. Other crew members were there, and the argument wasn't very parliamentary; Brennan was too tired for a fight, so he slipped out and walked to Mrs. Farrelly's. The walk cleared his head, which badly needed clearing.

It was almost midnight when he rang the doorbell. He saw the light go on behind the glass panels that flanked the door; then the door opened and Mrs. Farrelly stood blinking at him. She was fully dressed, in a black dress. As soon as she saw Brennan she started to cry, and he knew what must have happened.

He stepped inside and put an arm around her shoulder, waiting until the sobbing stopped. She leaned her head against him. "You were the only one," she said. "You were the only one was ever nice about his poetry."

Brennan kept his arm around her. "Would you make me some coffee?" he asked.

"Honest to God," she said, stepping away from him, "I forgot all about it. I got some on."

He followed her through the dark hallway and into the lighted kitchen. The coffee had boiled over and the lid of the pot was rattling over the bubbling sounds.

Brennan sat down at the table and waited. She wiped off the smeared sides of the pot, brought cups from the pantry, and poured. Brennan lighted a cigarette, waiting for his coffee to cool.

"I buried Farrelly yesterday," she said.

She sat down, her chair close to Brennan. "The end came suddenly," she said, relishing the formal obituary phrase, "though, like I told you, I seen it coming. He fell over in the street coming from the library and they took him to Bellevue. He didn't even know me when they let me see him. He just cried and stared up at the ceiling. And then he screamed a lot—and then he didn't do anything. He just passed away."

She was quite dry-eyed now, and enjoying telling him about it. Brennan said how sorry he was.

"I know," she said. "I told my sister Hattie and Nell and all them snotnoses came to the wake about you. I told them you *know* about poetry. We waked him here, and I like to screamed listening to Hattie blabbering about it was a blessed release, and Nell with her 'it's the will of God and he's at peace at last.' And I wouldn't give them the satisfaction of crying or taking on or anything. I just sat in there in the front room the whole three days and looked at him. He was laid out nice, in his good blue serge. And he looked so young. He was a fine-looking man, Farrelly was."

She waited for Brennan to agree. "A fine-looking man," he echoed.

"And I'd look at Farrelly, and then I'd look at that big bruiser Hattie's married to, with the black hairs sticking out from his collar, and no gentleness to him at all and no brains in his thick head to understand poetry. And when I'd look at Farrelly again, I'd almost cry, thinking: it may be the will of God, but I hope He knows what He's doing—taking away a man that never did anyone a day's harm and could make up poetry right in the middle of the dirty streets and never take his mind off it for anything else, only his glass of whisky now and again—taking away a man like that and leaving only the slobs of men that laugh at poetry."

She pushed back her chair and stood up. "He's gone now and it can't hurt him if I show it to you. I don't care if it never gets printed up in books. The hell with the clicks. You been nice. I'll show it to you."

She went out and Brennan could hear her footsteps on the stairs. He stared into the grounds in his coffee cup. When she came back she was carrying a cardboard carton, which she placed on the table. She raised the covers, and Brennan saw that the box was filled with paper, tied in bundles. "This is only some of it," Mrs. Farrelly told him, lifting out a bundle and undoing the ribbon that bound it. She handed it to Brennan and her hand shook.

He glanced at the top sheet of lined tablet paper such as school children use. The handwriting was large and legible, not beautiful but painstakingly neat, as though it were an exercise in penmanship. Brennan read the opening lines on the top sheet: —

> Yet once more, O ye Laurels, and once more
> Ye Myrtles brown, with Ivy never-sear,
> I com to pluck your Berries harsh and crude,
> And with forc'd fingers rude,
> Shatter your leaves before the mellowing year.

He riffled the sheets, glancing at the titles carefully written in block capitals at the top of the pages: Kubla Khan, Lines Composed a Few Miles Above Tintern Abbey, Lines Written Among the Euganean Hills, On First Looking into Chapman's Homer, The Lotos-Eaters, The Blessed Damozel, Chorus from Atalanta in Calydon, The Hound of Heaven. . . .

He looked up at Mrs. Farrelly. "I can't read them all now," he said, smiling.

She smiled back. "Sure you can't. You take all the time you want." She put her hand on Brennan's arm. "You read some of the first one. I seen you. Is it good poetry?"

Brennan lifted his free hand and touched her cheek gently. "The best," he said.

Questions and Suggestions

    1. Felix Krull realized the great difference between appearance and reality. Does Brennan also become conscious of a disparity between the ideal and the actual?

2. Once he knows the truth about Farrelly, why does Brennan remain silent?
3. Why was Farrelly interested in poetry? Were Mrs. Farrelly's sisters right in their evaluation of him?
4. What did Mrs. Farrelly and Brennan have in common?
5. How important were moral codes to Mrs. Farrelly?
6. From whose point of view is the story told? Why?
7. Study Mrs. Farrelly's diction and her figures of speech. Does she sound authentic?

Ideas for Writing

1. Contrast Mrs. Farrelly with the wife in William Inge's play *Come Back, Little Sheba.*
2. Mrs. Farrelly admires poetry without understanding it. Analyze this American tendency to respect the unknown.
3. Study the attitude toward poetry held by the people in your community, or the reactions of students in a college dormitory to a reading of Dylan Thomas's poems.
4. "A person has their passions."
5. Compare or contrast Mrs. Farrelly with your landlady.
6. "You go to college," the old man said. "My pa liked books too. Come and see 'em." Were you disappointed in what you found?
7. Does knowledge give a greater sense of security than does money?

THE DEATH OF GEORGE GROSZ

HILTON KRAMER

For several years Hilton Kramer (1928–) has been an editor of *Arts.* Born in Gloucester, Massachusetts, he studied at Syracuse, Columbia, the New School for Social Research, Harvard, and Indiana. A contributor to a number of magazines, Mr. Kramer is one of the most perceptive critics of American art and artists.

George Grosz died in Germany on July 6, 1959, at the age of sixty-six. He had just returned to his native country after twenty-seven years in the United States. In May, on the eve of his departure, he was presented with a gold medal by the American Academy of Arts and Letters in a ceremony which was notable for, among other things, the fact that Grosz, sharing the platform with Aldous Huxley, denounced satire as a trivial form of art. The irony was that the audience, because of a mix-up in the loud-speaker system and Grosz's own deportment on the occasion, took this earnest denunciation as a joke. The scene was, in fact, a little cruel and grotesque. To put it another way, it was in Grosz's early style.

Nobody pretends any longer that Grosz lived up to his early reputation once he established residence in this country as a refugee. The attempts a few years ago to elevate the pathetic efforts of his "American period" to the status of a major art were all addressed to our political sentiments. The truth is that the American atmosphere depressed Grosz's talents. Coming to America saved his life perhaps, but it did not save his art. Once installed in the American milieu, he was curiously divided between commercialism on the one hand and a retrograde dream of "fine art" on the other. He had either lost confidence in the satirical impulse, or he found perhaps that there was no vehicle here which allowed for its full expression. Whatever the cause, George Grosz never succeeded in improving on his earlier achievements in Germany. The crisis which inspired this early work, and which he criticized so boldly, was apparently the only soil in which his talent could flower.

His early work remains without equal in the quality of its sardonic, even cruel wit, its devastating social commentary, and the expressive power by which the wit and social commentary are made memorable. Yet it is true that the genre which Grosz practiced at the height of his powers, in the period of the First World War and the twenties, is not the highest form of art. All his life Grosz was himself haunted by that fact, and it led him finally, with the official gold medal in hand, to denounce satire with great bitterness.

Yet the question persists: Can we really get along without it? It is possible to say, perhaps, that we have gotten along without it for a good many years now. Certainly there is no artist one can point to on the scene today—or in the period since the Second World War—who has wielded the satirical knife with anything like its old force. Saul

Steinberg comes closest, but even his most brilliant drawings fail us in this regard. In the end they always turn on the subject of *taste,* and a criticism of taste, rather than the values which inspire it, sooner or later reduces itself to trivialities, revealing a partisanship with what is ostensibly criticized. Other artists with reputations for graphic satire have either, like Ben Shahn, discredited themselves through commercialism or, like Jack Levine, mistakenly inflated their small ideas for heroic, old-master subjects. The graphic artist who is also a social satirist, an honest observer, a partisan of humane values, and who is yet modest enough to sustain his art at something below the highest level of expression and still fierce enough to endow his vision with its own intensity: this kind of artist is now dead. When George Grosz died this summer, he had already been a kind of ghost for years. The genre had been declared obsolete.

Is it too much to suggest that the disappearance of this type of artist from the scene is yet another evidence of the moral conformity of our times? Certainly we have no lack of artists who function at something lower than the highest levels, but none of them would consider it even honorable to undertake the tasks which once made Grosz justly famous. A word—or better still, a shrug—about the thirties is supposed to answer this question. Yet the matter is not so easily disposed of. It is even possible that the absence of an intense, secondary art of this kind today may account for some of the vacuities which are clearly visible at the "highest" levels.

Questions and Suggestions

1. Why did George Grosz denounce satire so bitterly near the end of his life?
2. Explain why he had for years been a "kind of ghost."
3. Does Kramer believe that a healthy society can get along without satire? Explain why satire need not be "a trivial form of art."
4. Define *sarcasm, irony, sardonic wit, genre,* and *taste.*

Ideas for Writing

1. After consulting reproductions of Grosz's early work, discuss the facets of German society that he attacked. If your library has a record collection, listen to the recording of *Mahagonny.* In this opera Bertolt Brecht and Kurt Weill also pointed out

evils that existed in the same society that Grosz knew and
disliked.

2. Follow Saul Steinberg through a number of issues of *The
New Yorker* to discover what American tastes he satirizes.
For another paper, compare his attitude with that of Randall
Jarrell as it appears in the essay included in this text or in
his novel dealing with academic life, *Pictures from an Insti-
tution: A Comedy.*

3. Do you know the work of Jules Pfeiffer or Charles Addams?
Are their interests similar to those of the poet Ogden Nash?

4. Analyze the subjects depicted by such nationally famous
cartoonists as Herblock and Bill Mauldin. Do their cartoons
probe into questions of what we truly value as Americans?

5. Does your environment foster any forms of secondary art?
Who are the local Michelangelos and da Vincis who will
make your city, centuries from now, a mecca for art-lovers?

6. Contrast two essays that discuss the Guggenheim Museum—
Hilton Kramer's "Month in Review," *Arts,* December, 1959;
and Lewis Mumford's "What Wright Hath Wrought," *The
New Yorker,* December 5, 1959.

GENUFLECTION IN THE SUN

S. J. PERELMAN

Sidney Joseph Perelman (1904–) excites many readers by his
amazing command of the English language. After graduating
from Brown, he wrote for a number of the humorous magazines
then flourishing. In 1929, as soon as his first book was published,
he and his wife, the sister of Nathanael West, hied off to Hollywood where Perelman wrote a scenario, jokes for the Marx
brothers, and many of his own essays. In addition to his satirical
pieces and his superb parodies, Perelmen has in recent years
become the best writer on the ancient art of boxing.

"I am not a teetotaler and enjoy a good snort as well as the next
one, but for sheer delight and ecstasy in the region of the tonsils none

of them can even begin to compare with that strange combination
of syrup, ice cream and carbonated water skillfully proportioned and
compounded by some Master Dispenser at my favorite Liggett fountain.

"I can see him now, this delicate and brilliant chemist, his head
tilted forward slightly as his ear reaches for my order—'All black,
please.'

" 'All black!' Already his hand has whisked a large-sized tumbler
whose narrowed round bottom was scientifically designed to aid the
magical blending of all the weird component parts of the soda. Under
the chocolate syrup faucet it goes. See how the rich, dark brown goo
covers a third of the bottom of the glass, clinging lovingly to the side.

"Now a splash of cream and the first of a series of wonderful amal-
gams has taken place. The dark chocolate is lighter in tone, more fluid,
better prepared for the life infusion that follows—the fizzer.

"Here is surely the secret of this nectar for the Gods of America,
the genius touch of this unknown benefactor of mankind. The Master
Dispenser is all concentration now, for this is a solemn moment, the
aerating of the milk and chocolate mixture with the wire-thin stream
of vital and living fizz. It hisses into the glass as he turns it carefully
to all points of the compass. Under the impulse of this injection, the
liquid suddenly begins to bubble and boil and heave, seething with a
new and inner life of its own. Whereas a moment ago it was somber
and viscous, now it is light, merry, purposeful, and gay.

"Plop! Into its joyously heaving bosom is dropped a rounded gobbet
of smooth, rich ice cream.

"Now the Master Dispenser approaches the climax. Infected by his
own artistry, he swings the glass and turns on the soda faucet, his eye
keen to the task of producing perfection. As the charged water joins
the composition, great, luscious brown bubbles begin to rise in the
glass. Higher and Higher under the watchful gaze of the Super Dispenser. Not yet . . . not yet . . . NOW! A corona of pure aerated chocolate flavor stands an inch high above the glass, a crown of sweet nothing,
too superb in texture and flavor for words. A spoon, two straws, and
there it is vibrant, pulsating—ready. . . .

"Ah, Ye Gods of Gluttony! That first taste, the mouthful of froth,
the sweet of the chocolate, the brisk tang of the soda, the ecstasy of
the now-you-have-it, now-you-haven't, which sends you on for fulfillment into the first bite of ice cream irrigated with the lovely fluid of
the soda.

"Rich though these rewards be, they are nothing to the grand finale, the climax of enjoyment, when with froth gone, ice cream gone, you discard the straws, lift the glass, tilt back your head and subject your tonsils to the first superb shock of the pure Ichor of the soda, syrup, bubble water, water, melted ice cream, all blended into one Ambrosia of flavor, action and chill.

"What is there to match it? Where is it to be found? Who, oh, who, is the great, great man who thought it all up for the likes of you and me?"—*From a Liggett menu.*

Two miles south of Corona del Mar, I saw looming up ahead the Piggy-Wig Drive-In they had told me in Balboa to watch for. Narrowly missing a Hupmobile driven by an old harpy in curlers, who interpreted my left-hand signal as an invitation to sleep with her, I swerved off the Coast Highway and pulled up alongside it. A heavy miasma of frying lard and barbecued ribs drifted across the wheel of asphalt radiating from the structure; somewhere inside, the sepulchral voice of Patti Page sniveled a plaint about a doggie in a window. Three lackluster carhops, manifestly chosen for their resemblance to porkers, were seated under a bong tree made of papier-mâché, and as one languidly rose and undulated toward me, I noticed a curled pink celluloid tail protruding from her scientifically designed narrowed round bottom, which bobbled as she moved.

"Villa Jacaranda?" she repeated, swallowing a yawn. "What is it— a motel?" I explained I was looking for the residence of Willard Inchcape, the writer. "I wouldn't know, I'm sure," she returned with disdain. "There's some bohemians up that dirt road there. They all sculp or weave or something."

I thanked her and, resisting an impulse to order a slice of quince to see whether it came with a runcible spoon, a form of cutlery that has always pricked my curiosity, drove on. The road straggled into the foothills past a cluster of aggressive ranch-style homes—each equipped with an incinerator adapted for those murders in which southern California seems to excel—and terminated at a high wall of whitewashed brick. Over the massive gate was a chemically aged plastic shingle bearing the legend "Villa Jacaranda" in Carborundum Old Style. I pushed the gate open and stepped down into a garden choked with poinsettias. Their foliage was so lush that it veiled the outlines of the house beyond, but in a patch of greensward at the far end there was visible a woman laboring at a sculptor's table. As I approached, she turned and I beheld a portly matron of fifty-odd in a green smock, with an uncompromising henna bob and Hashimura Togo spectacles.

"Mrs. Inchcape?" I asked. "I phoned from Los Angeles."

"Oh, yes," she said energetically. "You're the man who wanted to talk to Willard. Come in." She laid her graving tool on the stand, a gesture that automatically drew my eye to the object she was modeling. It was the head of a Scotch collie, carved from a block of castile soap with such fidelity to nature that I had no difficulty repressing a start.

"Aha," I commented with a portentous frown, aware that she was watching me closely. "Er—is that an actual portrait or more of an idealized conception, as it were?"

"Half and half," said Mrs. Inchcape. "I based it on our Timmy. He passed on several years ago."

"You don't say," I murmured, attempting to mingle respect for her bereavement with a note of philosophic fatalism.

"Yes, he's buried right where you're standing." I jerked sidewise, remorseful at having desecrated a tomb. "Do you like it?"

I cocked my head and nodded emphatically. "You certainly got him down cold," I said. Then, conscious of the ambiguity of my critique, I added hurriedly, "What I mean is you sure got him dead to rights." I felt the perspiration start on my forehead. "Of course, I never knew Timmy—"

"You bet you didn't," said Mrs. Inchcape. "If he were alive, you'd never be in this garden. He'd have torn you limb from limb."

"Well, well," I said, feigning admiration for her pet's loyalty. "I guess his death was a real loss."

"I can't imagine to whom," she returned. "He bit everybody, right up to the man who chloroformed him. But I suppose you're one of those people who get sentimental about animals."

It impressed me as singular that she should be immortalizing a beast she abhorred, but I decided not to pry. "Is Mr. Inchcape home?" I asked, looking around. "I wouldn't like to disturb him if he's working."

"Don't get fidgety, he'll be along in a minute," she said, motioning toward a bench. "Sit down while I clean up this mess. Did you ever hear of Daniel Chester French?"

"The sculptor?"

"Well, I certainly don't mean Daniel Chester French the upholsterer," she said with asperity. "The one who did the statue of 'Memory' at the Metropolitan. I studied with him for two years, and let me tell you, young man, there wasn't a mean bone in his body." I tried to recall anything discreditable I had ever heard about French, and failed. "Your ears remind me of his. The way they're articulated to the head."

"Gee," I said, feeling it was incumbent on me to exhibit some sign of elation. "I've never been told that before. You—ah— It must have been a great privilege to know Mr. French."

"That depends on how you look at it," said Mrs. Inchcape acidly. She lapsed into a tight-lipped silence, dusting chips of soap from the stand and casting me an occasional suspicious glance.

Suddenly a man's voice, tremulous with excitement, resounded through the shrubbery. "Rowena!" it called. "Where are you—in the patio?" Her hail of response, easily audible in Mazatlán, flushed up my quarry, a leathery old gentleman with an Armagnac nose, a black velvet tam, and a smoking jacket. In one hand he clenched a Tyrolean porcelain pipe fluttering a pair of green tassels and in the other a typewritten sheet that bristled with interlineations. "Just listen to this, honey bun!" he crowed. "It's the copy for Mother Stentorian's Fish Kebabs, and if I do say so, it's a sockdolager. I couldn't get the exact poetic throb at first—"

"This geezer here's waiting for you," said his wife laconically.

"Well, he's got a stomach—let him hear it, too!" said Inchcape jovially. He rotated toward me. "You the party called me about my ice-cream-soda tribute?"

"I am, sir," I said, extending my hand, "and I've come to tell you it's the finest thing since Baudelaire's *Flowers of Evil*. I just wanted to pay my respects to a great poet."

"Thank you, son, thank you," he replied, his face suffused with pleasure. "But if you think that was good, get ready for a real treat." He adjusted a pince-nez secured to his lapel by a silver chain, cleared his throat, and began declaiming in a rich, fruity baritone: " 'Up from the silent, sunless depths of the seven seas into Mother Stentorian's spotless antiseptic kitchens come the hake, the scrod, the plaice, the fluke, the cream of the finny tribe, briny-fresh and jam-packed with succulent vitamins, to tickle the gourmet palate. Man alive, watch these yumdingers, these dorsal dainties, tumble from the nets in silver iridescence, splendid largess from Nature's treasure-trove, yearning to sputter in butter and ravish the jaded esophagus! Here in this hygienic temple of the culinary art, under the watchful yet kindly eye of Mother Stentorian, they are portioned into appetizing mouth-size chunks, sprinkled with mace, dill, rape, capsicum, and rose leaves, and precooked on skewers over aromatic fires of specially processed driftwood imported from faraway Armenia.' "

"Jiminetty," I ejaculated as he paused for breath. "That's inspired, Mr. Inchcape! You can almost taste the crisp, savory—"

"Wait, you haven't heard anything yet," he broke in. "I'm just warming up. Then each individual kebab, its delectable goodness sealed in, is wrapped in gleaming chlorophane—cellophane from which all harmful chlorophyll has been extracted—by deft-fingered, full-bosomed girls pledged to change their uniforms every hour. Now comes the most vital phase in the preparation of Mother Stentorian's Matchless Fish Kebabs. Science has discovered that these fishy shasliks—or, more properly, fishliks—acquire a mysterious added tang when impregnated with the folk songs of Asia Minor. Consequently, before your personalized package of kebabs is handi-packed, it is locked into a special tone chamber—a musical autoclave, so to speak—where it is saturated with rollicking airs like "The Well-Tufted Ottoman," "Sohrab and Rustum Were Lovers," and "Sister, Shake That Amphigouri." Why deny yourself any longer the color and enchantment of the Near East you've always secretly hungered for? Simply perfume your house with the odor of cold mutton fat, heat up a box of Mother Stentorian's Genuine Fish Kebabs, and become part of the world's most ancient culture. As you squat on your hams greedily engorging these zestful tidbits, you, too, will be at one with Shadrach, Meshach, and Abednego, with Nineveh and Tyre.' "

Mrs. Inchcape was the first to break the silence when her husband had concluded. "Will he be staying for lunch?" she demanded, nodding in my direction.

"Why, I can't really say," hesitated Inchcape, obviously derailed. "We haven't had a chance—"

"No, no, thank you," I said hastily. "I'm bound for La Jolla. I'll be leaving very soon."

"Then I'll just make a soybean *pizza* for two," Mrs. Inchcape announced, departing. "Come when I call you, now. It's no good cold."

The bard looked so stricken that first aid was indicated at once. "Mr. Inchcape," I said, "this may sound insincere, but when you were reading that, you brought a lump to my throat. It's tremendous. Absolutely symphonic."

"You think it jells, do you?" he asked eagerly.

"Good heavens, man, it sings!" I said. "They'll be quoting you in advertising circles for years to come. The lyricism—the imagery! It's a downright classic, I promise you."

"Oh, shucks, it's only a pastiche," said Inchcape, buffing his nails

on his sleeve. "I mean with a theme as limited as kebabs you don't have
the scope, naturally. Now, the ice-cream soda—there I had material
to work with. I employed a kind of a cosmic approach, if you noticed."

"It struck me right away," I confessed. "First the syrup, then the
cream, then the fizz. Like architecture."

"Each symbolizing a step in the universal creative process," he
pointed out. "Fire, earth, and water, all uniting to produce bliss everlasting, or, in the wider sense, the Promethean spark."

"And the whole compounded by a Master Dispenser," I recalled.
"Yes, the mystical analogy was perfect. Did you ever get any figures
from Liggett's? Were there many conversions?"

"You mean abstainers who took up ice-cream soda as a result?"
queried Inchcape. "Frankly, it *was* rather impressive; in fact, for a
while they considered having prayers with the sandwiches, but the
customers balked." He shrugged. "Ah, well, between you and me, I was
shooting at the aesthetic angle more than the religious."

"You hit the bull's-eye, in any case," I declared. "Tell me, how did
you happen to get into inspirational writing?"

He pondered for a moment before replying. "Well, it was sort of a
call," he said reflectively. "I had my own business up in Hollywood,
a few doors from Grauman's Egyptian, on the Boulevard. We eternalized baby shoes—you know, dipped them in bronze for ashtrays and
souvenirs. The work was creative, but somehow I felt I wasn't realizing
my potentialities. Then one day I came across a copy of Elbert Hub-
bard's magazine, *The Philistine,* and his style reacted on me like a long,
cold drink of sauerkraut juice. Right there, I made up my mind to
follow in the footsteps of the Sage of East Aurora, and I never deviated
one hair from my resolve. Which I'm thankful to say that Rowena—
that's Mrs. Inchcape—has always been my shield and my buckler,
urging me on and giving unselfishly of her artistic judgment. She's a
very gifted woman, as you can see for yourself."

"And a very gracious one," I agreed. "Well, I must be moving on,
Mr. Inchcape. Much obliged for the preview of Mother Stentorian's
Fish Kebabs. I'll be on the lookout for them."

"Yes, I hear they're quite tasty," he said. "Sure you won't stay and
take potluck with us? Rowena can fix you a mock omelet or some
toasted dates or something."

"No, thanks a million," I said, backing through the poinsettias.
"Well, goodbye, sir, and long may you flourish." I got into my rented
convertible, switched on a commercial for atomic laxatives, and drove

down to the coast road. As I passed the Piggy-Wig Drive-In, I saw two persons costumed as an owl and a pussycat dancing hand in hand on the edge of the asphalt. At least, I thought I saw them, but it may have been only a mirage. That southern California sunlight can be pretty tricky at times.

Questions and Suggestions

1. What contrasting views concerning art do the carhop, Mrs. Inchcape, Willard, and the pilgrim hold? What do you infer from this sketch about Perelman's concept of art?
2. What does this humorous account of a pilgrimage reveal about the use and abuse of art?
3. Would Perelman and Pyke have similar reactions to the Liggett "chemist"?
4. Are there sacrilegious overtones in the Liggett blurb?
5. Point out a number of clichés that add to the humor. How do such references as "chemically aged plaster shingle," "Carborundum Old Style," "Master Dispenser," "inspirational writing," "we eternalized baby shoes," and "a mock omelet" contribute to the satire?
6. List the American follies that Perelman attacks.

Ideas for Writing

1. Describe a restaurant, store, or privately-owned park or museum that uses "art" to attract the public.
2. Do any of the local restaurants and drive-ins vie with each other in being horrendously ugly? Have any of them employed their own Willards to write and design the copy for their menus?
3. What is the dress of the local bohemians?
4. Use examples to show the distinctions you make between good and bad taste.
5. Should museums buy and exhibit contemporary works of art? For support of your argument, study the title essay in Ananda K. Coomaraswamy's *Why Exhibit Works of Art?*
6. In view of what you have studied in this section of your text, write a paper explaining what you believe the purpose of art to be.
7. Imagine a foreign observer's reaction to one of your pseudo-intellectual acquaintances. Oliver Goldsmith used the device of an imaginary Chinese traveler to comment on English pretensions to culture. The following paragraphs from Letter 104 of *The Citizen of the World*, 1762, should give you additional ideas:

Our scholars in China have a most profound veneration for forms. A first-rate beauty never studied the decorums of dress with more assiduity; they may properly enough be said to be clothed with wisdom from head to foot; they have their philosophical caps, and philosophical whiskers; their philosophical slippers, and philosophical fans; there is even a philosophical standard for measuring the nails; and yet, with all this seeming wisdom, they are often found to be mere empty pretenders.

A philosophical beau is not so frequent in Europe; yet I am told that such characters are found here. I mean such as punctually support all the decorums of learning, without being really very profound, or naturally possessed of a fine understanding who labour hard to obtain the titular honours attending literary merit, who flatter others in order to be flattered in turn, and only study to be thought students.

A character of this kind generally receives company in his study, in all the pensive formality of slippers, night-gown, and easy chair. The table is covered with a large book, which is always kept open, and never read; his solitary hours being dedicated to dozing, mending pens, feeling his pulse, peeping through the microscope, and sometimes reading amusing books, which he condemns in company. His library is preserved with the most religious neatness, and is generally a repository of scarce books, which bear a high price, because too dull or useless to become common by the ordinary methods of publication.

Such men are generally candidates for admittance into literary clubs, academies, and institutions, where they regularly meet to give and receive a little instruction, and a great deal of praise. In conversation they never betray ignorance, because they never seem to receive information. Offer a new observation, they have heard it before, pinch them in argument, and they reply with a sneer.

Yet, how trifling soever these little arts may appear, they answer one valuable purpose, of gaining the practisers the esteem they wish for. The bounds of a man's knowledge are easily concealed, if he has but prudence; but all can readily see and admire a gilt library, a set of long nails, a silver standish, or a well-combed whisker, who are incapable of distinguishing a dunce.

part seven ✖ *Expressions of the self*

CORN-PONE OPINIONS

MARK TWAIN

Samuel Langhorne Clemens (1835–1910) took his pseudonym from the expression the river men used when they tested the Mississippi for its depth. Twain was born in Florida, Missouri, but spent most of his youth in Hannibal. His formal education was most rudimentary, but he had enough experiences to satisfy the needs of any writer. His state of mind could move from jokes and pranks to pessimistic reflections; however, he found his greatest satisfaction in recalling the days of an earlier America, the days of his youth.

Fifty years ago, when I was a boy of fifteen and helping to inhabit a Missourian village on the banks of the Mississippi, I had a friend whose society was very dear to me because I was forbidden by my mother to partake of it. He was a gay and impudent and satirical and delightful young black man—a slave—who daily preached sermons from the top of his master's woodpile, with me for sole audience. He imitated the pulpit style of the several clergymen of the village, and did it well, and with fine passion and energy. To me he was a wonder. I believed he was the greatest orator in the United States and would some day be heard from. But it did not happen; in the distribution of rewards he was overlooked. It is the way, in this world.

He interrupted his preaching, now and then, to saw a stick of wood; but the sawing was a pretense—he did it with his mouth; exactly imitating the sound the bucksaw makes in shrieking its way through the wood. But it served its purpose; it kept his master from coming out to see how the work was getting along. I listened to the sermons from the open window of a lumber room at the back of the house. One of his texts was this:

"You tell me whar a man gits his corn pone, en I'll tell you what his 'pinions is."

I can never forget it. It was deeply impressed upon me. By my mother. Not upon my memory, but elsewhere. She had slipped in upon me while I was absorbed and not watching. The black philosopher's idea was that a man is not independent, and cannot afford views which might interfere with his bread and butter. If he would prosper, he must train with the majority; in matters of large moment, like politics and religion, he must think and feel with the bulk of his neighbors, or suffer damage in his social standing and in his business prosperities. He must restrict himself to corn-pone opinions—at least on the surface. He must get his opinions from other people; he must reason out none for himself; he must have no first-hand views.

I think Jerry was right, in the main, but I think he did not go far enough.

1. It was his idea that a man conforms to the majority view of his locality by calculation and intention.

This happens, but I think it is not the rule.

2. It was his idea that there is such a thing as a first-hand opinion, an original opinion, an opinion which is coldly reasoned out in a man's head, by a searching analysis of the facts involved, with the heart unconsulted, and the jury room closed against outside influences. It may be that such an opinion has been born somewhere, at some time or other, but I suppose it got away before they could catch it and stuff it and put it in the museum.

I am persuaded that a coldly-thought-out and independent verdict upon a fashion in clothes, or manners, or literature, or politics, or religion, or any other matter that is projected into the field of our notice and interest, is a most rare thing—if it has indeed ever existed.

A new thing in costume appears—the flaring hoopskirt, for example—and the passers-by are shocked, and the irreverent laugh. Six months later everybody is reconciled; the fashion has established itself; it is admired, now, and no one laughs. Public opinion resented it before, public opinion accepts it now, and is happy in it. Why? Was the resentment reasoned out? Was the acceptance reasoned out? No. The instinct that moves to conformity did the work. It is our nature to conform; it is a force which not many can successfully resist. What is its seat? The inborn requirement of self-approval. We all have to bow to that; there are no exceptions. Even the woman who refuses from first to last to wear the hoopskirt comes under that law and is its slave; she could not wear the skirt and have her own approval; and that she *must* have, she cannot help herself. But as a rule our self-approval has its source in but one place and not elsewhere—the approval of other people. A person of vast consequences can introduce any kind of novelty in dress and the general world will presently adopt it—moved to do it, in the first place, by the natural instinct to passively yield to that vague something recognized as authority, and in the second place by the human instinct to train with the multitude and have its approval. An empress introduced the hoopskirt, and we know the result. A nobody introduced the bloomer, and we know the result. If Eve should come again, in her ripe renown, and reintroduce her quaint styles—well, we know what would happen. And we should be cruelly embarrassed, along at first.

The hoopskirt runs its course and disappears. Nobody reasons about it. One woman abandons the fashion; her neighbor notices this and follows her lead; this influences the next woman; and so on and so on, and presently the skirt has vanished out of the world, no one knows how nor why; nor cares, for that matter. It will come again, by and by; and in due course will go again.

Twenty-five years ago, in England, six or eight wine glasses stood grouped by each person's plate at a dinner party, and they were used, not left idle and empty; to-day there are but three or four in the group, and the average guest sparingly uses about two of them. We have not adopted this new fashion yet, but we shall do it presently. We shall not think it out; we shall merely conform, and let it go at that. We get our notions and habits and opinions from outside influences; we do not have to study them out.

Our table manners, and company manners, and street manners change from time to time, but the changes are not reasoned out; we merely notice and conform. We are creatures of outside influences; as a rule we do not think, we only imitate. We cannot invent standards that will stick; what we mistake for standards are only fashions, and perishable. We may continue to admire them, but we drop the use of them. We notice this in literature. Shakespeare is a standard, and fifty years ago we used to write tragedies which we couldn't tell from — from somebody else's; but we don't do it any more, now. Our prose standard, three quarters of a century ago, was ornate and diffuse; some authority or other changed it in the direction of compactness and simplicity, and conformity followed, without argument. The historical novel starts up suddenly, and sweeps the land. Everybody writes one, and the nation is glad. We had historical novels before; but nobody read them, and the rest of us conformed—without reasoning it out. We are conforming in the other way, now, because it is another case of everybody.

The outside influences are always pouring in upon us, and we are always obeying their orders and accepting their verdicts. The Smiths like the new play; the Joneses go to see it, and they copy the Smith verdict. Morals, religions, politics, get their following from surrounding influences and atmospheres, almost entirely; not from study, not from thinking. A man must and will have his own approval first of all, in each and every moment and circumstance of his life—even if he must repent of a self-approved act the moment after its commission, in order to get his self-approval *again:* but, speaking in general terms, a man's self-approval in the large concerns of life has its source in the approval of the peoples about him, and not in a searching personal examination of the matter. Mohammedans are Mohammedans because they are born and reared among that sect, not because they have thought it out and can furnish sound reasons for being Mohammedans; we know why Catholics are Catholics; why Presbyterians are Presbyterians; why Baptists are Baptists; why Mormons are Mormons; why thieves are thieves; why monarchists are monarchists; why Republicans are Republicans and Democrats, Democrats. We know it is a matter of association and sympathy, not reasoning and examination; that hardly a man in the world has an opinion upon morals, politics, or religion which he got otherwise than through his associations and sympathies.

Broadly speaking, there are none but corn-pone opinions. And broadly speaking, corn pone stands for self-approval. Self-approval is acquired mainly from the approval of other people. The result is conformity. Sometimes conformity has a sordid business interest—the bread-and-butter interest—but not in most cases, I think. I think that in the majority of cases it is unconscious and not calculated; that it is born of the human being's natural yearning to stand well with his fellows and have their inspiring approval and praise—a yearning which is commonly so strong and so insistent that it cannot be effectually resisted, and must have its way.

A political emergency brings out the corn-pone opinion in fine force in its two chief varieties—the pocketbook variety, which has its origin in self-interest, and the bigger variety, the sentimental variety—the one which can't bear to be outside the pale; can't bear to be in disfavor; can't endure the averted face and the cold shoulder; wants to stand well with his friends, wants to be smiled upon, wants to be welcome, wants to hear the precious words, *"He's* on the right track!" Uttered, perhaps by an ass, but still an ass of high degree, an ass whose approval is gold and diamonds to a smaller ass, and confers glory and honor and happiness, and membership in the herd. For these gauds many a man will dump his life-long principles into the street, and his conscience along with them. We have seen it happen. In some millions of instances.

Men think they think upon great political questions, and they do; but they think with their party, not independently; they read its literature, but not that of the other side; they arrive at convictions, but they are drawn from a partial view of the matter in hand and are of no particular value. They swarm with their party, they feel with their party, they are happy in their party's approval; and where the party leads they will follow, whether for right and honor, or through blood and dirt and a mush of mutilated morals.

In our late canvass half of the nation passionately believed that in silver lay salvation, the other half as passionately believed that that way lay destruction. Do you believe that a tenth part of the people, on either side, had any rational excuse for having an opinion about the matter at all? I studied that mighty question to the bottom—came out empty. Half of our people passionately believe in high tariff, the other half believe otherwise. Does this mean study and examination, or only feeling? The latter, I think. I have deeply studied that question, too—and didn't arrive. We all do no end of feeling, and we mistake it for thinking. And out of it we get a aggregation which we consider a boon. Its name is Public Opinion. It is held in reverence. It settles everything. Some think it the Voice of God.

Questions and Suggestions

1. Locate a passage that summarizes Twain's view about the source of opinions and their effect upon human beings. Can this passage also serve as the thesis statement?
2. Study the paragraph that begins "Our table manners. . . ." What variety appears in the structure of the sentences?
3. How many major divisions do you find in the essay? List the reasons why Twain uses the example of Jerry.
4. Are you conscious of the transitional devices? Does the essay build to a climax?
5. Although Twain wrote this essay in 1900, it was not published until after his death. Does he wish to irritate, instruct, or entertain his reader? Does he mix banter with seriousness?
6. Do you believe that Twain himself was capable of making an "independent verdict"?
7. Do we still rely upon public opinion to settle many of our problems? If so, cite examples. Do you take issue with his views?

Ideas for Writing

1. Contrast Twain's view of man's nature with that expressed in Thoreau's "Civil Disobedience."
2. Write an essay in which you demonstrate how a method for some campus problem might be solved—such as changing the procedures of final examinations or revising the rules for dormitory life. Consider the dubious results if, to reach the decisions, all the students were polled, regardless of class or interests.
3. Explain why your own religious or political beliefs might be "a matter of association and sympathy, not reasoning and examination." What do the latter intellectual processes involve?
4. Have any of your friends deliberately conformed to the view of the majority? When he chose to conform, did he "dump his life-long principles into the street"?
5. Has mob-rule ever dominated the life of your city or town? Is there anything wrong with a political society where one man feels he must say, "But my vote means nothing at all"?

MIDDLEBROW

VIRGINIA WOOLF

Spending most of her life in cultural circles, Virginia Stephen Woolf (1882–1941), the daughter of Sir Leslie Stephen, a celebrated literary figure, received the greater part of her education from her father's books. Her husband, Leonard Woolf, is a well-known economist, essayist, and publisher. For many years their home served as a literary mecca for the writers, painters, and economists who came to be known as the Bloomsbury Group. A number of readers believe that her witty, sensitive, and incisive essays are even superior to her celebrated works of fiction.

To the Editor of the "New Statesman"

SIR,

Will you allow me to draw your attention to the fact that in a review of a book by me (October) your reviewer omitted to use the word Highbrow? The review, save for that omission, gave me so much pleasure that I am driven to ask you, at the risk of appearing unduly egotistical, whether your reviewer, a man of obvious intelligence, intended to deny my claim to that title? I say "claim," for surely I may claim that title when a great critic, who is also a great novelist, a rare and enviable combination, always calls me a highbrow when he condescends to notice my work in a great newspaper; and, further, always finds space to inform not only myself, who knows it already, but the whole British Empire, who hang on his words, that I live in Bloomsbury? Is your critic unaware of that fact too? Or does he, for all his intelligence, maintain that it is unnecessary in reviewing a book to add the postal address of the writer?

His answer to these questions, though of real value to me, is of no possible interest to the public at large. Of that I am well aware. But since larger issues are involved, since the Battle of the Brows troubles, I am told, the evening air, since the finest minds of our age have lately been engaged in debating, not without that passion which befits a noble cause, what a highbrow is and what a lowbrow, which is better and which is worse, may I take this opportunity to express my opinion and at the same time draw attention to certain aspects of the question which seem to me to have been unfortunately overlooked?

Now there can be no two opinions as to what a highbrow is. He is the man or woman of thoroughbred intelligence who rides his mind at a gallop across country in pursuit of an idea. That is why I have always been so proud to be called highbrow. That is why, if I could be more of a highbrow I would. I honour and respect highbrows. Some of my relations have been highbrows; and some, but by no means all, of my friends. To be a highbrow, a complete and representative highbrow, a highbrow like Shakespeare, Dickens, Byron, Shelley, Keats, Charlotte Brontë, Scott, Jane Austen, Flaubert, Hardy or Henry James—to name a few highbrows from the same profession chosen at random—is of course beyond the wildest dreams of my imagination. And, though I would cheerfully lay myself down in the dust and kiss the print of their feet, no person of sense will deny that this passionate preoccupation of theirs—riding across country in pursuit of ideas—often leads to disaster. Undoubtedly, they come fearful croppers. Take Shelley— what a mess he made of his life! And Byron, getting into bed with first one woman and then with another and dying in the mud at Missolonghi. Look at Keats, loving poetry and Fanny Brawne so intemperately that he pined and died of consumption at the age of twenty-six. Charlotte Brontë again—I have been assured on good authority that Charlotte Brontë was, with the possible exception of Emily, the worst governess in the British Isles. Then there was Scott—he went bankrupt, and left, together with a few magnificent novels, one house, Abbotsford, which is perhaps the ugliest in the whole Empire. But surely these instances are enough—I need not further labour the point that highbrows, for some reason or another, are wholly incapable of dealing successfully with what is called real life. That is why, and here I come to a point that is often surprisingly ignored, they honour so wholeheartedly and depend so completely upon those who are called lowbrows. By a low-brow is meant of course a man or a woman of thoroughbred vitality who rides his body in pursuit of a living at a gallop across life. That is why I honour and respect lowbrows—and I have never known a highbrow who did not. In so far as I am a highbrow (and my im-perfections in that line are well known to me) I love lowbrows; I study them; I always sit next the conductor in an omnibus and try to get him to tell me what it is like—being a conductor. In whatever company I am I always try to know what it is like—being a conductor, being a woman with ten children and thirty-five shillings a week, being a stock-broker, being an admiral, being a bank clerk, being a dressmaker, being a duchess, being a miner, being a cook, being a prostitute. All that lowbrows do is of surpassing interest and wonder to me, because, in so far as I am a highbrow, I cannot do things myself.

This brings me to another point which is also surprisingly over-looked. Lowbrows need highbrows and honour them just as much as highbrows need lowbrows and honour them. This too is not a matter that requires much demonstration. You have only to stroll along the Strand on a wet winter's night and watch the crowds lining up to get into the movies. These lowbrows are waiting, after the day's work, in the rain, sometimes for hours, to get into the cheap seats and sit in hot theatres in order to see what their lives look like. Since they are lowbrows, engaged magnificently and adventurously in riding full tilt from one end of life to the other in pursuit of a living, they cannot see themselves doing it. Yet nothing interests them more. Nothing mat-ters to them more. It is one of the prime necessities of life to them—to be shown what life looks like. And the highbrows, of course, are the only people who can show them. Since they are the only people who do not do things, they are the only people who can see things being done. This is so—and so it is I am certain; nevertheless we are told—the air buzzes with it by night, the Press booms with it by day, the very donkeys in the fields do nothing but bray it, the very curs in the streets do nothing but bark it—"Highbrows hate lowbrows! Lowbrows hate highbrows!"—when highbrows need lowbrows, when lowbrows need highbrows, when they cannot exist apart, when one is the complement and other side of the other! How has such a lie come into existence? Who has set this malicious gossip afloat?

There can be no doubt about that either. It is the doing of the middlebrows. They are the people, I confess, that I seldom regard with entire cordiality. They are the go-betweens; they are the busy-bodies who run from one to the other with their tittle tattle and make all the mischief—the middlebrows, I repeat. But what, you may ask, is a middlebrow? And that, to tell the truth, is no easy question to answer. They are neither one thing nor the other. They are not highbrows, whose brows are high; nor lowbrows, whose brows are low. Their brows are betwixt and between. They do not live in Bloomsbury which is on high ground; nor in Chelsea, which is on low ground. Since they must live somewhere presumably, they live perhaps in South Kensington, which is betwixt and between. The middlebrow is the man, or woman, of middlebred intelligence who ambles and saunters now on this side of the hedge, now on that, in pursuit of no single object, neither art itself nor life itself, but both mixed indistinguishably, and rather nastily, with money, fame, power, or prestige. The middlebrow curries favour with both sides equally. He goes to the lowbrows and tells them that while he is not quite one of them, he is almost their friend. Next moment he rings up the highbrows and asks them with equal geniality whether he may not come to tea. Now there are highbrows—I myself have known duchesses who were highbrows, also charwomen, and they have both told me with that vigour of language which so often unites the aristocracy with the working classes, that they would rather sit in the coal cellar, together, than in the drawing-room with middlebrows and pour out tea. I have myself been asked— but may I, for the sake of brevity, cast this scene which is only partly fictitious, into the form of fiction?—I myself, then, have been asked to come and "see" them—how strange a passion theirs is for being "seen"! They ring me up, therefore, at about eleven in the morning, and ask me to come to tea. I go to my wardrobe and consider, rather lugubriously, what is the right thing to wear? We highbrows may be smart, or we may be shabby; but we never have the right thing to wear. I proceed to ask next: What is the right thing to say? Which is the right knife to use? What is the right book to praise? All these are things I do not know for myself. We highbrows read what we like and do what we like and praise what we like. We also know what we dislike—for example, thin bread and butter tea. The difficulty of eating thin bread and butter in white kid gloves has always seemed to me one of life's more insuperable problems. Then I dislike bound volumes of the classics behind plate glass. Then I distrust people who call both Shakespeare and Wordsworth equally "Bill"—it is a habit moreover that leads to confusion. And in the matter of clothes, I like people either to dress very well; or to dress very badly; I dislike the correct thing in clothes. Then there is the question of games. Being a highbrow I do not play them. But I love watching people play who have a passion for games. These middlebrows pat balls about; they poke their bats and muff their catches at cricket. And when poor Middlebrow mounts on horseback and that animal breaks into a canter, to me there is no sadder sight in all Rotten Row. To put it in a nutshell (in order to get on with the story) that tea party was not wholly a success, nor altogether a failure; for Middlebrow, who writes, following me to the door, clapped me briskly on the back, and said, "I'm sending you my book!" (Or did he call it "stuff?") And his book comes—sure enough, though called, so symbolically, *Keepaway,** it comes. And I read a page here, and I read a page there (I am breakfasting, as usual, in bed). And it is not well written; nor is it badly written. It is not proper, nor is it improper—in short it is betwixt and between. Now if there is any sort of book for which I have, perhaps, an imperfect sympathy, it is the betwixt and between. And so, though I suffer from the gout of a morning—but if one's ancestors for two or three centuries have tumbled into bed dead drunk one has deserved a touch of that malady—I rise. I dress. I proceed weakly to the window. I take that book in my swollen right hand and toss it gently over the hedge into the field. The hungry sheep—did I remember to say that this part of the story takes place in the country?—the hungry sheep look up but are not fed.

But to have done with fiction and its tendency to lapse into poetry— I will now report a perfectly prosaic conversation in words of one syllable. I often ask my friends the lowbrows, over our muffins and honey, why it is that while we, the highbrows, never buy a middlebrow book, or go to a middlebrow lecture, or read, unless we are paid for doing so, a middlebrow review, they, on the contrary, take these middle-brow activities so seriously? Why, I ask (not of course on the wireless), are you so damnably modest? Do you think that a description of your lives, as they are, is too sordid and too mean to be beautiful? Is that why you prefer the middlebrow version of what they have the impu-dence to call real humanity?—this mixture of geniality and sentiment stuck together with a sticky slime of calves-foot jelly? The truth, if you would only believe it, is much more beautiful than any lie. Then again, I continue, how can you let the middlebrows teach *you* how to write?— you, who write so beautifully when you write naturally, that I would give both my hands to write as you do—for which reason I never attempt it, but do my best to learn the art of writing as a highbrow should. And again, I press on, brandishing a muffin on the point of a tea spoon, how dare the middlebrows teach *you* how to read—Shake-speare for instance? All you have to do is to read him. The Cambridge ed:tion is both good and cheap. If you find *Hamlet* difficult, ask him to tea. He is a highbrow. Ask Ophelia to meet him. She is a lowbrow.

---

* Keepaway is the name of a preparation used to distract the male dog from the female at certain seasons.

Talk to them, as you talk to me, and you will know more about
Shakespeare than all the middlebrows in the world can teach you—I
do not think, by the way, from certain phrases that Shakespeare liked
middlebrows, or Pope either.

To all this the lowbrows reply—but I cannot imitate their style
of talking—that they consider themselves to be common people without education. It is very kind of the middlebrows to try to teach them
culture. And after all, the lowbrows continue, middlebrows, like other
people, have to make money. There must be money in teaching and
in writing books about Shakespeare. We all have to earn our livings
nowadays, my friends the lowbrows remind me. I quite agree. Even
those of us whose Aunts came a cropper riding in India and left them
an annual income of four hundred and fifty pounds, now reduced,
thanks to the war and other luxuries, to little more than two hundred
odd, even we have to do that. And we do it, too, by writing about anybody who seems amusing—enough has been written about Shakespeare
—Shakespeare hardly pays. We highbrows, I agree, have to earn our
livings; but when we have earned enough to live on, then we live.
When the middlebrows, on the contrary, have earned enough to live
on, they go on earning enough to buy—what are the things that
middlebrows always buy? Queen Anne furniture (faked, but none
the less expensive); first editions of dead writers—always the worst;
pictures, or reproductions from pictures, by dead painters; houses in
what is called "the Georgian style"—but never anything new, never
a picture by a living painter, or a chair by a living carpenter, or books
by living writers, for to buy living art requires living taste. And, as
that kind of art and that kind of taste are what middlebrows call
"highbrow," "Bloomsbury," poor middlebrow spends vast sums on sham
antiques, and has to keep at it scribbling away, year in, year out, while
we highbrows ring each other up, and are off for a day's jaunt into
the country. That is the worst of course of living in a set—one likes
being with one's friends.

Have I then made my point clear, sir, that the true battle in my
opinion lies not between highbrow and lowbrow, but between highbrows and lowbrows joined together in blood brotherhood against the
bloodless and pernicious pest who comes between? If the B.B.C. stood
for anything but the Betwixt and Between Company they would use
their control of the air not to stir strife between brothers, but to broadcast the fact that highbrows and lowbrows must band together to ex-
terminate a pest which is the bane of all thinking and living. It may

be, to quote from your advertisement columns, that "terrifically sensitive" lady novelists overestimate the dampness and dinginess of this
fungoid growth. But all I can say is that when, lapsing into that stream
which people call, so oddly, consciousness, and gathering wool from
the sheep that have been mentioned above, I ramble round my garden
in the suburbs, middlebrow seems to me to be everywhere. "What's
that?" I cry. "Middlebrow on the cabbages? Middlebrow infecting that
poor old sheep? And what about the moon?" I look up and, behold, the
moon is under eclipse. "Middlebrow at it again!" I exclaim. "Middlebrow obscuring, dulling, tarnishing and coarsening even the silver edge
of Heaven's own scythe." (I "draw near to poetry," see advt.) And
then my thoughts, as Freud assures us thoughts will do, rush (Middlebrow's saunter and simper, out of respect for the Censor) to sex, and
I ask of the sea-gulls who are crying on desolate sea sands and of the
farm hands who are coming home rather drunk to their wives, what
will become of us, men and women, if Middlebrow has his way with
us, and there is only a middle sex but no husbands or wives? The next
remark I address with the utmost humility to the Prime Minister.
"What, sir," I demand, "will be the fate of the British Empire and
of our Dominions Across the Seas if Middlebrows prevail? Will you not,
sir, read a pronouncement of an authoritative nature from Broadcasting
House?"

Such are the thoughts, such are the fancies that visit "cultured
invalidish ladies with private means" (see advt.) when they stroll in
their suburban gardens and look at the cabbages and at the red brick
villas that have been built by middlebrows so that middlebrows may
look at the view. Such are the thoughts "at once gay and tragic and
deeply feminine" (see advt.) of one who has not yet "been driven out
of Bloomsbury" (advt. again), a place where lowbrows and highbrows
live happily together on equal terms and priests are not, nor priestesses,
and, to be quite frank, the adjective "priestly" is neither often heard
nor held in high esteem. Such are the thoughts of one who will stay
in Bloomsbury until the Duke of Bedford, rightly concerned for the
respectability of his squares, raises the rent so high that Bloomsbury
is safe for middlebrows to live in. Then she will leave.

May I conclude, as I began, by thanking your reviewer for his very
courteous and interesting review, but may I tell him that though he did
not, for reasons best known to himself, call me a highbrow, there is
no name in the world that I prefer? I ask nothing better than that all
reviewers, for ever, and everywhere, should call me a highbrow. I will

do my best to oblige them. If they like to add Bloomsbury, W.C.1, that
is the correct postal address, and my telephone number is in the
Directory. But if your reviewer, or any other reviewer, dares hint that
I live in South Kensington, I will sue him for libel. If any human being,
man, woman, dog, cat or half-crushed worm dares call me "middlebrow" I will take my pen and stab him, dead.

Yours etc.,

Virginia Woolf.

Questions and Suggestions

1. Distinguish between highbrows and lowbrows. How do middlebrows differ from the other two? Of the three, which ones
   would be likely to agree with "corn-pone opinions"?
2. How does Virginia Woolf organize her letter? Is her style
   appropriate to a highbrow, as she defines him?
3. When you begin to analyze the transitional devices, do you
   observe that she often uses a "free association" between her
   ideas? Is this method effective?
4. What did she dislike about the reviewer? What is the effect
   of the final sentence?
5. On what side of the "true battle" does she find the British
   Broadcasting Corporation? Can you draw parallels with radio
   or television presentations in America?
6. Explain the several references to *see advt.*

Ideas for Writing

1. Discuss the idea that "to buy living art requires living taste."
2. Has mass production had any effect upon the artifacts in your
   own house, in the lounge of your dormitory, or in the home
   of a friend?
3. Are the "beatniks" only another manifestation of middle-
   browism?
4. What benefits would our society derive from a cultural aristocracy?
5. Analyze our society for the presence of the three classes. Can
   you describe representative specimens? In this connection see
   Russell Lynes, "High-Brow, Low-Brow, Middle-Brow," *Life*,
   April 11, 1949.
6. Write a letter to a friend who has mistakenly placed you in a
   wrong social or intellectual category. To get a clearer idea of
   what you might wish to say about yourself, read some of the
   essays in Jacques Barzun's *The House of Intellect*, or Maurice
   Baring's "High-Brows and Low-Brows" in *Lost Lectures*.

THE TASTE OF THE AGE

RANDALL JARRELL

Poet, novelist, short story writer, and critic, Randall Jarrell (1914–), who has been a professor of English in several institutions, studied at Vanderbilt, in his native city, Nashville, Tennessee. He has not, however, spent all of his time in academic surroundings: he served during World War II in the Air Corps, he has been literary editor of several magazines, and he has been Consultant in Poetry to the Library of Congress. His poems have won a number of awards.

When a man looks at the age in which he lives—no matter what age it happens to be—it is hard for him not to be depressed by it. The taste of the age is always a bitter one. "What kind of a time is this when one must envy the dead and buried!" said Goethe about his age; yet Matthew Arnold would have traded his own time for Goethe's almost as willingly as he would have traded his own self for Goethe's. How often, after a long day witnessing elementary and secondary education, School Inspector Arnold came home, sank into what I hope was a Morris chair, looked round him at the Age of Victoria, that Indian summer of the Western world, and gave way to a wistful, exacting, articulate despair!

We say that somebody doesn't know what he is missing; Arnold, pretty plainly, didn't know what he was having. The people who live in a Golden Age usually go around complaining how yellow everything looks. Maybe we, too, are living in a Golden or, anyway, Gold-Plated Age, and the people of the next age will say ruefully: "We never had it so good." And yet the thought that they will say this isn't so reassuring as it might be. We can see that Goethe's and Arnold's ages weren't so bad as Goethe and Arnold thought them: after all, they produced

From *The Saturday Evening Post,* July 26, 1958. This essay was number 8 in a series entitled "Adventures of the Mind." Reprinted by permission of the author.

Goethe and Arnold. In the same way, our times may not be so bad as we think them: they have produced us. Yet this, too, is a thought that isn't so reassuring as it might be.

A Tale of Two Cities begins by saying that the times were, as always, "the best of times, the worst of times!" If we judge by wealth and power, our times are the best of times; if the times have made us willing to judge by wealth and power, our times are the worst of times. But we still judge by more: by literature and the arts, science, education. How are literature and the arts, and their audience, and the education that helps to prepare this audience, getting along in the United States?

In some ways this audience has improved tremendously. Think of that small, round, profitable thing, the long-playing record. Today it is as easy to get Falstaff or Boris Godunov or Ariadne auf Naxos, or Landowska playing The Well-Tempered Clavier, or Schnabel playing Beethoven's sonatas, as it used to be to get Mischa Elman playing Humoresque. Several hundred thousand Americans bought Toscanini's recording of Beethoven's Ninth Symphony. Some of them played it only to show how faithful their phonographs are. But many more really listened to it; many more bought, got to know and love, compositions that a few years ago nobody but musicologists had even read the scores of.

The greatest influence on American ballet, today, is the greatest choreographer who ever lived, George Balanchine; and we who, twenty-five years ago, would have had to say, "American ballet? What American ballet?" can say today, "Yes, American ballet. Is there a better?"

We Americans are producing paintings and reproductions of paintings, painters and reproductions of painters, museum directors and gallery goers, in almost celestial quantities. Most of the painters are bad or mediocre—this is so, necessarily, in any art at any time—but the good ones find shelter in numbers, are bought and looked at like the rest. A restaurant, today, will order a mural by Miró in as easy and matter-of-fact a spirit as, twenty-five years ago, it would have ordered one by Maxfield Parrish. The president of a paint factory goes home, sits down by his fireplace—it looks like a chromium aquarium set into the wall by a wall-safe company that has branched out into interior decoration, but there is a log burning in it, he calls it a fireplace, let's call it a fireplace too—the president sits down, folds his hands on his stomach, and stares relishingly at two paintings by Jackson Pollock that he has hung on the wall opposite him. He feels at home with them; in fact, as he looks at them he not only feels at home, he feels as if he were back at the paint factory.

This president's employees may not be willing to hang a Mondrian in the house, but they will wear one, if you make it into a tie or a sport shirt; and if you make it into a sofa, they will lie on it. They and their wives and children will sit on a porcupine, if you first exhibit it at the Museum of Modern Art and say that it is a chair. The great new art form of our age is the chair: if Hieronymus Bosch, if Christian Morgenstern, if the Marquis de Sade were living at this hour, what chairs they would be designing!

Our architecture is flourishing too. A mansion, today, is what it is, not because a millionaire has dreamed of the Alhambra, but because an architect has dreamed of the marriage of Frank Lloyd Wright and a silo. We Americans have the best factories anyone has ever designed; we have many schools, post offices and public buildings that are, so far as one can see, the best factories anyone has ever designed; we have many delightful, or efficient, or extraordinary houses. The public that lives in the houses our architects design is a tolerant, adventurous public: you can put a spherical gas tower on aluminum stilts, divide it into rooms, and quite a few people will be willing to crawl along saying, "Is this the floor? Is this the wall?" to make a down payment, and to call it home.

But in the arts that utilize words——

But here you may interrupt me, saying: "You've praised or characterized or joked about our music, dancing, painting, furniture and architecture; yet each time you've talked about things that apply to hundreds of thousands, not to hundreds of millions. Most people don't listen to classical music, but to rock-and-roll or hillbilly songs or some album named Music to Listen to Music By; they see no ballet except a television ballet or some musical comedy's last echo of Rodeo. When they go home they sit inside chairs like imitation-leather haystacks, chairs that were exhibited not at the Museum of Modern Art, but at a convention of furniture dealers; if they buy a picture they buy it from the furniture dealer, and it was the furniture dealer who painted it; and their houses are split-level ranch-type rabbit warrens. Now that you've come to the 'arts that utilize words,' will you keep on talking about the unhappy few or will you talk about the happy many?"

About the happy many. I'll mention, and then leave for good, such inspiriting things as paper-bound books, off-Broadway plays, our many good writers. But when we talk about tens of millions of readers,

hundreds of millions of hearers and viewers, we are talking about a
new and strange situation; and to understand it we need to go back
to the days of Matthew Arnold and Queen Victoria.

We all remember that Queen Victoria, when she died, in 1901, had
never seen a helicopter, penicillin, television. Yet she had seen rail-
roads, electric lights, the telegraph—she came midway in the industrial and technological revolution that has transformed our world. But
there are many things that Queen Victoria never saw because she came
at the very beginning of another half-technological, half-cultural revolution. For example:

If the young Victoria had said to the Duke of Wellington, "Sir, the
Bureau of Public Relations of our army is in a deplorable state," he
would have answered, "What is a Bureau of Public Relations, ma'am?"
When he and his generals wanted to tell lies, they had to tell them
themselves; there was no organized institution set up to do it for them.
But of course Victoria couldn't have made this remark, since she had
never heard of public relations; she had never heard of a commentator,
a soap opera, a quiz program. Queen Victoria—think of it!—had
never heard a singing commercial, never seen an advertisement beginning "Science says," and if she had, she would probably have retorted,
"And what, pray, does the Archbishop of Canterbury say? What does
dear good Albert say?"

When some comedian or wit told Queen Victoria jokes, they weren't
supplied him by six well-paid gag writers, but just occurred to him.
When Disraeli and Gladstone sent her lovingly or respectfully inscribed
copies of their new books, they had written the books themselves. There
they were, with the resources of an empire at their command, and they
wrote the books themselves! And Queen Victoria had to read the books
herself: nobody was willing—or able—to digest them for her in The
Reader's Digest, to make movies of them, or to make radio or television
programs of them, so that she could experience them painlessly and
effortlessly. In those days people, so to speak, chewed their own food
or went hungry; we have changed all that.

Queen Victoria never went to the movies and had an epic costing
eight million dollars injected into her veins. She never Adjusted herself
to her Group, or Shared the Experience of her Generation, or breathed
a little deeper to feel herself a part of the Century of the Common
Man—she was a part of it for almost two years, but she didn't know
that that was what it was.

Isn't it plain that it is all these lacks that made Queen Victoria so old-fashioned, so awfully and finally different from us, rather than the fact that she never flew, or took insulin, or had a hydrogen bomb dropped on her? Queen Victoria in a DC-7 would be Queen Victoria still—I can hear her saying to the stewardess, "We do not wish Dramamine"; but a Queen Victoria who listened every day to John's Other Wife, Portia Faces Life, and Just Plain Bill—that wouldn't be Queen Victoria at all!

There has not been one revolution, an industrial and technological one—there have been two; and this second revolution might be called the Revolution of the Word. People have learned to process words, too—words, and the thoughts and attitudes they embody. One sees in stores ordinary old-fashioned oatmeal or cocoa; and, beside it, another kind called Instant Cocoa, Instant Oats. Much of our literature is Instant Literature: the words are short, easy, instantly recognizable words; the thoughts are easy, familiar, instantly recognizable thoughts; the attitudes are familiar, already-agreed-upon, instantly acceptable attitudes. And if this is so, can these productions be either truth or— really—literature? The truth is sometimes complicated or hard to understand; different from what we expected; difficult to accept. Literature can almost be defined as the union of a wish and a truth, or as a wish modified by a truth. But this Instant Literature is a wish reinforced by a cliché, a wish proved by a lie. The makers of Instant Literature— whether it is a soap opera, a Saturday Evening Post serial, or a historical, sexual best seller—treat us as advertisers treat the readers of advertisements; they humor us, flatter our prejudices, pull our strings, show us that they know us for what they think us to be: impressionable, emotional, ignorant, somewhat weak-minded Common Men. They fool us to the top of our bent; and if we aren't fooled, they dismiss us as a statistically negligible minority.

The greatest American industry is the industry of using words. We pay tens of millions of men of words—writers, advertisers, commentators, politicians—to spend their lives lying to us, or telling us the truth, or supplying us with a nourishing medicinal compound of the two. We are living in the middle of a dark wood—a bright Technicolored forest—of words, words, words. It is a forest in which the wind is never still: there isn't a tree in the forest that is not for every moment of its life, of our lives, persuading or seducing or overawing us into buying this, believing that, voting for the other.

And yet, the more words there are, the simpler the words get. The words are processed as if they were baby food and we babies; all we have to do is open our mouths and swallow. Most of our mental and moral food is predigested, spoon-fed. E. M. Forster has said: "The only thing we learn from spoon-feeding is the shape of the spoon." Not only is this true; soon, if anything doesn't have the shape of that spoon we won't swallow it, we can't swallow it. Our century has produced some great and much good literature, but the habitual readers of Instant Literature cannot read it; nor can they read the great and good literature of the past.

Each year Harper's, The Saturday Evening Post, and the Sunday supplements seem more nearly the same magazine. Each year they depend less on fiction, on the writer's or reader's imaginative or creative powers, and more on fact, on familiar or unfamiliar information which efficient, indistinguishable authors organize into articles. Such articles are part of The Reader's Digest even before the Digest reprints them: they are, literally, pre-Digested.

If Queen Victoria had got to read The Reader's Digest—awful thought!—she would have loved it; and it would have changed her. Everything in The Reader's Digest sounds like everything else in The Reader's Digest: so, soon, Queen Victoria would listen to dear good Albert, to the Archbishop of Canterbury, and would feel dissatisfied because they didn't sound like The Reader's Digest. Everything in the world, in such magazines, is a timely, reassuring, immediately comprehensible anecdote, full of human interest. Queen Victoria would notice that Albert kept quoting, from Shakespeare—that the Archbishop of Canterbury kept quoting, from the Bible—things that were very different from anything in The Reader's Digest: sometimes these sentences were not reassuring, but disquieting, sometimes they had big words or hard thoughts in them, sometimes the interest in them wasn't human, but literary or divine. After a while Queen Victoria would want Shakespeare and the Bible—would want Albert, even—digested for her beforehand by The Reader's Digest. And a little farther on in this process of digestion, she would look from them to some magazine the size of your hand, called Quick or Pic or TV Guide, and a strange half-sexual yearning would move like musk through her veins, and she would —— But I cannot, I will not say it. You and I know how she and Albert will end: sitting before the television set, staring into it, silent; and inside the set, there are Victoria and Albert, staring into the television camera, silent, and the master of ceremonies is saying to them, "No, I think you will find that Bismarck is the capital of North Dakota!"

But while she still reads, Victoria can get a rewritten Bible, Shakespeare in comic books. Only the other day I read of an interesting attempt to rewrite Shakespeare "for students":

Philadelphia, Pa. Feb. 1 (AP)

Two high-school teachers have published a simplified version of Shakespeare's Julius Caesar and plan to do the same for Macbeth. Their goal is to make the plays more understandable to youth. The teachers, Jack A. Waypen and Leroy S. Layton, say if the Bible can be revised and modernized, why not Shakespeare? They made 1,122 changes in Julius Caesar from single words to entire passages. They modernized obsolete words and expressions and substituted "you" for "thee" and "thou."

Shakespeare had Brutus say in Act III, Scene I:

"Fates, we will know your pleasures;
That we shall die, we know; 'tis but the time
And drawing days out, that men stand upon."

In the Waypen-Layton version, Brutus says:

"We will soon know what Fate decrees for us.
That we shall die, we know. It's putting off
The time of death that's of concern to men."

Not being Shakespeare, I can't find a comment worthy of this— project. I am tempted to say in an Elizabethan voice: "Ah, wayward Waypen, lascivious Layton, lay down thine errant pen!" And yet if I said this they would only reply earnestly, uncomprehendingly, reprovingly: "Can't you give us some *con*structive criticism, not *de*structive? Why don't you say *your* errant pen, not *thine*? And *lascivious!* Mr. Jarrell, if you *have* to talk about that type subject, don't say *lascivious* Layton, say *sexy* Layton."

Even Little Red Riding Hood is getting too hard for children, I read. The headline of the story is CHILD'S BOOKS BEING MADE MORE SIMPLE. Miss Olga Curtis has interviewed Julius Kushner, the publisher of children's books; he tells Miss Curtis that "nonessential details have disappeared from the 1953 Little Red Riding Hood story. Modern children enjoy their stories better stripped down to basic plot—for instance, Little Red Riding Hood meets wolf, Little Red Riding Hood escapes wolf." [Her name seems a nonessential detail. Why not call the child Red, and strip the story down to Red meets wolf, Red escapes? At this rate one could tell a child all of Grimm's Tales between dinner and bedtime.] . . . Modernizing old favorites, Kushner said, is fundamentally a matter of simplifying. Kushner added that today's children's books are intended to be activity games as well as reading matter. He mentioned books that make noises when pressed, and books with pop-up three-dimensional illustrations as examples of publishers' efforts to make each book a teaching aid as well as a story.

A great deal of the knowledge that educated—and many uneducated —people used to have in common has disappeared or is rapidly disappearing. Fairy tales, myths, history—the Bible, Shakespeare, Dickens, the Iliad are, surprisingly often, things most of an audience won't understand an allusion to. These things were the ground on which the people of the past came together; much of the wit or charm or elevation of any writing or conversation with an atmosphere depends upon this presupposed, easily and affectionately remembered body of common knowledge. Because of it we understand things, feel about things, as human beings and not as human animals.

Who teaches us all this? Our families, our friends, our schools, society in general. Most of all, we hope, our schools. When I say schools I mean colleges and high schools and grammar schools. But the last two are the most important. Most people still don't go to college, and those who do don't get there until they are seventeen or eighteen. "Give us a child until he is seven and he is ours," a Jesuit is supposed to have said; our grammar schools and high schools have a child for ten years longer, and then he is—whose? Shakespeare's? Leroy S. Layton's? The Reader's Digest's?

College teachers complain about their students' lack of preparation just as, each winter, they complain about the winter's lack of snow. Winters don't have so much snow as winters used to: things are going to the dogs and always have been. The teachers tell one another stories about the things their students don't know; it surprises you, after a few thousand such stories, that the students manage to find their way to the college.

One dark, cold, rainy night—the sort of night on which clients came to Sherlock Holmes—I read in a magazine that winters don't have so much snow as winters used to: according to meteorologists, the climate is changing. Maybe students are changing too. Hearing one fifth-grade child say to another, "What does E come after in the alphabet?" makes a great, and perhaps unfair, impression on one. The child may not be what is called a random sample.

I thought of some other samples I had seen, and I wasn't sure whether they were random. That winter I had talked with some fifth- and some eighth-grade students; I had gone to one of their classes; I had even gone caroling with some, and had been dismayed at all the carols I didn't know—it was a part of my education that had been neglected.

I was not dismayed at the things the children didn't know, I was overawed; there were very few parts of their education that had not been neglected. Half the fifth-grade children didn't know who Jonah was; only a few had heard of King Arthur. When I asked an eighth-grade student she laughed at me; she said, "Of course I know who King Arthur was." My heart warmed to her "of course." But she didn't know who Lancelot was, didn't know who Guinevere was; she had never heard of Galahad. I left the Knights of the Round Table for history: she didn't know who Charlemagne was.

She didn't know who Charlemagne was! And she had never heard of Alexander the Great; her class had "had Rome," but she didn't remember anything about Julius Caesar, though she knew his name. I asked her about Hector and Achilles. She had heard the name Hector, but didn't know who he was; she had never heard of "that other one."

But these had been questions of literature or European history; maybe there are more important things for students to know. I found that the little girl who didn't know who Charlemagne was had been taught to conduct a meeting, to nominate, and to second nominations; she had been taught—I thought this, though farfetched, truly imaginative—the right sort of story to tell an eighteen-month-old baby; and she had learned in Domestic Science to bake a date pudding, to make a dirndl skirt and, from the remnants of the cloth, a drawstring carry-all. She could not tell me who Charlemagne was, it is true, but if I were an eighteen-month-old baby I could go to her and be sure of having her tell me the right sort of story.

I said to myself, as I was getting into the habit of saying about each new eighth-grade girl I talked to: "She must be an exception"; pretty soon I was saying, "She *must* be an exception." If I had said this to her teacher she would have replied: "Exception indeed! She's a nice, normal, well-adjusted girl. She's one of the drum majorettes and she's vice president of the Student Body; she's had two short stories in the school magazine and she made her own formal for the Sadie Hawkins dance. She's an exceptionally normal girl!" And what could I have replied? "But she doesn't know who Charlemagne was"?

How many people cared whether or not she knew who Charlemagne was? How much good would knowing who Charlemagne was ever do her? Could you make a dirndl out of Charlemagne? Make, even, a drawstring carryall? There was a chance that someday, on a quiz program, someone would ask her who Charlemagne was. If she knew, the audience would applaud in delight, and the announcer would give her a refrigerator; if she didn't know, the audience would groan in sympathy, and the announcer would give her a dozen cartons of soap powder.

Another eighth-grade girl had shown me her Reader—a popular and unusually literary Reader. It has in it, just as readers used to have in them, The Man Without a Country and The Legend of Sleepy Hollow and Evangeline; and the preface to Adventures for Readers says about them:

> The competition of movies and radios has reduced the time young children spend with books. It is no longer supposed, as it once was, that reading skills are fully developed at the end of the sixth grade. . . . Included are The Man Without a Country, The Legend of Sleepy Hollow, and Evangeline. These longer selections were once in every eighth-grade reading book. They have disappeared because in the original they are far too difficult for eighth-grade readers. . . . In their simplified form they are once more available to young people to become a part of their background and experience.

In the next edition of Adventures for Readers, I thought, the editors will have to say "the competition of movies, radios and television": I thought of this thought for some time. But when I thought of Longfellow's being "in the original" far too difficult for eighth-grade students, I—I did not know what to think. How much more difficult everything is than it used to be!

I remembered a letter, one about difficult writers, that I had read in The Saturday Review:

> I have been wondering when somebody with an established reputation in the field of letters would stand tiptoe and slap these unintelligibles in the face. Now I hope the publishers will wake up and throw the whole egotistical, sophist lot of them down the drain. I hope that fifty years from now nobody will remember that Joyce or Stein or James or Proust or Mann ever lived.

Once I had read a London Times, printed in 1851, that had in it a review of a new book by Alfred Tennyson. The reviewer said, after several unfavorable sentences: "Another fault is not peculiar to In Memoriam; it runs through all Mr. Tennyson's poetry—we allude to his obscurity."

The reviewer would not have alluded to Longfellow's obscurity; those Victorians for whom everything else was too difficult still understood, and delighted in, Longfellow. But Tennyson had been too obscure for some of them, just as Longfellow was getting to be too obscure for some of us.

This better-humored writer of the London Times had not hoped that in fifty years nobody would remember that Tennyson had ever lived; and this is fortunate, since he would not have got his wish. But I thought that the writer to The Saturday Review might already be getting a part of his wish. How many people there were who did not remember—who indeed had never learned—that Proust or James or Mann or Joyce had ever lived! How many of them there were, and how many more of their children there were, who did not remember—who indeed had never learned—that Jonah or King Arthur or Galahad or Charlemagne had ever lived! And in the end all of us would die, and not know, then, that anybody had ever lived; and the writer to The Saturday Review would have got not part of his wish but all of it.

And if, meanwhile, some people grieved to think of so much gone and so much more to go, they were the exception. Or, rather, the exceptions: millions of exceptions. There were enough exceptions to make a good-sized country; I thought, with pleasure, of walking through the streets of that country and having the children tell me who Charlemagne was.

I decided not to think of Charlemagne any more. . . . My samples weren't really random; I was being exceptionally unjust to that exceptionally normal girl and the school that had helped to make her so. My quarrel was not so much with her education as with her world, and our quarrels with the world are like our quarrels with God: no matter how right we are, we are wrong. *But who wants to be right all the time?* I thought, smiling; and said good-by to Charlemagne with the same smile.

Instead of thinking, I looked at The New York Times Book Review; there in the midst of so many books I could surely forget that some people don't read any. And as Rilke says, we are—some of us are—"beaten at/ By books as if by perpetual bells"; we can well, as he bids us, "rejoice/ When between two books the sky shines to you, silent." In the beginning was the Word, and man has made books of it.

I read quietly along, but the book I was reading was continued on page 47; and as I turned to it I came to a two-page advertisement of the Revised Standard Version of the Bible. It was a sober, careful, authorized sort of advertisement, but it was, truly, an advertisement. It said:

> In these anxious days, the Bible offers a practical antidote for sorrow, cynicism, and despair. But the King James version is often difficult reading.
> If *you* have too seldom opened your Bible because the way it is

> written makes it hard for you to understand, the Revised Standard
> Version can bring you an exciting new experience.
> Here is a Bible so enjoyable you find you pick it up twice as
> often.

Tennyson and Longfellow and the Bible—what was there that wasn't
difficult reading? And a few days before that, I had torn out of the
paper—I got it and read it again, and it was hard for me to read it—a
Gallup Poll that began: "Although the United States has the highest
level of formal education in the world, fewer people here read books
than in any other major democracy. Fewer than one adult American
in every five was found to be reading a book at the time of the survey.
[Twenty years ago 29% were found to be reading a book; today 17%
are.] In England, where the typical citizen has far less formal schooling
than the typical citizen here, nearly three times as many read books.
Even among American college graduates fewer than half read books."

It went on and on; I was so tired that, as I read, the phrase "read
books" kept beating in my brain, and getting mixed up with Charlemagne; compared to other major monarchs, I thought sleepily, fewer
than one fifth of Charlemagne reads books. I read on as best I could,
but I thought of the preface to Adventures for Readers, and the letter
to The Saturday Review, and the advertisement in The New York
Times Book Review, and the highest level of formal education in the
world; and they all went around and around in my head and said to
me an advertisement named Adventures for Non-Readers:

> In these anxious days, reading books offers a practical antidote
> for sorrow, cynicism, and despair. But books are often, in the
> original, difficult reading.
> If *you* have too seldom opened books because the way they are
> written makes them hard for you to understand, our Revised
> Standard Versions of books, in their simplified, televised form,
> can bring you an exciting new experience.
> Here are books so enjoyable you find you turn them on twice
> as often.

I shook myself; I was dreaming. As I went to bed the words of the
eighth-grade class' teacher, when the class got to Evangeline, kept
echoing in my ears: "We're coming to a long poem now, boys and girls.
Now don't be babies and start counting the pages." I lay there like a
baby, counting the pages over and over, counting the pages.

> For readers who wish to pursue this subject further the following
> books are recommended:
> Jarrell, Randall. Poetry and the Age. Vintage. 95¢

Lynes, Russell. Snobs. Harper Taste-makers. $1.00. Harper.
Freud, Sigmund. Civilization and Its Discontents. Anchor. $1.25
Auerbach, Erich. Mimesis. Anchor. $1.45
Linton, Ralph. The Study of Man. Appleton. $5.00

Questions and Suggestions

1. Restate Jarrell's distinction between "Literature" and "Instant Literature." What does he mean by "Revolution of the Word" and "the makers of Instant Literature"?
2. What fallacies does he attack?
3. Why does he dislike *The Reader's Digest*? Is his reference to it both figurative and literal?
4. Summarize his ideas about the differences in Victorian and American cultures. Do you believe he offers an honest appraisal of both? To learn more about Victorian times, read Lytton Strachey's *Queen Victoria*.
5. Why does Jarrell think present educational practices are not so good as those of several decades ago?
6. What bearing on the essay does the question in the third paragraph have?
7. What methods does Jarrell use to produce unity? Do you think he used a formal or an informal outline or no outline at all in writing the essay?
8. What is the tone?

Ideas for Writing

1. Explain why your father or uncle believes in keeping alive his knowledge of how to make a chair, to make dyes out of herbs, to tie his own flies, or to tend a garden. Are you aware that any knowledge has passed or is passing from our communities as the older generations die?
2. Visualize through a point of view similar to Jarrell's some member of your family who dotes on *The Reader's Digest* or *The Saturday Evening Post*. Observe a college friend who reveals much about himself as he talks about the magazines to which his family subscribes. Or observe a specific family that buys its books and records from grocery stores, with coupons, or from the varied clubs.
3. Why wasn't the study of languages as important in your high school as the courses in domestic science or shop?
4. Evaluate your preparation for college reading and writing.
5. What distinguishes a good or great college from a mediocre one? For further enlightenment, read John Henry Newman's *The Idea of a University*.

THINGS

D. H. LAWRENCE

The son of a coal miner, David Herbert Lawrence (1885–1930), one of the most influential writers of this century, was born in Eastwood, Nottinghamshire, and attended Nottingham University. Except for a brief period, after the publication of his first novel, *The White Peacock,* he made his living by writing. He and his wife Frieda traveled in many parts of the world, including a lengthy stay in New Mexico. A writer who often transmuted facts into fiction, Lawrence may have had the American writer Mabel Dodge Luhan in mind when he created Mrs. Melville.

They were true idealists, from New England. But that is some time ago: before the war. Several years before the war, they met and married; he a tall, keen-eyed young man from Connecticut, she a smallish, demure, Puritan-looking young woman from Massachusetts. They both had a little money. Not much, however. Even added together, it didn't make three thousand dollars a year. Still—they were free. Free!

Ah! Freedom! To be free to live one's own life! To be twenty-five and twenty-seven, a pair of true idealists with a mutual love of beauty, and an inclination towards "Indian thought"—meaning, alas, Mrs. Besant—and an income a little under three thousand dollars a year! But what is money? All one wishes to do is to live a full and beautiful life. In Europe, of course, right at the fountain-head of tradition. It might possibly be done in America: in New England, for example. But at a forfeiture of a certain amount of "beauty." True beauty takes a long time to mature. The baroque is only half-beautiful, half-matured. No, the real silver bloom, the real golden-sweet bouquet of beauty had its roots in the Renaissance, not in any later or shallower period.

Therefore the two idealists, who were married in New Haven, sailed

From *The Lovely Lady.* Copyright 1933 by the Estate of D. H. Lawrence. Reprinted by permission of The Viking Press, Inc.

at once to Paris: Paris of the old days. They had a studio apartment
on the Boulevard Montparnasse, and they became real Parisians, in the
old, delightful sense, not in the modern, vulgar. It was the shimmer of
the pure impressionists, Monet and his followers, the world seen in
terms of pure light, light broken and unbroken. How lovely! How lovely
the nights, the river, the mornings in the old streets and by the flower-
stalls and the book-stalls, the afternoons up on Montmartre or in the
Tuileries, the evenings on the boulevards!

They both painted, but not desperately. Art had not taken them by
the throat, and they did not take Art by the throat. They painted: that's
all. They knew people—nice people, if possible, though one had to take
them mixed. And they were happy.

Yet it seems as if human beings must set their claws in *something*. To
be "free," to be "living a full and beautiful life," you must, alas, be
attached to something. A "full and beautiful life" means a tight attachment to *something*—at least, it is so for all idealists—or else a certain
boredom supervenes; there is a certain waving of loose ends upon the
air, like the waving, yearning tendrils of the vine that spread and rotate,
seeking something to clutch, something up which to climb towards the
necessary sun. Finding nothing, the vine can only trail, half-fulfilled,
upon the ground. Such is freedom!—a clutching of the right pole. And
human beings are all vines. But especially the idealist. He is a vine, and
he needs to clutch and climb. And he despises the man who is a mere
potato, or turnip, or lump of wood.

Our idealists were frightfully happy, but they were all the time
reaching out for something to cotton on to. At first, Paris was enough.
They explored Paris *thoroughly*. And they learned French till they almost felt like French people, they could speak it so glibly.

Still, you know, you never talk French with your *soul*. It can't be
done. And though it's very thrilling, at first, talking in French to
clever Frenchmen—they seem *so* much cleverer than oneself—still, in
the long run, it is not satisfying. The endlessly clever *materialism* of the
French leaves you cold, in the end, gives a sense of barrenness and incompatibility with true New England depth. So our two idealists felt.

They turned away from France—but ever so gently. France had disappointed them. "We've loved it, and we've got a great deal out of it.
But after a while, after a considerable while, several years, in fact, Paris
leaves one feeling disappointed. It hasn't quite got what one wants."

"But Paris isn't France."

"No, perhaps not. France is quite different from Paris. And France

is lovely—quite lovely. But *to us,* though we love it, it doesn't say a
great deal."

So, when the war came, the idealists moved to Italy. And they loved
Italy. They found it beautiful, and more poignant than France. It
seemed much nearer to the New England conception of beauty: something pure, and full of sympathy, without the *materialism* and the
cynicism of the French. The two idealists seemed to breathe their own
true air in Italy.

And in Italy, much more than in Paris, they felt they could thrill
to the teachings of the Buddha. They entered the swelling stream of
modern Buddhistic emotion, and they read the books, and they practised
meditation, and they deliberately set themselves to eliminate from their
own souls greed, pain, and sorrow. They did not realize—yet—that
Buddha's very eagerness to free himself from pain and sorrow is in itself a sort of greed. No, they dreamed of a perfect world, from which
all greed, and nearly all pain, and a great deal of sorrow, were
eliminated.

But America entered the war, so the two idealists had to help. They
did hospital work. And though their experience made them realize more
than ever that greed, pain, and sorrow *should* be eliminated from the
world, nevertheless the Buddhism, or the theosophy, didn't emerge very
triumphant from the long crisis. Somehow, somewhere, in some part
of themselves, they felt that greed, pain, and sorrow would never be
eliminated, because most people don't care about eliminating them, and
never will care. Our idealists were far too western to think of abandoning all the world to damnation, while they saved their two selves. They
were far too unselfish to sit tight under a bho-tree and reach Nirvana in
a mere couple.

It was more than that, though. They simply hadn't enough *Seitzfleisch*
to squat under a bho-tree and get to Nirvana by contemplating anything,
least of all their own navel. If the whole wide world was not going to
be saved, they, personally, were not so very keen on being saved just
by themselves. No, it would be so lonesome. They were New Eng-
landers, so it must be all or nothing. Greed, pain, and sorrow must either
be eliminated from *all the world*, or else, what was the use of eliminating them from oneself? No use at all! One was just a victim.

And so, although they still *loved* "Indian thought," and felt very
tender about it: well, to go back to our metaphor, the pole up which
the green and anxious vines had clambered so far now proved dry-
rotten. It snapped, and the vines came slowly subsiding to earth again.

There was no crack and crash. The vines held themselves up by their own foliage, for a while. But they subsided. The beanstalk of "Indian thought" had given way before Jack and Jill had climbed off the tip of it to a further world.

They subsided with a slow rustle back to earth again. But they made no outcry. They were again "disappointed." But they never admitted it. "Indian thought" had let them down. But they never complained. Even to one another, they never said a word. They were disappointed, faintly but deeply disillusioned, and they both knew it. But the knowledge was tacit.

And they still had so much in their lives. They still had Italy—dear Italy. And they still had freedom, the priceless treasure. And they still had so much "beauty." About the fulness of their lives they were not quite so sure. They had one little boy, whom they loved as parents should love their children, but whom they wisely refrained from fastening upon, to build their lives on him. No, no, they must live their own lives! They still had strength of mind to know that.

But they were now no longer so very young. Twenty-five and twenty-seven had become thirty-five and thirty-seven. And though they had had a very wonderful time in Europe, and though they still loved Italy —dear Italy!—yet: they were disappointed. They had got a lot out of it: oh, a very great deal indeed! Still, it hadn't given them quite, not quite, what they had expected. Europe was lovely, but it was dead. Living in Europe, you were living on the past. And Europeans, with all their superficial charm, were not really charming. They were materialistic, they had no real soul. They just did not understand the inner urge of the spirit, because the inner urge was dead in them, they were all survivals. There, that was the truth about Europeans: they were survivals, with no more getting ahead in them.

It was another bean-pole, another vine-support crumbled under the green life of the vine. And very bitter it was, this time. For up the old tree-trunk of Europe the green vine had been clambering silently for more than ten years, ten hugely important years, the years of real living. The two idealists had *lived* in Europe, lived on Europe and on European life and European things as vines in an everlasting vineyard.

They had made their home here: a home such as you could never make in America. Their watchword had been "beauty." They had rented, the last four years, the second floor of an old Palazzo on the Arno, and here they had all their "things." And they derived a profound, profound satisfaction from their apartment: the lofty, silent, ancient rooms with windows on the river, with glistening, dark-red floors, and the beautiful furniture that the idealists had "picked up."

Yes, unknown to themselves, the lives of the idealists had been running with a fierce swiftness horizontally, all the time. They had become tense, fierce hunters of "things" for their home. While their souls were climbing up to the sun of old European culture or old Indian thought, their passions were running horizontally, clutching at "things." Of course they did not buy the things for the things' sakes, but for the sake of "beauty." They looked upon their home as a place entirely furnished by loveliness, not by "things" at all. Valerie had some very lovely curtains at the windows of the long *salotto*, looking on the river: curtains of queer ancient material that looked like finely-knitted silk, most beautifully faded down from vermilion and orange, and gold, and black, down to a sheer soft glow. Valerie hardly ever came into the *salotto* without mentally falling on her knees before the curtains. "Chartres!" she said. "To me they are Chartres!" And Melville never turned and looked at his sixteenth-century Venetian bookcase, with its two or three dozen of choice books, without feeling his marrow stir in his bones. The holy of holies!

The child silently, almost sinisterly, avoided any rude contact with these ancient monuments of furniture, as if they had been nests of sleeping cobras, or that "thing" most perilous to the touch, the Ark of the Covenant. His childish awe was silent and cold, but final.

Still, a couple of New England idealists cannot live merely on the bygone glory of their furniture. At least, one couple could not. They got used to the marvellous Bologna cupboard, they got used to the wonderful Venetian bookcase, and the books, and the Siena curtains and bronzes, and the lovely sofas and side-tables and chairs they had "picked up" in Paris. Oh, they had been picking things up since the first day they landed in Europe. And they were still at it. It is the last interest Europe can offer to an outsider: or to an insider either.

When people came, and were thrilled by the Melville interior, then Valerie and Erasmus felt they had not lived in vain: that they still were living. But in the long mornings, when Erasmus was desultorily working at Renaissance Florentine literature, and Valerie was attending to the apartment: and in the long hours after lunch; and in the long, usually very cold and oppressive evenings in the ancient palazzo: then the halo died from around the furniture, and the things became things, lumps of matter that just stood there or hung there, *ad infinitum,* and said nothing; and Valerie and Erasmus almost hated them. The glow of beauty, like every other glow, dies down unless it is fed. The idealists still dearly loved their things. But they had got them. And the sad fact is, things that glow vividly while you're getting them, go almost quite cold after a year or two. Unless, of course, people envy them very much, and the museums are pining for them. And the Melvilles' "things," though very good, were not quite so good as that.

So, the glow gradually went out of everything, out of Europe, out of Italy—"the Italians are *dears*"—even out of that marvellous apartment on the Arno. "Why, if I had this apartment, I'd never, never even want to go out of doors! It's too lovely and perfect." That was something, of course—to hear that.

And yet Valerie and Erasmus went out of doors: they even went out to get away from its ancient, cold-floored, stone-heavy silence and dead dignity. "We're living on the past, you know, Dick," said Valerie to her husband. She called him Dick.

They were grimly hanging on. They did not like to give in. They did not like to own up that they were through. For twelve years, now, they had been "free" people living a "full and beautiful life." And America for twelve years had been their anathema, the Sodom and Gomorrah of industrial materialism.

It wasn't easy to own that you were "through." They hated to admit that they wanted to go back. But at last, reluctantly, they decided to go, "for the boy's sake."—"We can't *bear* to leave Europe. But Peter is an American, so he had better look at America while he's young." The Melvilles had an entirely English accent and manner; almost; a little Italian and French here and there.

They left Europe behind, but they took as much of it along with them as possible. Several van-loads, as a matter of fact. All those adorable and irreplaceable "things." And all arrived in New York, idealists, child, and the huge bulk of Europe they had lugged along.

Valerie had dreamed of a pleasant apartment, perhaps on Riverside Drive, where it was not so expensive as east of Fifth Avenue, and where all their wonderful things would look marvellous. She and Erasmus house-hunted. But alas! their income was quite under three thousand dollars a year. They found—well, everybody knows what they found. Two small rooms and a kitchenette, and don't let us unpack a *thing!*

The chunk of Europe which they had bitten off went into a warehouse, at fifty dollars a month. And they sat in two small rooms and a kitchenette, and wondered why they'd done it.

Erasmus, of course, ought to get a job. This was what was written on the wall, and what they both pretended not to see. But it had been the strange, vague threat that the Statue of Liberty had always held over them: "Thou shalt get a job!" Erasmus had the tickets, as they say. A scholastic career was still possible for him. He had taken his exams brilliantly at Yale, and had kept up his "researches," all the time he had been in Europe.

But both he and Valerie shuddered. A scholastic career! The scholastic world! The *American* scholastic world! Shudder upon shudder! Give up their freedom, their full and beautiful life? Never! Never! Erasmus would be forty next birthday.

The "things" remained in warehouse. Valerie went to look at them. It cost her a dollar an hour, and horrid pangs. The "things" poor things, looked a bit shabby and wretched, in that warehouse.

However, New York was not all America. There was the great clean West. So the Melvilles went West, with Peter, but without the things. They tried living the simple life, in the mountains. But doing their own chores became almost a nightmare. "Things" are all very well to look at, but it's awful handling them, even when they're beautiful. To be the slave of hideous things, to keep a stove going, cook meals, wash dishes, carry water and clean floors: pure horror of sordid anti-life!

In the cabin on the mountains, Valerie dreamed of Florence, the lost apartment; and her Bologna cupboard and Louis-Quinze chairs, above all, her "Chartres" curtains, stood in New York and costing fifty dollars a month.

A millionaire friend came to the rescue, offering them a cottage on the California coast—California! Where the new soul is to be born in man. With joy the idealists moved a little farther west, catching at new vine-props of hope.

And finding them straws! The millionaire cottage was perfectly equipped. It was perhaps as labour-savingly perfect as is possible: electric heating and cooking, a white-and-pearl-enamelled kitchen, nothing to make dirt except the human being himself. In an hour or so the idealists had got through their chores. They were "free"—free to hear the great Pacific pounding the coast, and to feel a new soul filling their bodies.

Alas! the Pacific pounded the coast with hideous brutality, brute force itself! And the new soul, instead of sweetly stealing into their bodies, seemed only meanly to gnaw the old soul out of their bodies. To

feel you are under the fist of the most blind and crunching brute force:
to feel that your cherished idealist's soul is being gnawed out of you,
and only irritation left in place of it: well, it isn't good enough.

After about nine months, the idealists departed from the Californian
west. It had been a great experience, they were glad to have had it.
But, in the long run, the West was not the place for them, and they
knew it. No, the people who wanted new souls had better get them.
They, Valerie and Erasmus Melville, would like to develop the old
soul a little further. Anyway, they had not felt any influx of new soul,
on the Californian coast. On the contrary.

So, with a slight hole in their material capital, they returned to
Massachusetts and paid a visit to Valerie's parents, taking the boy
along. The grandparents welcomed the child—poor expatriated boy
—and were rather cold to Valerie, but really cold to Erasmus. Valerie's
mother definitely said to Valerie, one day, that Erasmus ought to take
a job, so that Valerie could live decently. Valerie haughtily reminded
her mother of the beautiful apartment on the Arno, and the "wonderful" things in store in New York, and of the "marvelous and satisfying life" she and Erasmus had led. Valerie's mother said that she
didn't think her daughter's life looked so very marvellous at present:
homeless, with a husband idle at the age of forty, a child to educate, and
a dwindling capital: looked the reverse of marvellous to *her*. Let
Erasmus take some post in one of the universities.

"What post? What university?" interrupted Valerie.

"That could be found, considering your father's connections and
Erasmus's qualifications," replied Valerie's mother. "And you could
get all your valuable things out of store, and have a really lovely home,
which everybody in America would be proud to visit. As it is, your
furniture is eating up your income, and you are living like rats in a
hole, with nowhere to go to."

This was very true. Valerie was beginning to pine for a home, with
her "things." Of course she could have sold her furniture for a substantial sum. But nothing would have induced her to. Whatever else
passed away, religions, cultures, continents, and hopes, Valerie would
never part from the "things" which she and Erasmus had collected
with such passion. To these she was nailed.

But she and Erasmus still would not give up that freedom, that
full and beautiful life they had so believed in. Erasmus cursed America. He did not *want* to earn a living. He panted for Europe.

Leaving the boy in charge of Valerie's parents, the two idealists once more set off for Europe. In New York they paid two dollars and looked for a brief, bitter hour at their "things." They sailed "student class"— that is, third. Their income now was less than two thousand dollars, instead of three. And they made straight for Paris—cheap Paris.

They found Europe, this time, a complete failure. "We have returned like dogs to our vomit," said Erasmus; "but the vomit has staled in the meantime." He found he couldn't stand Europe. It irritated every nerve in his body. He hated America too. But America at least was a darn sight better than this miserable, dirt-eating continent; which was by no means cheap any more, either.

Valerie, with her heart on her things—she had really burned to get them out of that warehouse, where they had stood now for three years, eating up two thousand dollars—wrote to her mother she thought Erasmus would come back if he could get some suitable work in America. Erasmus, in a state of frustration bordering on rage and insanity, just went round Italy in a poverty-stricken fashion, his coat-cuffs frayed, hating everything with intensity. And when a post was found for him in Cleveland University, to teach French, Italian, and Spanish literature, his eyes grew more beady, and his long, queer face grew sharper and more rat-like, with utter baffled fury. He was forty, and the job was upon him.

"I think you'd better accept, dear. You don't care for Europe any longer. As you say, it's dead and finished. They offer us a house on the college lot, and mother says there's room in it for all our things. I think we'd better cable 'Accept'."

He glowered at her like a cornered rat. One almost expected to see rat's whiskers twitching at the sides of the sharp nose.

"Shall I send the cablegram?" she asked.

"Send it!" he blurted.

And she went out and sent it.

He was a changed man, quieter, much less irritable. A load was off him. He was inside the cage.

But when he looked at the furnaces of Cleveland, vast and like the greatest of black forests, with red and white-hot cascades of gushing metal, and tiny gnomes of men, and terrific noises, gigantic, he said to Valerie:

"Say what you like, Valerie, this is the biggest thing the modern world has to show."

And when they were in their up-to-date little house on the college lot of Cleveland University, and that woebegone débris of Europe,

Bologna cupboard, Venice book-shelves, Ravenna bishop's chair, Louis-Quinze side-tables, "Chartres" curtains, Siena bronze lamps, all were arrayed, and all looked perfectly out of keeping, and therefore very impressive; and when the idealists had had a bunch of gaping people in, and Erasmus had showed off in his best European manner, but still quite cordial and American; and Valerie had been most ladylike, but for all that, "we prefer America"; then Erasmus said, looking at her with queer sharp eyes of a rat:

"Europe's the mayonnaise all right, but America supplies the good old lobster—what?"

"Every time!" she said, with satisfaction.

And he peered at her. He was in the cage: but it was safe inside. And she, evidently, was her real self at last. She had got the goods. Yet round his nose was a queer, evil, scholastic look, of pure scepticism. But he liked lobster.

Questions and Suggestions

1. Does Lawrence want you to like the Melvilles, feel pity for them, despise them, or merely recognize the superficiality of their ideals?

2. Does he treat them as types or as individuals?

3. What are some of Lawrence's favorite theories, his special hates? How does he weave these ideas into the theme of the story?

4. What does he think, at least in general, about idealists? Does he believe that " 'Indian thought' had let them [the Melvilles] down"? Does he think that when they were in Florence they actually lived a " 'full and beautiful life' "? Did they ever become "real Parisians"? What does he mean when he says that their lives "had been running . . . horizontally, all the time"?

5. What had Melville's father hoped for in his son when he named him Erasmus? How successful a teacher at Cleveland University would Erasmus (Dick) Melville be?

6. Although Lawrence uses many fragments and you may find his punctuation to be almost a personal affair, point out a number of strong sentences that make his story move rapidly.

7. Explain how he sometimes creates the flavor of talk without the use of quotation marks.

8. Comment on his use of repetition.

9. What matters does Lawrence treat humorously?

Ideas for Writing

1. In what ways do the Melvilles remind you of people whom you know? Have some of your friends left the university or your home town in order that they might "live" in Greenwich Village, San Francisco, Taos, or Paris?

2. What influence has Zen Buddhism had on your campus? Is there some other fad which the students feel they must follow if they are to be "in"?

3. Why does the attractive girl who is a B student often have an easier time in getting married than the equally attractive girl who is an A student?

4. Do you visit in any house that has been decorated by an "interior architect"? What effect does it have upon you?

5. What was your reaction to a friend's description of his trip to Europe when he avoided the tourists and became just one of the "natives"?

6. Use examples that will leave no doubt in your reader's mind that you are describing a cultural snob or a dilettante.

THE MIND OF MAN

JOHN STEINBECK

Born in Salinas, California, John Steinbeck (1902–), who studied at Stanford, varies the mood often in *East of Eden,* an ambitious novel centered around the Trask family. A prolific and most versatile writer, both in form and content, and the winner of a Pulitzer Prize for *The Grapes of Wrath,* Steinbeck lost a job as a young reporter because he failed to give all the facts that his editor demanded. During World War II, however, he wrote some of the finest accounts to come from any Theater of Operations, some of these essays being included in *Once There Was a War.*

Sometimes a kind of glory lights up the mind of a man. It happens to nearly everyone. You can feel it growing or preparing like a fuse burning toward dynamite. It is a feeling in the stomach, a delight of the nerves, of the forearms. The skin tastes the air, and every deep-drawn breath is sweet. Its beginning has the pleasure of a great stretching yawn; it flashes in the brain and the whole world glows outside your eyes. A man may have lived all of his life in the gray, and the land and trees of him dark and somber. The events, even the important ones, may have trooped by faceless and pale. And then—the glory—so that a cricket song sweetens his ears, the smell of the earth rises chanting to his nose, and dappling light under a tree blesses his eyes. Then a man pours outward, a torrent of him, and yet he is not diminished. And I guess a man's importance in the world can be measured by the quality and number of his glories. It is a lonely thing but it relates us to the world. It is the mother of all creativeness, and it sets each man separate from all other men.

I don't know how it will be in the years to come. There are monstrous changes taking place in the world, forces shaping a future whose face we do not know. Some of these forces seem evil to us, perhaps not in themselves but because their tendency is to eliminate other things we hold good. It is true that two men can lift a bigger stone than one man. A group can build automobiles quicker and better than one man, and bread from a huge factory is cheaper and more uniform. When our food and clothing and housing all are born in the complication of mass production, mass method is bound to get into our thinking and to eliminate all other thinking. In our time mass or collective production has entered our economics, our politics, and even our religion, so that some nations have substituted the idea collective for the idea God. This in my time is the danger. There is great tension in the world, tension toward a breaking point, and men are unhappy and confused.

At such a time it seems natural and good to me to ask myself these questions. What do I believe in? What must I fight for and what must I fight against?

Our species is the only creative species, and it has only one creative instrument, the individual mind and spirit of a man. Nothing was ever created by two men. There are no good collaborations, whether in music, in art, in poetry, in mathematics, in philosophy. Once the miracle of creation has taken place, the group can build and extend it, but the group never invents anything. The preciousness lies in the lonely mind of a man.

And now the forces marshaled around the concept of the group have declared a war of extermination on that preciousness, the mind

of man. By disparagement, by starvation, by repressions, forced direction, and the stunning hammerblows of conditioning, the free, roving
mind is being pursued, roped, blunted, drugged. It is a sad suicidal
course our species seems to have taken.

And this I believe: that the free, exploring mind of the individual
human is the most valuable thing in the world. And this I would fight
for: the freedom of the mind to take any direction it wishes, undirected. And this I must fight against: any idea, religion, or government which limits or destroys the individual. This is what I am and
what I am about. I can understand why a system built on a pattern
must try to destroy the free mind, for that is one thing which can by
inspection destroy such a system. Surely I can understand this, and I
hate it and I will fight against it to preserve the one thing that separates us from the uncreative beasts. If the glory can be killed, we
are lost.

Questions and Suggestions

1. What is the narrator's thesis?
2. How does Steinbeck's narrator define or perhaps limit the
   concept of the "freedom of the mind"? In this context how
   important is the word "undirected"?
3. Measure the Melvilles by the number and strength of their
   "glories." Did any idea limit or destroy them? Were they ever
   creative?
4. Who are "the uncreative beasts"?
5. Most people grant that a political state can limit and destroy
   an individual. Do you think that a religion can do the same?
6. Cite several examples that show how through the influence
   of the assembly line "mass method is bound to get into our
   thinking and to eliminate all other thinking."
7. What societies "have substituted the idea collective for the
   idea God"? What changes does such a substitution bring
   about?
8. Read Dylan Thomas's "The Force That Through the Green
   Fuse Drives the Flower" and see if you think the speaker
   could have had this poem in mind when he spoke of the
   "glory [that] lights up the mind of a man."

Ideas for Writing

1. Do you have any friends who "by disparagement, by starvation, by repressions, forced direction, and the stunning hammerblows of conditioning" have been ruined as potentially
   valuable members of society?

2. How is "brainwashing" accomplished and what lasting effects does it have? Read Dr. Robert J. Lifton's *Thought Reform*, a study based on interviews that he had with forty individuals who had undergone the treatment.

3. Since coming to college have you made any ill-advised efforts to conform? What effect do teachers and administrators have upon the conformity of the student body? Why is there more or less conformity among college students than among high school students?

4. What can you say about the loneliness of the individual who fights to be himself? Have you noticed yourself as having more respect than you formerly had for the student who tries to remain an individual?

5. If you have ever worked on an assembly line, compare your experiences with those that Harvey Swados uses in his collection of stories, *On the Line*.

6. Should every man be entitled to his own opinions?

THE MORALS OF EXTERMINATION

LEWIS MUMFORD

Although Lewis Mumford (1895–), who was born in Flushing, New York, attended several colleges and universities, he never received a degree. Because of his astute books and essays that deal with American architecture, many readers mistakenly think he received his training as an architect or as a city planner. The author of many influential and far-ranging works, Mumford, a social philosopher, is chiefly concerned with education, politics, philosophy, and religion. For many years he has opposed fascistic tendencies and, if you consult his essays in *Air Affairs*, you will see that he has long been an opponent of extermination bombing.

Since 1945, the American government has devoted the better part of our national energies to preparations for wholesale human extermination. This curious enterprise has been disguised as a scien-

From *The Atlantic Monthly*, October 1959. Reprinted by permission of the author.

tifically sound method of ensuring world peace and national security, but it has obviously failed at every point on both counts. Our reckless experimental explosion of nuclear weapons is only a persuasive salesman's sample of what a nuclear war would produce, but even this has already done significant damage to the human race. With poetic justice, the earliest victims of our experiments toward genocide—sharing honors with the South Pacific islanders and the Japanese fishermen—have been our own children, and even more, our children's prospective children.

Almost from the beginning, our investment in nuclear weapons has been openly directed against a single country, Soviet Russia. In our government's concern with the self-imposed problem of containing Russia and restricting by force alone the area of Communist penetration, we have turned our back on more vital human objectives. Today the political and military strategy our leaders framed on the supposition that our country had a permanent superiority in nuclear power is bankrupt, so completely that the business probably cannot be liquidated without serious losses.

As things stand now, we are not able to conduct even a justifiable police action, as a representative of the United Nations, with the backing of a majority of the nations, without the permission of Russia and China. When they refuse permission, as they did in Korea, the limited war our strategists fancy is still open to us turns into an unlimited humiliation, as the painful truce that continues in Korea should remind us, for every original issue remains unsettled. But if we challenge that veto, our only recourse is to our absolute weapons, now as fatal to ourselves and the rest of mankind as they would be to Russia and China. The distinguished army combat generals who have publicly recognized this state of impotence have been forced out of the armed services.

This situation should give us pause. While every scientific advance in nuclear weapons and intercontinental missiles only widens to planetary dimensions the catastrophe we have been preparing, our leaders still concentrate the nation's efforts on hastening these advances. Why, then, do we still listen to those mistaken counsels that committed us to the Cold War, though our own military plans have wiped out the possibility of war itself and replaced it by total annihilation as the only foreseeable terminus of the tensions we have done our full share to produce? By what standard of prudence do we trust our lives to political, military, and scientific advisers who have staked our national existence on a single set of weapons and have already lost that shortsighted gamble, even if they become desperate enough to use these weapons or remain blind enough to believe that they can conceal that loss by not using them?

What was it that set in motion the chain reaction of errors, miscalculations, delusions, and compulsions that have pushed us into the impossible situation we now occupy? Every day that we delay in facing our national mistakes adds to both the cumulative dangers that threaten us and the difficulty of undoing them.

The first step toward framing a new policy is to trace our path back to the point where we adopted our fatal commitment to weapons of mass extermination. This moral debacle, it is important to remember, was not a response to any threat by Russia or by Communism; still less was it imposed by Russia's possession of similar weapons. Actually, the acceptance of extermination antedated the invention of the atom bomb.

The principles upon which the strategy of extermination was based were first enunciated by fascist military theorists, notably General Douhet, who believed, like our own Major Seversky, that a small air force could take the place of a large army by confining its efforts to mass attacks on civilians and undermining the national will to resist. This reversion to the vicious Bronze Age practice of total war was a natural extension of fascism's readiness to reintroduce terrorism and torture as instruments of government. When these methods were first carried into action, by Mussolini in Abyssinia, by Hitler in Warsaw and Rotterdam, they awakened horror in our still morally sensitive breasts. The creed that could justify such actions was, we thought correctly, not merely antidemocratic but antihuman.

In the midst of World War II a moral reversal took place among the English-speaking Allies, such a transposition as happened by accident in the final duel in *Hamlet,* when Hamlet picks up the weapon Laertes had poisoned in advance in order to make sure of his enemy's death. The fascist powers became the victims of their own strategy, for both the United States and Britain adopted what was politely called "obliteration bombing," which had as its object the total destruction of great cities and the terrorization and massacre of their inhabitants.

By taking over this method as a cheap substitute for conventional warfare—cheap in soldiers' lives, costly in its expenditure of other human lives and in the irreplaceable historic accumulations of countless lifetimes—these democratic governments sanctioned the dehumanized techniques of fascism. This was Nazidom's firmest victory and democracy's most servile surrender. That moral reversal undermined the eventual military triumph of the democracies, and it has poisoned our political and military policies ever since.

Civilized warfare has always been an atrocity per se, even when practiced by gallant men fighting in a just cause. But in the course of five thousand years certain inhibitions and moral safeguards had been set up. Thus, poisoning the water supply and slaying the unarmed inhabitants of a city were no longer within the modern soldier's code, however gratifying they might once have been to an Ashurbanipal or a Genghis Khan, moral monsters whose names have become infamous in history. Overnight, as it were, our own countrymen became such moral monsters. In principle, the extermination camps where the Nazis incinerated over six million helpless Jews were no different from the urban crematoriums our air force improvised in its attacks by napalm bombs on Tokyo. By these means, in a single night, we roasted alive more people than were killed by atom bombs in either Hiroshima or Nagasaki. Our aims were different, but our methods were those of mankind's worst enemy.

Up to this point, war had been an operation conducted by military forces against military targets. By long-established convention, a token part, the army, stood for the greater whole, the nation. Even when an army was totally defeated and wiped out, the nation it represented lived to tell the tale; neither unarmed prisoners nor civilians were killed to seal a defeat or celebrate a victory. Even our air force, the chief shaper of our present policy, once prided itself on its pin-point bombing, done in daylight to ensure that only military targets would be hit.

As late as the spring of 1942, as I know by personal observation, a memorandum was circulated among military advisers in Washington propounding this dilemma: If by fighting the war against Japan by orthodox methods it might require five or ten years to conquer the enemy, while with incendiary air attacks on Japanese cities Japan's resistance might be broken in a year or two, would it be morally justifiable to use the second means? Now it is hard to say which is more astonishing, that the morality of total extermination was then seriously debated in military circles or that today its morality is taken for granted, as outside debate, even among a large part of the clergy.

More than any other event that has taken place in modern times this sudden radical change-over from war to collective extermination reversed the whole course of human history.

Plainly, the acceptance of mass extermination as a normal outcome of war undermined all the moral inhibitions that have kept man's murderous fantasies from active expression. War, however brutal and devastating, had a formal beginning and could come to an end by some formal process of compromise or surrender. But no one has the faintest notion how nuclear extermination, once begun, could be brought to an end. Still less can anyone guess what purpose would be accomplished by it, except a release by death from intolerable anxiety and fear. But this is to anticipate. What is important to bear in mind is that atomic weapons did not bring about this first decisive change; they merely gave our already de-moralized strategy a more effective means of expression.

Once extermination became acceptable, the confined tumor of war, itself an atavistic pseudo-organ, turned into a cancer that would invade the blood stream of civilization. Now the smallest sore of conflict or hostility might fatally spread through the whole organism, immune to all those protective moral and political restraints that a healthy body can mobilize for such occasions.

By the time the atom bomb was invented our authorities needed no special justification for using it. The humane pleas for withholding the weapon, made by the atomic scientists, suddenly awakened to a moral crisis they had not foreseen while working on the bomb, were automatically disposed of by well-established precedent, already three years in operation. Still, the dramatic nature of the explosions at Hiroshima and Nagasaki threw a white light of horror and doubt over the whole process; for a moment a sense of moral guilt counteracted our exorbitant pride. This reaction proved as short-lived as it was belated. Yet it prompted Henry L. Stimson, a public servant whose admirable personal conduct had never been open to question, to publish a magazine article defending the official decision to use the atom bomb.

The argument Mr. Stimson advanced in favor of atomic genocide— a name invented later but studiously reserved for the acts of our enemies—was that it shortened the war and saved perhaps more than a million precious American lives. There is no need here to debate that highly debatable point. But on those same practical, "humanitarian" grounds, systematic torture might be employed by an advancing army to deter guerrilla fighters and to blackmail the remaining population into accepting promptly the torturer's terms.

That only a handful of people ventured to make this criticism indicates the depth of moral apathy to which our countrymen had sunk in less than a dozen years. The Those who used this illustration, however, were not surprised to find that the French, themselves the victims of Hitler's carefully devised plans of torture and mass extermination, would authorize the use of military torture in Algeria a decade later. Our own country had forecast that depravity by our national conduct. This conduct still remains without public examination or repentance, but, unfortunately, retribution may not lie far away. Should it come, Civil Defense estimates have established that it will at once wipe out forty million American lives for the one million we once supposedly saved.

Let us be clear about cause and effect. It was not our nuclear weapons that committed us to the strategy of extermination; it was rather our decision to concentrate on the methods of extermination that led to our one-sided, obsessive pre-occupation with nuclear weapons. Even before Russia had achieved a single nuclear weapon, we had so dismantled our military establishment that we lacked sufficient equipment and munitions to fight successfully such a minor action as that in Korea.

The total nature of our moral breakdown, accurately predicted a half century ago—along with the atom bomb—by Henry Adams, can be gauged by a single fact: most Americans do not realize that this change has taken place or, worse, that it makes any difference. They have no consciousness of either the magnitude of their collective sin or the fact that, by their silence, they have individually condoned it. It is precisely as if the Secretary of Agriculture had licensed the sale of human flesh as a wartime emergency measure and people had taken to cannibalism when the war was over as a clever dodge for lowering the cost of living—a mere extension of everyday butchery. Many of our professed religious and moral leaders have steadily shrunk from touching this subject; or, if they have done so, they have naïvely equated mass extermination with war and have too often given their blessing to it, for reasons just as specious as those our government has used.

It is in relation to this gigantic moral collapse that our present devotion to nuclear weapons and their equally dehumanized bacterial and chemical counterparts must be gauged.

When we abandoned the basic moral restraints against random killing and mass extermination we enlarged the destructive capacities of our nuclear weapons. What was almost as bad, our pride in this achievement expressed itself in an inverted fashion by our identifying our safety and welfare with the one-sided expansion of our weapons system. Thus we surrendered the initiative to our instruments, confusing physical power with rational human purpose, forgetting that machines and weapons have no values and no goals, above all, no limits and no restraints except those that human beings superimpose on them.

The one thing that might have rectified our government's premature exploitation of atomic power would have been a public assize of its manifold dangers, even for wider industrial and medical use. As early as the winter of 1945-1946 the Senate Atomic Energy Committee made the first full inquiry into these matters, and the physicists who appeared before this committee gave forecasts whose accuracy was fully confirmed in the tardy hearings that have just taken place before a joint congressional committee. Almost with one voice, these scientists predicted that Soviet Russia would be able to produce a nuclear bomb within five years, possibly within three. On that basis, the nations of the world had three "safe" years to create through the United Nations the necessary political and moral safeguards against the misuse of this new power.

There was no salvation, the more alert leaders of science wisely pointed out, on purely national terms. Naturally, Russia's totalitarian isolationism and suspicion made it difficult to arrive at a basis for rational agreement, but our own sense of holding all the trump cards did not lessen this difficulty. All too quickly, after the Russian rejection of our generous but politically unsound Baruch proposal, our country used Russian hostility as an excuse for abandoning all further effort. Even before we had openly committed ourselves to the Cold War itself—a now obsolete pre-atomic military concept—our leaders preferred to build a threatening ring of air bases around Russia rather than to pursue with patient circumspection a course directed toward securing eventual understanding and cooperation. So the difficult became the impossible.

As late as 1947 this situation, though grave, was not disastrous. Our very mistakes in turning to mass extermination were capable, if openly and honestly faced, of leading both ourselves and the world back to the right path. Up to then, our totalitarian weapons system had not yet consolidated its position or threatened our free institutions; the organs of democratic society, invigorated rather than depressed by the war, had not yet been enfeebled by official secrecy, repression, suspicion, craven conformism, or the corruptions of absolute power, shielded from public criticism. Meanwhile, unfortunately, the strategy of mass extermination, which did not bear public discussion or open assessment, was rapidly taking shape.

For a brief moment, nevertheless, our leaders seized the political initiative, though they were handicapped by ambivalent intentions and contradictory goals. Our contribution to organizing the United Nations, though it had been originally proposed by the United States, was as cagey and inept as Russia's, for the frustrating Council veto was an American conception. Under a more imaginative leadership two other, admirable American proposals came forward, UNRRA and the Marshall Plan. Both these agencies had great potentialities, for at first we had the intelligence to offer their benefits even to Communist countries.

Had we followed these efforts through, they might have permanently increased the whole range of international cooperation. In wiser executive hands, these initiatives would not have been prematurely terminated. Rather, they would have been employed to reduce world tensions and to win general assent to a program for giving all nations the prefatory exercises in magnanimity and understanding essential to the re-establishment of moral order and the control of our demoralizing weapons. But even in their brief, limited application these agencies did far more to fortify the assisted nations against oppressive Communist dictatorship than all the billions we poured into NATO and SEATO to build up futile armaments for wars neither we nor our allies were capable of fighting. Witness our long series of backdowns and letdowns: Czechoslovakia, Korea, Vietnam, Poland, East Germany, Hungary, Egypt.

In our commitment to the strategy of extermination, under a decision made when General Eisenhower was Chief of Staff, the United States rejected the timely warnings of the world's leading scientists and the common counsels of humanity. Instead of holding a series of world conferences in which the dangers of nuclear energy could be fully canvassed, not alone by physicists but by thinkers in every threatened field, our official agencies deliberately played down these dangers and used every available mode of censorship to restrict the circulation of the knowledge needed for such an appraisal. In this obstinate desire to exploit nuclear power solely for our national advantage, our government relied upon insistent publicity and indoctrination to build up a false sense of security. Instead of regaining our moral position by ceasing the reckless experiments whose mounting pollution justified a world-wide apprehension, we flatly denied the need for any such cessation and allowed Russia, after it had come abreast of us, to take the moral lead here. Even at a recent United Nations conference, which clearly demonstrated the dangers, our own representatives helped vote down the Russian preamble to the conclusions of the conference, which called for a cessation of all further nuclear testing.

To explain this obstinate commitment to the infamous policy of mass extermination one must understand that its side reactions have proved as demoralizing as its central purpose. Within a bare decade, the United States has built up a huge vested interest in mass extermination—in the weapons themselves and in the highly profitable manufacture of electronic equipment, planes, and missiles designed to carry them to their destination. There are tens of thousands of individual scientists and technicians engaged in nuclear, bacteriological, and chemical research to increase the range and effectiveness of these lethal agents, though we boast we already have a stockpile of nuclear weapons capable of wiping out the entire planet. There are also corporate bodies —the air force, the Atomic Energy Commission, great industrial corporations, and extravagantly endowed centers of research—whose powers and presumptions have been constantly widened along with their profit and prestige. While the show lasts, their careers depend on our accepting the fallacious assumptions to which they have committed us.

All these agents now operate in secret totalitarian enclaves, perfecting their secret totalitarian weapons, functioning outside the processes of democratic government, immune to public challenge and criticism or to public correction. Whatever the scientific or technical competence of the men working in this field, their sedulous restriction of interest and the limited conditions under which they work and have contact with other human beings do not foster wisdom in the conduct of life. By vocational commitment they live in an underdimensioned and distorted world. The sum of their combined judgments is still an unbalanced judgment, for moral criteria have, from the start, been left out of their general directives.

Is it any wonder that even in the narrow segments of science where they claim mastery our nuclear officials have made error after error? They have again and again been forced to reduce their estimate of the "permissible" limit of exposure to radiation, and on the basis of knowledge already available they will have to reduce these estimates still further. Thus, too, they made an error that startled themselves, in their undercalculating the range and the lethal fall-out of the hydrogen bomb, and they sought to cover that error by concealment and calumny, at first denying the plight of the Japanese fishermen they had injured. Some have even used their authority as scientists to give pseudo-scientific assurances about biological changes that no one will be able to verify until half a century has passed. Furthermore, in matters falling within their province of exact knowledge, the judgment of these authorities has repeatedly proved erroneous and mischievous.

All this should not surprise us: neither science nor nuclear energy endows its users with superhuman powers. But what should surprise us is the fact that the American nation has entrusted its welfare, safety, and future existence to these imprudent, fallible men and to those who have sanctioned their de-moralized plans. Under the guise of a calculated risk, our nuclear strategists have prepared to bring on a calculated catastrophe. At some unpredictable moment their sick fantasies may become unspeakable realities.

Does anyone really think that, unless a miracle supervenes, there can be a more favorable outcome to the overall policy we have been pursuing? If this policy had a color of excuse before Russia had achieved her first nuclear weapon in 1949, it became thoroughly discredited in Korea in 1950 and became suicidal as soon as Russia's superiority in rocket missiles was established. The fact that Russia now has equal or better weapons of extermination and has joined us in these same insane preparations doubles our danger but does not halve our original guilt. Neither does it nullify our willful stupidity in now clinging to an obsolete, discredited strategy, based on a negation of morality and a defiance of common sense.

The only possible justification of our continued reliance upon weapons of total extermination would be that they do no present harm and would never be used by either side under any extremity of provocation. Can any mature mind comfort itself with either hope? Even our experimental explosion of nuclear bombs, at a rate of more than two for Russia's one, has poisoned our babies' milk, upset the delicate ecological balance of nature, and, still worse, defiled our genetic heritage. As for the possibility that nuclear weapons will never be used, our children in school know better than this every time they are put through the sadistic mummery of an air-raid drill and learn to "play disaster." Such baths of fear and hostility are gratuitous assaults against the young, whose psychological damage is already incalculable; their only service is to bar more tightly the exits that would permit a real escape.

There are people who would defend these plans on the grounds that it is better to die nobly, defending democracy and freedom, than to survive under Communist oppression. Such apologists perhaps exaggerate the differences that now exist between our two systems, but they err even more seriously in applying to mass extermination a moral standard that was defensible only as long as this death was a symbolic one confined to a restricted number of people on a small portion of the earth. Such a disaster, as in the bitter-end resistance of the Southern Confederacy, was still relatively minor and retrievable; if the original resolve to die were in fact an erroneous one, in a few generations it could be corrected. Nuclear damage, in contrast, is cumulative and irretrievable; it admits no belated confession of error, no repentance and absolution.

Under what canon of sanity, then, can any government, or any generation, with its limited perspectives, its fallible judgment, its obvious proneness to self-deception, delusion, and error, make a decision for all future ages about the very existence of even a single country? Still more, how can any one nation treat as a purely private right its decision on a matter that will affect the life and health and continued existence of the rest of mankind?

There are no words to describe the magnitude of such insolence in thought or the magnitude of criminality involved in carrying it out. Those who believe that any country has the right to make such a decision share the madness of Captain Ahab in *Moby Dick*. For them Russia is the White Whale that must be hunted down and grappled with. Like Ahab in that mad pursuit, they will listen to no reminders of love, home, family obligation; in order to kill the object of their fear and hate they are ready to throw away the sextant and compass that might give them back their moral direction, and in the end they will sink their own ship and drown their crew. To such unbalanced men, to such demoralized efforts, to such dehumanized purposes, our government has entrusted, in an easily conceivable extremity, our lives. Even an accident, these men have confessed, might produce the dire results they have planned, and more than once has almost done so. To accept their plans and ensuing decisions, we have deliberately anesthetized the normal feelings, emotions, anxieties, and hopes that could alone bring us to our senses.

No one can guess how a sufficiently wide recovery of moral responsibility and initiative might be brought about. Neither can one predict at what moment our nation will see that there is no permissible sacrifice of life, either in experimental preparation of these vile weapons or in a final conflict whose very method would nullify every rational end. Certainly it seems doubtful that popular pressure would bring about such a change in government policy, except under the emotion of a shattering crisis, when it might well be too late. But great leadership, exerted at the right moment, might clear the air and illuminate the territory ahead. Until we actually use our weapons of extermination, there is nothing that we have yet done that cannot be undone, except for the existing pollution of our food and our genetic heritage with strontium 90 and carbon 14. But we must make a moral about-face before we can command a political forward march.

Yet if once the American nation made such evaluation of the morality of extermination, new policies and appropriate decisions would quickly suggest themselves. This would do more to effect an immediate improvement in the relations between the two powers now committed to preparing for mutual extermination than endless parleys between their heads of government.

A moral about-face does not demand, as those whose minds are congealed by the Cold War suppose, either a surrender to Russian Communism or a series of futile appeasements; neither does it mean any increase in the dangers under which we now live: just the contrary. Those who see no other alternatives are still living in the pre-nuclear world; they do not understand that our greatest enemy is not Russia but our treacherous weapons, and that our commitment to these weapons is what has prevented us from conceiving and proposing the necessary means for extending the area of effective freedom and, above all, for safeguarding mankind from meaningless mutilation and massacre.

No dangers we might face once we abandoned the very possibility of using mass extermination would be as great as those under which we now live; yet this is not to say that a bold change of policy would be immediately successful, or that before it had time to register its full effects in other countries it might not tempt Russia to risk measures to extend over other areas its own monolithic system of minority single-party government. But need I emphasize that these possible penalties could hardly be worse than those our government meekly accepted in Czechoslovakia, Poland, and Korea, at a time when we still hugged the illusion of wielding absolute power through our monopoly of nuclear weapons? While sober judgment need not minimize these transitional difficulties and possible losses, one must not underestimate, either, the impact of a new policy, wholly concerned to re-establish the moral controls and political cooperations necessary to enable mankind to halt the threatening misuse of the extraordinary powers that it now commands.

Even in a purely military sense, this changed orientation might produce the greatest difficulties for those Communist governments who misunderstood its intention and sought to turn it to their private national advantage. Russia would no more be able to escape the impact of our humane plans and moralized proposals than it was able to avoid the impact and challenge of our nuclear weapons. If we rallied the forces of mercy, human-heartedness, and morality with the vigor with which we have marshaled the dehumanized forces of destruction, what government could stand against us and face its own people, however strong its cynical suspicions and misgivings?

This is not the place or the moment to spell out a new policy which would start with the complete renunciation of weapons of mass extermination and go on to build constructive measures addressed to all those tasks which the Cold War has caused us to leave in abeyance. Fortunately, George Kennan, the only official or ex-official who has yet had the courage to admit our earlier miscalculations, has already sketched in, with some boldness, the outlines of a better policy, and his proposals might be amplified and enlarged in many directions once we had overcome our official obsession with Russia and our fixation on mass extermination as an ultimate resource.

But the key to all practical proposals lies in a return to human feelings and sensitivities, to moral values, and to life-regarding procedures as controlling factors in the operation of intelligence. The problems our nation has tried to solve by mechanical weapons alone, operated by a detached and de-moralized mechanical intelligence, have proved insoluble by those means. A great leader would know that the time has come to reinstate the missing human factor and bring forth generously imaginative proposals addressed to mankind's survival and working toward its further development.

Questions and Suggestions

1. According to Mumford's impassioned plea for national sanity and morality, what was "democracy's most servile surrender" and what was it that "reversed the whole course of human history"?

2. How persuasive are his reasons for distrusting the "nuclear strategists," the political leaders, and the military advisers?

List his reasons under three headings. What is their cumulative effect?

3. Do you agree with Mumford's belief that there may not be great differences between the governments of the two major powers?

4. Before America entered World War II, a number of civilians feared that a war to destroy the evils of fascism would result in a permanent loss of some of our own democratic ideals. Do any of Mumford's points seem to bear out this fear?

5. Why is Mumford disappointed with the clergy? What does he think is wrong with us as a people? What are the causes of America's "moral apathy"? Does Steinbeck's essay help you reach an answer?

6. Reread Rabi's essay in light of Mumford's. Do they reach any similar conclusions?

7. How successful is Mumford's rejoinder to Stimson's argument for the use of the bomb? What happened to Captain Ahab? Is the analogy appropriate to the context?

8. See what your library has concerning the scientists' plea that the atomic bomb not be used. What happened to Dr. Robert Oppenheimer? What stand did Einstein take? What happened to the men who flew on the first atomic bombing raid over Hiroshima? In addition, look in the December, 1959, issue of *The Atlantic* for the reactions of some readers to Mumford's article.

Ideas for Writing

1. Use examples to show why the end may or may not justify the means.

2. What have friends and relatives told you about the Korean War? What did World War II mean to your family?

3. Consult the chapters in your rhetoric that deal with persuasion and diction. Then study the sections in *Time, Newsweek, U.S. News and World Report,* or other magazines that deal with politics. How objective are the reports? Do you find any inferences or judgments being presented as facts, any logical fallacies, any non-verifiable statements?

4. Do we need to have a greater freedom of the press, radio, and television? Listen to a newscaster and see if through his choice of words and tone of voice he tells you what you should think about a particular situation.

5. If your library subscribes to any foreign newspapers, consult several issues and see if you find important news items about this country which the papers you normally read failed to report or else reported but slanted in a particular direction.

For further insight into the inadequacies of the American press, read Arnold Beichman's "Report from America" in *Encounter*, March, 1961.

CAN MEN LIVE WITHOUT WAR?

VANNEVAR BUSH

The grandson of a whaling captain and the son of a Universalist minister, Dr. Vannevar Bush (1890–), who was born in Everett, Massachusetts, is a graduate of Tufts, Harvard, and the Massachusetts Institute of Technology. As a young man he taught mathematics and electrical engineering and did research for the Navy. In addition to being the vice-president of M.I.T. and Dean of the Engineering College, Dr. Bush, an important inventor and the recipient of many honors, has an international reputation for the leadership that he gave to the National Defense Research Committee and the Office of Scientific Research and Development, for the growth of the Carnegie Institution during the years of his presidency, and for the important administrative part he played in the development of atomic energy.

Nearly fifty years ago William James wrote an essay which he called "The Moral Equivalent of War." Since then many things have happened: there have been two world wars, a crippling depression, and now a phenomenal burst of fairly solid prosperity. The whole art of war has been profoundly altered by the application of science. A new kind of empire has arisen, rigidly controlled and avowedly bent on world conquest. The old colonial empires have disintegrated, and a new spirit of nationalism pervades lands that were once inarticulate. Most important of all, there is a growing understanding of what war may mean, and a deep yearning among all peoples for peace. It is proper, therefore, to review the arguments which James advanced and to do so in the light of the new circumstances.

James foresaw, with a clarity which was remarkable, that war would sometime end. At a time when warfare and the applications of science were poles apart, he said, "And when whole nations are the armies, and the science of destruction vies in intellectual refinement with the sciences of production, I see that war becomes absurd and impossible from its own monstrosity."

And so he turned to what might follow, with evident apprehension that men would become soft—that the virility which had brought the race thus far would give place to flat insipidity.

He first stated the case of the apologists for war, better than they themselves had stated it, repeating the only alternatives they offered: "a world of clerks and teachers, of co-education and zo-ophily, of 'consumers' leagues' and 'associated charities,' of industrialism unlimited, and feminism unabashed. No scorn, no hardness, no valor any more! Fie upon such a cattleyard of a planet."

With this extreme point of view he evidently had a genuine sympathy, for he added: "So far as the central essence of this feeling goes, no healthy minded person, it seems to me, can help to some degree partaking of it. Militarism is the great preserver of our ideals of hardihood, and human life with no use for hardihood would be contemptible. Without risks or prizes for the darer, history would be insipid indeed; and there is a type of military character which every one feels that the race should never cease to breed."

But when he then sought a moral equivalent for war he was far from convincing. His alternative was the struggle with nature as a substitute for the struggle between men and nations. Rugged though the struggle with nature sometimes is, we can hardly believe that it would fully serve to keep the red blood flowing hot in our veins, and to release the adrenalin which is the messenger between a virile mind and a fighting body. For the conquest of nature today involves only relatively few of us, and it is becoming an intellectual effort rather than a matter of brute strength. So James left me, at least, disappointed with his alternative and bewildered. Let us review his line of argument, in the present setting, and see whether there may be a way out of the dilemma.

His first point may indeed now be underlined. We strive for peace today with conviction and intensity, for great wars must cease if we are to pursue further the path of progress. And our striving is by no means hopeless. If great wars are outlawed—not by treaty, perhaps, but by a general realization of their absurdity—secondary wars will go on for a time by conventional means, and nations will maintain their postures of readiness to fight. But the end of all war is now definitely in sight for the first time in human history. No nation can today attack its prepared neighbor with the expectation of profiting immensely and securing a place in the sun, as has been attempted twice within our memory. The result today would be devastation for all, cities utterly destroyed, populations killed and maimed, starvation and disease rampant. That this is the brute fact is now obvious to the most obtuse. Nor can a tyrant or ruling clique, by bringing on a war, hope to advance their private interests or provide a diversion from popular discontent; no modern all-out war will leave in power anywhere those who perpetrated it.

War might, to be sure, come by accident, and this we must guard against assiduously. Little wars with the foolhardy use of weapons of mass destruction could lead to a great war; and if tempers rise, we shall need to curb the trigger-happy fools among us. Were we so gullible as to let down our guard too soon and invite a surprise mass attack which would prevent our retaliation and end the conflict at a single stroke, the invitation might be seized upon by those who still think of conquering the world by force of arms. It is not impossible that a group of desperate men could pull the temple down on all of us. But the conditions and concepts which brought on most of the great wars of history have now disappeared. We are all on notice, if we can read or listen, that indulgence in all-out war would be suicide. Self-preservation is a very powerful primary urge, and an understanding of the present monstrosity of war is increasing among the masses of people in spite of both iron and bamboo curtains. There is certainly more chance than ever before that we may now look forward to peace. In fact, we may conclude that we can have peace if we are not utterly gullible or careless.

The second point made by James also deserves emphasis. The main argument of the apologists for war has vanished as science has stepped into the picture. Whatever else may happen, the glamour of war is gone.

Where do the virtues of war lie today? Is courage needed to watch a radar screen or adjust a guided missile? Where is the daring of the soldier when the folks at home encounter equal risks? When one man guides a plane that can destroy a city, what becomes of the infectious influence of comradeship, the sense of being engaged with many others 'n a common hazardous campaign, the identification of self with a group which could inspire, or was supposed to inspire, even the common soldier with ideals and courage? Great war has become complex and must now be fought at a distance, if at all. It has lost forever those qualities that once had a real appeal for the red-blooded man.

Do we then look forward to some sort of Utopia? James had little use for Utopias, for he wrote in "The Dilemma of Determinism": —

> Why does the painting of any paradise or utopia, in heaven or on earth, awaken such yawnings for nirvana and escape? The white-robed harp-playing heaven of our sabbath-schools, and the ladylike tea-table elysium represented in Mr. Spencer's Data of Ethics, as the final consummation of progress, are exactly on a par in this respect,—lubberlands, pure and simple, one and all. . . . If *this* be the whole fruit of the victory, we say; if the generations of mankind suffered and laid down their lives; if prophets confessed and martyrs sang in the fire, and all the sacred tears were shed for no other end than that a race of creatures of such unexampled insipidity should succeed, and protract . . . their contented and inoffensive lives,—why, at such a rate, better lose than win the battle, or at all events better ring down the curtain before the last act of the play, so that a business that began so importantly may be saved from so singularly flat a winding-up.

We need have little fear of any such dismal outcome. Struggles will not cease even if armed conflict ends. Between nations there will continue to be political jockeying for position and very intense economic competition. We shall still need to cope with penetration and subversion and face the difficult task of guiding our friends among the younger nations to positions of true independence and stability.

Nor will struggle and conflict end in our internal affairs. We shall have much to quarrel about.

Our racial antagonisms have by no means vanished. We hope we have learned to avoid great depressions, but on this score we should by no means be sanguine. Whether we can maintain full employment without forcing inflation remains to be seen. The division of our product between capital, labor, and management can still lead to paralyzing strikes. We have narcotics, juvenile delinquency, defiance of law. The preservation of our liberties demands eternal vigilance. If we are easygoing, a swollen bureaucracy will certainly regiment us. Our political contests can still be embittered and sordid.

If war ceases, it will be a different sort of world; and the apologists for war usually overlook one of its primary attributes, the ending of which might greatly influence our lives in subtle ways. During the past two decades this country has forged ahead at an unprecedented rate until it stands as the unquestioned leader of the free world, power-ful, disciplined, even wise as it attempts to press further by lifting its neighbors with it. War and the fear of war produced this result—produced also our present great prosperity. And this did not occur because of war profits; for there are no such things as war profits for a country as a whole; war merely wastes man's goods and man's labor. In many nations the waste has overbalanced all else, but we were fortunate. Our advance has come about because the nation became internally united and went to work, because secondary quarrels were submerged or tempered in the common cause, because public opinion forced the channeling of all effort in a single direction, because men's spirits rose and their blood ran hot as they faced together an enemy that all could recognize. Where would we now be had there been no such cement to hold us together during the past twenty years—if we had worked at cross-purposes, occupied ourselves with petty quarrels, or succumbed to the vices of intrigue and treachery?

Does this mean that, if peace comes and the fear of war is lifted, we shall again return to all the old quarrels and become a nation divided, split into factions with animosity and petty intrigues para-mount? Does it mean that we shall lose the vision of a happy and prosperous nation, brought about by our own unity and determination, in which we can approach our disagreements objectively and in a spirit of relative good will? Does it mean that we shall forget how to battle with one another vigorously and with full conviction and determination, but standing up, and shall again thrash about in the mire of mutual suspicion? Do biting and kicking have to take the place of honest blows given and received?

The citizens of this country have shown that they take most of the guarantees of the Bill of Rights for granted, that they see no real danger to our primary liberties or any need to be keenly on the alert to preserve them; and in this complacency lies danger. But there is one element of the free life that is not taken for granted at all, that is highly valued, and that men are willing to fight for, if necessary, without question. This element is the opportunity for an individual to rise as far as his talents, health, and determination will take him, without artificial barriers of any kind.

We have by no means reached perfection in this regard. There are still artificial barriers of race, birth, and resources. Nor would we banish the paternal instinct, forbid the father to aid his son to make a good start in life, or frown on any effort of a man to help one of his fellows. There is a fundamental difference between this mutual aid—even the banding together of groups with mutual interests for mutual advancement—and the throwing of artificial obstacles in the path of a young man struggling to rise by his own efforts. We shall always have with us those who will drift, who will refuse to pull their weight in the boat, to whom opportunity means nothing; but the problem of their place in society is not one that concerns us here. It is the artificial obstacle in the path of the ambitious and able that we would banish, and this has not as yet been fully accomplished.

But we have proceeded much farther toward the ideal than ever before in any country at any time. The workman at the bench recognizes the artificial limitations that surround him; and his own ambitions may be ended. But he knows, too, that for his son, his neighbor's son, or the bright attractive boy down the street there are genuine opportunities to rise to positions of influence and satisfaction. Luck, the caprice of men in high places, loyalty to dependents, an insidious bacterium or virus—any one of these may stop him in his tracks. Only a few will have the ambition to rise and the skill and personality that must go with it. But the opportunity is there, and it is real. The son of a tailor on the east side may become the honored surgeon, respected by men of power, loved by patients who owe their lives to him. The peddler of bananas may come to rule an industrial empire he has built. The painter's helper may become a labor leader and treat on equal terms with the captains of industry. The haberdasher may become president. It has happened. The bans and taboos are less than they ever were before. This is the land of opportunity, and we had better keep it so and enhance this central aspect of our liberty.

It is this which may yet bind us together in the ideal of brotherhood among men, not as a vague generality to which we pay lip service but as a living reality, exemplified by the opportunity for all to develop their talents to the utmost for their own benefit and the benefit of their fellow men.

We look forward to living in a new sort of world. The flowering of science, which has rendered war absurd, is also giving us wealth, comfort, and freedom from disease of the body or the mind. Our contests for position in the intricate fabric of society need no longer require that the unsuccessful shall suffer want and distress.

When individual progress is artificially barred, when men are divided into classes with impenetrable barriers, when men are serfs or slaves, or fettered by false restraint so that they cannot move, struggles on any subject are bound to be bitter. When a man knows that if he loses out, in competition with his fellows, those he loves will be ill-nourished and neglected, he must fight too desperately to care for the conventions of fairness and decency.

But when artificial barriers are gone, and men may rise if they have what it takes—when there is a floor beneath which no man need fall, a floor that will ensure a decent life—then the contests of men with one another may well be on a different plane. The key is the preservation and enhancement of individual opportunity in all its forms. Few will rise, for few are the places to fill at the top. But all will have dignity and satisfaction; and those who prefer for any reason to remain in humble and peasant status will do so by choice.

We can have peace. And with it we can have prosperity, greater than the world has even seen, with a distribution of its blessings that preserves the necessary order of an industrial society while avoiding both arrogant opulence and cringing poverty. As we attain these things, whenever we do, shall we return to petty bickering and strife, sordid intrigue, and bitter recriminations? Or shall we tackle our problems as men, vigorously, with courage and convictions, pulling no punches, but with decency and fairness? We may, indeed, be able to rise to the latter if we keep our senses and our objectivity—and, above all, if we open the door of opportunity wide so that we battle as free men, in the pride and dignity to which only free men may aspire.

Here, indeed, may be an acceptable equivalent for war, preserving and enhancing in our people those virile attributes which conquered the old frontiers and built an industrial civilization beyond compare. When the foolhardy nature of international combat is fully recognized and great wars are banished, we may still struggle with nature and with one another and thus keep the vitality of the race from being sapped by insipid ease. If we do so as free men, independent, proud, seizing our opportunity in an open field from which artificial barriers have been removed, we may find that struggle, so necessary for the health of our race, can be entered upon in decency and dignity, and the vulgarity of war may give place to strife for worthy causes conducted with fairness and good will.

Yet, having said this, we have not come to the end of the matter. Man needs to exercise his virile attributes—in sport, in coping with the hazards of the wilderness, in honest and decent conflict with his fellows for just and worthy causes. No man has fully lived who has not experienced the fear, the exultation, of meeting great odds and struggling to prevail. But no man has fully lived who has not also experienced the joy of close association with worthy fellows or who has not known the thrill of individual creation. He who can say honestly to himself that he has discovered a set of facts or a relation between phenomena not known to any man before him in all history, and that by his insight and skill he has made them comprehensible to the human intellect— such a man experiences the same uplift of spirit as the one who first climbs a high mountain or first runs a mile in four minutes. And when the accomplishment results not from the lonely acts of individual genius but from the efforts of a team or group having mutual trust and confidence, supplementing one another's skills, compensating for one another's weaknesses, carrying the unfortunate over the rough places, heartening the leader by steadfast support—then all members of the group enjoy a satisfaction transcending that of accomplished creation, a satisfaction of success in their margin of effort to attain something that was beyond the capacity of any individual.

If war ends, we must still have outlets for our inherited energies; we need only attempt to render them dignified and worthy. But we shall also have increased opportunities for other satisfactions, not so intense but far more lasting and substantial. The unifying bond of war will be gone, but it can give place to a nobler bond, less universal, far more genuine and strong. This can appear in the midst of diverse careers. To me, naturally, the field of science stands out uniquely in its opportunities.

The country will be full of struggle and conflict as diverse causes are fought over. As individuals and citizens we enter if our consciences and inclinations so dictate. And by entering we may help to raise the level of the contests and render them worthy. But research centers such as the Carnegie Institution stand aside from all this.

Within the institutions dedicated to scientific research lies opportunity for the individual. They do not care about a man's origins— his country, race, or religion. They seek men who have an ambition to rise to the heights in their scientific professions, and insist, moreover, that among their talents should be a large measure of ability to rise by effective collaboration with others. They want men of generous instinct, and men who are devoted to science because they believe that the life of a scientist yields more satisfaction than any other career on earth and contributes more genuinely to the public weal. When they find a young man of this sort they welcome him with open arms. After that no artificial barrier stands in his path. He can rise as rapidly and as high in his profession as his own effort, judgment, and skill will carry him. He will be judged only according to the estimation in which he is held by fellow scientists—his peers. The requirements are rigorous, but the opportunity these institutions offer is real and complete. We must always keep it so.

No more war? Peace is indeed in sight if we are wise. But not an end of contest or struggle. And certainly not an end of opportunity, which may render the lives of those who follow us not insipid but virile, not belligerent but creative.

Questions and Suggestions

1. Why is Dr. Bush disappointed in James's alternative to war?
2. What, according to Bush, must man do if he is to live without war? What advantages will a warless world offer?
3. What reasons does he give for his hope that a time of peace may soon mark our lives? Does his recognition that there is a growing "new spirit of nationalism" seem to offer any contradictions to his conviction that there is "a deep yearning among all peoples for peace"? How convinced are you that even "the most obtuse" know that "great wars" are absurd?
4. Contrast Bush and Mumford's views of the American people. Do they come to the same conclusions about our scientific and political leaders? Wherein are Bush and Whitman alike? Do Bush and Steinbeck agree about the value of collaboration, the power of a "swollen bureaucracy," and the effects of complacency?
5. Do you find any statements in the essay with which a "second-class" American citizen might take issue? For example, are you convinced that "the institutions dedicated to scientific research . . . do not care about a man's origins—his country, race, or religion"? Is it possible for an Austrian-born scientist to have better chances in being appointed to such an institution than an equally creative scientist who is an American-born Negro?

Ideas for Writing

1. Between 1890 and 1914, many men left Europe in order to avoid military conscription. Although the draft law is relatively new in America, why have we come to take it for granted? Does the period of military service act as the " 'great preserver of our ideals of hardihood,' " or does it soften and weaken the draftees? What place should the R.O.T.C. have on the campus? Does army life foster the escaping of responsibilities?

2. Intellect or brawn—which is the best preserver of our way of life? What arguments can you propose for the substitution of compulsory education in place of the years of military service? Should a series of tax-supported national institutions of higher learning be established?
3. What did one of your friends learn from his experiences with the Peace Corps?
4. Do older people seem more prone than youth to advocate war? Do you know any person with vested interests who seems to support a desire for war? Do newspapers help push us toward "the brink of war"?

A HANGING

GEORGE ORWELL

Born in India, Eric Blair (1903–1950), who is best known by his pseudonym of George Orwell, has come to be recognized as one of the most important essayists and novelists of our times. After spending several years at Eton, Orwell served with the Imperial Police in Burma from 1922 until 1927, giving up the post because of poor health and his distrust of all forms of imperialism. Active in the Spanish Civil War, he came to have a horror of politics. The publication of *Animal Farm,* a political fable, and his penetrating attack on totalitarian states, *Nineteen Eighty-Four,* made Orwell a spokesman for moral, personal values wherever English books are read.

It was in Burma, a sodden morning of the rains. A sickly light, like yellow tinfoil, was slanting over the high walls into the jail yard. We were waiting outside the condemned cells, a row of sheds fronted with double bars, like small animal cages. Each cell measured about ten feet by ten and was quite bare within except for a plank bed and

From *Shooting an Elephant and Other Essays.* Copyright 1945, 1946, 1949, 1950 by Sonia Brownell Orwell. Reprinted by permission of Harcourt, Brace & World, Inc., and Martin Secker & Warburg Limited.

a pot for drinking water. In some of them brown silent men were squatting at the inner bars, with their blankets draped round them. These were the condemned men, due to be hanged within the next week or two.

One prisoner had been brought out of his cell. He was a Hindu, a puny wisp of a man, with a shaven head and vague liquid eyes. He had a thick, sprouting moustache, absurdly too big for his body, rather like the moustache of a comic man on the films. Six tall Indian warders were guarding him and getting him ready for the gallows. Two of them stood by with rifles and fixed bayonets, while the others handcuffed him, passed a chain through his handcuffs and fixed it to their belts, and lashed his arms tight to his sides. They crowded very close about him, with their hands always on him in a careful, caressing grip, as though all the while feeling him to make sure he was there. It was like men handling a fish which is still alive and may jump back into the water. But he stood quite unresisting, yielding his arms limply to the ropes, as though he hardly noticed what was happening.

Eight o'clock struck and a bugle call, desolately thin in the wet air, floated from the distant barracks. The superintendent of the jail, who was standing apart from the rest of us, moodily prodding the gravel with his stick, raised his head at the sound. He was an army doctor, with a grey toothbrush moustache and a gruff voice. "For God's sake hurry up, Francis," he said irritably. "The man ought to have been dead by this time. Aren't you ready yet?"

Francis, the head jailer, a fat Dravidian in a white drill suit and gold spectacles, waved his black hand. "Yes sir, yes sir," he bubbled. "All iss satisfactorily prepared. The hangman iss waiting. We shall proceed."

"Well, quick march, then. The prisoners can't get their breakfast till this job's over."

We set out for the gallows. Two warders marched on either side of the prisoner, with their rifles at the slope; two others marched close against him, gripping him by arm and shoulder, as though at once pushing and supporting him. The rest of us, magistrates and the like, followed behind. Suddenly, when we had gone ten yards, the procession stopped short without any order or warning. A dreadful thing had happened—a dog, come goodness knows whence, had appeared in the yard. It came bounding among us with a loud volley of barks, and leapt round us wagging its whole body, wild with glee at finding so many human beings together. It was a large woolly dog, half Airedale, half pariah. For a moment it pranced round us, and then, before anyone could stop it, it had made a dash for the prisoner and, jumping up, tried to lick his face. Everyone stood aghast, too taken aback even to grab at the dog.

"Who let that bloody brute in here?" said the superintendent angrily. "Catch it, someone!"

A warder, detached from the escort, charged clumsily after the dog, but it danced and gambolled just out of his reach, taking everything as part of the game. A young Eurasian jailer picked up a handful of gravel and tried to stone the dog away, but it dodged the stones and came after us again. Its yaps echoed from the jail walls. The prisoner, in the grasp of the two warders, looked on incuriously, as though this was another formality of the hanging. It was several minutes before someone managed to catch the dog. Then we put my handkerchief through its collar and moved off once more, with the dog still straining and whimpering.

It was about forty yards to the gallows. I watched the bare brown back of the prisoner marching in front of me. He walked clumsily with his bound arms, but quite steadily, with that bobbing gait of the Indian who never straightens his knees. At each step his muscles slid neatly into place, the lock of hair on his scalp danced up and down, his feet printed themselves on the wet gravel. And once, in spite of the men who gripped him by each shoulder, he stepped slightly aside to avoid a puddle on the path.

It is curious, but till that moment I had never realized what it means to destroy a healthy, conscious man. When I saw the prisoner step aside to avoid the puddle I saw the mystery, the unspeakable wrongness, of cutting a life short when it is in full tide. This man was not dying, he was alive just as we are alive. All the organs of his body were working—bowels digesting food, skin renewing itself, nails growing, tissues forming—all toiling away in solemn foolery. His nails would still be growing when he stood on the drop, when he was falling through the air with a tenth-of-a-second to live. His eyes saw the yellow gravel and the grey walls, and his brain still remembered, foresaw, reasoned—reasoned even about puddles. He and we were a party of men walking together, seeing, hearing, feeling, understanding the same world; and in two minutes, with a sudden snap, one of us would be gone—one mind less, one world less.

The gallows stood in a small yard, separate from the main grounds of the prison, and overgrown with tall prickly weeds. It was a brick erection like three sides of a shed, with planking on top, and above that two beams and a crossbar with the rope dangling. The hangman, a grey-haired convict in the white uniform of the prison, was waiting beside his machine. He greeted us with a servile crouch as we entered. At a word from Francis the two warders, gripping the prisoner more closely than ever, half led half pushed him to the gallows and helped him clumsily up the ladder. Then the hangman climbed up and fixed the rope round the prisoner's neck.

We stood waiting, five yards away. The warders had formed in a rough circle round the gallows. And then, when the noose was fixed, the prisoner began crying out to his god. It was a high, reiterated cry of "Ram! Ram! Ram! Ram!" not urgent and fearful like a prayer or cry for help, but steady, rhythmical, almost like the tolling of a bell. The dog answered the sound with a whine. The hangman, still standing on the gallows, produced a small cotton bag like a flour bag and drew it down over the prisoner's face. But the sound, muffled by the cloth, still persisted, over and over again: "Ram! Ram! Ram! Ram! Ram!"

The hangman climbed down and stood ready, holding the lever. Minutes seemed to pass. The steady, muffled crying from the prisoner went on and on, "Ram! Ram! Ram!" never faltering for an instant. The superintendent, his head on his chest, was slowly poking the ground with his stick; perhaps he was counting the cries, allowing the prisoner a fixed number—fifty, perhaps, or a hundred. Everyone had changed color. The Indians had gone grey like bad coffee, and one or two of the bayonets were wavering. We looked at the lashed, hooded man on the drop, and listened to his cries—each cry another second of life; the same thought was in all our minds: oh, kill him quickly, get it over, stop that abominable noise!

Suddenly the superintendent made up his mind. Throwing up his head he make a swift motion with his stick. "Chalo!" he shouted almost fiercely.

There was a clanking noise, and then dead silence. The prisoner had vanished, and the rope was twisting on itself. I let go of the dog, and it galloped immediately to the back of the gallows; but when it got there it stopped short, barked, and then retreated into a corner of the yard, where it stood among the weeds, looking timorously out at us. We went round the gallows to inspect the prisoner's body. He was dangling with his toes pointed straight downwards, very slowly revolving, as dead as a stone.

The superintendent reached out with his stick and poked the bare brown body; it oscillated slightly. "*He's* all right," said the superintendent. He backed out from under the gallows, and blew out a deep breath. The moody look had gone out of his face quite suddenly. He glanced at his wrist-watch. "Eight minutes past eight. Well, that's all for this morning, thank God."

The warders unfixed bayonets and marched away. The dog, sobered and conscious of having misbehaved itself, slipped after them. We walked out of the gallows yard, past the condemned cells with their waiting prisoners, into the big central yard of the prison. The convicts, under the command of warders armed with lathis, were already receiving their breakfast. They squatted in long rows, each man holding a tin panikin, while two warders with buckets marched round ladling out rice; it seemed quite a homely, jolly scene, after the hanging. An enormous relief had come upon us now that the job was done. One felt an impulse to sing, to break into a run, to snigger. All at once everyone began chattering gaily.

The Eurasian boy walking beside me nodded towards the way we had come, with a knowing smile: "Do you know, sir, our friend [he meant the dead man] when he heard his appeal had been dismissed, he pissed on the floor of his cell. From fright. Kindly take one of my cigarettes, sir. Do you not admire my new silver case, sir? From the boxwalah, two rupees eight annas. Classy European style."

Several people laughed—at what, nobody seemed certain.

Francis was walking by the superintendent, talking garrulously: "Well, sir, all hass passed off with the utmost satisfactoriness. It was all finished—flick! like that. It iss not always so—oah, no! I have known cases where the doctor wass obliged to go beneath the gallows and pull the prissoner's legs to ensure decease. Most disagreeable!"

"Wriggling about, eh? That's bad," said the superintendent.

"Ach, sir, it iss worse when they become refractory! One man, I recall, clung to the bars of hiss cage when we went to take him out. You will scarcely credit, sir, that it took six warders to dislodge him, three pulling at each leg. We reasoned with him. 'My dear fellow,' we said, 'think of all the pain and trouble you are causing to us!' But no, he would not listen! Ach, he wass very troublesome!"

I found that I was laughing quite loudly. Everyone was laughing. Even the superintendent grinned in a tolerant way. "You'd better all come out and have a drink," he said quite genially. "I've got a bottle of whisky in the car. We could do with it."

We went through the big double gates of the prison into the road. "Pulling at his legs!" exclaimed a Burmese magistrate suddenly, and burst into a loud chuckling. We all began laughing again. At that moment Francis' anecdote seemed extraordinarily funny. We all had a drink together, native and European alike, quite amicably. The dead man was a hundred yards away.

Questions and Suggestions

1. Why does Orwell not wait until the end of the essay to inform you that this particular hanging changed his ideas? What made him suddenly realize "the unspeakable wrongness" of hanging a man? Why is it significant that his conversion occurred through the death of a Hindu rather than through the death of an Englishman?

2. What reaction does Orwell want you to have toward the superintendent, the Eurasian boy, and Francis? What details and devices does Orwell use to achieve his purpose?

3. Does the second paragraph contain any elements of irony? How does the paragraph prepare you for further descriptive elements in the essay?

4. Study carefully a number of Orwell's figures of speech. Remove them from the sentences. What has happened to the prose?

Ideas for Writing

1. If you have undergone a conversion similar to Orwell's, what was responsible for the change?

2. Does the fear of capital punishment actually deter would-be criminals?

3. Because the death penalty has been abolished in some states, what reasons would you give for advocating that the law be removed from the statute books in all states? What arguments would you use if you wished to have public executions restored?

4. Should reform schools be abolished? Are there any occasions when the parents of juvenile offenders should be sent to prison rather than their children?

5. Do you know anyone who was tried before he appeared in court? Do our courts handle the problem of justice impartially? What happened at a trial which you attended?

6. How valid are Albert Camus's arguments against capital punishment in "Reflections on the Guillotine"? This important essay appeared in the *Evergreen Review,* Vol. I, No. 3, in

1957, the year Camus was awarded the Nobel Prize in Literature. Read Arthur Koestler's *Reflections on Hanging* to see why he believes judges support the death penalty.

WORK

ERIC GILL

Artist and craftsman in many mediums, Eric Rowland Gill (1882–1940) was born in Brighton, England. Still quite young when he realized there should be no distinction between the artist and the average worker, Gill briefly turned to the Fabians but before long came to distrust all forms of politics as offering any solution to man's problems. In 1913 he became a convert to Catholicism. His numerous books clearly demonstrate his conviction that man must solve his own social problems.

As usual it is necessary to begin at the beginning. Work, as the dictionary says, is "the exertion of energy, physical or mental." In common speech, however, we distinguish between the exertion of energy for the sake of pleasure or recreation, and the same exertion when it is made for the sake of or as a means to the earning or procuring of the means of living. The former we commonly call play; the word work we commonly reserve for those occupations by means of which we get food, clothing, and shelter—the necessaries of life.

It is clear, therefore, that work is a good thing, for that which enables us to live must be good. We must assume that to live is good and that therefore to work is good. And we may freely agree with the Apostle when he says: "if any man will not work neither let him eat," for to eat what the labour of others has produced is, unless freely given, a form of robbery and, as the same Apostle says elsewhere: "he that stole, let him now steal no more; but rather let him labour, working with his hands the thing which is good. . . ."

God has made the world and he has made man such that labour, that is to say, work, is necessary for life, and God cannot have made necessary that which in itself is bad. Moreover, as Solomon, inspired by the Holy Spirit, said: ". . . nothing is better than for a man to rejoice in his work, and this is his portion."

Now it follows from these things that nothing which truly subserves our life can be bad, and therefore there can be no form of necessary work which is in itself degrading. In these latter days we have to be more than usually clear in our minds about this. The idea is prevalent that physical labour is a bad thing, a thing to be avoided, a thing from which we may rightly seek release. We cannot discuss the question of work, the question of the factory system, of the machine, of the arts, until we have right notions as to the nature of physical labour itself. For there can be nothing made, either for man's service or for his pleasure, which is not, at bottom, dependent upon some amount of physical labour for its existence. Even in the most highly organized industrial world, with all the necessaries of life made by machines minded by machines, there will have to be at least the makers of machines and the machine overseers, and there will have to be designers of machines and designers of machine products. Further, there will have to be all the army of officials and administrators, and all the doctors, lawyers, and school teachers, and all these professional persons will be dependent upon a subordinate army of clerks and typists. Then there will be the transport workers of all kinds, and in all these occupations there will be a basis of actual physical labour. So the question remains as before: is physical labour good or bad? Is it a thing to be reduced to a minimum because it is in itself a bad thing, unworthy of "the mystical mug called man," or is it in itself a good thing and only bad when it is done under bad conditions, conditions physically or hygienically unhealthy or morally bad, or when the product is inferior or unsuitable for human use?

Now, as we have seen, according to Christian doctrine, physical labour is not in itself bad, but, on the contrary, because it is necessary for the preservation and continuance of human life, it is in itself good and may be and should be holy and sacred. We have to start with this doctrine. At every turn our object must be to sanctify rather than to exclude physical labour, to honour it rather than to degrade it, to discover how to make it pleasant rather than onerous, a source of pride rather than of shame. And we have to begin by realizing that, in itself and in a Christian society, there is no kind of physical labour, no kind whatsoever, none, which is either derogatory to human beings or incapable of being sanctified and ennobled. There is no kind of physical labour which is at one and the same time truly necessary to human life and necessarily either unduly onerous or unpleasant. This is the first thing to grasp, and it is perhaps the most difficult to-day. For considering the conditions of industrialized life in Europe and America, and according to the special kind of town mind which industrialism has begot and fostered (if we may thus, though unwillingly, ennoble a mechanism by speaking of it in such terms), there is nothing to be said about physical labour except that it is to be avoided as much as possible.

In sports and pastimes physical exertion is delighted in, but in the things we do to earn our living we regard the elimination of physical exertion as desirable in itself and a mark of good civilization. We regard physical labour as barbarous. We regard the sight of hundreds of men and girls doing simple repetitive operations requiring the minimum of strength and the minimum of intelligence as a sign of advancement from the primitive life of savages to the full stature of man made in God's image.

We are not concerned in this article to discuss the historical causes of our industrialism, its origin in the greed of manufacturers and merchants and its development under the sway of banks and financiers. The one and only point here is the nature of work in itself, and our object is to rebut the common belief, which industrialism must necessarily encourage, that, as an eminent Catholic writer has recently said: "*such manual work is, of itself, subhuman drudgery.*" This is not only untrue but subversive of the whole Christian doctrine of man. Unfortunately, in the circumstances of our industrial world, nothing could seem more obvious common sense. When we consider the working life of the millions of factory-hands, of shop assistants and clerks, of transport workers, and of the agricultural labourers on our degraded farms, it is obvious that much of the work is, indeed, subhuman drudgery and it cannot but seem a good thing that, by the use of machinery, at least the physical pain has been eliminated. So it has come about that we have come to believe that physical labour is in itself bad. We seek to reduce it to a minimum, and we look to our leisure time for all enjoyable exercise of our human bodies. We do not notice the contradiction. For if physical labour is a thing rightly to be eliminated from work because it is derogatory then it should rightly be eliminated from play also, which is absurd.

It should be obvious that it is not physical labour which is bad, but the proletarianism by which men and women have become simply "hands," simply instruments for the making of money by those who own the means of production, distribution, and exchange. And those who argue in favour of the still further elimination of physical labour on the ground that much manual work is, of itself, subhuman drudgery are either playing into the hands of those for whose profit the mechanical organization of industry has been developed, or they are playing into the hands of the communists and others who look to the Leisure State as the *summum bonum*.

We must return again and again to the simple doctrine: physical labour, manual work, is *not* in itself bad. It is the necessary basis of all human production and, in the most strict sense of the words, physical labour directed to the production of things needed for human life is both honourable and holy. And we must remember that there are no exceptions. It is frequently said in extenuation of industrialism that, for instance, modern sanitary engineering has not only lessened the danger of disease, but has done away with much unpleasant and degrading labour in the disposal of sewage. It is said that with sawing and lifting machinery we have done away with the unduly arduous; that with the power-loom we have done away with the slave labour of the old weavers. And in the domestic world we claim to have released the housewife and the mother from many or all of those labours known as "domestic drudgery," thus setting her free for "higher things." In all these cases we forget that we had, first of all, by the conditions of town life or commercial exploitation so degraded these various kinds of labour that they were no longer capable of being viewed as pleasant and still less as sacred. And having thus degraded labour, making men and women into mere "hands" and beasts of burden, instruments of profit-making, having allowed, and even encouraged, the growth of the monstrous conglomerations we still call towns and cities, we turn round and curse the very idea of labour. To use the body, our arms and legs and backs, is now held to be derogatory to our human dignity. This then, is the first thing, and it is at the very base of the Christian reform for which we stand, that we return to the honouring of bodily labour.

We have said nothing about the spiritual and creative and personal side of human work. Greatly as we have dishonoured and corrupted and destroyed the arts and crafts of men, reducing the workman to a "subhuman condition of intellectual irresponsibility," the root of the matter is in the dishonouring of physical work, and until we have eradicated the prevailing notion that some kinds of work are, of their nature, subhuman drudgery, all discussion of human labour is futile.

But it is relevant to note that in what are generally agreed to be the "highest" forms of human production, "the fine arts," those of painting and sculpture, for example, physical labour is still honoured. In spite of the tendency in recent centuries for sculptors to relegate the actual job of stone-carving to hired labourers (and among painters the grinding of pigments and the preparing of the material to be painted on is now generally done in factories by machinery) nevertheless, it is still recognized that if the thing to be made is to be as good as it can be, the artist himself must use his own hands to do the work. With regard to this the supporters of industrialism say, of course, that in the fine arts the thing made depends for its quality upon the actual personality of its maker, while in ordinary objects of human use this is not so. But apart from the fact that in a normal society "the artist is not a special kind of man, but every man is a special kind of artist," and that, therefore, there is no such hard distinction between the fine arts and others, the point here is this: "that certain kinds of work which, in other circumstances, we regard as drudgery, which could be done by machinery if we so chose, are not so done. In fact, when the nature of the work demands it we willingly endure what our mechanistically-minded reformers find derogatory to human dignity and even delight in it and honour it, and it is only dullness of mind and lack of imagination which prevents the said reformers from seeing that *all* things made could be, and should be, regarded as we regard the products of artists."

It is impossible in a short article to show how these contentions apply throughout the whole world of labour. We can but repeat that in all those cases where it seems that mechanization has brought release from "sub-human drudgery," the drudgery is not inherent in the nature of the work, "of itself," but in the sub-human conditions consequent upon commercialism, industrialism, and the abnormal growth of cities. Whether or no we continue the present mechanistic trend or decide to deliberately restrict machinery (though the possibility of so doing is doubtful) depends ultimately upon the line we take with regard to the ownership of land and work-shops. In a later article we shall see how the ownership of property is the chief means to the resuscitation of the dignity of physical labour and also of the quality of things made.

Questions and Suggestions

1. How is the method of deductive reasoning used in the first paragraph?
2. What sentence patterns and rhythms echo the style of the King James version of the Bible?
3. What are the points in Gill's argument that "physical labour, manual work, is *not* in itself bad"?
4. Although Gill does not mention Karl Marx by name, how do you know that he heartily disapproves of the German's theories of work? Why has the factory system not proved to be the panacea that nineteenth century economists thought it would be?
5. In what ways can pride be restored to the factory laborer, to the farmer?
6. How does the work of an artist differ from that of the man on the assembly line?

Ideas for Writing

1. What would happen to you if suddenly all the assembly lines in America stopped?
2. Americans love imitations.
3. Use examples to show how highbrows, middlebrows, and lowbrows differ in their attitudes toward assembly-line products.
4. What ironies are involved in the life of a commuter?
5. If you agree with Gill's argument, read the latter part of Mohandas K. Gandhi's *Autobiography* to see why he urged the Hindu women to reintroduce carders, spinning wheels, and looms into their homes.
6. Read Robert Frost's "Two Tramps in Mud-Time" and state his theory of work.

THE POWER OF LAUGHTER: WEAPON AGAINST EVIL

SEAN O'CASEY

In six autobiographical volumes, most of which are banned in Ireland, Sean O'Casey (1880–), who is self-taught, presents a vivid account of his life, from his birth in Dublin, to the more recent years when he has come to be considered, in spite of some iconoclastic views, one of the major dramatists of the twentieth century. His first major plays were produced by the Abbey Theatre, but because his fifth play caused a riot and because he already felt himself to be an exile among the Irish, O'Casey moved to England. That removal, however, has not lessened his gift for dialogue, his humanity, or his distrust of fools.

Laughter is wine for the soul—laughter soft, or loud and deep, tinged through with seriousness. Comedy and tragedy step through life together, arm in arm, all along, out along, down along lea. A laugh is the loud echo of a sigh; a sigh the faint echo of a laugh. A laugh is a great natural stimulator, a pushful entry into life; and once we can laugh, we can live. It is the hilarious declaration made by man that life is worth living. Man is always hopeful of, always pushing towards, better things; and to bring this about, a change must be made in the actual way of life; so laughter is brought in to mock at things as they are so that they may topple down, and make room for better things to come.

People are somewhat afraid of laughing. Many times, when laughter abounded, I have heard the warning remark, "Oh, give it a rest, or it'll end in a cry." It is odd how many seem to be curiously envious of laughter, never of grief. You can have more than your fill of grief, and nobody minds: they never grudge your grief to you. You are given the world to grieve in; laughter is more often confined to a corner. We are more afraid of laughter than we are of grief. The saying is all wrong—it should be "Grieve, and the world grieves with you; laugh, and you laugh alone." Laughter may be a bad thing; grief is invariably a good or a harmless one.

Laughter tends to mock the pompous and the pretentious; all man's boastful gadding about, all his pretty pomps, his hoary customs, his wornout creeds, changing the glitter of them into the dullest hue of lead. The bigger the subject, the sharper the laugh. No one can escape it: not the grave judge in his robe and threatening wig; the parson and his saw; the general full of his sword and his medals; the palled prelate, tripping about, a blessing in one hand, a curse in the other; the politician carrying his magic wand of Wendy windy words; they all fear laughter, for the quiet laugh or the loud one upends them, strips them of pretense, and leaves them naked to enemy and friend.

Laughter is allowed when it laughs at the foibles of ordinary men, but frowned on and thought unseemly when it makes fun of superstitions, creeds, customs, and the blown-up importance of brief authority of those going in velvet and fine linen. The ban on laughter stretches back to the day when man wore skins and defended himself with the stone hammer. Many enemies have always surrounded laughter, have tried to banish it from life; and many have perished on the high gallows tree because they laughed at those who had been given power over them. Hell-fire tried to burn it, and the weeping for sins committed did all that was possible to drown it; but laughter came safely through the ordeals of fire and water; came smiling through. The people clung to laughter, and held it safe, holding both its sides, in their midst; out in the field, at home in the mud hovel, under the castle wall, at the very gateway of the Abbey.

Every chance of leisure the medieval peasant and worker snatched from his fearsome and fiery labor was spent in low revelry, banned by the church, deprecated by the grandees; the hodden gray put on and colorful ribbons, and the hours went in making love, listening to and singing ditties mocking spiritual pastor and master, and whirling rapturously and riotously round the beribboned maypole. The bawl of the ballad came into the Abbey or Priory Church, and poured through the open windows of the Castle Hall, irritating and distracting the lord and his lady poring over the pictured book of hours. In story whispered from ear to ear, in song sung at peasant gatherings, they saw themselves as they were seen by their people, and they didn't like it; they weren't amused, for these things ate into their dignity, made them nearer to the common stature of common men, who learned that the grand and the distant ones were but a hand's span away from themselves.

Nothing could kill or stay laughter, or hold it fast in one place. It spread itself out all over the world, for, though men show their thoughts in many different manners and modes, they all laugh the same way.

When Christianity became a power, and took the place of the

Roman Empire, they closed the theaters, deeming them places of surly rioting and brazen infamy, destroying souls, displeasing God, and hindering holiness on its dismal way. Bang, bang went the doors, shutting poor Satan in with the shadows. The dispersed actors became wandering minstrels, and whereas before they had been thorns in the Church's fingers, now, in songs of laughter, satire, and ridicule, they shot arrows into her breast and into her two thighs. A lot of the minor clergy joined them, and added their songs, too, to the ballads of the minstrels, ridiculing and damaging the rulers of both Church and State. Footsore, tired, hungry, and ragged, they laughed their way along the highway of lord and bishop; they put a laughable ban on everything they knew, all they had heard of, laughing on, though the end of many was a drear death in a ditch, with the curse of the Church as a hard pillow for a stiffening head.

Nothing seems too high or low for the humorist; he is above honor, above faith, preserving sense in religion and sanity in life. The minstrels thought (as we should think, too) that "The most completely lost of all days is that on which one hasn't laughed." So, if you get a chance in the hurry and complexity of life, laugh when the sun shines, when the rain falls, or even when the frost bites the skin or touches the heart with a chill.

Laughter has always been a puzzle to the thinker, a kind of a monkey-puzzle, a tree that doesn't look like a tree at all, but is as much a tree as any other one. Philosophers and sages have stopped up many and many a night, seeking an explanation, trying out a definition of comedy; but have gone to bed no wiser, and dead tired, while man kept on laughing, content to enjoy it, and never bothering his head as to what it was. Crowds of thinkers have set down big theories about laughter and comedy, among them the great Aristotle, Plato, Socrates, Jamblichus, and Kant; but though all of them were often blue in the face thinking it out, none of them got to the bottom of its mystery.

One American writer has connected laughter with Salvation; and maybe he isn't far wrong. He says: "The Church will prosper not through diminishing its requirements upon its members, nor in punishing them too severely for their delinquencies, but in showing mercy and kindness. Mercy is a flexible connective between the ideal and the real; it is a proper manifestation of the comic spirit. God, too, has a sense of humor: is He not revealed unto us as full of compassion, long-suffering, and merciful?" That is Dudley Zuver's opinion, and a new and odd one it will be to many. Not to David Lyndsay, the Scottish poet of the sixteenth century, who saw God near breaking his sides laughing at a rogue of an old woman who got past the indignant St. Peter by the use of her ready and tricky tongue.

It is high time and low time that we made a sense of humor an attribute of whatever God there may be. Why, at times, the whole earth must present a comic picture to whatever deity may be watching its antics. There's the United Nations, for instance, never more divided than now in conference, sub-conference, committee, sub-committee, this council and that council, trying out one question, and making a thousand more questions out of their discussions. What fools these mortals be!

It is odd—significant, too—that in any litany whatsoever, Catholic or Protestant, Methodist or Baptist, there isn't a single petition for a sense of humor. There are petitions for everything, ideal conditions and real conditions; for everything except a sense of humor. If they petitioned for this, and got it, then the other petitions wouldn't be so many, for they would understand themselves more clearly, and cease to pester God to do things for them that they could do in an easier and better way for themselves. They would become more tolerant, would priest and parson, more understanding, more sociable, and, in many ways, more worthy of heaven and of earth. So let all who pray ask for what most of them need badly, a sense of humor to lighten their way through life, making it merrier for themselves and easier for others. Then there will be something in the carol's greeting—God rest you merry, gentlemen!

Even Shakespeare seems to be somewhat shy of laughter; even he. He rarely—save in the play, *Troilus and Cressida*—goes all out for the mockery of the heroic and the nobility. He often dismisses his clowns with a scornful gesture, as if half apologizing for their existence. He gives a semi-comic and partly-pathetic touch to the death of Falstaff, his supreme comic character, and makes poor Bardolph swing by the neck from the end of a rope for stealing a silver pyx out of a church during the campaign in France. Mistress Quickly and Doll Tearsheet suddenly become shadows; so does Poins. Only the ranting Pistol is left to eat the leek, and then creep away from life forever. Shakespeare kept ridicule warm for the lower class, recognizing in his middle-class way that to criticize the nobility by comic characterization might be danger-ous, by letting the peasant and poor worker know what they really looked like. Yet, by and large, we can warmly feel how Shakespeare loved his rascals, a love so deep that, in their drawing, he made them live forever.

Where was laughter born, and when was it first heard? No one seems to know. We don't even know what it is. A baby knows how to cry before it learns to laugh. Its first smile is regarded as a miracle. So it is—the greatest and most valuable miracle born amongst men, though one thinker, Vico, says that "laughter is an attribute of second-rate minds." Let it be, then, for it is a lovely humor. It is so intensely human: however we may differ in color, in thought, in manners, in ideologies, we all laugh the same way; it is a golden chain binding us all together. The human mind will always be second-rate in the sense of still having to learn. To rise above humor is to rise above partiality, and no human being can do this; we are all partial, one way or another. We do not seek to be gods; we are content to be good men and good women; useful, neighborly, and fond of life, rounding it off with a big laugh and a little sleep.

The conscious humorist, said Vico, is a very low fellow. We're all very low fellows, for all of us, some time or another, are conscious humorists. And well we are, for our souls' sake, and for the sake of man's sanity. We couldn't live without comedy. Let us pray: Oh, Lord, give us a sense of humor with courage to manifest it forth, so that we may laugh to shame the pomps, the vanities, the sense of self-importance of the Big Fellows that the world sometimes sends among us, and who try to take our peace away. Amen.

Questions and Suggestions

1. This essay deals with the history, nature, and value of laughter. According to what you learned from your history texts, how valid do you find O'Casey's description of the Middle Ages? Does what he includes give a true or false picture to that period? If you want to know more about the laughter and disrespect that some of the writers of the Middle Ages felt toward their own society, read some of François Villon's poems, Rabelais's *Gargantua and Pantagruel,* and Desiderius Erasmus's *The Praise of Folly.*

2. Should O'Casey be more specific about the nature of laughter?

3. Explain the meaning of the topic sentence in the fourth paragraph. Is he too disrespectful toward philosophers, sages, priests, parsons, politicians, and the "Big Fellows"? What changes would he make in contemporary theology?

4. Summarize his views of Shakespeare's use of humor.

5. Does this essay help explain why George Grosz was not a successful artist when he lived in America? Consider the Melvilles in Lawrence's "Things" in light of O'Casey's belief

in laughter. Do you think that Emerson would agree with Vico
or with O'Casey?

Ideas for Writing

1. If you agree with O'Casey that some people are afraid to laugh,
   that many are "envious of laughter," base an essay upon your
   own experiences with such people.
2. What was your reaction to the person who laughed at your
   own creeds or customs?
3. How much laughter should there be in the classroom?
4. Who are some of the present enemies of laughter? What do
   you mean when you say that a person has a "sense of humor"?
   Are any of your relatives, friends, or classmates too serious?
5. What are your reasons for advocating that a "court jester" be
   hired for the United Nations, the Senate, the House cf Representatives, the state legislature, or your own city council?
6. Attempt a parody of a politican or a prelate's sense of his
   self importance.
7. Explain why you either look down upon or support the use
   of "low revelry."
8. What distinguishing marks does the B.M.O.E. have?

LIFE WITHOUT PRINCIPLE

HENRY DAVID THOREAU

The son of a pencil manufacturer, Henry David Thoreau (1817–
1862), who lived in Concord, Massachusetts, was far from being
the well-known writer during his lifetime that he has since become. A naturalist almost from birth, he graduated from Harvard
and was on easy terms of friendship with Emerson and some of
the Transcendentalists. At Walden Pond from 1845 to 1847, he
proved to his own satisfaction that man need not sacrifice his
search for the meaning of life to his efforts to find economic
security. He usually wrote his books from the jottings he had
earlier made in his journals.

From *Miscellanies*. This essay, published posthumously, first appeared in *The Atlantic Monthly*, October, 1863.

At a lyceum, not long since, I felt that the lecturer had chosen a theme too foreign to himself, and so failed to interest me as much as he might have done. He described things not in or near to his heart, but toward his extremities and superficies. There was, in this sense, no truly central or centralizing thought in the lecture. I would have had him deal with his privatest experience, as the poet does. The greatest compliment that was ever paid me was when one asked me what *I thought,* and attended to my answer. I am surprised, as well as delighted, when this happens, it is such a rare use he would make of me, as if he were acquainted with the tool. Commonly, if men want anything of me, it is only to know how many acres I make of their land,—since I am a surveyor,—or, at most, what trivial news I have burdened myself with. They never will go to law for my meat; they prefer the shell. A man once came a considerable distance to ask me to lecture on Slavery; but on conversing with him, I found that he and his clique expected seven eighths of the lecture to be theirs, and only one eighth mine; so I declined. I take it for granted, when I am invited to lecture anywhere,— for I have had a little experience in that business,—that there is a desire to hear what *I think* on some subject, though I may be the greatest fool in the country,—and not that I should say pleasant things merely, or such as the audience will assent to; and I resolve, accordingly, that I will give them a strong dose of myself. They have sent for me, and engaged to pay for me, and I am determined that they shall have me, though I bore them beyond all precedent.

So now I would say something similar to you, my readers. Since *you* are my readers, and I have not been much of a traveler, I will not talk about people a thousand miles off, but come as near home as I can. As the time is short, I will leave out all the flattery, and retain all the criticism.

Let us consider the way in which we spend our lives.

This world is a place of business. What an infinite bustle! I am awaked almost every night by the panting of the locomotive. It interrupts my dreams. There is no sabbath. It would be glorious to see mankind at leisure for once. It is nothing but work, work, work. I cannot easily buy a blank-book to write thoughts in; they are commonly ruled for dollars and cents. An Irishman, seeing me making a minute in the fields, took it for granted that I was calculating my wages. If a man was tossed out of a window when an infant, and so made a cripple for life, or scared out of his wits by the Indians, it is regretted chiefly because he was thus incapacitated for—business! I think that there is nothing, not even crime, more opposed to poetry, to philosophy, ay, to life itself, than this incessant business.

There is a coarse and boisterous money-making fellow in the outskirts of our town, who is going to build a bank-wall under the hill along the edge of his meadow. The powers have put this into his head to keep him out of mischief, and he wishes me to spend three weeks digging there with him. The result will be that he will perhaps get some more money to hoard, and leave for his heirs to spend foolishly. If I do this, most will commend me as an industrious and hard-working man; but if I choose to devote myself to certain labors which yield more real profit, though but little money, they may be inclined to look on me as an idler. Nevertheless, as I do not need the police of meaningless labor to regulate me, and do not see anything absolutely praiseworthy in this fellow's undertaking any more than in many an enterprise of our own or foreign governments, however amusing it may be to him or them, I prefer to finish my education at a different school.

If a man walk in the woods for love of them half of each day, he is in danger of being regarded as a loafer; but if he spends his whole day as a speculator, shearing off those woods and making earth bald before her time, he is esteemed an industrious and enterprising citizen. As if a town had no interest in its forests but to cut them down!

Most men would feel insulted if it were proposed to employ them in throwing stones over a wall, and then in throwing them back, merely that they might earn their wages. But many are no more worthily employed now. For instance: just after sunrise, one summer morning, I noticed one of my neighbors walking beside his team, which was slowly drawing a heavy hewn stone swung under the axle, surrounded by an atmosphere of industry,—his day's work begun,—his brow commenced to sweat,—a reproach to all sluggards and idlers,—pausing abreast the shoulders of his oxen, and half turning round with a flourish of his merciful whip, while they gained their length on him. And I thought, Such is the labor which the American Congress exists to protect,—honest, manly toil,—honest as the day is long,—that makes his bread taste sweet, and keeps society sweet,—which all men respect and have consecrated; one of the sacred band, doing the needful but irksome drudgery. Indeed, I felt a slight reproach, because I observed this from a window, and was not abroad and stirring about a similar business. The day went by, and at evening I passed the yard of another neighbor, who keeps many servants, and spends much money foolishly, while he adds nothing to the common stock, and there I saw the stone of the morning lying beside a whimsical structure intended to adorn this Lord Timothy Dexter's premises, and the dignity forthwith departed from the teamster's labor, in my eyes. In my opinion, the sun was made to light worthier toil than this. I may add that his employer has since run off, in debt to a good part of the town, and, after passing through Chancery, has settled somewhere else, there to become once more a patron of the arts.

The ways by which you may get money almost without exception lead downward. To have done anything by which you earned money *merely* is to have been truly idle or worse. If the laborer gets no more than the wages which his employer pays him, he is cheated, he cheats himself. If you would get money as a writer or lecturer, you must be popular, which is to go down perpendicularly. Those services which the community will most readily pay for, it is most disagreeable to render. You are paid for being something less than a man. The state does not commonly reward a genius any more wisely. Even the poet laureate would rather not have to celebrate the accidents of royalty. He must be bribed with a pipe of wine; and perhaps another poet is called away from his muse to gauge that very pipe. As for my own business, even that kind of surveying which I could do with most satisfaction, my employers do not want. They would prefer that I should do my work coarsely and not too well, ay, not well enough. When I observe that there are different ways of surveying, my employer commonly asks which will give him the most land, not which is most correct. I once invented a rule for measuring cord-wood, and tried to introduce it in Boston; but the measurer there told me that the sellers did not wish to have their wood measured correctly,—that he was already too accurate for them, and therefore they commonly got their wood measured in Charlestown before crossing the bridge.

The aim of the laborer should be, not to get his living, to get "a good job," but to perform well a certain work; and, even in a pecuniary sense, it would be economy for a town to pay its laborers so well that they would not feel that they were working for low ends, as for a livelihood merely, but for scientific, or even moral ends. Do not hire a man who does your work for money, but him who does it for love of it.

It is remarkable that there are few men so well employed, so much to their minds, but that a little money or fame would commonly buy them off from their present pursuit. I see advertisements for *active*

young men, as if activity were the whole of a young man's capital. Yet
I have been surprised when one has with confidence proposed to me,
a grown man, to embark in some enterprise of his, as if I had absolutely nothing to do, my life having been a complete failure hitherto.
What a doubtful compliment this to pay me! As if he had met me
half-way across the ocean beating up against the wind, but bound
nowhere, and proposed to me to go along with him! If I did, what
do you think the underwriters would say? No, no! I am not without
employment at this stage of the voyage. To tell the truth, I saw an
advertisement for able-bodied seamen, when I was a boy, sauntering
in my native port, and as soon as I came of age I embarked.

The community has no bribe that will tempt a wise man. You may
raise money enough to tunnel a mountain, but you cannot raise money
enough to hire a man who is minding *his own* business. An efficient
and valuable man does what he can, whether the community pay him
for it or not. The inefficient offer their inefficiency to the highest bidder,
and are forever expecting to be put into office. One would suppose
that they were rarely disappointed.

Perhaps I am more than usually jealous with respect to my freedom. I feel that my connection with and obligation to society are still
very slight and transient. Those slight labors which afford me a livelihood, and by which it is allowed that I am to some extent serviceable
to my contemporaries, are as yet commonly a pleasure to me, and I am
not often reminded that they are a necessity. So far I am successful. But
I foresee that if my wants should be much increased, the labor required
to supply them would become a drudgery. If I should sell both my
forenoons and afternoons to society, as most appear to do, I am sure
that for me there would be nothing left worth living for. I trust that
I shall never thus sell my birthright for a mess of pottage. I wish to
suggest that a man may be very industrious, and yet not spend his
time well. There is no more fatal blunderer than he who consumes the
greater part of his life getting his living. All great enterprises are self-
supporting. The poet, for instance, must sustain his body by his poetry,
as a steam planing-mill feeds its boilers with the shavings it makes.
You must get your living by loving. But as it is said of the merchants
that ninety-seven in a hundred fail, so the life of men generally, tried
by this standard, is a failure, and bankruptcy may be surely prophesied.

Merely to come into the world the heir of a fortune is not to be
born, but to be still-born, rather. To be supported by the charity of
friends, or a government pension,—provided you continue to breathe,—

by whatever fine synonyms you describe these relations, is to go into the almshouse. On Sundays the poor debtor goes to church to take an account of stock, and finds, of course, that his outgoes have been greater than his income. In the Catholic Church, especially, they go into chancery, make a clean confession, give up all, and think to start again. Thus men will lie on their backs, talking about the fall of man, and never make an effort to get up.

As for the comparative demand which men make on life, it is an important difference between two, that the one is satisfied with a level success, that his marks can all be hit by point-blank shots, but the other, however low and unsuccessful his life may be, constantly elevates his aim, though at a very slight angle to the horizon. I should much rather be the last man,—though, as the Orientals say, "Greatness doth not approach him who is forever looking down; and all those who are looking high are growing poor."

It is remarkable that there is little or nothing to be remembered written on the subject of getting a living; how to make getting a living not merely honest and honorable, but altogether inviting and glorious; for if *getting* a living is not so, then living is not. One would think, from looking at literature, that this question had never disturbed a solitary individual's musings. Is it that men are too much disgusted with their experience to speak of it? The lesson of value which money teaches, which the Author of the Universe has taken so much pains to teach us, we are inclined to skip altogether. As for the means of living, it is wonderful how indifferent men of all classes are about it, even reformers, so called,—whether they inherit, or earn, or steal it. I think that Society has done nothing for us in this respect, or at least has undone what she has done. Cold and hunger seem more friendly to my nature than those methods which men have adopted and advise to ward them off.

The title *wise* is, for the most part, falsely applied. How can one be a wise man, if he does not know any better how to live than other men?—if he is only more cunning and intellectually subtle? Does Wisdom work in a tread-mill? or does she teach how to succeed *by her example?* Is there any such thing as wisdom not applied to life? Is she merely the miller who grinds the finest logic? It is pertinent to ask if Plato got his *living* in a better way or more successfully than his contemporaries,—or did he succumb to the difficulties of life like other men? Did he seem to prevail over some of them merely by indifference, or by assuming grand airs? or find it easier to live, because his aunt remembered him in her will? The ways in which most men get their living, that is, live, are mere makeshifts, and a shirking of the real business of life,—chiefly because they do not know, but partly because they do not mean, any better.

The rush to California, for instance, and the attitude, not merely of merchants, but of philosophers and prophets, so called, in relation to it, reflect the greatest disgrace on mankind. That so many are ready to live by luck, and so get the means of commanding the labor of others less lucky, without contributing any value to society! And that is called enterprise! I know of no more startling development of the immorality of trade, and all the common modes of getting a living. The philosophy and poetry and religion of such a mankind are not worth the dust of a puffball. The hog that gets his living by rooting, stirring up the soil so, would be ashamed of such company. If I could command the wealth of all the worlds by lifting my finger, I would not pay *such* a price for it. Even Mahomet knew that God did not make this world in jest. It makes God to be a moneyed gentleman who scatters a handful of pennies in order to see mankind scramble for them. The world's raffle! A subsistence in the domains of Nature a thing to be raffled for! What a comment, what a satire, on our institutions! The conclusion will be, that mankind will hang itself upon a tree. And have all the precepts in all the Bibles taught men only this? and is the last and most admirable invention of the human race only an improved muck-rake? Is this the ground on which Orientals and Occidentals meet? Did God direct us so to get our living, digging where we never planted,—and He would, perchance, reward us with lumps of gold?

God gave the righteous man a certificate entitling him to food and raiment, but the unrighteous man found a facsimile of the same in God's coffers, and appropriated it, and obtained food and raiment like the former. It is one of the most extensive systems of counterfeiting that the world has seen. I did not know that mankind was suffering for want of gold. I have seen a little of it. I know that it is very malleable, but not so malleable as wit. A grain of gold will gild a great surface, but not so much as a grain of wisdom.

The gold-digger in the ravines of the mountains is as much a gambler as his fellow in the saloons of San Francisco. What difference does it make whether you shake dirt or shake dice? If you win, society is the loser. The gold-digger is the enemy of the honest laborer, whatever checks and compensations there may be. It is not enough to tell me that you worked hard to get your gold. So does the Devil work hard.

The way of transgressors may be hard in many respects. The humblest observer who goes to the mines sees and says that gold-digging is of the character of a lottery; the gold thus obtained is not the same thing with the wages of honest toil. But, practically, he forgets what he has seen, for he has seen only the fact, not the principle, and goes into trade there, that is, buys a ticket in what commonly proves another lottery, where the fact is not so obvious.

After reading Howitt's account of the Australian gold-diggings one evening, I had in my mind's eye, all night, the numerous valleys, with their streams, all cut up with foul pits, from ten to one hundred feet deep, and half a dozen feet across, as close as they can be dug, and partly filled with water,—the locality to which men furiously rush to probe for their fortunes,—uncertain where they shall break ground,—not knowing but the gold is under their camp itself,—sometimes digging one hundred and sixty feet before they strike the vein, or then missing it by a foot,—turned into demons, and regardless of each others' rights, in their thirst for riches,—whole valleys, for thirty miles, suddenly honeycombed by the pits of the miners, so that even hundreds are drowned in them,—standing in water, and covered with mud and clay, they work night and day, dying of exposure and disease. Having read this, and partly forgotten it, I was thinking, accidentally, of my own unsatisfactory life, doing as others do; and with that vision of the diggings still before me, I asked myself why I might not be washing some gold daily, though it were only the finest particles,— why I might not sink a shaft down to the gold within me, and work that mine. *There* is a Ballarat, a Bendigo for you,—what though it were a sulky-gully? At any rate, I might pursue some path, however solitary and narrow and crooked, in which I could walk with love and reverence. Wherever a man separates from the multitude, and goes his own way in this mood, there indeed is a fork in the road, though ordinary travelers may see only a gap in the paling. His solitary path across lots will turn out the *higher way* of the two.

Men rush to California and Australia as if the true gold were to be found in that direction; but that is to go to the very opposite extreme to where it lies. They go prospecting farther and farther away from the true lead, and are most unfortunate when they think themselves most successful. Is not our *native* soil auriferous? Does not a stream from the golden mountains flow through our native valley? and has not this for more than geologic ages been bringing down the shining particles and forming the nuggets for us? Yet, strange to tell, if a

digger steal away, prospecting for this true gold, into the unexplored
solitudes around us, there is no danger that any will dog his steps, and
endeavor to supplant him. He may claim and undermine the whole
valley even, both the cultivated and the uncultivated portions, his
whole life long in peace, for no one will ever dispute his claim. They
will not mind his cradles or his toms. He is not confined to a claim
twelve feet square, as at Ballarat, but may mine anywhere, and wash
the whole wide world in his tom.

Howitt says of the man who found the great nugget which weighed
twenty-eight pounds, at the Bendigo diggings in Australia: "He soon
began to drink; got a horse, and rode all about, generally at full gallop,
and, when he met people, called out to inquire if they knew who he
was, and then kindly informed them that he was 'the bloody wretch
that had found the nugget.' At last he rode full speed against a tree,
and nearly knocked his brains out." I think, however, there was no
danger of that, for he had already knocked his brains out against the
nugget. Howitt adds, "He is a hopelessly ruined man." But he is a
type of the class. They are all fast men. Hear some of the names of the
places where they dig: "Jackass Flat,"—"Sheep's-Head Gully,"—"Murderer's Bar," etc. Is there no satire in these names? Let them carry their
ill-gotten wealth where they will, I am thinking it will still be "Jackass
Flat," if not "Murderer's Bar," where they live.

The last resource of our energy has been the robbing of graveyards
on the Isthmus of Darien, an enterprise which appears to be but in its
infancy; for, according to late accounts, an act has passed its second
reading in the legislature of New Granada, regulating this kind of mining; and a correspondent of the "Tribune" writes: "In the dry season,
when the weather will permit of the country being properly pros-
pected, no doubt other rich *guacas* [that is, graveyards] will be found."
To emigrants he says: "Do not come before December; take the Isthmus
route in preference to the Boca del Toro one; bring no useless baggage,
and do not cumber yourself with a tent; but a good pair of blankets
will be necessary; a pick, shovel, and axe of good material will be
almost all that is required:" advice which might have been taken
from the "Burker's Guide." And he concludes with this line in Italics
and small capitals: "*If you are doing well at home,* STAY THERE,"
which may fairly be interpreted to mean, "If you are getting a good
living by robbing graveyards at home, stay there."

But why go to California for a text? She is the child of New England, bred at her own school and church.

It is remarkable that among all the preachers there are so few moral teachers. The prophets are employed in excusing the ways of men. Most reverend seniors, the *illuminati* of the age, tell me, with a gracious, reminiscent smile, betwixt an aspiration and a shudder, not to be too tender about these things,—to lump all that, that is, make a lump of gold of it. The highest advice I have heard on these subjects was groveling. The burden of it was,—It is not worth your while to undertake to reform the world in this particular. Do not ask how your bread is buttered; it will make you sick, if you do,—and the like. A man had better starve at once than lose his innocence in the process of getting his bread. If within the sophisticated man there is not an unsophisticated one, then he is but one of the devil's angels. As we grow old, we live more coarsely, we relax a little in our disciplines, and, to some extent, cease to obey our finest instincts. But we should be fastidious to the extreme of sanity, disregarding the gibes of those who are more unfortunate than ourselves.

In our science and philosophy, even, there is commonly no true and absolute account of things. The spirit of sect and bigotry has planted its hoof amid the stars. You have only to discuss the problem, whether the stars are inhabited or not, in order to discover it. Why must we daub the heavens as well as the earth? It was an unfortunate discovery that Dr. Kane was a Mason, and that Sir John Franklin was another. But it was a more cruel suggestion that possibly that was the reason why the former went in search of the latter. There is not a popular magazine in this country that would dare to print a child's thought on important subjects without comment. It must be submitted to the D.D.'s. I would it were the chickadee-dees.

You come from attending the funeral of mankind to attend to a natural phenomenon. A little thought is sexton to all the world.

I hardly know an *intellectual* man, even, who is so broad and truly liberal that you can think aloud in his society. Most with whom you endeavor to talk soon come to a stand against some institution in which they appear to hold stock,—that is, some particular, not universal, way of viewing things. They will continually thrust their own low roof, with its narrow skylight, between you and the sky, when it is the unobstructed heavens you would view. Get out of the way with your cobwebs; wash your windows, I say! In some lyceums they tell me that they have voted to exclude the subject of religion. But how do I know what their religion is, and when I am near to or far from it? I have walked into such an arena and done my best to make a clean breast of what religion I have experienced, and the audience never suspected what I was about. The lecture was as harmless as moonshine to them. Whereas, if I had read to them the biography of the greatest scamps in history, they might have thought that I had written the lives of the deacons of their church. Ordinarily, the inquiry is, Where did you come from? or, Where are you going? That was a more pertinent question which I overheard one of my auditors put to another once,—"What does he lecture for?" It made me quake in my shoes.

To speak impartially, the best men that I know are not serene, a world in themselves. For the most part, they dwell in forms, and flatter and study effect only more finely than the rest. We select granite for the underpinning of our houses and barns; we build fences of stone; but we do not ourselves rest on an underpinning of granitic truth, the lowest primitive rock. Our sills are rotten. What stuff is the man made of who is not coexistent in our thought with the purest and subtilest truth? I often accuse my finest acquaintances of an immense frivolity; for, while there are manners and compliments we do not meet, we do not teach one another the lessons of honesty and sincerity that the brutes do, or of steadiness and solidity that the rocks do. The fault is commonly mutual, however; for we do not habitually demand any more of each other.

That excitement about Kossuth, consider how characteristic, but superficial, it was!—only another kind of politics or dancing. Men were making speeches to him all over the country, but each expressed only the thought, or the want of thought, of the multitude. No man stood on truth. They were merely banded together, as usual one leaning on another, and all together on nothing; as the Hindoos made the world rest on an elephant, the elephant on a tortoise, and the tortoise on a serpent, and had nothing to put under the serpent. For all fruit of that stir we have the Kossuth hat.

Just so hollow and ineffectual, for the most part, is our ordinary conversation. Surface meets surface. When our life ceases to be inward and private, conversation degenerates into mere gossip. We rarely meet a man who can tell us any news which he has not read in a newspaper, or been told by his neighbor; and, for the most part, the only difference between us and our fellow is that he has seen the newspaper, or been out to tea, and we have not. In proportion as our inward life fails, we go more constantly and desperately to the post-office. You may depend on it, that the poor fellow who walks away with the greatest number of letters, proud of his extensive correspondence, has not heard from himself this long while.

I do not know but it is too much to read one newspaper a week. I have tried it recently, and for so long it seems to me that I have not dwelt in my native region. The sun, the clouds, the snow, the trees say not so much to me. You cannot serve two masters. It requires more than a day's devotion to know and to possess the wealth of a day.

We may well be ashamed to tell what things we have read or heard in our day. I do not know why my news should be so trivial,—considering what one's dreams and expectations are, why the developments should be so paltry. The news we hear, for the most part, is not news to our genius. It is the stalest repetition. You are often tempted to ask why such stress is laid on a particular experience which you have had,— that, after twenty-five years, you should meet Hobbins, Registrar of Deeds, again on the sidewalk. Have you not budged an inch, then? Such is the daily news. Its facts appear to float in the atmosphere, insignificant as the sporules of fungi, and impinge on some neglected *thallus,* or surface of our minds, which affords a basis for them, and hence a parasitic growth. We should wash ourselves clean of such news. Of what consequence, though our planet explode, if there is no character involved in the explosion? In health we have not the least curiosity about such events. We do not live for idle amusement. I would not run round a corner to see the world blow up.

All summer, and far into the autumn, perchance, you unconsciously went by the newspapers and the news, and now you find it was because the morning and the evening were full of news to you. Your walks were full of incidents. You attended, not to the affairs of Europe, but to your own affairs in Massachusetts fields. If you chance to live and move and have your being in that thin stratum in which the events that make the news transpire,—thinner than the paper on which it is printed,—then these things will fill the world for you; but if you soar above or dive below that plane, you cannot remember nor be reminded of them. Really to see the sun rise or go down every day, so to relate ourselves to a universal fact, would preserve us sane forever. Nations! What are nations? Tartars, and Huns, and Chinamen! Like insects, they swarm. The historian strives in vain to make them memorable. It is for want of a man that there are so many men. It is individuals that populate the world. Any man thinking may say with the Spirit of Lodin,—

> "I look down from my height on nations,
> And they become ashes before me;—
> Calm is my dwelling in the clouds;
> Pleasant are the great fields of my rest."

Pray, let us live without being drawn by dogs, Esquimaux-fashion, tearing over hill and dale, and biting each other's ears.

Not without a slight shudder at the danger, I often perceive how near I had come to admitting into my mind the details of some trivial affair,—the news of the street; and I am astonished to observe how willing men are to lumber their minds with such rubbish,—to permit idle rumors and incidents of the most insignificant kind to intrude on ground which should be sacred to thought. Shall the mind be a public arena, where the affairs of the street and the gossip of the tea-table chiefly are discussed? Or shall it be a quarter of heaven itself,—an hypæthral temple, consecrated to the service of the gods? I find it so difficult to dispose of the few facts which to me are significant, that I hesitate to burden my attention with those which are insignificant, which only a divine mind could illustrate. Such is, for the most part, the news in newspapers and conversation. It is important to preserve the mind's chastity in this respect. Think of admitting the details of a single case of the criminal court into our thoughts, to stalk profanely through their very *sanctum sanctorum* for an hour, ay, for many hours! to make a very barroom of the mind's inmost apartment, as if for so long the dust of the street had occupied us,—the very street itself, with all its travel, its bustle, and filth, had passed through our thoughts' shrine! Would it not be an intellectual and moral suicide? When I have been compelled to sit spectator and auditor in a courtroom for some hours, and have seen my neighbors, who were not compelled, stealing in from time to time, and tiptoeing about with washed hands and faces, it has appeared to my mind's eye, that, when they took off their hats, their ears suddenly expanded into vast hoppers for sound, between which even their narrow heads were crowded. Like the vanes of windmills, they caught the broad but shallow stream of sound, which, after a few titillating gyrations in their coggy brains, passed out the other side. I wondered if, when they got home, they were as careful to wash their ears as before their hands and faces. It has seemed to me, at such a time, that the auditors and the witnesses, the jury and the counsel, the judge and the criminal at the bar,—if I may presume him guilty before he is convicted,—were all equally criminal, and a thunderbolt might be expected to descend and consume them all together.

By all kinds of traps and signboards, threatening the extreme penalty of the divine law, exclude such trespassers from the only ground which can be sacred to you. It is so hard to forget what it is worse than useless to remember! If I am to be a thoroughfare, I prefer that it be of the mountain brooks, the Parnassian streams, and not the town sewers. There is inspiration, that gossip which comes to the ear of the attentive mind from the courts of heaven. There is the profane and stale revelation of the barroom and the police court. The same ear is fitted to receive both communications. Only the character of the hearer determines to which it shall be open, and to which closed. I believe that the mind can be permanently profaned by the habit of attending to trivial things, so that all our thoughts shall be tinged with triviality. Our very intellect shall be macadamized, as it were,—its foundation broken into fragments for the wheels of travel to roll over; and if you would know what will make the most durable pavement, surpassing rolled stones, spruce blocks, and asphaltum, you have only to look into some of our minds which have been subjected to this treatment so long.

If we have thus desecrated ourselves,—as who has not?—the remedy will be by wariness and devotion to reconsecrate ourselves, and make once more a fane of the mind. We should treat our minds, that is, ourselves, as innocent and ingenuous children, whose guardians we are, and be careful what objects and what subjects we thrust on their attention. Read not the Times. Read the Eternities. Conventionalities are at length as bad as impurities. Even the facts of science may dust the mind by their dryness, unless they are in a sense effaced each morning, or rather rendered fertile by the dews of fresh and living truth. Knowledge does not come to us by details, but in flashes of light from heaven. Yes, every thought that passes through the mind helps to wear and tear it, and to deepen the ruts, which, as in the streets of Pompeii, evince how much it has been used. How many things there are concerning which we might well deliberate whether we had better know them,—had better let their peddling-carts be driven, even at the slowest trot or walk, over that bridge of glorious span by which we trust to pass at last from the farthest brink of time to the nearest shore of eternity! Have we no culture, no refinement,—but skill only to live coarsely and serve the Devil?—to acquire a little worldly wealth, or fame, or liberty, and make a false show with it, as if we were all husk and shell, with no tender and living kernel to us? Shall our institutions be like those chestnut burs which contain abortive nuts, perfect only to prick the fingers?

America is said to be the arena on which the battle of freedom is to be fought; but surely it cannot be freedom in a merely political sense that is meant. Even if we grant that the American has freed himself from a political tyrant, he is still the slave of an economical and moral tyrant. Now that the republic—the *res-publica*—has been settled, it is time to look after the *res-privata*,—the private state,—to see, as the Roman senate charged its consuls, *"ne quid res-*PRIVATA *detrimenti caperet,"* that the *private* state receive no detriment.

Do we call this the land of the free? What is it to be free from King George and continue the slaves of King Prejudice? What is it to be born free and not to live free? What is the value of any political freedom, but as a means to moral freedom? Is it a freedom to be slaves, or a freedom to be free, of which we boast? We are a nation of politicians, concerned about the outmost defenses only of freedom. It is our children's children who may perchance be really free. We tax ourselves unjustly. There is a part of us which is not represented. It is taxation without representation. We quarter troops, we quarter fools and cattle of all sorts upon ourselves. We quarter our gross bodies on our poor souls, till the former eat up all the latter's substance.

With respect to a true culture and manhood, we are essentially provincial still, not metropolitan,—mere Jonathans. We are provincial, because we do not find at home our standards; because we do not worship truth, but the reflection of truth; because we are warped and narrowed by an exclusive devotion to trade and commerce and manufactures and agriculture and the like, which are but means, and not the end.

So is the English Parliament provincial. Mere country bumpkins, they betray themselves, when any more important question arises for them to settle, the Irish question, for instance,—the English question why did I not say? Their natures are subdued to what they work in. Their "good breeding" respects only secondary objects. The finest manners in the world are awkwardness and fatuity when contrasted with a finer intelligence. They appear but as the fashions of past days,—mere courtliness, knee-buckles and smallclothes, out of date. It is the vice, but not the excellence of manners, that they are continually being deserted by the character; they are cast-off clothes or shells, claiming the respect which belonged to the living creature. You are presented with the shells instead of the meat, and it is no excuse generally, that, in the case of some fishes, the shells are of more worth than the meat. The man who thrusts his manners upon me does as if he were to insist on introducing me to his cabinet of curiosities, when I wished to see himself. It was not in this sense that the poet Decker called Christ "the first true gentleman that ever breathed."

I repeat that in this sense the most splendid court in Christendom is provincial, having authority to consult about Transalpine interests only, and not the affairs of Rome. A prætor or proconsul would suffice to settle the questions which absorb the attention of the English Parliament and the American Congress.

Government and legislation! these I thought were respectable professions. We have heard of heaven-born Numas, Lycurguses, and Solons, in the history of the world, whose *names* at least may stand for ideal legislators; but think of legislating to *regulate* the breeding of slaves, or the exportation of tobacco! What have divine legislators to do with the exportation or the importation of tobacco? what humane ones with the breeding of slaves? Suppose you were to submit the question to any son of God,—and has He no children in the Nineteenth Century? is it a family which is extinct?—in what condition would you get it again? What shall a State like Virginia say for itself at the last day, in which these have been the principal, the staple productions? What ground is there for patriotism in such a State? I derive my facts from statistical tables which the States themselves have published.

A commerce that whitens every sea in quest of nuts and raisins, and makes slaves of its sailors for this purpose! I saw, the other day, a vessel which had been wrecked, and many lives lost, and her cargo of rags, juniper berries, and bitter almonds were strewn along the shore. It seemed hardly worth the while to tempt the dangers of the sea between Leghorn and New York for the sake of a cargo of juniper berries and bitter almonds. America sending to the Old World for her bitters! Is not the sea-brine, is not shipwreck, bitter enough to make the cup of life go down here? Yet such, to a great extent, is our boasted commerce; and there are those who style themselves statesmen and philosophers who are so blind as to think that progress and civilization depend on precisely this kind of interchange and activity,—the activity of flies about a molasses-hogshead. Very well, observes one, if men were oysters. And very well, answer I, if men were mosquitoes.

Lieutenant Herndon, whom our government sent to explore the Amazon, and, it is said, to extend the area of slavery, observed that there was wanting there "an industrious and active population, who know what the comforts of life are, and who have artificial wants to draw out the great resources of the country." But what are the "artificial wants" to be encouraged? Not the love of luxuries, like the tobacco and slaves of, I believe, his native Virginia, nor the ice and granite and other material wealth of our native New England; nor are "the great resources of a country" that fertility or barrenness of soil which produces these. The chief want, in every State that I have been into, was a high and earnest purpose in its inhabitants. This alone draws out "the great resources" of Nature, and at last taxes her beyond her resources; for man naturally dies out of her. When we want culture more than potatoes, and illumination more than sugar-plums, then the great resources of a world are taxed and drawn out, and the result, or staple production, is, not slaves, nor operatives, but men,—those rare fruits called heroes, saints, poets, philosophers, and redeemers.

In short, as a snow-drift is formed where there is a lull in the wind, so, one would say, where there is a lull of truth, an institution springs up. But the truth blows right on over it, nevertheless, and at length blows it down.

What is called politics is comparatively something so superficial and inhuman, that practically I have never fairly recognized that it concerns me at all. The newspapers, I perceive, devote some of their columns specially to politics or government without charge; and this, one would say, is all that saves it; but as I love literature and to some extent the truth also, I never read those columns at any rate. I do not wish to blunt my sense of right so much. I have not got to answer for having read a single President's Message. A strange age of the world this, when empires, kingdoms, and republics come a-begging to a private man's door, and utter their complaints at his elbow! I cannot take up a newspaper but I find that some wretched government or other, hard pushed and on its last legs, is interceding with me, the reader, to vote for it,—more importunate than an Italian beggar; and if I have a mind to look at its certificate, made, perchance, by some benevolent merchant's clerk, or the skipper that brought it over, for it cannot speak a word of English itself, I shall probably read of the eruption of some Vesuvius, or the overflowing of some Po, true or forged, which brought it into this condition. I do not hesitate, in such a case, to suggest work, or the almshouse; or why not keep its castle in silence, as I do commonly? The poor President, what with preserving his popularity and doing his duty, is completely bewildered. The newspapers are the ruling power. Any other government is reduced to a few marines at Fort Independence. If a man neglects to read the Daily Times, government will go down on its knees to him, for this is the only treason in these days.

Those things which now most engage the attention of men, as

politics and the daily routine, are, it is true, vital functions of human society, but should be unconsciously performed, like the corresponding functions of the physical body. They are *infra*-human, a kind of vegetation. I sometimes awake to a half-consciousness of them going on about me, as a man may become conscious of some of the processes of digestion in a morbid state, and so have the dyspepsia, as it is called. It is as if a thinker submitted himself to be rasped by the great gizzard of creation. Politics is, as it were, the gizzard of society, full of grit and gravel, and the two political parties are its two opposite halves,— sometimes split into quarters, it may be, which grind on each other. Not only individuals, but states, have thus a confirmed dyspepsia, which expresses itself, you can imagine by what sort of eloquence. Thus our life is not altogether a forgetting, but also, alas! to a great extent, a remembering, of that which we should never have been conscious of, certainly not in our waking hours. Why should we not meet, not always as dyspeptics, to tell our bad dreams, but sometimes as *eu*peptics, to congratulate each other on the ever-glorious morning? I do not make an exorbitant demand, surely.

Questions and Suggestions

1. What does Thoreau consider "the real business of life"?
2. Why does he believe it is a great blunder to spend most of one's life getting a living?
3. What does the title of the essay mean? Where does Thoreau most nearly state what he means by "principle"?
4. How do his views on work fit his thesis? Compare his views with those of Gill.
5. How do Thoreau's remarks about the obligation of a lecturer parallel Steinbeck's demand for intellectual freedom?
6. Summarize Thoreau's discussion of the proper kind of news.
7. Consider the excitement about Kossuth and think of parallel enthusiasms that have left behind only superficial tags or slogans.

Ideas for Writing

1. Report the reaction in your community to someone who, without following a set schedule for work, writes, paints, or does anything creative.
2. Define in well-developed paragraphs: (a) the wise man; (b) ordinary conversation; (c) the individual's debt to society; (d) man's greatest need.

3. Why would you like to emulate Thoreau? Why would your parents be opposed? If you become interested in Thoreau's belief in the value of the individual human being, you will profit from a study of Emerson's essays, especially "Self Reliance" and "The American Scholar."

4. What do you think would be Thoreau's reaction to some of our current problems?

5. Find sentences that are theses, such as, "The community has no bribe that will tempt a wise man"; ". . . a man may be industrious, yet not spend his time well"; ". . . as we grow old we live more coarsely," and develop one into a long essay.